REAL PHONIES

Real Phonies
Cultures of Authenticity in Post–World War II America

ABIGAIL CHEEVER

THE UNIVERSITY OF GEORGIA PRESS
Athens & London

© 2010 by the University of Georgia Press
Athens, Georgia 30602
www.ugapress.org
All rights reserved
Designed by Walton Harris
Set in 10.5/14 Minion Pro

Printed digitally in the United States of America

Library of Congress Cataloging-in-Publication Data

Cheever, Abigail, 1970–
Real phonies : cultures of authenticity in post–World War II America / Abigail Cheever.
     p.   cm.
Includes bibliographical references.
ISBN-13: 978-0-8203-3283-3 (alk. paper)
ISBN-10: 0-8203-3283-6 (alk. paper)
ISBN-13: 978-0-8203-3429-5 (pbk. : alk. paper)
ISBN-10: 0-8203-3429-4 (pbk. : alk. paper)
1. American literature — 20th century — History and criticism. 2. Self in literature. 3. Authenticity (Philosophy) in literature. 4. Literature and society — United States — History — 20th century. 5. Identity (Psychology) in literature. 6. Identity (Psychology) in motion pictures. 7. Agent (Philosophy) in literature. I. Title.
PS228.S36C47 2010
810.9'353 — dc22   2009024805

British Library Cataloging-in-Publication Data available

CONTENTS

Acknowledgments *vii*

Introduction: "Individuality in Name Only" *1*

1 Postwar Teenagers and the Attitude of Authenticity *23*

2 From Madness to the Prozac Americans *56*

3 "They Didn't Do It for Thrills": Serial Killing and the Problem of Motive *105*

4 Assimilation, Authenticity, and "Natural Jewishness" *141*

5 "The Man He Almost Is": Performativity and the Corporate Narrative *191*

Conclusion: "Collage Is the Art Form of the Twentieth Century" *239*

Notes *249*

Works Consulted *281*

Index *297*

ACKNOWLEDGMENTS

THIS BOOK BEGAN when Walter Benn Michaels challenged me to come up with something interesting to say about *The Catcher in the Rye*. I have benefited from the generosity of many people since that early attempt to work through some of the ideas under consideration here. Laura Browder, Christy Burns, Daniel S. Cheever Jr., Beth Crawford, Theo Davis, Frances Dickey, Lucinda Havenhand, Kathleen Hewett-Smith, Amy Hungerford, Oren Izenberg, John Marx, John D. Rockefeller V, Matthew Sewell, Gretchen Soderlund, Carol Summers, Sydney Watts, and Janet Winston all read and commented on these chapters at various points. Their careful attention substantially improved the manuscript, and I am grateful for their contributions. In particular, I am indebted to Jerome Christensen and Walter Benn Michaels for asking demanding questions and providing crucial guidance; to Deak Nabers for his willingness to read and discuss this manuscript at great length; and to Abby Aldrich Record, whose research assistance and support were fundamental to its completion.

I did much of the work on this volume at the University of Richmond, where numerous conversations with Thomas Allen, Joanna Drell, Elisabeth Gruner, Raymond Hilliard, Suzanne Jones, Edward Larkin, Peter Lurie, Ilka Saal, Louis Schwartz, Louis Tremaine, and Hugh West improved both my thinking and my days in the office. My students have actively engaged with these ideas in numerous contexts and provided a continual source of revelation and encouragement. I hope they realize how much they contributed to this project. I am also grateful to the participants in the annual Post-45 conference, who are rigorous and exacting in their study of this period. I have profited from their questions, their suggestions, and their scholarly example. Most recently, the anonymous readers for the University of Georgia Press were generous in their recommendations and unstinting with their advice.

Portions of chapter 2 and chapter 5 were published in *Twentieth-Century Literature* and *Arizona Quarterly*. I am grateful to those editors for letting me republish this material here.

My greatest thanks go to my parents, to whom I dedicate this book.

REAL PHONIES

INTRODUCTION:
"INDIVIDUALITY IN NAME ONLY"

WHEN HOLDEN CAULFIELD, the adolescent narrator of J. D. Salinger's *The Catcher in the Rye* (1951), searches for a scathing insult, he inevitably comes up with "phony": this is how the reader knows that Holden thinks the object of his scorn is ethically reprehensible, rather than just "a nasty guy" like his classmate Robert or "a touchy guy" like his cab driver. In a representative instance, Holden identifies his former headmaster at Elkton Hills as "the phoniest bastard I ever met in my life," who

> went around shaking hands with everybody's parents when they drove up to school. He'd be charming as hell and all. Except if some boy had little old funny looking parents . . . then old Haas would just shake hands with them and give them a phony smile and then he'd go talk, for maybe half an *hour*, with somebody else's parents. (13–14)[1]

Haas does two things here to warrant Holden's disdain, but only one might be accurately described as phony. First, he dislikes a student's parents for superficial reasons—because they are "little old funny looking" people—and second, he pretends to like them—"gives them a phony smile"—so as to conform to social standards of behavior. Would he still be a phony if he made explicit his preference for attractive parents? Probably not: in Holden's taxonomy such behavior would make Haas a jerk, not a phony. Liking or disliking people solely on the basis of appearance may be shallow, but it is not necessarily an ethical failing of the type Holden censors. For Holden, Haas's judgment is far less offensive than his social camouflage. As Holden views the situation, Haas knows enough about himself to recognize that he dislikes "funny looking" parents and enough about his situation to appreciate that such dislikes are not acceptable in a school headmaster. His interest in other people's appearance is thus secondary to his investment in his own. For Haas, it is more important *to act* properly than *to be* honest. The "phony smile"—his attempt to conceal his dislike behind a pretense of liking, to represent socially acceptable behavior when his judgments are not socially acceptable—is what Holden deplores. If the added insult lies in Haas's superficial judgments of persons, the original and far more serious injury is his hypocrisy.

As Holden Caulfield's use of the term exemplifies, the epithet "phony" was omnipresent during the postwar period in the United States. It was an easy appellation for individuals who appeared cynically to conform to codes of behavior for social approbation or advancement and appeared as a common label for a certain type of person in the writing, literature, and film of mid-twentieth-century America. An interest in the possibility of social pretense has been a part of American ideology since at least the mid-nineteenth century. Ralph Waldo Emerson and Henry Thoreau are only the most obvious of American writers and philosophers who celebrated a particularly American individuality that was conceived in opposition to the expectations of a social world. And their roots might potentially stem back as far as Rousseau's theories of natural man and the Enlightenment birth of the idea of a unique and individuated self. But such concerns took on a renewed urgency in the years immediately following World War II. Too close a symbiosis between the individual and the various social contexts with which he or she negotiated was, at best, a sign of insincerity and, at worst, of outright fraud. In its contemporary variations such as "poser" or "wannabe," contemporary Americans might maintain the same position of smug superiority in relation to others that buoyed Holden Caulfield in the early 1950s.

Yet the apparent transparency of the categorization—everyone imagines she or he knows what a phony is—obscures the complicated models of authenticity and selfhood that must be in place for charges of phoniness to make sense. Most simply, for phoniness to be possible, the self needs to have two components that are generally understood through metaphors of depth: an inner core and an outer façade. The former must be able to employ the latter for its own purposes, and that interior core must be considered authentic even as the exterior presentation must be mutable—at times an authentic representation, and at times a misleading pretense. Further, the phony is inevitably imagined as a social creature; an audience, or at least some sort of social or cultural context, motivates his performances. Finally, as Holden's discussion of Haas suggests, phoniness requires some degree of self-knowledge. It imagines that each individual operates as a self-cognizant agent who can differentiate quickly between his or her immediate inclinations and the behavioral expectations of a larger group. To deploy the term "phony" is therefore to tangle with the inevitably related concepts of authenticity, selfhood, and self-knowledge, and their interactions with social and cultural contexts.

Accordingly, the phony's literary, intellectual, and popular deployment serves a profound analytical index, a means to access the mid-century's conception of authenticity as it relates to persons. To discover who is a phony, and why, is likewise to deduce what constitutes a real or genuine person in mid-twentieth-century American culture. This book is thus centrally concerned with explicating the phenomenon of phoniness as it is imagined in the writing and films from the middle of the twentieth century to its end—from adolescents like Holden Caulfield to sports agents like Jerry Maguire. It utilizes the concept of the phony—and its equally problematic fellow traveler, the *real* phony (defined below)—to explore a fundamental evolution in the concept of the authentic self. By reading closely in a range of literary, nonfictional, and filmic genres, this volume follows a central development during the second half of the twentieth century: the movement from an existential emphasis on self-constitution to a more postmodern view of the self as an embodiment of culture. Authenticity in the postwar period is imagined as that which separates the individual from the social world, as what might be uniquely one's own rather than a consequence of social influence. By the end of the century, authenticity emerges as an acknowledgment of one's construction within cultural contexts and a sign of one's involvement with that cultural milieu. Furthermore, in charting the contours of this transformation, this text rewrites the critically accepted account of the period which imagines that, during the later twentieth century, authenticity was of declining concern for American social and cultural critics, writers, and filmmakers.

This account begins in the years after World War II, during which time authenticity operated as an index to one's profound uniqueness, the means by which an individual's separation and independence from his cultural contexts was judged. As Lionel Trilling observed of this period, "the word authenticity [came] so readily to the tongue" and its deployment suggested a "strenuous moral experience . . . a more exigent conception of the self and what being true to it consists in, a wider reference to the universe and man's place in it" (11). That place, furthermore, was thought to be fundamentally oppositional; authenticity required defining oneself against the expectations of society and culture. Yet by the end of the century, authenticity had evolved into a standard of belonging, a means to register the extent to which one successfully embodied an identity — be it racial, cultural, or any other type. If, in the 1950s, intellectuals and writers debated authentic versus phony selves, by the end of the century their questions addressed the authenticity of cultures — and whether or not the self or subject was embodying those cultures faithfully. In this book, I examine this evolution in authenticity from the vogue for French existentialism in the immediate postwar period (as explored in works by J. D. Salinger, Saul Bellow, Truman Capote, Patricia Highsmith, Elia Kazan, Jim Thompson, Sloan Wilson, and Richard Yates), in which authenticity and its opposites are explicitly addressed, to texts from the later part of the twentieth century (Don DeLillo, Judith Butler, Jacques Derrida, John Guare, and Elizabeth Wurtzel), whose interest in the idea of authenticity is potentially less explicit yet no less fundamental. Despite this significant transition, and despite the widely shared assumption that recent culturalist views of the self represent a sharp departure from earlier models of self and identity, what emerges is the overwhelming persistence of a common, profound engagement with the ideal of authenticity over the past half century.

Understanding both this engagement and its persistence foremost requires a reexamination of the concepts of phoniness and authenticity during the immediate postwar period. This concern has typically been understood by historians and cultural critics in terms of an omnipresent interest in middle-class conformity. A phony like Haas, for example, would appear to be a textbook conformist, a character who allows his apprehension about the opinion of others to dictate his self-presentation. Yet the novelists, social critics, and filmmakers of the 1950s and early 1960s were not, as has long been assumed, fundamentally worried about the ways in which individuals might be coerced or seduced into surrendering their differences. What really worried them was the thought that everyone might be the same to begin with. That is, they were concerned less with *conformity*—the idea that different people pretend to possess the cultural habits and beliefs of others in order to get along—than with *uniformity*—the possibility that everyone is, at bottom, fundamentally the same. The problem as these writers understood it was less one of behaving than of being.

To put this point slightly differently, writers as diverse as J. D. Salinger, on the one hand, and sociologist David Riesman on the other—whose study *The Lonely Crowd: A Study in the Changing American Character* (1953) was widely influential throughout the period—were less distressed by phonies like Haas, who conceals his ostensibly true individuality behind a social mask, than with individuals who might all be the same, but through no deliberate act of subterfuge. From this perspective, the potentially good thing about the phony is that he *needs* to alter his behavior to fit into the social realm. His subterfuge implies there is something about him that is not inherently social as such. His pretense thus suggests a formative critical distance between the individual and his contexts. But individuals who appear all the same through no effort at concealment or deception suggest a more serious problem. They profoundly challenge the widespread ideological belief in the individual, in the strongest sense of the word. It was far better to imagine that similarities among persons were the product of deliberate misrepresentation. Otherwise, one might have to confront the possibility that the individuals long thought to be the backbone of American culture were in fact not so individual after all.

This distress over the possibility of uncoerced similarities among persons, for example, would lead journalist William Whyte Jr. actually to celebrate conformity as the lesser of the two very present evils. In his bestselling book *The Organization Man* (1956), Whyte advocates the phoniness that Holden Caulfield found unacceptable as an efficient form of self-preservation amid the inevitable coercions of suburban and corporate life during the 1950s. "Surface uniformities" among groups, Whyte maintains, provide an extremely useful "protective coloration" (11) for the person who possesses a genuine individuality. As long as those uniformities do not extend below the surface to become in some way elemental, they would protect an individual distinctiveness that intellectuals thought was at risk. For Whyte, it is better to be phony than to be the same as everyone else.

To argue for uniformity as a central intellectual concern means recasting the traditional description of the 1950s that imagines the middle-class United States as a wasteland of conformity. If, in the popular imagination, the 1950s still connote a placid homogeny, "an orderly era, one with a minimum of social dissent . . . [in which] people seemed, more than anything else 'square' and largely accepting of given social covenants" (Halberstam x), social and intellectual historians have long discussed the falsity of that image. These historians were centrally concerned with rewriting that popular perception to expose the profound unease of postwar intellectuals, who were profoundly troubled by the ostensible psychic consequences of postwar prosperity. As John Patrick Diggins writes, "To survey intellectual life in the postwar era is to become aware that the America of these years cannot be encapsulated in simple epithets like 'consensus' and 'conformity' . . . however society may have been guiding itself — 'the bland leading the bland' as it was then put — the intellectual assumed a critical position toward it" (271).[2] For historians like Diggins and Halberstam, the 1950s were actually a time of fundamental uncertainty as writers and intellectuals attempted to come to terms with an emergent consumerism, the perceived threat to liberal democratic institutions posed by totalitarian regimes, and new and omnipresent mass cultural forms. The consequences of such forces were feared at all levels of American culture, from the broadest national institutions to the most specific individual. Yet to understand the concerns of these intellectuals as being simply about conformity is to overlook what was centrally at stake: the possibility that the idea of the unique American individual was not just hiding beneath a phony mask, but rather no longer existed at all.

The resulting apprehension about the American psyche produced a surprising number of works — literary, nonfictional, and cinematic, academic and mainstream — that directly or indirectly addressed the ostensible realness of persons. The most explicit employ a combination of sociology and psychology to diagnose a specific postwar American malaise. In addition to *The Lonely Crowd* and *The Organization Man*, studies such as C. Wright Mills's *White Collar* (1951), Herbert Marcuse's *Eros and Civilization: A Philosophical Inquiry into Freud* (1955), Erving Goffman's *The Presentation of Self in Everyday Life* (1959), and R. D. Laing's *The Divided Self* (1960) expressed a profound unease with a perceived sameness in the middle-class

American character, and a conviction that neither psychology nor sociology alone is adequate to address it fully.[3] As Erich Fromm explains in *The Sane Society* (1955): "Today we come across a person who acts and feels like an automaton; who never experiences anything which is really his; who experiences himself entirely as the person he thinks he is supposed to be" (16). To understand such individuals, it is not enough to consider their individual pathology — their "defect of . . . individuality" (16) — as a psychiatrist might. For such a person, one must also consider "the nature of the external conditions under which he lives and which he has to master if he is to survive" (81). The modern cultural moment subsequently emerges as a continual struggle for mastery between the individual and her conditions, and one that the individual is inevitably losing.

The causes to which these authors attribute the emergence of such persons amid these "external conditions" vary. For the psychoanalytically trained like Fromm, explanations are found in the premise outlined in Freud's *Civilization and Its Discontents*: "human nature and society can have conflicting demands." If man "lives under conditions which are contrary to his nature . . . he must either deteriorate and perish; or bring about conditions which are more in accordance with his needs" (Fromm 19). The sociologically oriented locate causes in large social forces: shifts in population growth and death rates (Riesman), the byproducts of postindustrial capitalism and the emergent service economy (Mills), and the rise of scientism and the discipline of human relations in American business life (Whyte). As much as their sources vary, the consequences are inevitably the same. All present a version of the argument that contemporary society is currently composed of an "other-directed" population (to adopt Riesman's term) that is a betrayal of American individualism and a danger to the nation's psychic prosperity.

Recent criticism has placed new importance on the relation between these hybrid psychological and sociological works and the larger field of postwar cultural production. As Deak Nabers has perceptively observed, in 1959 C. Wright Mills himself imagined "the sociological imagination" in terms inseparable from those one might use to describe the practice of literature: "The sociological imagination enables its possessor to understand the larger historical scene in terms of its meaning for the inner life and the external career of a variety of individuals" (*Sociological* 5).[4] For those possessed of such an imagination, there might be no significant distance between a sociological treatise and a novel. Recent studies by Morris Dickstein, Andrew Hoberek, and Leerom Medevoi, among others, view the connections between books like Riesman's *The Lonely Crowd* and the literature, film, and culture of the era as crucially important to dispelling the remaining myths about the period from the late 1940s to the early 1960s. As with the primary texts themselves, these contemporary scholars posit a variety of sources for this burgeoning postwar apprehension about the quality of the American character.[5] The organizational structures instituted during World War II that were never fully dismantled, the shifts in the middle class away from property ownership and toward white-collar labor, and the crucial geographic migrations from cities to suburbs are variously credited with producing a widespread cultural and intellectual preoccupation with the interior lives of American citizens.

My work here is less concerned with taking sides in the valuable debates on the sources of these preoccupations as with examining their distinctive contours and consequences. This book builds on the groundbreaking recent analyses of academic critics like Catherine Jurca and Timothy Melley in examining the counterintuitive ways in which authenticity was believed to operate. If writers like Herbert Marcuse or David Riesman were distressed not by conformity but rather by uniformity — not with the possibility of a nation of fakers and hypocrites, but rather with an America whose citizens evidenced a stultifying sameness — then understandings of how authenticity functions during the period need to be revised. For those committed to the most radical forms of individuality, the idea that similarities among persons are the consequence of social coercion is reassuring. It allows for the possibility of reform designed to liberate concealed differences among persons. But if individuals display a rank uniformity, not as a result of social oppression, but rather because of an essential similarity among members of a group, then American ideologies of uncompromising individuality must be fundamentally rethought. For a culture that mythologized itself as the proper home of creativity over derivation, radical independence over social entanglement, and invigorating differences over tedious homogeny, the possibility that the United States might have, in Erik Erikson's words, "instead of individualism, a mass-produced mask of individuality" (295) represents a profound challenge to its conceptualization. What stands out in these texts is that they all suggest a version of the same dilemma: is it possible that an individual can be *genuinely* the same as everyone else?

For a writer like Herbert Marcuse, the answer is that he cannot be. His study, *Eros and Civilization*, provides a representative example of how concerns over uniformity during the period are inevitably recast as concerns with conformity, so that a belief in the uniqueness of the individual can be maintained. Since, as Freud observed, "the price of progress in civilization is paid in forfeiting happiness" (78), Marcuse accounts for Americans' inauthentic individuality by historicizing Freud's repression of the individual instincts (Eros, Thanatos, etc.) within specific moments of social organization. He argues that Freud's cycles of civilization ("domination-rebellion-domination") are progressive only insofar as the forces of repression, "taken in by the superego until it coagulates into the powerful representative of established morality" (32), shift from individuals (from primal father to brother clan, and so on) to cultural institutions. As civilization advances, these forces grow increasingly impersonal and objective until "under the rule of economic, political, and cultural monopolies, the formation of the mature superego seems to skip the stage of individualization: the generic atom becomes directly a social atom" (97). While one solution might be to curb the repressive force of the superego—eliminating "surplus repression," the residue of earlier stages of civilization—by Marcuse's account, greater psychic freedom will not solve the problem. A chastened superego (allowing that such a thing were even possible) may result in *happier* individuals but not necessarily more *individuated* ones, since it is through the conflict with the superego that the individual becomes individual in the first place: "through the struggle with the father and mother as personal targets of love and aggression, the younger generation entered societal life with impulses, ideas and needs which were largely *their own*" (96, emphasis in original). This struggle may leave "painful scars" (96), but those scars are valuable inasmuch as they differentiate between selves, establishing a crucial degree of individual variation.

Marcuse's account of the perceived homogeny of Americans is emblematic of the challenges facing the social critics in the decades after World War II. So, too, is his causation, which sees an explicit connection between insufficiently individuated persons and consumer capitalism. Though its benefits are real—"private automobiles," "dozens of newspapers and magazines," "huge refrigerators filled with frozen foods" (100) — its costs to individuality (at the very least) are significant. Yet the challenge for Marcuse, and the social critics whom he exemplifies, is to make those costs actually seem to matter. Acknowledging that under the rule of these economic, political, and cultural monopolies the "general unhappiness has decreased rather than increased" (103), Marcuse dismisses such happiness as ultimately phony. Happiness is not, as one might have thought, "the mere feeling of satisfaction: it is the reality of freedom and satisfaction":

> The individual does not really know what is going on; the overpowering machine of education and entertainment unites him with all the others in a state of anesthesia from which all detrimental ideas tend to be excluded. And since knowledge of the whole truth is hardly conducive to happiness, such general anesthesia makes individuals happy. (104)

Committed to an a priori individuality that precludes the possibility that people might all genuinely enjoy the same types of education and entertainment, Marcuse cannot imagine that individuals could be authentically content with "innumerable gadgets which are all of the same sort" (100). The idea that people may actually prefer to live in the same way as their neighbors does not occur to him, with the problematic result that the individual can no longer be the final judge of the validity of her own happiness. The result is that happiness starts to look like a version of the older Marxist category of false consciousness, where anyone reasonably content with his lot evidences only that he does not really understand what is happening. Marcuse argues that, as a result, America "has individuality . . . in name only, in the specific representation of types (such as vamp, housewife, Ondine, he-man, career woman, struggling young couple), just as competition tends to be reduced to prearranged varieties in the production of gadgets, wrappings, flavors, colors, and so on" (103). Happiness, in this construction, is evidence not just of consumptive shallowness, but also of inauthenticity.

From one perspective, this formulation appears merely like a particularly severe form of social or cultural determinism that, like contemporary theories of performance, imagines the subject to be constructed entirely within and by cultural institutions. If this were the case, however, Marcuse would not describe these career women and Ondines as *types*, as representing rather than existing as these social roles. He would view them as *persons* — albeit persons who are all the same. It is only if one imagines that each individual is *essentially* individual in the strongest sense of the term that one can understand the similarities among persons as inevitably only representations — which is to say, as inevitably phony. In Marcuse's analysis, no one might authentically be a vamp. No matter how much the vamp experiences her "vampiness" as her own being, or a he-man believes his he-manliness is a fundamental part of who he is, both are still only performing a role. That they do not recognize these roles as such is itself a part of the tragedy. By Marcuse's account, a whole realm of authentic being exists to which the modern individual is systematically prevented from experiencing.

The result is that while Marcuse imagines he is protecting the individual subject from the coercions of late modernity, in fact he only protects the idea of an essential individuality as such — and often at the expense of the individual in whose name that protection occurs. The question thus becomes: why do he and the writers he typifies care about individuality in this particular way? Similarly, in *The Lonely Crowd* (1953), sociologist David Riesman also imagines that one could account for the homogeneity of persons through the expansion and depersonalization of cultural institutions. Yet his fears, unlike Marcuse's, are as much for the anesthetized he-man or career woman as for the culture that produced them. He argues that dramatic changes in "the way in which society secures some degree of conformity from the individual" (5) produced a fundamental shift in the mid-century character. Western Europeans from the Renaissance to the twentieth century were "inner directed" by "a psychological gyroscope . . . set by the parents and other authorities" that "keeps the inner directed person 'on course' even when tradition . . . no longer dictates his moves" (16). Yet in the years after World War II, an "other-directed" person has emerged in Western cultures, particularly in the middle- and upper-middle-class urban and suburban United States. This person "must be able to receive signals from far and near" that cue him to his culture's expectations. Internalizing "not a code of behavior but the elaborate equipment needed to attend to such messages," the other-directed person is "at home everywhere and nowhere, capable of a rapid if sometimes superficial intimacy with and response to everyone." Riesman explains: "This control equipment, instead of being like a gyroscope, is like a radar" (25). The other-directed are thus primed for a behavioral uniformity among their peers.

Underlying this description are many of the pejorative connotations that usually follow when phrases like "control equipment" and "superficial intimacy" are used to describe persons. To have an internal gyroscope implies the presence of an internalized ethical code that structures and guides behavior. Possessing radar suggests the absence of such abstract principles. Without such guiding ideals, only the behavior of others cues individual conduct. Yet Riesman remains ostensibly neutral with regard to the ethical status of "inner-" versus "other-" directed persons. After all, one cannot blame radar for not working like a gyroscope. Neither piece of equipment is chosen. What any individual possesses depends on the population demographics of her era. In Riesman's terms, the most one can hope for is to become autonomous. Describing three common character types that occur within these larger formulations—the adjusted, the anomic, and the autonomous—he differentiates among the degrees of social oppression on individual characters.[6] The adjusted are those "who respond in their character structure to the demands of their society or social class at its particular stage on the curve of population. Such people fit the culture as though they were made for it, as in fact they are" (Riesman 241–42). Anomics (from Durkheim's *anomique*, meaning "ruleless, ungoverned" [242]) are "constitutionally and psychologically unable to conform or feel comfortable" (243); they may be inner-directed in a society structured through other-direction, or vice versa. The autonomous are those "who on the whole are capable of conforming to the behavioral norms of their society . . . but are free to choose whether to conform or not" (242). Autonomous individuals thus maintain a healthy distance from the behavioral expectations put forth by their social context. Existing like a hidden, powerful species among the adjusted, they are hard to identify because of a carefully maintained camouflage. "We obviously know much less about [them]," Riesman notes: "Many will even deny that there are such people, people capable of transcending their culture at any time or in any respect" (245). Like Clark Kent hiding a secret identity, the autonomous "must work constantly to detach himself from shadowy entanglements" (257) that threaten his independence. The autonomous are thus in important respects phony, hiding their autonomous selves behind a veneer of compliance with social norms. Their capacity to *choose* compliance, however, makes all the difference. It is better to be phony than to be adjusted. It is better to conform than to be uniform.

But if the individual is not to be blamed for his status as either inner- or other-directed — adjusted, anomic, or autonomous — neither is he to be lamented entirely for his own sake. What stands out in Riesman's analysis is the relative insignificance of the individuals whose experiences purportedly motivated Riesman's investigation in the first place. Though "people may be compelled to behave in one way although their character structure compels them to behave in the opposite way," there is a bright side to such compulsion: "the disparity between socially required behavior and characterologically compatible behavior is one of the great levers of change" (29). One might imagine that for those persons whose role is to be just such a "great lever," Riesman's attitude would seem cavalier. His observation that "[f]ortunately, we know of no society like the one glumly envisaged by Aldous Huxley in *Brave New World*, where the social character types have been completely content in their social roles" (29), suggests that, at the very least, change is to be valued above contentment. Ultimately the society (whose change is presumed to be for the better) rather than the individual (whose contentment is of secondary concern) emerges as the more important entity. While one might easily imagine that someone would consider the needs of society as more important than the experience of any one of its members, it is rare to see an emphasis on individuality as a result.

Both *Eros and Civilization* and *The Lonely Crowd* thus illuminate many of the larger stakes of mid-century analyses of the American character. The reason that Marcuse, Riesman, and others discuss conformity rather than uniformity is because they are so committed to the ideal of individuality that the only way they can account for individuals who look, act, and talk the same is to imagine that they are compelled. That commitment, furthermore, illustrates how a paradoxical figure like the real phony might come into being. Yet it would take a novelist, not a sociologist, to delineate most incisively what the real phony, or archetypal 1950s person, would look like, and how her existence challenges not only the American ideology of individuality, but also the long-held Enlightenment principle of the uniqueness of the individual.

The term is best exemplified by Holly Golightly, Truman Capote's girl-about-town from *Breakfast at Tiffany's* (1958), whose paradoxical characterization as simultaneously real and fake exemplifies the complicated definitions of authenticity that were in play during this period. Overall, Capote's novel operates as a referendum on Holly's character, as the narrator recounts his yearlong attempt to discover who Holly Golightly is, not as a category of features — "hair sleek and short as a young man's," "eyes too large and tilted in the tapering face," "flat little bottom," "walk fast and straight" (to name a few) — but rather as an essence (6, 9). He fears she is only "'a crude exhibitionist,' 'a time waster,' [and] 'an utter fake'" (60). At first, the narrator's dilemma looks like another version of the problems one recognizes at the center of *The Catcher in the Rye* — how to know if someone is phony or authentic. Yet this problem is rapidly transformed into a question of essences, and is epitomized in a question posed to the narrator early on: "What do you think: is she or ain't she?" When the narrator asks "Ain't she what?" O. J. Berman responds "a phony," as if it is the most predictable question in the world. Capote's narrator protests (too much) that Holly never appears phony to him. Yet O. J. Berman, who discovered Holly outside of Los Angeles, improved her hillbilly accent, and tried to get her a career as an actress, contradicts him. "You're wrong," he explains. "She is a phony. But on the other hand you're right. She isn't a phony because she's a *real* phony" (28–29, emphasis added).

How can a phony be real? Holden's phonies require authenticity as the thing they are not. Without a notion of authentic selves, phonies could not exist. There would be nothing in comparison to which they might be judged to be phony. Continually dissimulating for social advancement, phonies are defined by their refusal to be themselves. Yet in introducing the concept of the real phony, Capote asserts that phoniness itself could operate as a genuine way of being. Berman himself acknowledges that this looks like a contradiction in terms: how might a person both be and not be herself at the same time? But Holly is different from the average phony. She actually "believes all this crap she believes" (29). This explanation places Holly in explicit contrast to Berman, and, by extension, to both Haas — who does not actually "believe all this crap" yet pretends to, for social benefit — and Holden — who in his condemnation of Haas implies that he wastes no time either believing or pretending to believe in "this crap" in the first place. The result is a model of persons in which beliefs sustained and beliefs *really* sustained are placed in antithesis. A phony performs social norms that do not represent her authentic identity, while a real person is someone who is all authenticity, for whom there is no difference between a performative and authentic self. Holly, however, is like a phony in that her beliefs are perfectly in accordance with social norms, but she is real insofar as those beliefs are all she has. There is no discernable authentic self to which her performative character might be compared. Phonies like Haas assume certain beliefs as an exterior cover for an authentic inner nature. Real phonies like Holly are phony all the way down.

The emergence of the real phony and his sociological counterparts (Riesman's other-directed, suburban middle class, Marcuse's representative types) thus provides a vivid starting point for exploring the dramatic changes to the concepts of phoniness and authenticity across the second half of the twentieth century. Central to this exploration is the way in which that concept has evolved. Though references to individual authenticity continue to appear, for example, in Steven Spielberg's *Catch Me If You Can* (2002), this categorical tenacity belies a series of fundamental revisions to the term. Authenticity in the postwar period was understood to separate the individual from her social context, so that Holly, in perfect alignment with her social world, cannot count as fully real despite her lack of dissimulation. By the end of the century, authenticity becomes a standard of belonging, a sign of one's alignment within a particular culture. To frame this in Capote's terms, in the early 1990s, Holly would no longer be a real phony. She would be just plain real—and would probably hang out with Paul Poitier, from John Guare's *Six Degrees of Separation* (1992), her characterological brother hailing from the end of the century. In texts such as Guare's, the subject or self becomes an embodiment of the culture, rather than the culture becoming the expression of a collective of subjects.

Yet what makes this shift compelling is the extent to which it is not merely a reversal of position—a change whereby authenticity comes to mark one's cohesion within, rather than one's separation from, a group—but rather a fundamental reconfiguration of the terms. That is, if in the 1950s the relevant questions concerned the individual and his relation to a social context or situation, by the 1980s the individual and his relation to his identity are at stake. While that identity may in fact be a group identity, it is not dependent on the group as such. A Jewish person would still be Jewish even if there were no other Jews, even as an African American would still be African American even if he were the only one.

How one moves from a notion of authenticity that separates the individual from his social context to one that celebrates cultural influence is arguably tied to the emergence of new models of the self that downplay the phenomenological experience of the individual in favor of ontologies arising from the theorization of postmodernity. As Fredric Jameson observes in *The Cultural Turn* (1998), recent cultural theorists have spent a great deal of time "exploring the notion that . . . individualism and personal identity is a thing of the past; that the old individual or individualist subject is 'dead'; and that one might even describe the concept of the unique individual and the theoretical basis of individualism as ideological" (6).[7] Applying such theories, critics generally correlate the emergence of postmodernity with a declining interest in authentic selfhood. While scholars such as Jeff Karem have illustrated the continued importance of authenticity in the production and reception of ethnic texts,[8] for the most part, critics of recent narrative fiction and film suggest that in the absence of a singular and unified self, authenticity as well appears as an absence, as a lost purity for which the contemporary subject mourns.[9] In the words of Timothy Melley, contemporary texts "rarely seem to *celebrate* the fragmentation of the self. Rather they depict the difficulty their characters have relinquishing liberal humanist assumptions about themselves" (15).[10]

Yet in the works under consideration here, authenticity is not a casualty of challenges to liberal humanism. Rather, concern with the realness of persons proliferates during this period despite a series of dramatic transformations in understandings of the self. In texts like *Six Degrees of Separation* or Don DeLillo's *The Names* (1982), authenticity is inevitably resurrected, but that resurrection occurs not through the rejection of new models of self, but rather by reconfiguring the terms. This period saw the emergence of new philosophical concepts (poststructuralism, interpellation, performance theory), psychological and sociological models (constructivism, biological determinism), and technological innovations (media, communications, biotechnology) that had radical consequences for notions of the unified self. If authenticity has held a consistent attraction for late-twentieth-century culture, that consistency is itself contingent upon a series of fundamental revisions to the concept — revisions themselves required to allow for rapidly transforming notions of selfhood. As theories of the self accommodated changes in philosophical, sociological, psychological, and technological knowledge during the late twentieth century, so the ideal of authenticity transformed to account for a subject understood first in existentialist, then poststructuralist and culturalist, and finally biological or performative terms.

The study that follows is not an exhaustive account of the past half century of American novels and films, or even of those directly engaging questions of phoniness. There are probably few books written in the past half century in which questions of authenticity and its opposites are not in some way raised, if not resolved. Instead, the works examined here generally concern themselves with questions as much metaphysical as quotidian, and for the most part they address the experience of the white middle class, rather than the experience of postwar racial, sexual, or class minorities. This is not to say that the concept of authenticity is not fundamental to a work like Ralph Ellison's *Invisible Man* (1952). To read *Invisible Man* in these terms would constitute an entire book in and of itself.[11] That said, this study is bounded to books and films that address the white middle class for two reasons: first, because this was the population imagined by cultural critics to be the most dangerously uniform, so in these texts the discussion of authenticity is most pronounced; and second, because such a circumscription supports the interests of depth rather than breadth. By restricting the number of texts under consideration, the contours of concepts like phoniness and authenticity are explored in greater detail to illuminate the progression in models of self and subject across the later twentieth century.

The following chapters examine five diverse and highly distinctive narrative genres that manifest the cultural history of authenticity: the literature of adolescence, the narrative discussion of depression, the serial-killer genre, stories of mid-century Jewish assimilation, and the narratives of corporate manners. What may look at first like profoundly disparate genres are revealed to be crucially united by a shared interest in the possibility of authenticity. These genres, furthermore, illustrate each of the central issues at stake in the consideration of authenticity: the issue of self-knowledge and the developing self, of metaphysical versus biological selfhood, of the relation between the self and its actions, of the interaction between the self and the institutions that surround it, and of the possibility of agency. In each chapter, the concept of authenticity thus becomes an index to and an instantiation of this culture's negotiations of the changing terrain of the self and its constitution.

The first chapter builds from the introduction by showing how the figure of the teenager crystallized the problems of uniformity. It argues that in the 1950s adolescence was conceived simultaneously as a developmental stage and a cultural type. Where the former suggests that the teenage self continually evolves—adolescence as something one goes through—the latter posits that adolescence operates like a religious, ethnic, or racial identity—a state of being that would presumably remain constant in time. This dual conception means the teenager is uniquely positioned to illustrate both the epistemological and ontological questions that are central to the period's understanding of the self. *The Catcher in the Rye* (1950) is analyzed within the tradition of the *bildungsroman* to demonstrate that with a developmental model of self, phoniness is presented as a problem of self-knowledge. If the self is continually changing, the novel asks, can a person know himself well enough to guard against phony behaviors? The solution is found in the existentialist concept of the situation, in which authenticity is guaranteed through the notion of the authentic choice. The chapter then examines the movement away from developmental accounts of the teenager and toward cultural models. It analyzes Erik Erikson's *Childhood and Society* (1950) alongside *Breakfast at Tiffany's* to suggest how the social circumstances in which one finds oneself might exert an inauthenticating influence on the developing self. The result is a situation in which it is taken for granted that, although Holly Golightly may experience herself as real, there is another real that is more real that Holly *should* be.

The second chapter examines the recent history of those conditions variously termed "mental illness," "madness," and "insanity" as vital sites for theorizing authentic selfhood in the past half century. Since these conditions reside on the boundary between metaphysical (melancholia, madness, etc.) and biological (mental illness) accounts of the self, they are uniquely positioned to illustrate the presumed challenges posed to authenticity by the fact of the physical body. It analyzes Sylvia Plath's *The Bell Jar* (written in 1963) in the context of Michel Foucault's *Madness and Civilization* (1961, English translation 1965), R. D. Laing's *The Divided Self* (1960), and Thomas Szasz's *The Myth of Mental Illness* (1961) to illustrate the privileged position granted to mental illness as the means whereby real phonies like Holly are made conscious of their inauthenticity. For Plath and others, such conditions are less a disease than a technology, a method through which the authentic self might be realized. The chapter compares Walker Percy's *The Thanatos Syndrome* (1987) with William Styron's *Darkness Visible* (1990) to suggest the competing views about a particular form of mental illness — depression — that exist toward the end of the century. If Percy exemplifies the mid-century's celebration of depression as a summons to authentic existence, Styron views depressive illness as precisely the opposite, an illness that interferes with the self's proper functioning. Styron illustrates the tendency to view depression as an impediment to genuine selfhood — an affliction that prevents the self from being itself. The chapter concludes with an analysis of *Prozac Nation* (1994) by Elizabeth Wurtzel, which imagines depression as a form of authenticity in its own right. The author suggests that the advent of Prozac and its family of pharmaceuticals, by helping to alleviate depressive symptoms — by removing the behaviors one associates with depression — enable depression as a new form of identity, independent of, and unrelated to, mere biological indicators.

The third chapter traces the transformation of the imagined murderers of the 1950s into the cinematic and fictional serial killers of the 1980s and 1990s. Though narratives about serial killers might seem a strange place to find debates over authenticity, their centrality to this project stems from the crucial role that motive plays in the genre. Since motive is the means through which the relation between individuals and their behaviors is inscribed and understood, serial-killing novels — with their emphasis on the inscrutability of motivation — are fundamentally concerned with the link between action and selfhood. Therefore the chapter asks: How does what a murderer does relate to what a murderer is? What are the implications of that relation for the concept of authenticity? Comparing Jim Thompson's *The Killer inside Me* (1952) and Patricia Highsmith's *The Talented Mr. Ripley* (1955), it illustrates two opposing versions of that relation. For Thompson, who Lou Ford is "inside" produces what Lou Ford does; for Highsmith, what Tom Ripley does produces the person he becomes — his murdered friend Dickie Greenleaf. Ripley thus embodies the existentialist claim that "human reality does not exist first in order to act later; but for human reality, to be is to act, and to cease to act is to cease to be" (Sartre, *Being* 615). Yet the novel leaves unanswered the questions: Why did Ripley need to murder Dickie? Why not become just like him in every way? The novel suggests that to be "just like" (the condition of phoniness), rather than to "just be" (the state of authenticity) is fundamentally unsatisfactory; this idea is then taken up by Don DeLillo's *The Names*, which explores the possibility of being real within poststructuralist ontologies of selfhood. In *The Names*, murderous violence is the means to repair what poststructuralists imagine as the inevitable violence of language—a violence that, in dividing the self from itself, renders authenticity impossible. The chapter concludes with a discussion of Thomas Harris's novels *Red Dragon* (1981) and *The Silence of the Lambs* (1988), in which murder, previously understood as either constitutive (Highsmith) or restorative (DeLillo) of the person, becomes instead *representative*, an illustration of being in the form of the serial killer.

The figure of the American Jew is the focus of the fourth chapter, which maps the relation between authenticity and Jewishness in mid-century America. It charts the implications of differing responses to the related (but not identical) concepts of Jewish passing or assimilation from the late 1940s to the early 1960s. These responses range from the existential model that fought to displace racial accounts of Jewishness immediately after World War II, to the uneasy portrayals of suburban Jewish life from the mid-1950s. Yet crucially, they also represent the shifting of the discourse of authenticity into a different register—one that imagines that the authenticity of individuals might be understood not in opposition to culture but rather in relation to it, as something that does not separate the self from its context but rather embeds the self within it. In that shift, furthermore, one can begin to perceive the fundamental transformation of authenticity as a concept that occurs toward the end of the twentieth century. The chapter begins by analyzing Elia Kazan's *Gentleman's Agreement* (1947) alongside *Anti-Semite and Jew* (1948), Jean-Paul Sartre's controversial discourse on Jewish authenticity. A passing narrative in which a gentile pretends to be a Jew, *Gentleman's Agreement* exposes how the existential definition of Jewishness ends up evacuating the category of all content, so that, in sociologist Daniel Bell's terms, "there is the word, Jew, but no feeling" (475) — and as a result, no actual Jews. The chapter then considers the problem of Jewish assimilation that the existential model of Jewishness all but guarantees through Saul Bellow's canonical novel *Seize the Day* (1956). Placing the existentialist model of self against models that base selfhood in history and culture, or in shared experiences among a generation, the novel ultimately locates Jewishness in terms of "the nerve of failure" — "the nerve to be oneself when that self is not approved of by the dominant ethic of a society" (Riesman, "Minority" 413). In *Seize the Day*, what makes the lead character most authentic is that which also makes him most Jewish: the fact that he stands up (however inadvertently) against the phony world. The chapter then considers Herman Wouk's best-selling novel of Jewish success, *Marjorie Morningstar* (1955), in which the lived reality of Jewish life in the suburbs is investigated for its putative phoniness. In *Marjorie Morningstar*, the very institutionalization of Jewish life in suburban belonging is feared to inauthenticate suburban Jews, but it counterintuitively emerges as the means of authentic Jewish survival.

The final chapter uses the literature of the corporation to address the recent interest in performance theory as a possible solution to the dilemmas of authenticity and agency. It illustrates how performativity, which is commonly thought to signal the demise of authenticity as an ideal, ultimately rehabilitates the concept by reconfiguring the terms. Richard Yates's *Revolutionary Road* (1961) and Cameron Crowe's *Jerry Maguire* (1996) are explored alongside contemporaneous theories of institutional influence by William Whyte, Erving Goffman, C. Wright Mills, Louis Althusser, and Judith Butler to consider how the professional subject is thought to be constituted through the institutions that surround him. For Whyte and Mills — whose personality market operates not unlike an early version of Althusserian interpellation — such institutional influence precludes the possibility of authenticity as such. Yet for Butler, authenticity is given a new life through the notion of a performative agency that outruns the conditions of its emergence. It then examines Butler's *The Psychic Life of Power* (1997) in the context of Cameron Crowe's Oscar-nominated film *Jerry Maguire* to illustrate the way in which such seemingly disparate texts evoke similar ideas about authenticity and agency. Though Judith Butler speaks of the poststructuralist subject and *Jerry Maguire* evokes a pop-psychologized identity, both are engaged in imagining ways that the subject or self might use institutions to become, as Jerry Maguire asserts, "the me I always wanted to be" (38). Authenticity thus becomes not an interior state to be discovered and lived, but rather a potentiality that is made all the more desirable for being unobtainable. The result is that contemporary performance theory, often understood as the answer to questions of authenticity, instead only reinscribes the very authenticity it purports to undermine.

1 POSTWAR TEENAGERS AND THE ATTITUDE OF AUTHENTICITY

JIM STARK FROM Nicholas Ray's *Rebel without a Cause* (1955) is one of mid-century America's iconic teenagers.[1] Along with Holden Caulfield and Johnny Strabler from Laslo Benedek's *The Wild One* (1953), Jim exemplifies the incoherent anguish that was thought to define the adolescent experience and that some feared was disappearing.[2] Also, like Holden, that anguish is caused in no small part by the pretenses of the adult world he must negotiate. Jim Stark's sincerity — "he doesn't say much," his friend Plato asserts, "but when he does, you know he means it" — is shown in dramatic comparison to his parents' glad-handing and social hypocrisy, and qualifies him to instruct them on the importance of "honor" and not "pretending."

The film opens at the police precinct where Jim has been arrested for underage public drinking. When his parents arrive in black tie from a party, the audience learns that the family has recently moved to avoid dealing with Jim's delinquency. He is the "phony excuse" (his term) that his parents use to avoid their own problems. Of those problems, the primary one from which all others are shown to emerge is that "she eats him alive and he takes it." Jim wishes his father "had the guts to knock Mom cold once, then maybe she'd be happy and stop picking on him." Horrified by this emasculation and desperate not to appear "chicken" like his father, Jim engages in hypermasculine displays to defend his honor from a local teenage gang — flick-knife fights, a chickie run — the latter of which ends in the death of Buzz, the gang's leader. His parents tell him not to talk to the police about the accident, insisting "you can't be idealistic your whole life." Instead, Jim challenges their hypocrisy: "I don't see how I can get out of it by pretending it didn't happen. . . . You tell me you want me to tell the truth. Now didn't you say that? You can't turn it off." When his father tells him, "You'll learn when you're older, Jim," he responds, "I don't want to learn that way."

By the end of the film, Jim's father ends up learning from Jim rather than vice versa. Jim imagines that he needs his father to tell him "how to be a man," but the film shows Jim as the more stereotypically masculine of the two. Over the course of one very long evening, Jim hides out from the gang who believe he ratted them out to the police; falls in love with Judy, the girl next door; fails to prevent Plato from shooting a gang member when they are found; convinces Plato to turn himself in to the police; and witnesses the police shooting Plato when they mistakenly believe he aims for them. Throughout all of these events, Jim is "strong" and "the kind of a person a girl wants" — "a man who can be gentle and sweet . . . someone who doesn't run away when you want them." As Jim weeps over Plato's fallen body, Jim's father pledges to "stand up" with Jim, and promises to "be as strong as you want me to be." The implication is that Jim's strength and sincerity, in a world where "nobody is sincere," inspires his father's transformation. Reversing the conventional account of maturation, the child models adult behavior for the parents and the parents — his newly re-masculinized father and visibly chastened mother — absorb the important lesson of adolescent authenticity.[3]

As *Rebel without a Cause* indicates, the idea that adolescents might illustrate authentic behavior for adults to learn from is a common one. In *The Catcher in the Rye*, this idea forms the basis of the novel's continued popularity into the twenty-first century. As Louis Menand observed, "people don't outgrow Holden's attitude, or not completely, and they don't want to outgrow it either" (84). The position that the adolescent assumes in relation to the world is imagined to be worthy of adults as well; not just a developmental stage, it becomes instead an approach that structures and defines all later stages. That attitude, "a modest degree of contempt" (84) for the rewards of middle-class life, is the crucial component of how mid-century American culture imagined individuals to retain a sense of authenticity. The idea that one has disdain for aspects of one's cultural milieu implies that one maintains a distance from that milieu even as he enjoys its benefits; it suggests that the beliefs and values of consumer culture have not been fully internalized. In modeling this attitude for its adolescent and adult readers alike, *The Catcher in the Rye* not only stages a form of reconciliation with the practical realities of adulthood, but it makes that reconciliation acceptable by suggesting a means whereby the individual might maintain his authenticity despite it — an authenticity that is continually reaffirmed through one's attitude of detachment.

This reconciliation accounts for the counterintuitive and often misunderstood cultural position that *The Catcher in the Rye* occupied in the second half of the twentieth century, as the socially sanctioned (which is to say, academically assigned) denunciation of society. The book produces the very uniformity of behavior it ostensibly condemns because it is a book that virtually an entire class of person — the middle-class American teenager — reads. Thinking of the novel in this way explains one of the more surprising facts of its publication — that it was originally intended for adults — and illustrates why adolescence emerges during the 1950s as the central location for consideration of phoniness and authenticity. If, in the popular imagination, Holden belongs to a time when "people started talking about 'alienation' and 'conformity' and 'the youth culture'" (Menand 85), the reason he remains so forcefully present past the end of the century is because the youth culture he represents is not exclusively a culture for youth. The mind-set that youth culture purports to instill — a healthy skepticism about adulthood and its putative hypocrisies — is something to which adults cling. More important, if adults do not "outgrow Holden's attitude" (84), then adolescence must be more than just a developmental stage, and youth culture must be more than just a metaphor for the values and rituals that teenagers use to define themselves away from their parents and toward their peer group. It must be a culture in the strong sense of the term, a collection of beliefs and practices that structure and give meaning to daily experience, with aspects that its members retain long after any particular maturation process has ostensibly ended.

This chapter examines how the cultural figure of the teenager crystallizes the problems inherent to the concept of the phony, the real phony, and the authentic selves to which they are ostensibly compared. It recasts the typical account of adolescence as merely a developmental stage to illustrate its dual representation in mid-century American culture: as both a process of maturation and a cultural community. Where the former suggests that the teenage self evolves through adolescence into adulthood, the latter suggests that adolescence operates like a religious, ethnic, or racial identity, an identification that would remain largely constant through time. This dual conception means that the teenager is uniquely positioned to illustrate both the epistemological and ontological questions that are central to the period's understanding of the self. Further, it illuminates the challenges to authenticity posed by each. Psychologists and sociologists have long noted that teenagers develop cultures all their own. This chapter revises these observations to demonstrate the ways in which those cultures are hoped to persist for the individual even after she leaves adolescence for adulthood. Most important, the chapter reveals the crucial role those cultures are imagined to play in safeguarding the adult against inauthenticity.

That the teenager became the subject of intense social and intellectual scrutiny during the postwar period is by now a critical commonplace. Studies of the history of adolescence in America generally agree that the period after World War II was crucial for the instantiation of the American teenager as a cultural phenomenon. Yet these accounts tend to understand the development of adolescence as a category, and the youth culture that attended to it, primarily as a consumer event.[4] The focus in the literature has thus been on the question of whether the American teenager produced the culture that attended him or vice versa. Historians debate whether teenagers, as a concept, preexisted the products and services marketed to them, or whether that market in fact produced the identity to which it ostensibly catered. These questions are outside the realm of this investigation. However, building off the consensus that by the late 1940s, "the teenage period of life—from ages thirteen to eighteen—took on the attributes of a mass cultural experience . . . with its own language, customs, and emotional traumas" (L. Cohen 319), this chapter thus considers the teenager not within the context of postwar American consumerism but rather amid the postwar concern for the possibility of an authentic self. Writing in 1959, Edgar Z. Friedenberg claimed, "Adolescents insult us by quietly flaunting their authenticity. They behave as if they did not even know that passion and fidelity are expensive, but merely assumed that everyone possessed them" (11). But what qualities of adolescence allow it to emerge as an exemplar of the authentic life still remain to be understood, as does the question of why adolescent authenticity during the period was thought to be particularly at risk.

I thus use two narratives about adolescence — *The Catcher in the Rye* and *Breakfast at Tiffany's* — to chart the phony's progression from Holden's model of the fully self-knowledgeable and seductively performative being who manipulates others for social gain, through its complication at Salinger's hands, to its emergence as the real phony, an authentic type all its own as embodied by Holly Golightly. Examining Holden's self-glorifying alienation as the only authentic individual in a phony world, the novel emerges as an extended thought experiment on the possibility of authenticity in a world in which complete self-knowledge is impossible. Though *The Catcher in the Rye* suggests that the self-knowledge about which Holden fantasizes is doomed to fail, it imagines a solution to the problem of phoniness in the form of a permanent adolescence. The teenager who emerges at the end of the novel conceives of adolescence less as a developmental stage than an approach to life, an "attitude" (Menand 84) that structures one's relation to world. If *The Catcher in the Rye* celebrates the possibilities of youth culture as a means to authenticity, then *Breakfast at Tiffany's* details the consequences of growing up and leaving the indeterminacy of the adolescent self behind. The product of a social context that is thought to deform rather than form individuals, the real phony exemplifies the contradictions inherent in imagining the self as simultaneously the result of and, crucially, still in opposition to, the culture that produces it.

To understand how the real phony emerges from her merely phony predecessor requires scrutinizing the discussions of adolescence and youth culture in the 1950s alongside the reconsideration of Freudian concepts to account for social influence on the psyche. Erik Erikson, the central psychological figure of the period, did what is now considered some of his most influential work on the ways in which cultural environments influence individual psychology. The range of child-rearing traditions in different cultures that Erikson's work mapped had profound consequences for Freud's traditional emphasis on family dynamics, suggesting that those dynamics themselves would need to be situated within a given cultural milieu.[5] The concept of the adolescent was likewise informed by the importation and popularization of existentialism in the late 1940s and 1950s. By virtue of his developmental needs, the figure of the teenager was thought to experience directly the relations that were thought crucial to the self's formation: the interactions between behavior and putative essences, between the self and its external contexts, and between the self and itself as it changes in time. Ultimately, the teenager — with Holden Caulfield as its representative figure — emerges as an existential hero during the period, because the identity work the teenager is imagined to be doing is exactly the type of work that the existentialist imagines that everyone should *always* be doing; that is the basis of authenticity as such.

In this chapter's first section, *The Catcher in the Rye* is situated alongside Jean-Paul Sartre's *Anti-Semite and Jew* to illustrate the existential model of self that grew increasingly popular during this period, and to work through the challenge to that model that Salinger's novel puts forth. Where *The Catcher in the Rye* progresses beyond the typical representation of existentialist ontology is in recognizing that such ontologies mirror precisely the theories of adolescent selfhood during the period. This similarity, furthermore, is not because all adolescents are thought to be natural existentialists (though they are), but rather because everyone, of all ages, is thought to be existentialist (or at least they should be). The result is that, insofar as everyone is an existentialist, everyone is also inevitably always an adolescent. By endorsing an existential model premised on the idea that, as the catchphrase would have it, "existence precedes essence," the novel imagines a way in which the individual might reconcile with the world of adulthood while at the same time maintaining a distance that marks out the space of the authentic self. The approach to the world that Holden advocates at the end of the novel appears less like the type of self-scrutiny in which the adolescent inevitably engages and more like the methodology or a handbook for the authentic life that the existentialist offers as a safeguard against inadvertent phoniness. The result is that adolescence becomes more than just a developmental stage. It emerges as a way of life.

I then consider in more detail the continuities that structure both the existentialist concept of the situation and the contemporaneous analyzes of adolescence by Erikson, sociologist Edgar Z. Friedenberg, and journalist Bette Friedan. In both, the individual struggle for authenticity models itself as a specifically developmental problem: a consequence of the interactions among the self, its constitutive influences, and time. My discussion exposes how the period's combined commitment to developmental narratives and a corrosive model of social influence suggests not only the source of Holden's epistemological dilemma, but also how Holly Golightly might come to be. As *Breakfast at Tiffany's* illustrates, real phonies like Holly Golightly, who are "given [their] character too soon" (55), thus exemplify individuals who are understood to be phony despite themselves—and yet are still held responsible for that inauthenticity. All his own experiences of Holly as "unique" (84) to the contrary, the narrator cannot imagine that the real phony might be as much an individual as anyone else—which is to say, as much an individual as anyone could be who develops in the context of the "self-contradictions in American history" (Erikson 287). To put it slightly differently, the novel imagines that though Holly experiences herself as real, there is another real that is somehow *more real* that Holly *should* be. Holly's own understanding of her authenticity has no relevance to its evaluation.

The Catcher in the Rye and the Deaf-Mute Solution

If, as Menand observes, adults who read *The Catcher in the Rye* reaffirm their detachment from the superficialities of adult life, it also reaffirms their detachment from at least some of the angst of adolescence.[6] In general, the strength of Holden's narrative voice encourages a form of submission to his point of view; sarcastic and full of the idiomatic speech and rhythms of mid-century teenagers, his voice invites the reader to agree with his assessments of people and places. Adult readers, though, are ostensibly better situated to recognize a potentially unreliable narrator when they find one, and to read through (or around) that voice to recognize that Holden is not so different from the phonies that he condemns. To adult readers, the novel's upper-middle-class New Yorkers—the phonies who like Alfred Lunt and Lynn Fontanne, Hollywood movies, and sanitized jazz performed for white audiences—may emerge as the corruptors of innocence, but they also might appear as the misunderstood victims of Holden's adolescent rage. How they are viewed depends on how Holden himself is viewed: as entirely blameless or the biggest phony of them all.

In a 1963 review of a later Salinger novel, Mary McCarthy provides a prototypical example of the latter position. She argues that for Holden, the characters of the novel are "divided into those who belong to the club and those who don't—the clean marlin, on one hand, and the scavenger sharks on the other" (35). From Holden's condescending point of view, "those who do not belong are 'born that way.' . . . They can't help the way they are, the way they talk: they are obeying a law of species" (36). But if Holden thinks the phonies are a separate species, it is not clear why he would call them phony, rather than merely different. McCarthy's metaphor of clubs and species assumes that Holden believes phonies constitute a different category of person from himself and others like him, even as marlins and sharks represent different categories of fish. Her metaphor implies not only that Holdens and marlins are different from phonies and sharks, but that they imagine themselves to be intrinsically better. The logic that McCarthy attributes to Holden is essentially a racialist one, based on a perceived ontology of persons, and the ethical force of her criticism comes from the fact that clubs in the 1950s excluded not marlins and sharks, but rather African Americans (a fact that is deplorable but not particularly surprising) and also Jewish Americans, an issue taken up in chapter 4. McCarthy's comparison is problematic for the reason that to judge a phony as such requires an assumption of similarity, not difference. If Holden believed that phonies were in fact "born that way," his ethical critique would lose its force. That an ethical judgment is weak does not, of course, prevent anyone from rendering it. There are many examples in which individuals are held responsible precisely for being, in McCarthy's terms, "born that way," despite the fact that the situation of one's birth would seem to be outside of one's sphere of influence. But this particular judgment of Holden's only makes sense if he assumes a sense of commonality with the phonies he condemns. His disgust rests upon a premise of shared humanity; the strength of his denunciation lies in the fact that phonies make choices that Holden presumably could make, but for ethical reasons never would.

McCarthy's critique highlights a central issue for analyses of *The Catcher in the Rye*. Holden can only perceive a phony's inauthenticity as such if he assumes a level of shared characteristics between them. Further, the presence of those shared characteristics suggests that Holden himself might not be as different from the phonies as he would like the reader to believe. What drives McCarthy's animosity toward *The Catcher in the Rye* is her conviction that Holden and the phonies are essentially the same; she condemns Holden's refusal to recognize that he and the phonies are not as different as he would like to believe. But while Holden himself never fully acknowledges this fact, the novel makes it obvious. To return to the example from the introduction, Holden describes his former headmaster Mr. Haas as "the phoniest bastard [he] ever met" (13–14) for giving the "little old funny looking parents" "a phony smile" and then favoring the better-dressed ones with conversation. Yet to accept Holden's account of events means that the reader need imagine Haas conducting a ruthless self-accounting in the moments before he approaches a student's parents. Haas would need to recognize that he dislikes funny-looking people and then quickly formulate a maneuver (highly transparent, as it turns out) to avoid them. But if one allows that Haas has not fully acknowledged his prejudice against the funny-looking, his quick getaway might appear less as an intentional subterfuge, and more as an only semiformulated instinct for escape. Presumably not all actions are as highly deliberative as Holden's model of phoniness would suggest. In fact, Holden himself performs a similar maneuver when he tells elaborate lies to the mother of a classmate on a train. He tells her that her universally detested son, "doubtless the biggest bastard that ever went to Pencey" (54), is beloved; he does so partially because he is "shooting the old crap around a little bit" (55) and partially as a cover for his own dislike of the boy since the mother seems nice. But to allow for a lack of total self-knowledge on Haas's part would enable exculpatory circumstances and would diffuse much of Holden's critique. It would be hard to blame Haas (though one still might dislike him) for avoiding the funny-looking parents if he is unaware of doing it. Holden's judgment of phonies requires that the phonies operate on a level of conscious choice that allows them to differentiate between how one might act and how others do so in similar situations.

Thus, while McCarthy is right to note that Holden's preoccupations are primarily classificatory—is Haas a phony or not?—ultimately the novel's interests best locate themselves in the larger questions that surround such categorizations. This interest is made more visible through Holden's difficulty in formulating a viable alternative to phoniness. He imagines himself to be crucially different from the phonies, yet he never succeeds in categorizing himself. His difficulty doing so suggests not only the permeability of what at first appear to be rigid ontological categories, but also the variables that complicate their easy construction and application. Those variables center on the problem of self-knowledge. After all, a person must know who he is in order to know which behaviors are authentic for him.

They also include the problem of development—the concept of a self that potentially changes over time. Knowing oneself is useful as a guide to authentic behavior only if who one is does not constantly change. For this reason, novels about adolescence emerge as key vehicles for considering these variables, because such novels presume a self that is under constant revision. Where *The Catcher in the Rye* might be said to depart from these generic formulations lies in its fundamental understanding that, during the period, these problems are not only the problems of adolescence—that they are part of what is conceived to be the nature of selfhood as such.

Of course, Holden is not the only one who has difficulty explicating what a state of authenticity might look like. Many recognize the theoretical problem; as Lionel Trilling acknowledges, authenticity "may well resist such efforts at definition" as one might try to make, but overall he tentatively states that it suggests "a more strenuous moral experience" with "a less acceptant and genial view of the social circumstances of life" and in which "much that was once thought to make up the very fabric of culture has come to seem of little account" (11).[7] Trilling rejects what others mean by "strenuous moral experience" as inseparable from the postwar attack on Freudian models of persons (a model he himself indirectly favors), arguing instead that "the therapeutic practice of psychoanalysis would seem to constitute a very considerable effort of self-knowledge, a strenuous attempt to identify and overcome in the mental life of the individual an inauthenticity which is not the less to be deplored because it is enforced and universal" (143). As Holden's condemnations of phonies would suggest, the practical reality of inauthenticity—that it is compulsory and collective—does nothing to mitigate its ethical failure.

Trilling makes three crucial observations on the idea of authenticity in the mid-twentieth century: first, that questions of self-knowledge in the postwar period are inextricable from and must wrestle with the Freudian model of conscious and unconscious life; second, that inauthenticity is defined as the final product of an intangible interaction between the individual and the social—that which "enforces" inauthentic behavior and toward which Americans have lost their "acceptant and genial view"; and third, that inauthenticity represents an ethical problem of the type Holden's disgust implies, in that the condition is made no less reprehensible by the fact that everybody's doing it. An advocate for psychoanalysis, Trilling objects to this ethical principle. As he explains, Freud's mature social theory finds a "newly discerned principle of inauthenticity" as the result of the interaction between society and the unconscious, "the extent of whose duplicity is suggested by its success in appropriating the reason and authority of society for its own self-serving principles" (150). In Trilling's account of psychoanalysis, inauthenticity results from the unconscious's use of social norms for "its own self-serving purposes" in the form of the superego. While it might be said to be the unconscious's choice to do so, it is not the individual's choice (since it all happens unconsciously). Regardless, society mandates such choices as a condition for successful social interaction.

None of these points fully address the more practical question of responsibility and blame at the heart of (at least) Holden's concerns. For example, if Haas does not know he is a phony, and if his choice to avoid the funny-looking parents operates as an unconscious one, Holden might not be in a position to condemn his behavior. The best he might do is to recommend he see an analyst. Holden does not believe in the unconscious per se—he rejects his own doctor's attempts to discuss his family life and "all that David Copperfield kind of crap" (1)—but even without a theory of the unconscious, his sense of self is arguably more complicated. The novel takes pains to illustrate that, consciously or otherwise, even Holden succumbs to something not unlike his definition of phoniness as a matter of course. In a representative instance, Holden admits that he "used to think [his former girlfriend Sally Hayes] was quite intelligent" (105), but he later decided "she's a pain in the ass" (106). Yet when they get together, "just to show you how crazy I am," Holden confesses, "I told her I loved her and all. It was a lie of course." But it is not a lie in the strictest sense of the word. As Holden explains, "the thing is, I *meant* it when I said it" (125) and insists that this fact constitutes "the terrible part" (134) of the whole experience. Holden cannot be called a phony here, because he does not deliberately deceive Sally in the manner he imagines Haas to do (although Holden may well be incorrect about Haas). Yet neither would anyone want to argue that this is authentic behavior of the type Trilling calls "a strenuous moral experience" (11). Rather Holden is just confused. How he behaves at any moment is contingent upon the social circumstances in which he finds himself and is susceptible to a terrific inconsistency.

In one sense, Holden's confusion is merely paradigmatic of the novel of adolescence as such, in which the fragmented adolescent self appears the inevitable product of juvenile ambivalence about middle-class social roles. Louis Menand identifies the concept of *Weltschmerz*—"the unhappiness of eternal disappointment in life as it is" (82)—as crucial to novels about adolescence. He argues that *The Catcher in the Rye* itself spawned a collection of "'Catcher in the Rye' rewrites, a literary genre all its own" (82). Whether *The Catcher in the Rye* genuinely introduced a new genre is open to debate. Its roots, however, arguably lie in the nineteenth-century *bildungsroman*, which Franco Moretti claims addressed a problem likewise familiar to writers such as David Riesman, Herbert Marcuse, and Erich Fromm: "a dilemma coterminous with modern bourgeois civilization: the conflict between the ideal of *self-determination* and the equally imperious demands of *socialization*" (15).[8] To put this in the mid-century terms addressed in this project, the problem is that "human nature and society can have conflicting demands" (Fromm 19). As the *bildungsroman* presents it, the resolution of this conflict requires not merely that the individual "subdue the drives that oppose the standards of 'normality.' It is also necessary that, as a 'free individual,' not as a fearful subject or but as a convinced citizen, one perceives the social norms *as one's own*. One must *internalize* them and fuse external compulsion and internal impulses into a new unity" (Moretti 16). Going through the motions of acquiescence is not enough. The subject must freely choose his own subjection.

Moretti's use of scare quotes around "normality" and "free individual" signals more than just skepticism about the bourgeois civilization demanding such socialization. It also indicates that his analysis is cognizant of (if not necessarily in full agreement with) the poststructuralist critique of the humanist self, a critique that disputes the possibility of the "free individual" as such. What once was called "internalization" looks from the perspective of postmodern theory more like interpellation, a point taken up in later chapters. However, *The Catcher in the Rye* departs from the genre of the classical *bildungsroman* by openly rejecting that genre's project of internalization. In so doing, Salinger's novel rejects as well one of the central tenets of the classical *bildungsroman*: the "idea of a gradual growth, a few steps at a time" (Moretti 46). In this sense the novel resembles more closely the late or counter-*bildungsroman*, works like Joyce's *The Portrait of the Artist as a Young Man* (1914) that were written in the years surrounding the First World War. In these novels, "[y]outh begins to despise maturity, and define itself in revulsion from it.... [Y]outh now looks for its meaning within itself: gravitating further and further away from adult age, and more and more toward adolescence, or preadolescence, or beyond" (Moretti 231). This refusal of adulthood thus became "the narrative form of what liberal Europe saw as an anthropological reversal from the individual as an autonomous entity to the individual as mere member of a mass.... [T]hat mass movements may be constitutive of individual identity — rather than merely destructive of it — was to remain an unexplored possibility of Western narrative" (232).

Moretti may not be correct to claim that Western narratives have never taken seriously the possibility that mass culture might produce genuinely individual individuals. Flirting with this possibility is precisely the project of *Breakfast at Tiffany's*. In *The Catcher in the Rye*, this revulsion from the realities of adult life constitutes a rejection of growth or development as such — a rejection of the idea that the self must inevitably change. Responding to his own propensity to "mean things when [he says] them," only to discover later that what he says "was a lie, of course" (125), Holden fantasizes a world of stasis, where the self would be as consistent as the panoramas he remembers from school trips to the Museum of Natural History. In that world, he remembers, "nobody moved. You could go there a hundred thousand times and that Eskimo would still be just finished catching those fish, the birds would still be on their way south, the deers would still be drinking out of the water hole. Nobody'd be different" (121). Even the fantasy terrifies, however, for Holden immediately recognizes that "the only thing that would be different would be you.... You'd have an overcoat on this time. Or the kid that was your partner in line had got scarlet fever and you'd have a new partner.... I mean you'd be *different* in some way" (121–22). The stasis of the panoramas serves only to underscore the lack of stasis for the adolescent, with the inevitable result that difference in and of itself becomes the only constant.

In a world where the possibility of self-knowledge appears increasingly suspect, waking up different from yourself looks entirely possible. As Holden rightly notes, the only way to assure authentic behavior is *never to behave*, to maintain an ideal of stasis that is itself unachievable. Nevertheless, it is Holden's fantasy. It forms the basis of his respect for James Castle, a classmate who kills himself (wearing Holden's sweater) rather than retract under duress a comment he made about a fellow student

(170). It motivates his desire to be "the catcher in the rye": the only "big kid" amid thousands of "little kids" whose job it is "to catch everybody if they start to go over the cliff" (173) — that is, if they start to grow up. After all, growing up and taking a job, even an altruistic one, opens oneself up to phoniness because "even if you did go around saving guys' lives and all, how would you know if you did it because you really wanted to save guys' lives, or because what you really wanted to do was be a terrific lawyer, with everybody slapping you on the back and congratulating you in court when the goddamn trial was over.... How would you know you weren't being a phony?" (172).

It is a good question. Since phoniness for Holden constitutes deception for social advancement, and complete self-knowledge is impossible, then any contact with the social runs the risk of inauthenticity. The result is a profound anxiety about motive — about whether one's actions stem from authentic impulses, or whether they are the product of external influences. Furthermore, this particular anxiety is not limited to Holden and his fellow adolescents during the 1950s. In *The Lonely Crowd* (1953), David Riesman describes the individual who would count as autonomous: a state in which one is able to evaluate the relative advantages and disadvantages to conforming and then choose between them. The autonomous are individuals who "may or may not conform outwardly" (243). But whichever the autonomous chooses, the important thing is that "he has a *choice*" (243, emphasis added), unlike the adjusted, who are unintentionally all the same. If autonomics choose to conform for strategic purposes, the adjusted are uniform. Their essential similarity is not a matter of choice; it just *is*. Like Holden, autonomics — when refusing "to bend the knee to custom" — are prone to self-doubt. They repeatedly ask themselves, "is this what I really want? Perhaps I only want it because ..." (256). This is because, in Riesman's view, "the autonomous ... live in a milieu in which people systematically question themselves in anticipation of the questions of others" (256). While the benefits of autonomy include the ability to separate oneself from one's context — to maintain a modicum of psychic independence — the disadvantages include a potentially never-ending self-scrutiny.

Given this anxiety about the true source of one's motivation, and the possibility that it derives from inauthentic sources, Holden's refusal of action makes more sense. His commitment to stasis—to a principled non-action—thus operates as a refusal of the social as such, insofar as all action is understood to be in some way social. Nevertheless, nonaction is a little bit harder in practice than in theory. As Holden's history teacher observes, "Life is a game that one plays according to the rules." Holden might think (but not vocalize), "Game my ass. Some game. If you get on the side where all the hot-shots are, then it's a game, all right. . . . But if you get on the other side, where there aren't any hot-shots, then what's a game about it?" (8). But contrary to his wishes, Holden's inability to win does not render life not a game—the nature of games is that someone must lose—and no one else will quit playing just because Holden says stop. Consequently all his attempts not to act, not to play the game on ethical grounds (it is not fair), only look as if he is playing badly. What Holden imagines as a principled refusal to participate, his teacher, and the larger culture in which he moves more generally, views only as poor sportsmanship.

But if Holden's rejection of growth—his rejection of a project of internalization in which the protagonist learns to "*desire* to do what [he] in any case *should* have done" (Moretti 21)—resembles the counter-*bildungsromans* of the World War I era, the alternative to such internalization that Holden adopts comes directly out of the intellectual climate in the years after World War II. In so doing, furthermore, the novel imagines a way in which one might retain the possibility of authenticity regardless of the self's inevitable existence within a particular social circumstance. Holden's situation is having no outside position from which he can register his objections, and it is a problem of which he is acutely aware. Although the solution he stumbles upon looks naïve, it constitutes an active choice of the type central to Sartrean existential philosophy's version of the ethical life. Holden decides:

> I thought what I'd do was, I'd pretend to be one of those deaf-mutes. That way I wouldn't have to have any of those goddam stupid useless conversations with anybody. If anybody wanted to tell me something, they'd have to write it on a piece of paper and shove it over to me. They'd get bored as hell doing that after a while, and then I'd be through with having conversations for the rest of my life. Everybody'd think I was just a poor deaf-mute bastard and they'd leave me alone. (198–99)

At first glance, it looks as if pretending to be a "deaf-mute bastard" constitutes explicit phoniness. All epistemological questions aside, one can assume that a person would know if he were an actual deaf-mute. Yet there is a way that Holden's decision to assume deaf-mute status might avoid the taint of phoniness precisely because it presents itself as a self-conscious, active choice based upon his situation, what Jean-Paul Sartre's *Anti-Semite and Jew* understands as the guarantor of individual authenticity despite the inevitability of external pressures.

Subscribing to a doctrine of radical self-making, that "existence precedes essence," Sartre argues that "man . . . is not definable" by his racial, economic, religious, or cultural background: "Man is nothing else but what he makes of himself" (*Existentialism* 28). As he explains, "human reality does not exist first in order to act later; but for human reality, to be is to act, and to cease to act is to cease to be" (*Being* 613). Taking the question "is the supreme value of human activity a *doing* or a *being*?" as fundamental, existential philosophy finds "no *given* in human reality, in the sense that temperament, character, passions, [or] principles of reason would be acquired or innate data existing in the manner of things. The empirical consideration of the human being shows him as an organized unity of conduct patterns or of 'behaviors'" (*Being* 558, 612–13).[9] Though the individual appears "'to be made' by climate and the earth, race and class, language and the history of the collectivity of which he is a part" (619), one's ontological freedom dictates that "the past is without force to constitute the present and to sketch out the future" (637). While the situation of one's birth, personal history, and cultural context "must account for the *substantial permanence* which we readily recognize in people . . . and which the person experiences in most cases as being his own," in fact "there is no character; there is only a project of oneself" (705) realized through one's acts and always open to revision.

This self-making does not take place in a vacuum; the individual is constrained by the situation in which she finds herself, and that situation may well give primacy to precisely the cultural or racial determinism that the existentialist refuses to imagine as constitutive. But if the individual cannot control her circumstances, or situation, she can control how she responds to those circumstances. Evaluations of authenticity will be made on the basis of those choices as such, not whether those choices align with a putative internal essence or being. Using the situation of the Jew returning to France after World War II as a representative instance, Sartre observed, "[i]f it is agreed that man may be defined as a being having freedom within the limits of a situation, then it is easy to see that the exercise of this freedom may be considered as authentic or inauthentic according to the choices made" (*Anti-Semite* 90). Insofar as the situation (or in Holden's terms, the game) limits the individual's freedom to respond, then Sartre maintains that the man acts authentically vis à vis his situation only in accepting it first and acting on it afterward. Thus, the only means for individuals to be authentic — not to "deal with their situation by running away from it" — is to embrace it in its totality, to maintain "a true and lucid consciousness ... in assuming the responsibilities and risks that it involves" (90). Behaviors, rather than essences, determine the authenticity of the individual; at each moment the individual's radical freedom allows her to transcend the limitations of her personal or cultural history to make the authentic choice.

What that authentic choice might be is open to debate. Sartre himself never completed the treatise on ethics that he promised as future work at the end of *Being and Nothingness*. His *Notebooks on an Ethics* represented decades of work that were published only posthumously. At the time of *The Catcher in the Rye*, a definition of existential authenticity would need to be extrapolated from those writings, like *Anti-Semite and Jew* and *Existentialism and Humanism*, which had been translated into English. Since a person "cannot be distinguished from his situation, for it forms him and decides his possibilities," it is still up to him "to give it meaning, by making his choices within it and by it" (Sartre, *Anti-Semite* 60). This valorization of choice appears to make sense when applied to the Jew as Jew; one can imagine the ways in which a Jew might "assert his claim" (91) in the face of a hostile situation. In chapter 4 of this volume, *Anti-Semite and Jew*'s implication for the mid-century representations of authentic Jewishness is explored further. But it makes less sense in *The Catcher in the Rye*. If one retains the capacity of hearing and speech, it is difficult to see how asserting one's claim as a deaf-mute might be authentic.

The answer lies in the existentialist's rejection of essences as fundamental to authenticity. Holden's situation is that he cannot communicate with the people around him; for all the good that speech and audition do him, he might as well *be* a deaf-mute. Since his situation "forms him and decides his possibilities," any choices he makes must be made "within it and by it." Thus, by this account, choosing to be a deaf-mute (when one is not a deaf-mute) constitutes the choice to be who one is even if one is not. Choosing, then, is more important than choosing correctly. In fact, choosing correctly is irrelevant to the task at hand. Holden chooses what he will not be—he chooses against phoniness—in the only way he can think of, by making literal a purely figurative aspect of his situation. When he attempts to communicate, no one hears him and, try as he might, he cannot understand what anyone else is saying. His situation (how not to play the game as a matter of principle) and his choice (to be a deaf-mute) meet Sartre's criterion, insofar as his choice is fully self-conscious and takes all responsibility for its consequences. As an existential thought experiment, the decision to become a deaf-mute constitutes, as Sartre claims authenticity must, "a moral decision, bringing certainty . . . on the ethical level" (*Anti-Semite* 141), which is precisely the level on which Holden registers his complaint.

While Holden's crusade against phoniness begins as a search for an adolescent notion of truth, it ends when truth itself is sacrificed to authenticity as the highest attainable goal. The confused adolescent must decide that it is more important to be authentic than to be honest—a decision that would seem at best counterintuitive. The novel avoids working through this dilemma by never allowing Holden to go through with this plan, and neither does it explain why. "I could probably tell you what I did after I went home, and how I got sick and all," Holden offers, "but I don't feel like it" (213). Yet Holden does seem to have made some sort of peace with the world that surrounds him. "About I all know," he confesses, "is I sort of *miss* everybody I told about" (214). Adolescent disdain has been replaced by a more adult nostalgia, yet crucially this nostalgia does not imply that Holden has fully succumbed to the conveniences of the phony world. By placing his reconciliation outside of even the indirect view of the reader, the novel avoids detailing the precise means through which Holden comes to terms with endemic phoniness. The reader knows that Holden has given up the fantasies of being either a deaf-mute or the catcher in the rye; he recognizes, for example, that if kids on the carousel "want to grab for the gold ring, you have to let them do it, and not say anything. If they fall off, they fall off" (211). But the reader does not know precisely why. However, neither does the novel's ending suggest that Holden has fully internalized the values and beliefs of adult culture. He has not, as the *bildungsroman* would have it, fused "external compulsion and internal impulses into a new unity" (Moretti 16), and adopted freely social norms as his own.

Instead, *The Catcher in the Rye* advocates an approach to social interaction that Sartre himself might have endorsed, suggesting a means through which one might maintain one's authenticity despite the inevitability of social influence. Repeatedly asked by his doctor if he is "going to apply [himself]" when he returns to school in September, Holden explains, "It's such a stupid question, in my opinion. I mean how do you know what you're going to do till you *do* it? The answer is, you don't. I *think* I am, but how do I know?" (213). He has a point. In a world in which "man is defined first of all as a being 'in a situation'. . . [that] forms him and decides his possibilities" (Sartre, *Anti-Semite and Jew* 59–60), it is impossible to know what the authentic choice will be until that situation — and the choices that arise from it — is presented. The existentialist model of self thus provides a means to bypass the problem of self-knowledge that plagued Holden from the beginning of the novel. Since there is no essential self to know, that Holden, or for that matter Haas — or any of the other phonies — do not know that self is only to be expected. One cannot know what one is going to do until one does it.

The Catcher in the Rye thus refuses the idea that one could know an authentic choice in advance of its presentation — that one could say because I am this type of person (marlin or shark, adolescent or headmaster), the authentic choice would be X. What the novel finally offers is less a state of being — phony or authentic — than an approach to the world designed to produce an authentic self. Or, as Louis Menand would put it, an "attitude" (84) with which one might continually evaluate one's situations and the opportunities for authenticity that exist therein. It is the attitude that Holden expresses when he worries that he "*meant* it when [he] asked her" (134) or when he rhetorically wonders "how would you know you were not being a phony?" (176). As becomes clear in the next section, in a situation in which social influence is both inevitable and inevitably corruptive, such an attitude is put forth as the only defense one has against the real phoniness that was feared to plague not just Holly Golightly but also the American character in the 1950s more generally.

Childhood and Society, Breakfast at Tiffany's, and the Real Phony

The existentialist model of self became increasingly well known during the late 1940s and early 1950s. American audiences first became familiar with Sartre's work through the mainstream rather than the academic press. Writing for *The New Yorker* in December 1945, Janet Flanner reported that, in Paris, "Sartre is automatically fashionable now among those who once found Surrealism automatically fashionable" (quoted in Fulton, 11–12). In the mid- to late 1940s, articles about Sartre and Beauvoir appeared in opinion magazines such as the *Partisan Review*, the *Nation*, and the *New Republic*; popular magazines such as *Life*, the *New York Times Magazine*, *Time*, and *Newsweek*; and fashion magazines such as *Vogue* and *Harper's Bazaar*. A number of Sartre's plays and novels were translated in the late 1940s; excerpts of *Nausea* appeared in the *Paris Review* in 1946; *The Flies*, *No Exit*, *The Age of Reason*, and *The Reprieve* were published in English in 1947; *No Exit* and *The Flies* were produced on Broadway and on college campuses.[10] However Sartre's first specifically philosophical work to appear in the United States was *Existentialism and Humanism* (1948), a short essay based on the popular lecture "L'Existentialisme est un Humanisme," in which Sartre outlined his concept of selfhood in broad terms.[11] As its catchphrase "existence precedes essence" implies, the essay argues that human beings are not constituted through the contingent circumstances of birth—be they racial, sociological, political, cultural, or anything else. Rather, human beings continually transcend mere facts and constitute themselves through the choices that they make. The result is, on the one hand, a radical freedom; on the other, a fundamental responsibility for oneself and one's actions: for one's authenticity as such.

It was not until the early 1950s that the nature of that responsibility was explicated fully for American audiences. "Bad Faith," the fourth section of *Being and Nothingness*, was translated and appeared as part of the volume *Existentialist Psychoanalysis* in 1953.[12] Developing more fully the ideas expressed in *Existentialism and Humanism*, Sartre's discussion of bad faith suggests the original source of the confused adolescent's inauthentic impulses. He may live in risk of acting in bad faith, but in fact that bad faith may not be entirely his responsibility. The product of a complicated relationship between the developing self and its external situation, the concept of bad faith further elaborates Sartre's account of the problem of inauthenticity. More important, it lays the groundwork for the way in which real phonies like Holly Golightly might come to be theorized by Capote and observers of 1950s adolescence.

Sartre defines bad faith as a particular type of falsehood. The traditional liar, he explains, is necessarily in "complete possession of the truth he is hiding" (*Psychoanalysis* 155) and "utilizes for its own profit the duality of myself and myself in the eyes of others" (157). This type of lie, for example, is precisely the behavior Holden originally attributes to his headmaster, Haas, who conceals his actual feelings about unattractive parents behind his simulation of polite behavior. Since the unattractive parents cannot read his mind, he presumably gets away with the subterfuge. However, the person who acts in bad faith — who lies not to others but rather to herself — also "must know the truth very exactly in *order* to conceal it more carefully," but that concealment must take place within "the unitary structure of a single project" (158–59), or consciousness. If Haas were to conceal his unacceptable opinions from himself, for example, he would need first to admit that he has those opinions, and only then reconceal them from his own consciousness — a consciousness that had acknowledged having them only moments before, precisely *in order* to conceal them. He would have to become other to himself, the other from whom the truth must be concealed. But this requires that one know the lie in order to know that it needs to be suppressed. How can one know without knowing one knows?

The theoretical impossibility of achieving this duality within "the unity of *a single* consciousness" (*Psychoanalysis* 158) is conveniently answered by psychoanalysis. Cutting "the psychic whole in two" (161), psychoanalysis substitutes "for the notion of bad faith, the idea of a lie without a liar" (163). That is, in Freud's theory, the dyad of self and other — one of whom knows the truth, one of whom does not — is replicated within the individual consciousness. The theory thus imagines the individual to be "in the same relationship to myself that the other has in respect to me"; for "the duality of the deceiver and the deceived," psychoanalysis substitutes the duality "of the 'id' and the 'ego'" (Sartre, *Psychoanalysis* 163). Yet at some point, Sartre argues, even if the psychic whole is divided, there must be a censor that mediates between the two functions, recognizing that one (the id) possesses knowledge that the other (the ego) cannot have. But how can that censor be conscious of the fact that the conscious must not be conscious of the lie?

The lie to oneself is thus from Sartre's perspective logically incoherent, and he argues instead that the individual in bad faith is doing something else: she manipulates "the double property of the human being, who is at once a facticity and a transcendence . . . affirming their identity while preserving their differences" (*Psychoanalysis* 175). By way of elaboration, Sartre introduces the example of the coquette, a young woman who wishes to continue to flirt with her suitor without engendering any consequences for her behavior. When faced with her suitor's very concrete sexual interest — a part of her situation, or "facticity" — the coquette "purifies his desire of anything humiliating by being willing to consider it only as pure transcendence, which she avoids even naming" (178) — as only a metaphysical respect for her being. Facticity becomes transcendence. Once she has rewritten his carnal desire as a metaphysical transcendence, she then "arrests this transcendence, she glues it down with all the facticity of the present; respect is nothing other than respect, it is an arrested surpassing which no longer surpasses itself toward anything" (178) like a carnal desire. Transcendence becomes facticity. To put it slightly differently, the coquette wants it both ways, and because humans are composed of both facticity and transcendence she can get it, by imagining first that the facts (carnal desire) are transcendent — they are a manifestation of respect — and then, that the transcendent (respect) is a fact — it cannot transcend itself to become carnal desire.

What Sartre argues against is the possibility of pure self-deception, but his objections are less to the logical inconsistencies inherent in Freud's division of consciousness than to the uses to which those divisions might be put.[13] Sartre's protest is not so much that Freud's model does not explain the experience of bad faith clearly (although he claims it does not) as that such a model enables a variety of excuses for at best ill-considered and at worst unethical behavior. It makes it entirely too easy to say, as Holden does, "*I meant* it when I said it" (125); to ignore the implications of one's actions when those implications are inconvenient, as Sartre's representative coquette does, who willfully "disarms the phrases of her suitor of their sexual background" (*Psychoanalysis* 173). Yet whose fault is it when one does act in bad faith? Sartre seems more than willing to condemn the coquette's actions as cowardly, but in *Anti-Semite and Jew* one learns that the inauthentic Jew requires a far more diffuse application of blame: "It is our eyes that reflect to him the unacceptable image that he wishes to dissimulate. It is our words and our gestures — *all* our words and *all* our gestures — our anti-Semitism, but equally our condescending liberalism that have poisoned him" (*Anti-Semite* 135). Despite Sartre's usual devotion to individual responsibility, he blames society for placing the Jew in his situation, and the subsequent mess he makes of it is to be expected.

The adolescent's private struggle with authenticity thus models itself as a developmental problem — a dangerous consequence of the interaction between the evolving self and the cultural circumstances in which that self is situated. More important, here one can begin to see why the adolescent herself emerges as a locus around which questions of authenticity are focused in the period — and how adolescence itself might crucially emerge as a type of permanent condition: an outlook or an attitude, rather than a developmental stage. If "conflict between the individual and society . . . is inherent in the development of personality," as Edgar Z. Friedenberg argues, then "adolescence is this conflict, no matter how old the individual is when it occurs. Adolescent conflict is the instrument by which an individual learns the complex, subtle, and precious difference between himself and his environment" (13). Loosening adolescence from a particular biological or chronological moment, Friedenberg thus identifies adolescence less as a developmental moment than an operative approach toward the expectations of one's environment — or to use Sartre's phrase, situation. Adolescence becomes, as it has for Holden and for Louis Menand, a way of addressing the world.

This view of adolescence was central to its primary mid-century theorizer, Erik Erikson. In *Childhood and Society* (1950), the definitive mid-century text on the subject, Erikson describes adolescence thusly: "what the regressing and growing, rebelling and maturing youths are now primarily concerned with is who and what they are in the eyes of a wider circle of significant people as compared with what they themselves have come to feel they are" (307). The project imagines a substantive disjunction between an inner self and a socially dictated persona, only this time the outer persona is not self-consciously assumed for social gain — as Holden fantasizes of Haas — but rather foisted on the unsuspecting self by a hostile outer world. Or, as Erikson explains, American mothers continually make the mistake of "standardizing and overadjusting children . . . creating, instead of individualism, a mass-produced mask of individuality" (295). The result is a generation of "automatons" (16), to use Erich Fromm's word, for whom the usual qualities of surface and depth have been reversed. Unlike Holden's phonies, who are superficially conformist and internally individual, Erikson's overadjusted adolescents are outwardly individual (wearing individuating "masks") and uniform (or "standardized") within.

Erikson's work was central to the theorization of adolescence that developed in the years after World War II, the years in which the teenager and youth culture became an increasingly omnipresent cultural phenomenon. Based on articles written throughout the 1940s, *Childhood and Society* was first published in 1950 and garnered increasing interest as the 1950s wore on. By 1963 it had become a central text for university courses in sociology, psychology, and social work (Friedman 240–41).[14] With it, Erikson joined the range of writers and scholars who were directly concerned with the problems of conformity and uniformity in American culture. His work was influenced by Erich Fromm and particularly David Riesman; in its interest in the deforming forces of mass society, it bears broad similarities to the work of Herbert Marcuse, Theodor Adorno, and Hannah Arendt (Friedman 20, 162, 174). However, Erikson's work differs from these other writers because he centers the emergence of authenticity or its opposites in the specific moment of adolescence, during which the teenager must develop an identity or live in a state of "role confusion." His theorization of the life cycle — the idea that psychic development takes place throughout life, not just in childhood as Freud had argued — places adolescence at the center of the self's development as the moment when one's sense of identity, as he came to formulate the term, is formed.

Erikson's project self-consciously engages with Freud's later work insofar as he is interested in "shifting its emphasis from the concentrated study of the conditions which blunt and distort the individual ego to the study of the ego's roots in social organization" (16). Comparing the "American identity" to that of other cultures — the Sioux and Yurok, the Russian, and the

German—he identifies in Americans a tendency of which Sartre would approve. The American, Erikson observes, "'will not commit himself to any identity as predetermined by the stigmata of birth'" (298). Erikson's first case study is the son of Jewish parents who recently moved to a predominantly gentile neighborhood in northern California (Friedman 202). Sam is a child with "a low tolerance of aggression," whose behavioral difficulties stem not only from "the whole milieu of these children of erstwhile fugitives from ghettos and pogroms" but also his particular situation amid both "his parents' conflict with their ancestors" and the family's decision to "dare the Jewish fate, by isolating itself in a Gentile town" (Erikson 30–31). "Going through a maturation stage characterized by a developmental intolerance of restraint" (31), Sam is prone to epileptic fits that end with loss of consciousness; Erikson discovers, "having worked with the mother also and learned her part of it," that "whatever deep 'psychic stimulus' may be present in the life of the young child, it is identical with his mother's most neurotic conflict" (30). Mirroring and amplifying his mother's neuroses, Sam is at risk of taking on a "predetermined" identity through the shaping forces of family, religion, and culture.

Sam's problem is here figured as a historical one; the Jewish history of being "erstwhile fugitives" established certain behavioral tendencies themselves reified in the culture and exacerbated by his parents' willingness to "dare the Jewish fate." Mother and child are thus identical insofar as her unresolved "conflict with her ancestors" is itself passed on to Sam in the form of a cultural situation or "social organization," manifested in Sam's failure to grow emotionally. In other words, the mother's failure to develop results in her child's equivalent failure; both are stuck in an earlier developmental stage. The implication is that all Jews in "conflict with their ancestors" are, emotionally speaking, children, but in this sense they are seen as no different from *all Americans*. Erikson's use of Sam as his paradigmatic example engenders the question of why the Jew is positioned as the representative American.[15] Yet the Jew is the perfect exemplar from Erikson's point of view, to the extent that every culture has some form of a history that perpetuates itself; the advantage of the Jews is, of course, that in the years after World War II their recent fate is well known. Only when one recognizes that, for Erikson, development within any culture is *by definition* isolating, alienating, and inauthenticating can Sam represent the American psyche.

Whatever else one imagines oneself to be, since one is inevitably isolated, one is inevitably a Jew. Consequently one can likewise understand how Haas (the phony) and Holly (the real phony) figure as universal anomalies. According to Erikson, being abnormal is the postwar norm.

Insofar as everyone is inevitably a Jew, however, everyone is also inevitably an adolescent. Erikson privileges adolescence as a developmental stage because the adolescent subject possesses a self-consciousness inaccessible to the child. It is the time when the patient — Jewish, white Anglo-Saxon Protestant, or otherwise — might repair earlier psychic damage. It is the moment when "all samenesses and continuities relied on earlier are more or less questioned again" (261). As Erikson explains, "the danger of this stage is role diffusion; as Biff puts it in *Death of a Salesman* 'I just can't take hold, Mom, I can't take hold of some kind of a life,'" resulting in "[y]outh after youth, bewildered by his assumed role, a role forced upon him by the inexorable standardization of American adolescence" (307). If the adolescent is lucky, he emerges "untouched and keeps his course: this will largely depend on the wife whom he — as the saying goes — chooses. Otherwise what else can he become but a childish joiner, or a cynical little boss, trying to get in on some big boss's 'insider track' — or a neurotic character, a psychosomatic case?" (323).

The adolescent then becomes a phony — "childish," "cynical," "a joiner" — but with a difference. Erikson stages a Sartrean moment of choosing in adolescence, the moment at which one elects it for one's own or fakes it for a lifetime, with the result that every individual over the age of eighteen might be understood as potentially phony, depending upon whether or not he is successfully developed. Lawrence J. Friedman has argued that this was an unintended consequence of the way Erikson presented the life cycle, which tended to make all of life's eight stages appear too linear and progressive, and too focused on adolescence as the central developmental moment: "the four stages that preceded [adolescence] seemed clearly to have involved working toward identity, while the subsequent three stages appeared to be governed by identity consolidation" (226). In fact, Erikson intended all of the stages to suggest a constant renegotiation of one's place in a social fabric (Friedman 227).

Yet in emphasizing "the neurotic character," Erikson moves the debate away from individual self-knowledge and evaluation, the forces behind the Sartrean emphasis on choice, and toward a model in which one might be phony despite oneself as the consequence of a developmental defect. Limiting individual responsibility, Erikson circumscribes individual freedom, making phoniness or authenticity a consequence of development as opposed to an individual ethical victory. His system thus suggests how one could be a phony without realizing it: a situation in which the best judge of individual authenticity may reside outside of the individual himself (for example: Holden evaluating Haas), in which the phony wearing "the mass-produced mask of individuality" (295) would have no idea that she was wearing the mask at all.

And what would that phony be, other than real? As the narrator of *Breakfast at Tiffany's* observes, Holly did not develop like other people.[16] Comparing Holly to a childhood acquaintance, he explains,

> The average person reshapes frequently; every few years our bodies undergo a complete overhaul—desirable or not, it is a natural thing that we should. All right, here were two people that never would. That is what Mildred Grossman had in common with Holly Golightly. They would never change because they had been given their character too soon; which, like sudden riches, leads to a lack of proportion: the one had splurged herself into a top-heavy realist, the other a lopsided romantic. (55)

Character, like the human body, continually evolves; this is a human universal, "a natural thing." There need be no ethical valence attached. Even as the body and the character are compared as similar if not identical entities, however, they are immediately contrasted again in Holly's case. What makes Holly unusual is not that she developed differently; she did, but only insofar as she did not *develop* at all. Like the panoramas at the Museum of Natural History, her character is static, stuck in an earlier stage. In moments when Holly is without make-up, she, the narrator comments, looks "not quite twelve years" (92); she must use powder and paint to get "every vestige of the twelve year old out of her face" (93). Because of this stasis, one would not argue that Holly's personality is authentic in precisely the terms Sartre advocates. Holly's character is real in that she is not faking it, but it is fake insofar as it comes entirely from outside herself, rather than as a product of her own making. Her character was "given . . . too soon" (55). The narrator continues, "I imagined them in a restaurant of the future, Mildred still studying the menu for its nutritional values, Holly still gluttonous for everything on it" (55), and his metaphor of consumption and ingestion makes clear what sudden riches only implies: those qualities that Holly possesses come to her entirely from the outside.

Breakfast at Tiffany's and the real phony thus explain by example an important distinction between two types of authenticity, which for lack of better terms shall be called internal versus superficial, the latter of which includes all the pejorative connotations attached to notions of superficiality. Internal authenticity would stem from the ostensibly natural process of growth and change that Capote describes; superficial authenticity, from ingesting wholly the character provided by a given cultural milieu. It's worth noting here that American female adolescents were thought particularly susceptible to the latter condition. That American girls were "given their character too soon" would form the central critique of Bette Friedan's *The Feminine Mystique* (1963) and become one of the central claims of the developing movement for women's rights. Acknowledging that "the image—created by the women's magazines, by advertisements, television, movies, novels, columns and books by experts on marriage and the family, child psychology, sexual adjustment and by the popularizers of sociology and psychoanalysis—shapes women's lives and mirrors their dreams" (34), Friedan censures the limitations that she argued have been artificially built into that image for the past two decades. Prewar images of women, she argues, showed them "independent and determined to find a new life of [their] own" (38). Comparatively, the image disseminated after World War II "makes certain concrete, finite, domestic aspects of feminine existence—as it was lived by women whose lives were confined, by necessity, to cooking cleaning, washing, bearing children—into a religion, a pattern by which all women must now live or deny their femininity" (43). For Friedan, the ingestion of this image produces precisely the type of stasis—the antigrowth—that Holden craves, Holly embodies, and her narrator laments. Describing research that found a sharp drop in the IQ levels of adolescent girls, Friedan notes that the record showed "repeated statements that 'it isn't too smart for a girl to be smart.'" She argues, "In a very real sense, these girls were arrested in their mental growth, at age fourteen or fifteen, by conformity to the feminine image" (174).

In important respects, Friedan's argument replicates the uncertainty that is at the center of Erikson's account of adolescence, and that haunts the narrator of *Breakfast at Tiffany's*. On one hand, Friedan acknowledges that culture will have a determining influence on the developing teenager; this is why she wants to change the image, rather than get rid of it entirely. On the other hand, neither Friedan nor the narrator can imagine that Holly (or the adolescent girls she represents) is not in some way harmed by this influence, regardless of its inevitability. Why should internal authenticity be so privileged, or why should superficial authenticity be such a bad thing? What's wrong with a society in which everyone wears a "mass-produced mask of individuality" (Erikson 295)? Presumably, individual experience carries some weight, and Holly, as a real phony, certainly experiences herself as authentic. Ultimately what matters to the individual is the real, not the phony, part of the combination. The "mass-produced mask" may create situations in which others know more about a person than she knows about herself—realness as a quality demands self-ignorance, but presumably somebody recognizes the mask as such—but Holly is hardly damaged by her lack of self-knowledge. As she would be the first to admit, she does fine in a world where "$350" can be made in a night with only "a few extra trips to the powder room" (Capote 56).

Nevertheless, anxiety about the "standardizing and overadjusting" of American youth runs throughout Erikson's work and dominates the conclusion of *Breakfast at Tiffany's*, manifesting itself as a fear of uniformity and the loss of a specifically American individuality. Those who conform choose to do so—and may also choose not to. Real phonies, who believe they make choices when they do not, are fundamentally uniform. The connection between real phonies and uniformity is reasonable if not automatic. If character might be understood as "given" by society, what makes individuals individual in the strong sense of the word? Just because everyone does the same thing at the same time (eat, sleep, work, play) does not mean everyone is the same, but it does leave open the question of where difference is to be located, especially if models of development grant primacy to social forces. The cultural notion of standardization and adjustment implies as much. Indeed, such standardization is implicit in the promise of Holden Caulfield's prep school, which boasts that "Since 1888 we have been molding boys into splendid, clear-thinking young men." Holden may think that that promise is "strictly for the birds" since anyone "that was splendid and clear-thinking . . . probably came to Pencey that way" (Salinger 2), but to argue this is to assume that boys bring fully formed characters with them, that each individual possesses his character in an essential as opposed to a developmental manner. As suggested above, not everyone shares this opinion. At the very least, the promise of "molding" is certainly part of the appeal of a school like Pencey for the funny-looking and the attractive parents alike who visit on Sundays.

At the same time, however, while one might recognize that uniformity among phonies, real or otherwise, suggests a potential problem, one must also acknowledge that this problem is not Holly's, but rather the narrator's. Because the novel is written in the first person, but not from Holly's point of view, one must read past the narrator's account to determine that Holly suffers no significant ill effects from her real phoniness. Those moments when she does indulge in something like introspection look, on one hand, like an acknowledgment of her lack of internal authenticity. A child bride in Oklahoma before she ran away to Hollywood, she comments to the narrator after her husband Doc comes to New York to take her home:

> Right up till the last minute Doc thought I was going to go with him. Even though I kept telling him: But, Doc, I'm not fourteen any more, and I'm not Lulamae. But the terrible part is (and I realized it while we were standing there) I am. I'm still stealing turkey eggs and running through a briar patch. Only now I call it having the mean reds. (69–70)

Such statements look like an acknowledgment of stasis, a recognition that she was given her character too soon by mass cultural influences, by the movie magazines that Doc blames for taking Holly away from him. "Ask me, that's what done it," he claims, "Looking at show-off pictures. Reading dreams. That's what started her walking down the road" (66). The only moments in which the novel imagines that Holly Golightly suffers from her real phoniness occurs when she experiences "the mean reds" — when "you're afraid and you sweat like hell, but you do not know what you're afraid of. Except that something bad is going to happen, only you do not know what it is" (37–38). The narrator identifies this sensation as "*angst*" (38). As sparsely defined as it is in the novel, it is the only indication that there might be some cost to Holly's construction entirely within cultural forms. Further, those moments of introspection have a familiar, corny aspect to them. Phrases like "I'm still stealing turkey eggs" (70) or, even worse, "it could go on forever. Not knowing what's yours until you've thrown it away" (103), suggest Holly is living her life from a cliched Hollywood script.

But even if the novel supports the narrator's sense of Holly as a real phony, Holly herself believes fully in her own authenticity. She acknowledges, "I'd rob a grave, I'd steal two bits off a dead man's eyes if I thought it would contribute to the day's enjoyment," but insists one should be honest: "Not law-type honest . . . but unto-thyself type honest. Be anything but a coward, a pretender, an emotional crook, a whore: I'd rather have cancer than a dishonest heart" (79). Whatever Holly thinks of herself, she does not think she is a phony. Her lack of self-consciousness gives the narrator great satisfaction in those moments when he is convinced that Holly is "an utter fake." After Holly insults the fiction he attempts to write—"Brats and niggers. Trembling leaves. Description. It does not mean anything," she argues—the narrator challenges Holly to describe "'something that means something. In your opinion." At first surprised that she offers *Wuthering Heights*, he then responds "with recognizable relief, 'oh . . . *the movie*'" (58–59, emphasis in original). Her composition entirely within cultural forms enables his feelings of superiority. He may not be able to get his fiction published, but at least he knows that *Wuthering Heights* was first a novel and only after then a movie.

Breakfast at Tiffany's thus makes clear that the problem of real phoniness is not necessarily a problem for the real phonies. It also makes clear why Holly in the 1950s could not herself be the narrator of her story; without a sense of development or change, the novel would have no means of moving forward. The focus of the story thus necessarily rests with the narrator, who possesses the capacity for development crucial to the *bildungsroman* as such. The novel operates on two levels—first as a referendum on Holly's phoniness and second as a love story—and the narrator's attempts to resolve the first level entirely motivate the feelings of the second. If the narrator has an epiphany, it occurs when he acknowledges to Holly that he loves her, yet the moment when Holly is most singled out—when she becomes the object of the narrator's love—allows for no definitive answer on the question of her individuality. Just fallen from a horse and probably concussed, the narrator remembers that "I saw several Hollys, a trio of sweaty faces so white with concern I was both touched and embarrassed."

Responding to her anxious queries, he finds the courage to state what is hinted at from the beginning: "'thank you. For saving my life. You're wonderful. Unique. I love you.' . . . She kissed me on the cheek. Then there were four of her and I fainted dead away" (84).

The moment embodies the various contradictions discussed above: when Holly is most individual, most "loved," she appears to the narrator not as one but four women, continually cloning before his eyes. The narrator's experience of his love, furthermore, mirrors Holly's experience of her selfhood: the narrator receives a blow to the head, realizes who he is (a man in love with Holly), and loses consciousness, all at the same time. While the rest of the novel exists primarily to tie up loose ends — Holly is forced to flee the country, the narrator remains behind to wonder about her — the final sentence speaks not only to the persistent unanswerability of these questions, but to the relentless desirability of an internalized authenticity (as opposed to a superficial or "given" authenticity) for its own sake, despite the fact that no coherent account has described why that type of authenticity need be privileged. Discovering that Holly's never-named cat, abandoned when she flees, has found himself a new owner, the narrator remembers the sculpture of Holly found in Africa and states, "Flanked by potted plants and framed by clean lace curtains, [the cat] was seated in the window of a warm-looking room: I wondered what his name was, for I was certain he had one now, certain he'd arrived somewhere he belonged. African hut or whatever, I hope Holly has, too" (105).[17]

The conclusion to *Breakfast at Tiffany's* illustrates two points that are not immediately obvious. As suggested above, the narrator conflates Holly's "real phoniness" with uniformity — a quality that presumably attaches itself to the phony as opposed to the real aspects of her character — implying that the socially given character inevitably encompasses the "standardization and overadjustment" Erikson laments in present-day adolescents. The narrator, his experiences of Holly as "unique" to the contrary, cannot imagine that the real phony might be as much an individual as anyone else; which is to say, as much an individual as anyone could be who develops in the context of the "self-contradictions in American history" (Erikson 287). The second point remains the irrelevance of the individual's own experience of authenticity to its ethical evaluation. As with the Sartrean individual — who may or may not possess an affective relation to aspects of his person that are not to be thought constitutive—Holly's self-conscious experience has no place in the narrator's evaluations. The point is not that Holly experiences herself as real, but rather that her construction entirely within and by social forms *invalidates* that particular authenticity. This also suggests that society has an active stake in the authenticity of its members that goes beyond individual well-being.[18] The real phony, who in one light might look like a cultural ideal—well-adjusted and polite—is not good enough by mid-century standards. Rather, it is far better to risk a society peopled entirely by alienated Holden Caulfields than (over-)adjusted Holly Golightlys.

The movement from Holden Caulfield to Holly Golightly during the 1950s thus illustrates how the figure of the teenager crystallizes the problem of phoniness and real phoniness, conformity versus uniformity, during the postwar era. Texts like *The Catcher in the Rye*, *Childhood and Society*, and *Breakfast at Tiffany's* illustrate the problems inherent in imagining the self as equally the result of and in opposition to the culture that produces it. If models of the self give primacy to cultural forces, and those forces are thought to be fundamentally deforming, it is unclear how a specifically individual authenticity might be maintained. Yet these texts also provide an answer to such problems by conceiving of adolescence as simultaneously a developmental stage—something that must be worked through—and a cultural type—something that becomes part of who one is, that forms the self and structures its relation to the world. Though adolescence inevitably must pass by, the attitude its culture imparts both enables a reconciliation with the hypocrisies of adulthood, and makes that reconciliation acceptable by guaranteeing one's authenticity despite it.

2 FROM MADNESS TO THE PROZAC AMERICANS

IS DR. MILES BENNELL CRAZY? In the opening scene of Don Siegel's 1955 movie *Invasion of the Body Snatchers*, he insists that he is not.[1] Trapped in an emergency room and attended by two police officers, a doctor, and a psychiatrist from the state mental hospital, Dr. Bennell insists on his sanity four times in the first minute of the film: "will you tell these fools I'm not crazy? . . . I'm not insane! . . . Listen. Doctor. Now you must listen to me. You must understand me. I am a doctor too. I am not insane. I am not insane!" ("Continuity" 32). One can hardly blame either his interrogators or the movie audience for disbelieving him. Disheveled, wild-eyed, and struggling, Miles Bennell does not look like a doctor, and the story he tells would be hard to believe under any circumstances. But one of the central purposes of the movie is to prove that the apparently crazy Dr. Bennell is, in fact, entirely sane. Encouraged by the psychiatrist to "tell [him] what happened," he explains, "It started, for me it started . . ." (32) as a slow dissolve brings us to the Santa Mira train station on the previous Thursday. The audience watches a cleaner and much more cheerful Dr. Bennell collect his luggage while he recounts in voice-over his early return from a medical conference at the request of his nurse. At this point, the flashback takes over the burden of narrative disclosure, which it largely maintains until the final two minutes of the film.

From its beginning, *Invasion of the Body Snatchers* addresses the problem of mental illness and its diagnosis. Even as the emergency-room doctors — and by extension, the film's audience — must decide whether Dr. Bennell is crazy, he too must determine the sanity of the rest of Santa Mira. The crisis that returns Dr. Bennell to his hometown is what the movie first calls "an epidemic of mass hysteria" (48); his patients have become convinced that their friends and relatives have been replaced by imposters. Dr. Bennell's job is to help his patient Wilma realize that her Uncle Ira really is her Uncle Ira. He explains, "No matter how [she] feel[s], he is" (43). "My business is people in trouble," he claims, and he promises to help Wilma realize that "that the trouble is inside [her]" (44). But the moments when Dr. Bennell determines the relative health of the townspeople go beyond mere differential diagnosis. Evaluating symptoms, he inadvertently circumscribes a boundary between the ostensibly sane and the so-called insane. More important, he begins a process that defines being "crazy" (Dr. Bennell's term), not merely by recourse to symptoms, but ultimately as a state of being, in and of itself.

This chapter is centrally concerned with such moments of diagnosis, because through these diagnoses, and the logic that informs them, the ontology of what is variously called insanity, mental illness, or madness can be parsed. The term chosen depends on what precisely this condition (or this constellation of conditions) is thought to be. To call it an illness, as Dr. Bennell does at first, is to understand it as a deviation from the norm, an affliction that ultimately prevents the self from its proper functioning, and that ideally would be cured, fixed, or in some way compensated for. Yet even if one accepts the idea of mental illness, one is left with the question of its source: does it stem from a bodily or moral weakness, or is it, in the words of novelist and essayist Walker Percy, "a wholly *appropriate* reaction" ("Crisis" 254) to the degradations of modern life?[2] At the other end of the spectrum is the term "madness," which, as the historian and philosopher Michel Foucault understands it in his 1961 study *Histoire de la Folie á l'âge Classique* (1961; abridged English translation, *Madness and Civilization*, 1965), is a way of being in its own right, a form of self that has been lost to us through the dominion of classical reason. If such states of being represent an alternative — but equally viable — version of human existence, then treatments of the type Dr. Bennell imagines are not cures, but rather coercion.

The competing ontologies of such conditions, as either mental illness or madness, are crucial for understanding the ways authenticity and self- or subjecthood interact during the mid-twentieth century. Analyzing the movement from madness to mental illness and then back again, the chapter illustrates that the ways that this phenomenon is defined suggest the complicated status that authenticity holds during the second half of the twentieth century. Novels such as Sylvia Plath's *The Bell Jar* (1963), Walker Percy's *The Moviegoer* (1961) and *The Thanatos Syndrome* (1987), as well as memoirs such as William Styron's *Darkness Visible: A Memoir of Madness* (1990) and Elizabeth Wurtzel's *Prozac Nation: Young and Depressed in America* (1994) all suggest the ambiguities in constructing an ontology of mental illness: is it a biological or metaphysical problem? An illness to be overcome or a means of realizing one's authenticity? The lack of clear definitions resulted in a variety of theorization during the second half of the twentieth century. In works by Plath, Percy, Foucault, and psychiatrists R. D. Laing and Thomas Szasz, mental illness emerges alternately as a reality to be experienced, a language to be harnessed, or a technology to be utilized. It is perhaps inevitable that the way these writers theorize these conditions are as telling for what it suggests about authentic self- or subjecthood as for any ostensible illness. The variety of explanations—from the philosophical to the biological—ultimately illustrates more about the ontology of selfhood than about insanity as such. Taken as a whole, the range of these accounts, incorporating the anti-institutionalism of Plath, the existentialism of Laing and Percy, and the communication theory of Szasz, demonstrates in miniature the range of popular and academic thinking about the self and its relation to authenticity during the postwar decades.

Further, these definitions illustrate how the interaction between authenticity and the self/subject evolved as the century came to a close. The genealogy of one particular branch of mental illness—depression—from the existential theories of the 1950s and 1960s to the Prozac-based accounts of the 1990s unveils a shift in notions of what constitutes an authentic individual. The change in emphasis from authentic selves to authentic identities charted in this chapter demonstrates a more extensive transformation in popular understandings of how the self is constituted and the role that cultural influences play in that constitution. As existentialism, with its ontology of being structured around a normative scale of authentic/inauthentic, retreated before multicultural models of persons that privilege culturally based characteristics, so depression shifted from an instrument to an identity—from a technology to realize authentic being to a way of being in and of itself. An existentialist writer such as Walker Percy thus harnesses depression as one symptom of personal inauthenticity and its treatment — psychotherapy — as one means to authentic existence. By comparison, the post-Prozac depression memoir, exemplified by Elizabeth Wurtzel's *Prozac Nation*, conceives of depression not as a hindrance to or a vehicle for realizing oneself, but rather as the self or subject itself. The advent of Prozac and its family of pharmaceuticals, by alleviating depression's symptoms — that is, by removing the behaviors one associates with depression — with fewer of the side effects associated with earlier medications, made possible the idea of depression as purified identity, independent of and unrelated to mere biological or behavioral indicators. In this way, depression, which a writer like Walker Percy imagines to be a solution to the problem of cultural construction, becomes itself just another identity category. To the list of relevant identities that demarcate selfhood at the end of the twentieth century, one can add the Prozac American.

Invasion of the Body Snatchers serves as an exemplary text with which to begin this discussion because it explicitly stages the same question that is at the center of *The Catcher and the Rye* and *Breakfast at Tiffany's*, and in the works of Herbert Marcuse, David Riesman, and others: can individuals genuinely be the same as everyone else? *Invasion of the Body Snatchers*, though, moves beyond a discussion of phonies and real phonies by adding a third concept — what the film calls "crazy" or "insane" — and thus provides an overt manifestation of the ways in which authenticity and mental illness, phoniness and sanity, are correlated during the period. Like Herbert Marcuse, *Invasion of the Body Snatchers* answers that question in the negative. The citizens of Santa Mira who are all the same are not genuinely so; they are the innocent victims of alien "seeds, drifting through space for years." Dr. Bennell and his girlfriend Becky eventually learn that these seeds, which "have the power to reproduce themselves in the exact likenesses of any form of life" ("Continuity" 87), have been replacing Dr. Bennell's patients with their duplicates while they sleep. These pod replacements precisely replicate their originals, save for the emotions. They take over "cell for cell, atom for atom. There's no pain . . . and you're reborn into an untroubled world . . . where everybody's the same" (88). Imagining a world in which "everybody's the same," and representing that uniformity as the product of an otherworldly influence, the movie thus forecloses on the possibility that individuals might be *legitimately* similar: that rather than being real phonies, they might just be real. That is, the movie never considers that maybe the townspeople just happen to enjoy doing the same things—that maybe, when individuals are free to do whatever they want, they'll likely choose to do what their neighbors are doing. Instead, their uncanny uniformity must be ascribed to a dangerous epidemic. In so doing, the movie likewise suggests that what looks like mental illness—a deviation from the mind's proper functioning—actually is not. What Dr. Kaufman, the town's psychiatrist, originally diagnoses as a "neurosis . . . [caused by] [w]orry about what's going on in the world" (48) is instead found to be a perfectly rational reaction to an extraordinary situation. The citizens, like Dr. Bennell, who seem most crazy are actually sane; the citizens who seem most sane are, in fact, alien impostors.

Invasion of the Body Snatchers thus correlates authenticity with insanity (or perceived insanity) and phoniness with sanity, hyperrationality, and the absence of emotion. In so doing, the film aligns itself with a variety of postwar writers whose representations of this problem are discussed below. Yet the movie goes a step further, imagining that the pod people are not only phonies—hiding their inhumanity behind a pretense of normality—but also real phonies of the type Holly Golightly represents. As Holly Golightly is simultaneously real and fake, authentic and inauthentic, so, too, the pods manage to be both themselves and other than themselves at the same time. That is, the pods are phony insofar as they pretend to be human with the still-unchanged portion of the Santa Mira population. The transformed Uncle Ira, for example, does not identify himself as a pod to his niece Wilma or to Dr. Bennell (45); he acts as if he cannot understand why Wilma is so upset with him. Similarly, Jimmy Grimaldi's mother insists Jimmy is just afraid of going to school, not that he fears "[s]he's not [his] mother" anymore (42). Concealing their inhumanity behind its pretense, the pods are not who (or what) they purport to be. Further, this gift for dissimulation appears integral to the pod constitution.[3] After Wilma herself becomes a pod, she informs Dr. Bennell that she cancelled her appointment with the town psychiatrist because when she "woke up this morning . . . everything was all right" (66), not because she had evolved into a new life form.

But if the pods are phony to the extent that they mimic humanity for strategic purposes, they are also real phonies of the type that Holly

Golightly embodies. Once the transformation has taken place, the original Uncle Ira, Wilma, and Jimmy Grimaldi no longer exist. The movie implies that the authentic human self has not been buried beneath a mechanistic podlike exterior, and it does not offer any means whereby the pods might be cured of pod-dom and return to human status. Pod-Wilma could not, for example, undergo treatment to go back to human-Wilma. Rather, that human self disappears entirely. For the pod person who emerges, being a pod is all there is. One might conclude then that the pods, if they experience themselves at all—if they have internality—experience themselves as real. It is only those humans who were present before the change who know that—as was said of Holly Golightly—there is *another* real that is *more* real that the pods are supposed to be, that the pod-Wilma is not the real Wilma. To put it slightly differently, the pods themselves are crucially real; only their previous status as ostensibly unique persons renders that realness ultimately phony.

The pods might thus more accurately be understood as representing a form of uniformity than of conformity. The "untroubled world" in which "everyone's the same" (88) that threatens to emerge under pod leadership is the product not of individuals *choosing* to diminish differences in the name of social cohesion (the nature of conformity), but rather of the absence of differences as such (the nature of uniformity). The person who conforms must possess individuating characteristics that she suppresses to accommodate social norms. Otherwise, she is not conforming, but rather being: the way she is just happens to be exactly the same as everyone else. The implications of this uniformity are most striking for the counterintuitive way it influences the nature of mental illness in the film. As real phonies, the pods reveal the extent in which authenticity and individuality are independent variables in *Invasion of the Body Snatchers*. While one might assume that to be authentic and to be individual is the same thing, for the pods authenticity is precisely the state of being like everyone else. That is, the pod people are authentic. It's just that their authentic selves are all the same. Nor for that matter is a phony automatically a conformist; one might, for example, be inauthentically iconoclastic.

The consequences of these observations are most arresting with regard to the "mass hysteria" that Dr. Bennell imagines to have overtaken the town. Surprisingly, in *Invasion of the Body Snatchers*, to fall victim to

1. Ben Marco awakens from his nightmare about brainwashing. *The Manchurian Candidate* (1962). MGM (Video & DVD).

this collective hysteria is one way of assuring one's authenticity. Only those individuals who have not become pods are afflicted with the "strange neurosis" that makes them think their friends have been replaced by impostors. What looks like a condition that produces conformity—that makes a person part of the mass by causing the same delusions in everyone—is actually a marker of an individual's authenticity, the means whereby one indicates her humanity. Succumbing to mass hysteria is the best way to illustrate that one is still human. Likewise, what might arguably look like a sign of individuality and strength of character—the ability to resist a form of group insanity—is instead the sign of one's (albeit real) phoniness and the loss of one's humanity embodied by the pods.

Invasion of the Body Snatchers is not the only postwar film to take up the idea that falling prey to an ostensible neurosis might be a sign of authenticity. In John Frankenheimer's *The Manchurian Candidate* (1962), the plot turns around the vivid nightmares experienced by Army Major Ben Marco (Frank Sinatra). Ben repeatedly dreams of being brainwashed during the Korean War by the Chinese Army to believe falsely that a fellow soldier, trained as an assassin, is actually a Medal of Honor winner. While his army superiors interpret his condition as a form of postcombat stress that requires a leave of absence, Ben insists that his dreams are evidence of an extensive brainwashing operation designed to position a Chinese operative in the United States. He swears, "There is something phony going on. There's something phony about me, about Raymond Shaw, about the whole Medal of Honor business." These suspicions are confirmed when fellow patrol member Al Melvin (James Edwards) reports that he, too, has been having virtually the same nightmare. In the shots of Ben and Al awakening from these nightmares, the *mise en scène*, narrative, and actors' movements

2. Al Melvin awakens from the same nightmare. *The Manchurian Candidate* (1962). MGM (Video & DVD).

closely mimic one another. In this case, the signs of a group hysteria — nervous breakdowns within an army unit — represent not conformity (everyone having the same nightmares) but rather an inner authenticity that is fighting to emerge from behind a phony façade.

The correlation between mental illness and authenticity — and by extension, sanity and inauthenticity — that *Invasion of the Body Snatchers* and *The Manchurian Candidate* construct is taken up at length in the rest of this chapter. It analyzes the assumption that, in the words of Walker Percy, "This is the age of anxiety because it is the age of the loss of self" ("Crisis" 254), and that mental illness serves as an important marker of authenticity. Yet *Invasion* takes that correlation one step further by counterintuitively aligning mental illness with a specifically bodily health, or at least control. Sanity is likewise associated with the loss of that control, and ultimately with the destruction of the body. In so doing, the movie raises a question about the ontology of mental illness that writers, filmmakers, and scholars would continue to debate throughout the remainder of the twentieth century. How one perceives of mental illness and its relation to authenticity ultimately hinges on how one defines these conditions as such: to what extent is mental illness actually an *illness* — that is, a biological rather than a metaphysical problem? And what is the relation of the self to the body that it inhabits or through which it is realized?

In *Invasion of the Body Snatchers*, one avoids becoming a pod — remains authentic — by disciplining the body away from its impulses. It is through the temptations of sleep and of sex that the pods replace their victims — hence the usefulness of Dr. Bennell's position as a doctor, a man trained to understand and manipulate biological processes. He can prescribe tranquilizers to calm the body ("Continuity" 41) and amphetamines

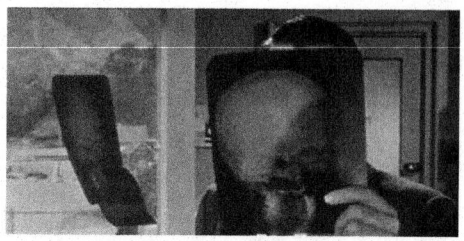

3. Shot of Dr. Miles Bennell examining the X-ray of the brain. *Invasion of the Body Snatchers* (1956). Republic Pictures.

to help it stay awake (82). But the movie's ambiguity about the "mass hysteria" that strikes Santa Mira — whether or not it should count as an illness — is embodied in a telling shot from early in the film. In a cut that brings us to Miles's office, the camera opens with a close-up of a skull X-ray that Miles is holding up to the light from the window. But what can Miles see? Can an X-ray, a technology that makes the mysteries of the body visible, expose the presence of mass hysteria? Is this the type of illness that Miles can or should treat? The film's answer, of course, is no. The mass hysteria is shown to be, in Walker Percy's words, a "wholly *appropriate* reaction" ("Crisis" 254) — which is to say, not an illness at all.

This position is illuminated in the film by the ambiguous position of Dr. Kaufman, the town psychiatrist and Miles's ostensible friend, who originally appears as a strong advocate for the mass-hysteria theory but later reveals himself as one of the leaders of the pods. In a world where mental health is associated with phoniness, psychiatry — which presumably exists to cure mental illnesses — ends up cultivating the inauthenticity of its patients in the name of individual adjustment and happiness. Psychiatry is rehabilitated somewhat in the conclusion to the framing narrative, which presents a much more sympathetic picture in Dr. Hill, the consultant from the state mental hospital. In response to the emergency room doctor's question, "What do you think? Will psychiatry help?" Dr. Hill replies, "If this is all a nightmare, yes" ("Continuity" 107). Luckily, at this moment an unconscious truck driver from Santa Mira is brought into the emergency room; the attending orderly comments on his "peculiar" cargo: "I never saw them before. They looked like great big seed pods" (108). As Dr. Bennell collapses in relief, Dr. Hill sounds the alarm and the world, presumably, is saved. Yet the indictment of psychiatry, and particularly the mental institutions in which its work was most thoroughly carried out, is characteristic of the immediate postwar period and is picked up in Sylvia Plath's harrowing account of psychiatric hospitalization, *The Bell Jar*. In the next section of this chapter, Plath's novel is examined in the context of the movement for deinstitutionalization that began in the mid-1950s and in relation to the attitudes toward mental illness that motivated some of that movement's most dramatic claims. Yet in some ways the novel goes further than the critics of institutional psychiatry: *The Bell Jar* imagines a mad cogito, in which existence takes place in the absence of rational thought — an existence premised specifically on the self's bodily and emotional, as opposed to cognitive, being.

The Bell Jar, Madness and Civilization, and the Mad Cogito

When it was first published in the United Kingdom in 1963, Sylvia Plath's *The Bell Jar* was described by Robert Taubman as "the first feminine novel in a Salinger mood" (Ames 262). The comparison would become commonplace by the time *The Bell Jar* appeared in the United States in 1972. Frances McCullough reports that the novel "quickly established itself as a female rite-of-passage novel, a twin to *The Catcher in the Rye*" (xii). The nine-year lapse before its American publication was possibly good for the novel, at least from the publisher's point of view. At the time of its U.S. publication, Plath was well-known for both her poetry and her suicide, which the novel was assumed to foreshadow. The women's movement had directed attention toward exactly the limitations in women's opportunities against which Esther Greenwood struggles. Questions about the putative *illness* of mental illnesses had become a topic of conversation for popular audiences through the works of R. D. Laing, Thomas Szasz, and A. Alvarez; the critically and commercially successful film version of *One Flew over the Cuckoo's Nest* (1975); and the publication of Stanford psychologist D. L. Rosenbaum's article "On Being Sane in Insane Places" (1973). Yet the context of the novel is properly the early 1960s when it was written; and the period Esther ostensibly describes — 1953, "the summer they electrocuted the Rosenbergs" (Plath 1) — is not so far from Holden's own.

The similarities between the two novels are obvious. Both are written in the first person by a middle-class adolescent remembering a specific experience. Both begin with the same narrative setup: the adolescent alone in New York City and undergoing an increasing alienation and isolation. Both narrators evidence a profound uneasiness about the adult American middle-class life that they are expected to join. As Holden fears entering the respectable upper-middle-class professions like the law, Esther imagines "the white, shining, identical, clapboard houses" of the suburbs, "with their interstices of well-groomed green," as "one bar after another in a large but escape-proof cage" (114). Esther even sounds like Holden at moments — for example, when she declares, "I'm stupid about executions" (1) or "I felt wise and cynical as all hell" (8). At the same time, Esther's story might be said to fill in some of the gaps in Holden's narrative. *The Bell Jar* presents the hospital scenes and ultimate reconciliation to adult life to which *The Catcher in the Rye* alludes but ultimately refuses to represent. Furthermore, *The Bell Jar* explicitly addresses the depression (and perhaps schizophrenia) from which Esther suffers, an issue that remains solidly in the background of Salinger's text.[4] The reader knows Holden writes from a hospital in California, but why he is there is never explicitly spelled out: either tuberculosis or depression might have caused his collapse. The reader does not know definitively whether Holden's problems go beyond the adolescent angst with which the 1950s were increasingly preoccupied. In comparison, in representing Esther's experience as an explicit mental breakdown, *The Bell Jar* moves its discussion beyond the by-then-familiar theorizations of adolescent development and toward a consideration of the nature of mental illness as such.

The idea that conditions like Esther's might have a nature rather than a pathology has always been a popular one, and the middle of the twentieth century offered no exception to this outlook. Yet the late 1950s and 1960s saw a profound shift in how mental illness was treated in the United States, marking a corollary shift in what these conditions were thought to be. In 1963, the Mental Retardation and Community Mental Health Centers Construction Act marked the beginning of a decades-long project to reduce the population of institutionalized mental health patients by treating them in local mental health centers. Such treatment centers ideally would allow these patients to live independently in nurturing communities while still receiving therapeutic care. As a result of this legislation, the number of institutionalized patients declined by 57 percent in the years between

1965 and 1975; this number dropped by another 64 percent by 1980 (Gillon 97). The ultimate failure of these centers (and the communities that surrounded them) to meet the needs of the chronically mentally ill has been well documented.[5] For this study, the shift in definitions that motivated that project is crucial. As Steven M. Gillon explains, the law grew out of an understanding of mental illness as "not biological but an outgrowth of unresolved tension, much of it caused by environmental stress" (88). Emphasizing "the social roots of illness," the law imagined "that poverty and a lack of opportunity, not genes, were the principal culprits" (115). If these conditions were caused by social problems, their cures would be found within communities, not in isolation from them.

The idea behind the deinstitutionalization of mental patients — that such conditions needed to be thought of as something other than biological illness — had its intellectual roots in a series of books published during the period when *The Bell Jar* was written. R. D. Laing's *The Divided Self* (1960), Thomas Szasz's *The Myth of Mental Illness* (1961), and Michel Foucault's *Madness and Civilization* (English translation, 1965) all support Szasz's contention that although "psychoanalysis has been concerned with man's relationship to his fellow man, and to the group in which he lives . . . this concern has been obscured by an ostensibly medical orientation" (10). For these authors, the various forms of mental illness (depression, schizophrenia, bipolar disorders, etc.) look less like biological problems than social ones — and more specifically, as problems of language. According to Szasz, "Psychiatry, using the methods of communication analysis, has much in common with the sciences concerned with the study of languages and communicative behavior" (3). To imagine schizophrenia, for example, as a type of language — a form of communication — and a therapist as a translator transforms the therapeutic moment from one of diagnosis into one of interpretation and explication. As Szasz explains, when "a person speaks a language other than our own, we do not usually look for the 'cause' of his peculiar linguistic behavior. . . . It follows, then, that if hysteria is regarded as a special form of communicative behavior, it is meaningless to inquire into its 'causes.' As with languages, we shall only be able to ask how hysteria was *learned* and what it *means*" (11–12).[6] The metaphor figures the patient not as ill but rather as foreign — someone whose linguistic and communicative habits may be different from one's own.

For R. D. Laing, the problem is less that the patient's language is unfamiliar than that the psychiatrist's is; the linguistic jargon employed by the psychiatric sciences ignores that which is most crucial about the patient: his essential integration. "As a psychiatrist," he explains, "I run into a major difficulty at the outset: how can I go straight to the patients if the psychiatric words at my disposal keep the patient at a distance from me?" (18). Medical language, he complains, "consists of words which split man up verbally" (19); they are "designed to isolate and circumscribe the meaning of a patient's life to a particular clinical entity" (18). "There are, of course, many descriptions of depersonalization and splitting in psychopathology," Laing states. Yet traditional psychiatric diagnosis and treatment mirrors that depersonalization, "distort[ing] the person . . . by its own premises." It must "presuppose that the objectification . . . imposed by thinking of a fictional 'thing' or system, is an adequate conceptual correlate of the other as a person" (23–24). That is, in assuming a psyche; in dividing that psyche into an ego, an id, and a superego; and in applying that model indiscriminately to all patients, the psychiatrist replicates within his therapeutic approach the patient's own difficulty in understanding herself as a singular and unified whole. The patient, an "already shattered Humpty-Dumpty . . . cannot be put together again by any number of hyphenated or compound words: psycho-physical, psycho-somatic, psycho-biological, [or] psycho-pathological" (20). Laing argues instead for an existential approach to therapy, because "only existential thought has attempted to match the original experience of oneself in relationship to others in one's world by a term that adequately reflects this totality. Thus, existentially, the concretum is seen as a man's *existence, his-being-in-the-world*" (19).[7] Thinking of the patient as a cohesive entity, rather than a system in which certain parts are malfunctioning, existential psychotherapy provides a means of recognizing "all the time [the patient's] distinctiveness and differentness, his separateness and loneliness and despair" (38). The implied pathos structures Laing's account as a whole; the patient emerges as a victim of a medical orientation, rather than its beneficiary.

Yet it remains unclear in Laing's analysis how this existential recognition might help to cure any *particular* instance of mental illness. This omission makes more sense when one realizes that Laing is not precisely arguing for a cure. When contemporary psychiatric jargon speaks of "social or biological *failure* of adjustment, or *mal*-adaptation of a particularly radical kind," Laing argues, "it implies a certain standard way of being human to which the psychotic cannot measure up" (27). Laing himself thinks less in terms of standards of normality than alternatives to that norm; after all, "the cracked mind of the schizophrenic may *let in* light which does not enter the intact minds of many sane people whose minds are closed" (27). Hence the attitude of the book as a whole, which offers a therapeutic approach less interested in curing schizophrenia (or any other form of mental illness) than in understanding and improving its existence on its own terms, recognizing that the patient's *"being-in-the-world"* may be legitimate. He claims, "one must bear in mind that deterioration and disintegration are only one outcome of the initial schizoid organization. Quite clearly, authentic versions of freedom, power, and creativity can be lived out" (89). If authenticity exists within the patient's *being-in-the-world*, efforts to "cure" that form of being risk the oppression and coercion of an authentic selfhood.

The "authentic versions" of freedom, power, and creativity that might be lost through institutionalized cures preoccupy *The Bell Jar*. The novel links Esther's condition with the rhetoric of nonuniformity circulating during the postwar period, associating mental illness and authenticity, and sanity and inauthenticity, in a manner familiar to the viewers of *Invasion of the Body Snatchers*. Esther's breakdown begins when she wins a summer internship with a fashion magazine publisher in New York. What should be every American girl's dream — "drinking martinis in a skimpy, imitation, silver-lamé bodice stuck on to a big, fat, cloud of white tulle, on some Starlight Roof, in the company of several anonymous young men with all-American bone structures" (2) — illustrates the distance between the lives conjured up by the magazines that Holly Golightly cannot stop reading and Esther's own ill-formed desires and ambitions.

Esther's uncertainty about the opportunities available to women is summarized in a description of a magazine layout picturing all the interns "with props to show who they wanted to be" (101). Betsy, who had been imported "straight from Kansas with her bouncing blonde ponytail and Sweetheart-of-Sigma-Chi smile" (6), poses with an ear of corn "to show she wanted to be a farmer's wife" (101); Hilda, who "moved like a mannequin" (99) and "stared at her reflection in the glossed shop windows as if to make sure, moment by moment, that she continued to exist" (100), holds "the bald, faceless head of a hatmaker's dummy to show she wanted to design hats" (101). The ease with which these young woman embody their socially sanctioned roles invites the reader to wonder if they, too, are not as empty as the "hatmaker's dummy" Hilda holds. By comparison, Esther, when asked what she wants to be, says she does not know. Life choices appear to Esther as so many figs on a tree; "One fig was a husband and a happy home and children, and another fig was a famous poet and another fig was a brilliant professor. . . . I wanted each and every one of them," Esther explains. But "choosing one meant losing all the rest," and indecision means "starving to death, just because I couldn't make up my mind which of the figs I would choose" (77).

The forms of femininity institutionalized in these magazines makes Esther sick, both psychically and physically. Psychically, she experiences a period of ill-defined mental illness that the summer initiates (Esther is never actually given a diagnosis) and that includes a nearly successful suicide attempt and extended hospitalization. Physically, she receives food poisoning at a *Ladies' Day* magazine luncheon, carefully prepared in the "Food Testing Kitchens" (25) where recipes are tested for publication. As Maria Farland argues, in *The Bell Jar* "established institutions and the conformity they enforce are embodied in the psychiatric institution and the boundaries it inscribes between normal and pathological individuals. For Plath, madness emerges as a kind of liberation from social imperatives, particularly the restrictions that society imposes on middle class women" (248).[8] Esther's insanity operates partially as a reaction to, and partially as an escape from, the limitations of mid-century American women's roles.

Where *Invasion of the Body Snatchers* symbolizes this pressure through the uniformity of the pod person, *The Bell Jar* relies upon metaphors of totalitarianism, institutionalization, and state-sponsored violence. Yet those metaphors too turn on images of uniformity, rather than conformity. The *Ladies Day* food poisoning turns the bathroom stall into a "glittering white torture-chamber" (44). Marriage is imagined as "being brainwashed," after which one lives one's life "numb as a slave in some private, totalitarian state"

(85). Childbirth is like a "long, blind, doorless and windowless corridor of pain" (66) that women are drugged into forgetting by male doctors, lest one risks "the end of the human race" (65). Esther's face after crying seems "to be peering from the grating of a prison cell after a prolonged beating" (102). Perhaps most notoriously, Esther's experience of electroshock therapy—"something bent down and took hold of me and shook me like the end of the world. Whee-ee-ee-ee-ee, it shrilled, through an air crackling with blue light, and with each flash a great jolt drubbed me till I thought my bones would break and the sap fly out of me like a split plant" (143)—is reminiscent of her fantasy of the Rosenbergs' execution: "being burned alive all along your nerves" (1). The victims of such violence become not individuals suppressing their individuality to conform to social expectations, but rather figures *without* internality—figures whose internality has been suppressed, removed, or potentially never existed in the first place. They are "mannequins" (99) and "bald faceless heads" (101), "brainwashed" (85) and "drugged" (66). Psychiatric institutionalization produces "men and women . . . and boys and girls" with "a uniformity to their faces, as if they had lain for a long time on a shelf" (141). In the most vivid example, it creates young women like Valerie, whose "perpetual, marble calm" (192), air of belonging "in a Girl Scout camp," and "intense interest" in a "tatty copy of *Vogue*" (188)—the type of magazine where Esther herself could find no place—are a consequence of a lobotomy. Another type of pod person, Valerie is a real phony. Though she experiences herself as real, there is another real—the kind of real provided by a frontal lobe—that she is supposed to be but to which she can never return. Postsurgery, Valerie is absent of emotion, also like the pods; she is not "angry any more" and plans never to leave the hospital, because she "like[s] it [t]here" (192). She is so thoroughly "adjusted" (*Lonely* 243), to use Riesman's term, that she is beyond making choices about her own uniformity.

Yet Esther's ill-defined condition is not only a mark of her authenticity. *The Bell Jar*'s careful delineation of Esther's subjectivity includes its own rumination on the nature of mental illness, in terms of the relation between the mind and body. Where Laing and Szasz deemphasize biological definitions in favor of metaphysical ones, Plath reasserts the primacy of the body, defined emotionally rather than rationally. The above images of totalitarian coercion insist on Esther's existence as a bodily one, even as

Esther's understanding of herself is one of profound disintegration, a radical mind-body dualism. Describing an attempt to strangle herself, Esther observes:

> I saw that my body had all sorts of little tricks, such as making my hands go limp at the crucial second, which would save it, time and again, whereas if I had the whole say, I would be dead in a flash.
>
> I would simply have to ambush it with whatever sense I had left or it would trap me in its stupid cage for fifty years without any sense at all. (159)

Passages such as these figure the body as a separate, independent entity, an entity with its own priorities that do not necessarily correspond to Esther's. The body becomes "it," an autonomous unit that might be understood as having a "say" in Esther's future, and that can lay a "trap" for her mind and imprison it "in its stupid cage." For Esther, the body is fundamentally separate from the mind (or "head"). "If only something were wrong with my body it would be fine," she explains. "I would rather have anything wrong with my body than something wrong with my head" (182). The assumption—that the body can be sick without the head, and, more important, that the head can be sick without the body—suggests the independence of these two aspects of existence. In these moments Esther evidences what R. D. Laing terms "unembodiment" (66), a condition in which "the individual experiences his self as being more or less divorced or detached from his body. *The body is felt more as one object among other objects in the world than as the core of the individual's own being*" (69). Such an orientation is not, in Laing's opinion, necessarily "abnormal and pathological"; disembodiment might represent merely "another way of being human" (66).

Representing Esther as fundamentally "unembodied," however, the novel does not merely render in narrative form the commonly recognized psychiatric symptoms of the 1950s. Instead, it rewrites the Cartesian cogito—*Cogito ergo sum* (I am thinking, therefore I exist)—to emphasize existence in the absence of rational thought, and to validate ostensibly mad existence as a legitimate form of selfhood. Descartes' cogito subordinates bodily existence in favor of a rational being that he argues is impervious to doubt. *The Bell Jar* reverses this hierarchy, and ends up validating a bodily and emotional life regardless of whether that life is lived rationally. This rewriting takes place in two crucial moments of the novel: during her second suicide attempt and then again at the novel's conclusion when Esther attends the funeral of fellow patient and successful suicide, Joan Giling. In the former instance, she describes planning to drown herself:

> I thought I would swim out until I was too tired to swim back. As I paddled on, my heartbeat boomed like a dull motor in my ears.
> I am I am I am. (158)

In the latter example, Esther imagines Joan's grave and the coffin as it is lowered into the ground:

> There would be a black, six-foot-deep gap hacked in the hard ground. That shadow would marry this shadow, and the peculiar, yellowish soil of our locality seal the wound in whiteness, and yet another snowfall erase the traces of newness in Joan's grave.
> I took a deep breath and listened to the old brag of my heart.
> I am, I am, I am. (243)

For the novel, "I am" is a "brag" of the heart and the heartbeat rather than the mind; its repeated assertions of self figure the heart at the core of human existence. Further, the heart's traditional status as both the physical source of being and the symbolic location of the emotions establish the self as a bodily and emotional entity, a physical and spiritual being rather than a purely cognitive one. Descartes originally established the cogito as a guarantee against radical doubt. If the speaker can be sure of nothing else — the reliability of sensory impressions, the reality of the external world — he can be sure that, while he is thinking, he himself exists. Descartes thus forsakes the body because of its inbuilt capacity for error, linking existence only with reason, and imagining in the latter the guarantee of the former. Such a statement is part of Descartes' overall project which, as philosophers and historians of philosophy have long argued, seeks to assert the value of a God-given power of reason. Foreshortening and rewriting the cogito into an overt statement of self that does not depend on rational thought, Plath joins those thinkers and writers who want the state of insanity to look like an alternative form of selfhood — to be madness rather than mental illness.

Plath is not the only postwar writer to imagine an alternative to a Cartesian existence guaranteed against doubt through its capacity for rational thought. In *La Histoire de la Folie á l'Âge Classique* (1961; abridged, translated, and published in English as *Madness and Civilization: A History of Insanity in the Age of Reason* in 1965), Foucault identifies in Descartes' work a dismissal of madness—a radical othering of the mad—that he takes as representative of the eighteenth century more broadly, a time in which "men, in an act of sovereign reason, confine their neighbors, and communicate and recognize each other through the merciless language of non-madness" (ix). In Roy Boynes's paraphrase, Foucault imagines that Descartes, "instead of finding something in the thought of the mad that could not be false," and therefore legitimating mad existence, "effectively declares that 'I who think cannot be mad'" (46), peremptorily dismissing the mad from consideration. Their dismissal from civic and social life, in the form of forced incarceration, followed soon after.

Foucault's indictment of Descartes is part of a larger project to chart the "history of unreason," mapping the philosophical and intellectual thinking about madness that girded the broad changes in policy enacted during the eighteenth century. In the Middle Ages and the Renaissance, "Madness and the madmen became major figures, in their ambiguity" (13), figures who existed alongside the reasonable as reminders of the limitations of reason and knowledge, the vain presumptions of human beings, and the dangers of unruly passions. During the "great confinements" of the eighteenth century, "madness was perceived on the social horizon of poverty, of incapacity for work, of inability to integrate with the group" and was "sequestered and, in the fortress of confinement, bound to Reason, to the rules of morality and to their monotonous rights" (64). If the nineteenth century instantiated the release of madness from the prison house, the movement was less emancipatory than it might originally appear. Madness was promptly reconfined in the asylum; in the hospital, "Madness no longer exists except as *seen*. . . . The science of mental disease, as it would develop in the asylum, would always be only of the order of classification. It would not be a dialogue" (250, emphasis in original). Instead of trying to find the essence of madness, nineteenth-century physicians sought only to order madness on their own terms through systems of standardization and categorization.

This absence of a dialogue with the mad motivates Foucault's entire project. While scholars have raised legitimate questions about Foucault's historical accuracy, his philosophical interest in the possibility of representing mad existence is generally recognized as the most fascinating (if profoundly problematic) aspect of the study. Like R. D. Laing, for whom the language of psychiatry prevents genuine communication with the insane, and for whom the insane's "separateness, loneliness and despair" (38) evokes constant sympathy, Foucault's history is permeated by the pathos involved in imagining that silence. He states in the preface,

> In the serene world of mental illness, modern man no longer communicates with the madman.... the constitution of madness as a mental illness, at the end of the eighteenth century, affords the evidence of a broken dialogue, posits the separation as already effected, and thrusts into oblivion all those stammered, imperfect words without fixed syntax in which the exchange between madness and reason was made. (x)

Foucault's openly stated goal is to conduct "an archeology of that silence" (xi); yet, more important, he wished, in Derrida's phrase, "to write a history of madness *itself. Itself* . . . [he] wanted madness to be the *subject* of his book in every sense of the word: its theme and its first-person narrator, its author, madness speaking about itself" ("Cogito" 33–34).[9] Derrida imagines Foucault to want to write less a history or philosophical inquiry, or even a novel—or perhaps even a novel like *The Bell Jar*, which everyone assumes to be autobiographical—than a memoir itself penned by the mad, written from within that particular subjectivity, that alternative form of selfhood. This wish, in Derrida's terms, is itself "the *maddest* aspect of [Foucault's] project" (34). Derrida argues that, by using language (spoken or written text) to expose the structures through which reason imprisons madness, one inevitably repeats that imprisonment, because language itself is inevitably of the order of reason. Putting reason on trial for its inhumanity toward madness is impossible, because "by the simple fact of their articulation the proceedings and the verdict unceasingly reiterate the crime" (35). By Derrida's account, any attempt to free madness through language only reimprisons that madness within the confining syntax of reason.

Yet if Derrida is right to note that Foucault's goal of an unmediated encounter with madness is fundamentally flawed, Foucault's (failed) effort illuminates the "stammered, imperfect words without fixed syntax" (Foucault x) through which *The Bell Jar*'s own representation of madness attempts (and also fails) to be expressed. That is, the novel adopts the only rhetorical strategy available "to say madness itself" while still having recourse to language. Like Foucault, Plath in *The Bell Jar* chooses to make language — or at least orthographical language — function as a metaphor for her illness. When she first voices the repeated "I am," Esther is arguably at her most mad — she is in the very process of trying to commit suicide — and the phrases are repeated without the use of commas to separate each instance: "I am I am I am" (158). Her failure to maintain orthographic rules at this moment is mirrored in her first visit to a psychiatrist, Dr. Gordon, who she is convinced will recognize her madness if he looks at her writing. This recognition will happen not because of the content of the writing but rather because the handwriting itself is suddenly illegible: writing a letter, Esther's "hand made big, jerky letters like those of a child, and the lines sloped down the page from left to right almost diagonally, as if they were loops of string lying on the paper" (130). While she is not happy to describe "not sleeping and not eating and not reading," she is "bothered most of all" (130) by showing him her handwriting, because it will provide proof that "[she] should be locked up" (135). Her inability to conform to norms of discourse — to use Derrida's terminology, her inability to render transparent the materiality of the signifier — is for Esther definitive proof of her own madness.

By comparison, at the end of the novel when Esther is about to be released, her repetition of the "old brag of [her] heart" is phrased correctly, with commas separating each of the clauses: "I am, I am, I am" (237). The implication is that the return of (relative) sanity marks itself through the capacity to manipulate correctly the formal rules of orthography — to exist, as it were, within the ostensibly totalitarian systems that Plath in *The Bell Jar* originally set out to indict: linguistic, psychiatric, gendered, and so on. It is worth noting that, like Foucault, Plath, too, would have failed here in Derridean terms; the earlier phrasing (without commas) is unorthodox, but neither is it *exterior* to a linguistic system. Plath also failed to speak "madness itself," even through her careful linguistic representation of its specificity.

Yet the novel leaves uncertain whether reconciliation within these systems implies total capitulation to them. If the return of proper orthography marks Esther's readiness for the world outside the institution, she remains aware of the fragility of any boundary designed to separate the sane and the insane. Offered by her mother the opportunity to "act as if this all were a bad dream," Esther insists on the relevance of these experiences: "Maybe forgetfulness, like a kind snow, should cover them. But they were a part of me. They were my landscape" (237). She does not know "that someday — at college, in Europe, somewhere, anywhere — the bell jar, with its stifling distortions wouldn't descend again" (241), and she recognizes that there is not much difference between the women at the asylum and her college classmates "playing bridge and gossiping and studying in the college . . . those girls, too, sat under bell jars of a sort" (238). Such observations suggest Esther's awareness of the arbitrariness of the types of lines Dr. Bennell blithely draws to separate the hysterical from the normal in Santa Mira — an awareness that one would not necessarily associate with the brainwashed, the drugged, or the lobotomized individuals whose essential uniformity, the novel suggests, enables a successful existence within the narrow opportunities for women.

The novel thus takes pains to emphasize Esther's distance from her cultural milieu even as she reenters the outside world. Her reunion with mainstream American life is less the wholehearted convergence of a wedding — "I wasn't getting married," Esther remarks — than the unwitting capitulation of a rebirth, about which the baby presumably has as little say as she did the first time. "There ought to be," Esther thinks, as she waits to be released, "a ritual for being born twice — patched, retreaded, and approved for the road" (244). At the same time, as Maria Farland points out, the representative moments of Esther's cure involve the development of precisely the type of self-regulatory behaviors that Foucault identifies as crucial to the psychiatric view of madness as mental illness — behaviors through which the patients are "gradually adapting themselves to [society's] disciplinary practices" (Farland 254). For Farland, this figuration suggests that Plath's most devastating critique of psychiatry's authoritarian regimes extends "into the contractual therapeutic model" (254) advocated by such anti-institutionalization figures as Thomas Szasz. Esther's reconciliation, therefore, inevitably involves at least *some* form of submission to the uniforming influences of postwar, middle-class culture, with its limited and limiting roles for women. To figure this reconciliation in terms similar to those that marked Holden's reconciliation to adult life at the end of *The Catcher in the Rye*, Esther, however regulated, emerges with "an attitude" (Menand 84) toward the realities of adulthood. She knows her "landscape" (Plath 237) — its fragility ("someday . . . the bell jar, with its stifling distortions [might] descend again" [241]) and omnipresence ("those girls, too, sat under bell jars of a sort" [238]). That attitude allows her the kind of autonomy that David Riesman describes in *The Lonely Crowd*: "The person here defined as autonomous may or may not conform outwardly, but whatever his choice, he pays less of a price, and he has a choice: he can meet both the culture's definitions of adequacy and those which (to a still culturally determined degree) slightly transcend the norm for the adjusted" (242–43). What matters at the end of *The Bell Jar* is not whether Esther is conforming or not, but rather whether she is *choosing* to conform or not — whether, that is, her conformity is conformity and not uniformity. Unlike Valerie, she can choose to leave the hospital, choose to what ("still culturally determined") degree she will "transcend the norm," and thus still count as an individual in the strongest sense of the term.

The Bell Jar thus suggests that compromise requires capitulation but that capitulation is acceptable as long as it is freely elected. The observation in parenthesis Riesman provides — "(to a still culturally determined degree)" — implies the illusory nature of such choices and, by extension, such individuality. It also suggests Riesman's own unwillingness to own fully the consequences of such an observation: otherwise, why place the observation in parentheses? Plath's novel, in keeping with R. D. Laing and Michel Foucault, represents Esther's condition less as mental illness than as madness, and appears not to doubt the authenticity of the individuality it implies.

The next section of this chapter examines the 1987 novel *The Thanatos Syndrome* by existentialist writer Walker Percy, which picks up where Plath's novel left off by imagining a wide-scale, coerced treatment of a particular population of the mentally ill — the clinically depressed. Both novels figure involuntary treatment as a form of authoritarian control. Yet where Plath believes such cures produce an inauthentic *uniformity*, Percy contends that these treatments produce an equally inauthentic *identity*, suggesting the distance traveled in understandings of self- or subjecthood between the early 1960s and the late 1980s.

The Thanatos Syndrome and the Genocide of the Depressed

Walker Percy's final novel, *The Thanatos Syndrome* (1987), is about a group of rogue scientists who use Na-24, familiarly known as heavy sodium, to poison the water supply of a small community in southern Louisiana as an experiment in behavioral engineering.[10] The opening of the novel mirrors the beginning of *Invasion of the Body Snatchers*: Dr. Tom More (allusion presumably intended), a psychiatrist returning to Feliciana Parish after two years in state prison, discovers that his former patients are not as he recalls. Nothing too dramatic, he asserts, but he notices that in Mickey, Ella, and Donna "there has occurred a sloughing away of the old terrors, worries, rages, a shedding of guilt like last year's snakeskin, and in its place is a mild fond vacancy" (21). As with Dr. Bennell, Tom is surprised to discover that those patients who appear most healthy are in fact the most troubled: they have been "cured" by the heavy sodium. For a psychiatrist, it is difficult to imagine this would come as bad news—unless, of course, one considers the loss of one's livelihood as bad. In this case, what's good for the patient is not so good for the doctor, or at least the doctor's practice. But a world in which the mentally anguished are no longer "worrying the same old bone" (21) sounds like the optimistic vision of a world without depression (if not other forms of mental illness) that will mark post-Prozac memoirs like that of William Styron and Elizabeth Wurtzel, which are discussed later.

The novel acknowledges the irony inherent in an evil scheme designed to make people happy, to cure the depressed. As Tom explains to his cousin, epidemiologist Dr. Lucy Pendergast, when she asks about possible symptoms in the exposed population, "Actually, it would be abatement of symptoms—of . . . anxiety, depression, stress, insomnia, suicidal tendencies, chemical dependence." Lucy's response is understandably incredulous: "That's a big help. How in hell can I frame a question in those terms?" (180). To place her sarcasm in a larger context, how does one isolate and identify contentment and well-being as a problem? If heavy sodium could achieve what psychotherapy only rarely accomplishes, what, precisely, is Tom so worried about?

It is a good question. What is the conspirators' crime? They cure depression. Even if its method of distribution is highly suspect, the cure of a debilitating disease should hardly count as a serious offense.[11] Yet the extremity of Tom's (and by extension, Percy's) reaction can be accounted for by a simple disparity. Like Szasz, Laing, and Plath, Percy does not imagine depression to be an illness at all. In "The Coming Crisis in Psychiatry" (1957), Percy claims that "Anxiety . . . is under one frame of reference, a symptom to be gotten rid of; under the other, it may be a summons to authentic existence, to be heeded at any cost" (259). What to Dr. Kaufman, the pod psychiatrist of *Invasion of the Body Snatchers*, appears as the alleviation of unnecessary suffering, to Percy constitutes a deprivation. Giving voice to a version of the theories of insanity implicit in *Invasion of the Body Snatchers* and *The Bell Jar*, in which "mass hysteria" or "madness" are legitimate forms of human existence, Percy argues for a depression that is not an illness but rather a vehicle to authentic selfhood. He imagines depression as the means whereby inadvertent phoniness — the residue of social development — is "sloughed" off and the authentic self emerges as from "last year's snakeskin." Having claimed in 1957 that "this is the age of anxiety because it is the age of the loss of self" ("Crisis" 254), thirty years later Percy makes this belief literal by representing a world in which individuals are robbed of selfhood in the name of superficial contentment, in which depression is rendered obsolete through the self's removal.

By this account, the problem with diverting heavy sodium into the water supply is not that it violates any civil rights — although it does — nor that such violations are warranted given current social conditions — they may or may not be — but rather that heavy sodium deprives the individual of his self and by extension his humanity. Describing those patients exposed to the additive, Tom observes, "there is something missing, not merely the old terrors, but a sense in each of her — her what? her self?" (21). At first it is difficult to ascertain what Tom intends by this "self"; the language he uses to describe the differences is, as one might expect, vague: "distant and ironed out," "somehow — diminished" (85). If Mickey or Ella still look like Mickey or Ella, and still possess all of Mickey's or Ella's memories and experiences, what is missing? None of the patients cease to exist on the medication; they merely evidence attitudinal changes. Mickey, for example, abandons her agoraphobia in favor of sexual aggressiveness. Donna — like Valerie, the lobotomized inmate in Esther's asylum — previously suffered from constant anger; and like Valerie, on Na-24 that anger is replaced by a relaxed nonchalance (and, it turns out, sexual aggressiveness). But both patients are understood to be fundamentally changed.

The variance is not merely one of personality. Neither becomes a different person; rather they cease to be *persons* at all. They have lost self-consciousness, "that peculiar trait of humans by which they utter sentences and which makes them curious about how they look in the mirror — when a chimp will look behind the mirror for another chimp" (22). They have also lost what Percy in the novel calls "context": they will answer any question, no matter how random, because they no longer concern themselves with its motivation. Mickey, for example, tells Tom where St. Louis is, but as Tom observes, "Now, everybody knows where St. Louis is, but people don't answer the question Where is St. Louis?, asked out of the blue, without wanting to know why you ask" (9). Perhaps most startling, Tom's patients show a remarkable aptitude for mathematical calculation: Mickey's "eyes go up into her eyebrows, as if she were reading a printout" (9) when she calculates the date of Easter in the upcoming year; Donna's "eyes move a little, as if she were consulting a map over [Tom's] head" (18) when she determines the precise distance of Cut Off, Louisiana, from New Orleans; and Tom's wife has developed a remarkable ability to "calculate the exact probabilities of where the cards are" (63) playing tournament bridge. These women answer questions as if "consulting, so to speak, their own built in computer readouts," whereas untreated persons, Tom explains, "would want to know why [the questioner] wanted to know. You'd want to relate the question to your — self" (22). But how can a human being lose her self?

The question has relevance outside the parameters of *The Thanatos Syndrome*. As Fredric Jameson observes, one of the consequences of the constellation of intellectual concepts, stylistic tropes, and technological advances that are loosely grouped under the heading of postmodernity has been the so-called death of the subject. As Jameson notes, whether or not such a unique self ever properly existed is open to debate. The loss of that self or subject (whether ideological or actual), however, did not produce a concurrent loss of fascination with that self or subject, in either its always-illusory or already-lost forms. Killing off the liberal humanist ideologies of individualism did not mean that the idea of the self or subject disappeared along with it; rather, it required that contemporary thinkers and writers construct that subject along different terms. If the self/subject was no longer to be thought of as "a unique personality and individuality" (Jameson, *Cultural* 6), how should it be conceived? What constitutes a human being without it?

As it turns out, in *The Thanatos Syndrome* the better question is: What's left of a human being when the self disappears? Na-24, Tom explains, causes "suppression of cortical function" in the "posterior speech center, Wernicke's area, Bodmann 39 and 40," the part of the brain that is "the locus of self-consciousness, the 'I,' the utterer, the 'self'" (22). Tom himself has done research into this phenomenon; he wrote a paper "on the effect of heavy-sodium fallout on the inhibitory function of the cerebral cortex on sexual behavior" (22), a study that the coconspirators themselves reference twice (28, 63). The beginning of the novel continually reasserts the geography and chemistry of mental functioning; in addition, it emphasizes Tom's competence amid "the Texas brain mechanics, M.I.T. neurone circuitrists" (16) who chart the geography of mood. Tom himself hesitates to speak of the self as a substantive entity, separate from the materiality of the brain, and ostentatiously separates the word from the rest of the sentence through the use of scare quotes, dashes, and question marks: "'self,'" "— self," "self?". Despite this hesitancy, Percy in *The Thanatos Syndrome* ultimately rejects biological accounts of the self in favor of more metaphysical considerations. Reflecting on the changes in his field, Tom comments that "old-fashioned shrinks are out of style and generally out of work. . . . we have been mostly superseded by brain engineers, neuropharmacologists, chemists of the synapses. And why not? If one can prescribe a chemical and overnight turn a haunted soul into a bustling little body, why take on such a quixotic quest as pursuing the secret of one's very self?" (13). Juxtaposing both the "soul" and the "self" with the "bustling little body" of the medicated, Percy implies two things: first, that the soul and the body are extricable, and hierarchically related, with the soul/self ruling over the body; and second, that treating the latter somehow occludes the former — otherwise, why would he not refer to the person on medication as a "bustling little soul"? The shift from soul to body suggests that only if the soul is gone would the body take precedence. The novel thus rejects the possibility that human beings could merely be the sum of its biological data even as it foregrounds biological functioning by illustrating the effects of heavy sodium on brain chemistry.

Removing the self with a dose of heavy sodium causes more than just the loss of self-consciousness, context, and the desire for self-knowledge. All subsequent desires also undergo significant revision.[12] Describing the success of an initiative medicating a low-income, African American neighborhood of Baton Rouge with Na-24, Dr. Bob Comeaux (one of the co-conspirators) asks Tom, "would you laugh at me if I told you what we've done is restore the best of the Southern Way of Life?" (197). For Comeaux, the image of blacks and whites living contentedly beside one another, the former laboring peacefully under the benevolent supervision of the latter, is realized in neighborhoods formerly marked by "a thousand young punks hanging out in the streets," (197) who are now committed to "Cottage industries, garden plots . . . [to be] Plumber's helpers, mechanic's helpers." These African American teenagers are working "not because somebody forces them—we ain't talking Simon Legree here boss," but importantly, "of their own accord" (198). Comeaux's comparison to slavery here is important, for the situations are formally but not materially different. If the worst of the "Southern Way of Life" deprived slaves of selfhood by refusing them the status of persons, its best (at least according to Comeaux) deprives the descendants of slaves of selfhood by replacing one set of desires with another. While they may possess the formal status of persons that was denied their ancestors (the concern of slavery's opponents), their material status remains essentially the same (the goal of slavery's advocates) because their desire for economic independence (at the very least) is tempered and controlled by heavy sodium. If slavery removed the legal self and left the essential self, Na-24 removes the essential self and leaves the legal self.

Dr. Comeaux's crude fantasy of "the best of the Southern Way of Life" notwithstanding, however, what is immediately apparent in these descriptions is that the novel references not so much to a return to slavery—a late-nineteenth-century fantasy—but rather to Africa—a specifically twentieth-century one. For if the African Americans in Dr. Comeaux's experiment have lost a certain selfhood through their exposure to Na-24, they've retained what can only be described as an identity. As Dr. Comeaux explains,

> Have you driven by the old project in Baton Rouge lately? . . . You know what you'd see now? . . . Green! Trees, shrubs, flowers, garden plots — one of the anthropologists on our board noted a striking resemblance to the decorative vegetation of the Masai tribesman — and guess what they've done with the old cinder-block entrances? . . . They're now mosaics, bits of colored glass from Anacin bottles, taillights, whatever, for all the world like — can't you guess? . . . The African bower bird, Tom. Lovely! (198–99)

Correlating the renewal of the African American urban community with the reemergence of so-called traditional African culture, *The Thanatos Syndrome* satirizes the multicultural and specifically Afrocentric movements of the 1980s that sought to reawaken a spirit within African Americans through the "language, dress, behavior, and games . . . derived from [an] African heritage" (Asante, *Afrocentricity* 21). African Americans exhibit on Na-24 a predisposition to certain artistic forms: "the decorative vegetation of the Masai tribesmen," and "The African bower bird."[13] That such a predisposition exists forms the basis of a particular version of Afrocentric philosophy; as Molefi Kete Asante explains, "Whether you are speaking of the Brazilian, Jamaican, Cuban, Haitian, or United States African, they all share the same experience or forms of experience . . . the same source of energy" (*Idea* 183). But what Maulana Karenga sees as the emergence of American "Blacks' real self, hidden under layers of false roles and identities imposed by the dominant society" (346), the novel represents as the moment of the self's radical absence, when identity takes over. And perhaps most compellingly, what for Asante represents freedom — in this case, from the Eurocentric ideals that constitute a "most pernicious kind of enslavement because the person . . . never see[s] clearly for himself" (*Afrocentricity* 40) — *The Thanatos Syndrome* represents as a new form of slavery — the enslavement to identity — in which the slave acts entirely "of his own accord" (198).

The novel's hostility to Afrocentricity is not in and of itself surprising. Afrocentric interpretations of culture and history were frequently made the scapegoat category for what some viewed as the extremes of multiculturalism and identity politics during the 1980s and 1990s.[14] What proves more interesting are the competing definitions of selfhood around which such hostility appeared. If, as Molly Anne Rothenberg and Joseph Valente claim, "Postmodern forms of feminist, postcolonial, and queer theory have deployed a radical social constructivism in order to challenge existing normative hierarchies by showing their underlying categories of intelligibility to be fundamentally arbitrary, invidious, and unstable" (413), the rise of multiculturalism suggests that their project was only half successful. Certainly, identity politics derived at least some of its force from the emphasis on social construction that emerged after the unified subject had disappeared as a theoretical possibility. But multiculturalism's resultant emphasis on the socially constructed subject appeared to reinstantiate something very like the essential self that postmodern theorists had set out to dismiss. While the vast majority of proponents of multiculturalism disdain arguments positing, in Henry Louis Gates Jr.'s words, "a mystically shared essence called blackness" (114), there remains a consensus among scholars writing that: first, individuals are crucially constructed through their cultural communities; and second, contemporary studies of culture need to compensate for the fact that, until now, "no women and people of color were ever able to discover the reflection or representation of their images, or hear the resonances of their cultural voices" (Gates 111). While those in favor of so-called traditional American culture argue that literature and the humanities "[*transcend*] accidents of class, race, and gender" — they "speak to us all," as Lynne Cheney, former head of the National Endowment for the Humanities declared (quoted in Fish, 258) — the multicultural project seeks precisely to challenge who "us all" might be, noting, as Stanley Fish does, that "it is obvious who will *not* get a say, those for whom matters of class, race, ethnicity and gender are of paramount importance" (258–59, emphasis in original). If one takes *The Thanatos Syndrome* seriously, however, one can imagine that Walker Percy would agree with *neither* of these two perspectives. For Percy, there is no guarantee that African American students will respond better to African American than Anglo- or Asian American literature, that in the fullness of selfhood they will create an African bower bird and not an Elizabethan sonnet. So to understand literature merely as an opportunity for identic consolidation — in which African Americans read Toni Morrison, Anglo-Americans read John Updike, and Jewish Americans read Saul Bellow — is to deprive it of its most powerful role as an aid to identic expansion. It is the nature of the human — not the humanities, as Cheney would have it — to transcend the limitations imposed by historical or cultural contingencies.

This commitment to the individual transcendence of sociological circumstances is itself a predictable outgrowth of the postwar existentialism with which Percy's work has been traditionally associated.[15] Objecting to the sociological or cultural constructivist assumption that human beings have fixed or definable natures, Percy maintains that "to the degree that a person perceives himself as an example of, a specimen of, this or that type of social creature or biological genotype, to precisely this same degree does he come short of being himself" ("State" 151). Like Sartre in *Being and Nothingness*, the individual's acceptance of his facticity as the total of his being overlooks that which defines humans as separate from other forms of being — the capacity of transcendence, of moving beyond the merely contingent aspects of existence. Authenticity is not a matter of being true to a hidden but essential innermost being. Rather, authenticity exists in a continued striving toward transcendence. Thus, for Percy the term "authentic" characterizes not a temperament or an essence but rather a commitment and a process; any theory of being "can only prove true to itself by seeing the human existent for what, at its minimum reach, it really is — not a quantifiable integer, a receptacle of biological needs and so susceptible to fixed inductions, but a transcending reality" ("Symbol" 286–87).

This is not to say that Percy attaches no importance to race or culture as aspects of selfhood. Nor is it to say that Percy merely disagrees with the multicultural privileging of culture at the expense of other influences. Percy is not, for instance, a neo-Marxist who believes that contemporary emphasis on race and ethnicity distracts attention from the real problem of economics; such an argument would not question that culture has a place in the construction of self- or subjecthood, but would assert that its role is exaggerated at the expense of other influences (like class status). Rather Percy's ontology of the human does not allow for either race, class, or culture to occupy anything other than a minor role, suggesting a hierarchy between the self and the identic categories it contains. Percy would most likely agree with those critics who maintain, as Diana Fuss paraphrases, "that biological determinism and social determinism are two sides of the same coin: both posit an utterly passive subject subordinated to the shaping influence of either nature or culture, and both disregard the unsettling effects on the psyche" (6). The structure of the novel—combining a medical response to insanity with a cultural side effect of the treatment—allows Percy in *The Thanatos Syndrome* to satirize *both* biological and cultural constructionism at the same time. To do so, furthermore, the novel utilizes the very tool that helped inaugurate the poststructuralist moment par excellence.

Having postulated in 1985 that the "common complaint of the age" stems from "an ontological impoverishment," Percy allegorizes this impoverishment in terms of the representational capacities of language.[16] For example, Father Smith, an elderly priest in charge of monitoring a smoke station for signs of fire, illustrates this analysis of the human condition by performing a word-association test. He names various national or cultural categories—"Irish," "Negro," "Jew"—and asks Tom to free associate. In response to the word "Irish" Tom says, "Bogs, Notre Dame, Pat O'Brien, begorra"; in response to the word "Negro" Tom says, "Africa, niggers, minority, civil rights"; in response to the word "Jew" he says, "Israel, Bible, Max, Sam, Julius, Hebrew, Hebe, Ben" (121–22). Father Smith then explains the significance of the results:

> Unlike the other test words, what you associated with the word *Jew* was Jews. Jews you have known . . . What you associated with the word sign *Irish* were certain connotations, stereotypical Irish stuff in your head. Same for Negro. If I had said Spanish, you'd have said something like guitar, castanets, bullfights and such. I have done the test on dozens. Thus these word-signs have been evacuated, deprived of meaning something real. Real persons. Not so with Jews. (122)

Most "word-signs" that represent identities are "deprived of meaning something real." They connote a series of ethnic types divorced from any specific embodiments of that ethnicity. But in Father Smith's (incoherent) logic, the word "Jew" still manages to represent "something real"—specific persons as opposed to mere cultural types. This notion of language partakes of a Christian theology that understands the word to have been given by God and made flesh through Christ's embodiment. The continued capacity of the Jewish person to be embodied in the world "Jew" (as evidenced in the word association test) represents the continued fact of

God's existence, since it is only God who has the capacity to make the word flesh. As the last remaining identity-marker that might represent individuals rather than an abstract class, category, or theory, the word "Jew" and the individuals to which it refers, "the original chosen people of God," are proof of God's continued relevance: "they are a sign of God's presence which cannot be evacuated" (123). Accordingly, Father Smith argues, to destroy the Jew would be to destroy the remaining proof of God. He thus asserts that "the holocaust was a consequence of the sign that could not be evacuated" (126) — could not, that is, be reduced to a mere cultural stereotype and thus required the infinitely more drastic means of the Final Solution. By extension, for Father Smith the capacity of the Jews to survive the Holocaust suggests that they possess an exemplary status among persons: they are the authentic self itself, undiluted by cultural identity or ethnic connotation.

It is worth noting here that Father Smith's linguistics are neither particularly sophisticated nor coherent; the novel would appear to offer them less as a potential new area for linguistic research than as a means to establish the role Jews will play as the embodiment of authenticity. That the Jews should personify such authenticity stems from their status as the primary victims of the Holocaust rather than any essential quality possessed by Jews. To imagine such a quality would seem to go against everything ostensibly argued for in *The Thanatos Syndrome*: that individuals do not have fixed or definable natures, they contain no "quantifiable integers," but are instead "transcending realities" ("Symbol" 287). Neither, one imagines, is Percy's point that Jews are not subject to national stereotypes that haunt African Americans, the Irish, and the like. Rather, the analogy that Percy seeks is between the wholesale medication of a community (the community of the depressed) with the wholesale murder of a community (the community of European Jews). The widespread medication of a population, for *The Thanatos Syndrome*, is a type of holocaust. The experiment in Na-24 constitutes the genocide of the depressed.

Ultimately, then, the individual should strive to the status of the Jew. Of the three states of being that the novel presents — the person-as-depressive (Tom's patients before heavy sodium), the person-as-identity (the African Americans taking Na-24), and the person-as-authentic-self (the Jews) — only the last embodies "something real." The ethical order validated by the Jews' continued "sign of God's presence" mandates the search for authentic existence above all else. To possess *merely* an identity suggests not only complacency but an ethical crime. Yet the person-as-depressive is not as far off in his quest for authenticity as one might think. As Tom claims, each patient "has the means of obtaining . . . the patient's truest unique self" (16–17). If the existentialist believes, in David E. Cooper's phrase, that "the true self . . . is not just an inner self somehow occluded by a false, superficial one, but a self you should strive to become," that "the self-estranged person is not distanced from a self he actually possesses but from a goal which he should be pursuing" (96), then Percy's commitment to depression-as-vehicle makes perfect sense. Percy imagines depression to operate as an invitation to process: the means whereby the self summons the individual and the individual "can come to themselves, without chemicals" (17). Answering that summons is the reason for Binx Bolling's search in Percy's novel *The Moviegoer* (1961), and constitutes "what anyone would undertake if he were not sunk in the everydayness of his own life" (13).

At the end of *The Thanatos Syndrome*, after Feliciana returns to its preconspiracy malaise, Mickey returns to Dr. More's couch and asks, "'Do you remember that dream I had? I had it again'" (371). The return of the dream invokes for Mickey the reawakening of the self to its own internality. Yet for Percy the dream constitutes only the beginning of the self's journey to authenticity. Tom's encouraging "Well?" is then repeated three times: the novel ends with the words "Well well well" (372) to emphasize the wrongness of understanding depression as an illness, the rightness of a world where depression is possible. *The Thanatos Syndrome* thus provides a veritable lament for a world without depression, for the loss of the self—or the loss of the search—around which Percy's career has been in many respects defined.

Darkness Visible, *Prozac Nation*, and the Prozac Americans

Percy's fear of a medication, widely available, that might eradicate depression itself seems remarkably prescient. Written two years before Prozac became available by prescription to the general population, *The Thanatos Syndrome* foreshadows many of the professional debates about Prozac in the psychiatric community and their lay interpretation in the mainstream media. By ostensibly curing depression, Prozac and its family of psychopharmaceuticals — the SSRIs — provided easily recognizable data to support those doctors who had long asserted the biological basis of all forms of insanity. If the 1960s were marked by the substitution of social for biological models of mental illness, with the closing of the asylums as the result, the 1990s saw a reverse trend, in which biological accounts took precedence over interpersonal ones. Advocates argued that no longer did one need to commit to years of therapy to deal with a mood disorder; now one only needs to take a pill that can be prescribed by a general practitioner rather than a psychiatrist. Further, Prozac promised that other forms of mental illness might be cured as easily. It opened up the prospect that other wonder drugs — drugs to cure schizophrenia, bipolar disorders, obsessive-compulsive conditions, and the like — might with time also be discovered.

Yet as Prozac made possible a purely biological definition of depression and other forms of insanity, it likewise required that doctors, writers, and those suffering from depression consider what biological accounts of these illness might mean for notions of self- or subjecthood. As Dr. Peter Kramer recalls in his best-selling *Listening to Prozac* (1993), his introduction of the term "cosmetic psychopharmacology" brought him instant notoriety as a psychiatrist unafraid to discuss "how [Prozac] went beyond treating illness to changing personality, how it entered into our struggle to understand the self" (xviii). Six years before Kramer considered the questions brought on by Prozac's success, Percy divined the issues that Prozac would raise, illustrating what later appeared as a widespread interest in the ethical consequences of medication that purported to go beyond happiness to alter selfhood.[17] In Kramer's cosmetic psychopharmacological nightmare, a woman who wished to be less shy, more socially aggressive, and comfortable with strangers would take Prozac "to cure her" of those aspects of her self. "Prozac does not just brighten mood," Kramer claims, "it allows a woman with the traits we now consider 'overly feminine,' in the sense of passivity and a tendency to histrionics, to opt, if she is a good responder, for a spunkier persona" (270–71). On the one hand, Kramer easily sympathizes with the person trapped and limited by shyness, unable to make friends or have relationships: no one would want to deny this individual what is generally considered a healthy social life. On the other hand, Kramer's discomfort stems from the fear that the shy woman is asked "to be someone she's not" (270) and is encouraged to take Prozac as a means to submit to cultural standards.

For Percy, the alternative to depression is identity — an ontology of persons that defines the individual as a fixed composite of certain biological and sociological contingencies. For Kramer, it is conformity (as it was for Riesman, Marcuse, and Erikson): he fears that "a mood elevator for dysthymics [individuals with persistent, low-grade depression], at least one that works through altering temperament, will necessarily be a drug that induces 'conformity.'" In this sense, Kramer's fears are most similar to the type that Sylvia Plath or Michel Foucault expressed thirty years previously; he fears the enforcement of norms that would wipe out alternative forms of being: the shy, the obsessive, the depressed, the mad. Yet Kramer qualifies his use of the term "conformity," stating that he uses "quotation marks because here it means conformity to traits society rewards, which might well be rebelliousness, egocentricity, radical self-confidence, or other qualities that lead to behaviors we normally call nonconformist" (269). He thereby accounts for the idea of the "inauthentically iconoclastic," a possibility that is implicitly foreclosed at least in Marcuse's discussion. Since Marcuse imagines that authenticity is inevitably constructed in *opposition* to the social, the idea of an inauthenticity that contradicted social norms — or of a society that rewards traits that ostensibly work against it — remains unexplored.

Yet the discrepancy between Percy's and Kramer's views, between identity and conformity, is crucial to understanding contemporary notions of the self or subject, and the distance those notions have traveled since the 1950s. What Kramer questions are the philosophical standards for self-identity; he wants to know how much an individual can change — to be liked, to fit in — and still remain the same. It is the Jekyll-and-Hyde question: is Jekyll/Hyde two people or one person with a particularly severe mental illness?[18] Kramer questions at what point an individual becomes a different person and which one — pre- or post-Prozac — is to be considered "real." The original, which is to say, the depressed person? The person whom the patient likes more? The person whom everyone else likes more? But for Percy the criterion of self-identity does not apply. His model of selfhood is inherently dynamic; it takes as given the self's continual change. For Percy, the individual on medication does not have two selves — a Jekyll and a Hyde, a pre- and a post-Prozac—between which one need differentiate. Rather, he has no self at all. The fault lies not in the change, but in the loss of the capacity to change, the insistence that there is a permanent answer to questions regarding the nature of the self. But both authors take at their core the idea that depression is more than an illness, involving a complicated negotiation between the individual and the community in which he operates. And while Kramer has been criticized for the extremity of his examples—few individuals have the dramatic results with Prozac that he describes—his fears encapsulate what Percy imagined five years earlier: depression is traditionally understood as something importantly *more* than a biological condition, a sign of or means to the self rather than a hindrance to daily life.

As it turns out, both authors were wrong to imagine that with a medical cure for depression, it might actually disappear. As William Styron's memoir, *Darkness Visible: A Memoir of Madness* (1990), suggests, the tendency to view depression predominantly in medical—which is to say biological—terms was well established by the late 1980s, even before Prozac came along. Published three years after *The Thanatos Syndrome*, *Darkness Visible* evidences the same interest in the medicalization of depression, only Styron is strongly supportive of the trend. Recounting the circumstances that led to his exploration of his own experience of mental illness, Styron claims he decided to write his memoir as a horrified response to Primo Levi's suicide in 1987—only his horror was not at the suicide itself, but rather the published reaction to it. Styron claims, "It was as if this man whom [scholars and writers] had all so greatly admired, and who had endured so much at the hands of the Nazis . . . had by his suicide demonstrated a frailty, a crumbling of character they were loath to accept. In the face of a terrible absolute—self-destruction—their reaction was helplessness and (the reader could not avoid it) a touch of shame" (32–33). In a fit of "annoyance" with such ignorance, Styron wrote an editorial for the *New York Times* arguing that "the pain of severe depression is quite unimaginable to those who have not suffered it" and "to the tragic legion who are compelled to destroy themselves there should be no more reproof attached than to the victims of terminal cancer" (33). The response was "equally spontaneous—and enormous" by Styron's account. A Stonewall riots for the secretly depressed, his article expressed "no particular originality or boldness" (33), he confesses, yet "the overwhelming reaction made me feel that inadvertently I had helped unlock a closet from which many souls were eager to come out and proclaim that they, too, had experienced the feelings I had described" (34). Concluding that to educate his audience about depression represented a worthwhile reason "to have invaded my own privacy," Styron decided that the time was appropriate to "chronicle some of my own experiences with the illness" (34).

Taken as a whole, *Darkness Visible* is defined by such moments of self- and communal discovery. Its references to cancer and locked closets allude to both Susan Sontag's *Illness as Metaphor* and the historic shame associated with homosexuality (and repudiated by the gay rights movement) to describe the experience of the depressed. Yet to look more closely at these two analogies is to expose an ambiguity in Styron's text. *Darkness Visible* represents depression as simultaneously an illness and an identity; it is at once a disease—like cancer—foreign to the individual and invasive of the self, and a way of life—like homosexuality—thought both essential and constitutive of one's being. While not necessarily contradictory, the two accounts suggest substantially different understandings of what depression is and how most accurately to represent the depressed. For example, invoking Sontag's *Illness as Metaphor*, Styron contends that depression is only properly understood as something that happens to and in spite of its victim. Sontag's account censures any description of illness that correlates the identity of the patient with the identity of the ailment, protesting that "the notion that disease expresses the character" (46) is too easily converted into the notion "that the character causes the disease," with the result that "people are encouraged to believe that they get sick because they (unconsciously) want to, and that they can cure themselves by the mobilization of will" (57). The analogy Sontag adopts to describe "the lurid metaphors" with which "the kingdom of the ill" has been "landscaped" harnesses images of ethnicity and identity to illustrate their inappropriateness: such descriptions, Sontag maintains, evoke "not real geography, but stereotypes of national character" (4, 3).

If any disease were to engage the unconscious desires, it seems likely that depression would be the one, but Styron, like Sontag, argues that depression disregards character, and when forced to choose among the few available accounts of the disease, he favors those that emphasize biological as opposed to psychological factors. He argues depression "strikes indiscriminately at all ages, races, creeds and classes" (35) with no regard for identity, behavior, or lifestyle, and he provides representative case histories in order to emphasize its eclectic reach. As he states, "the occupational list (dressmakers, barge captains, sushi chefs, cabinet members) of its patients is too long and tedious to give here; it is enough to say that few people escape being a potential victim" (35). If the character of the individual has little ability to affect the onslaught of depression, however, depression does possess the ability to affect the character of the individual—with Primo Levi's suicide providing the most extreme example. While few argue that suffering from cancer creates an essentially different person, Styron understands depression to alter fundamentally the person of the depressed.[19] Not just behaviors change; the individual suffering from depression is, in a crucial sense, no longer himself. Describing a trip to Paris in which he offended his host by accepting an invitation to and then canceling an award luncheon at which he was the guest of honor, Styron claims:

> my behavior was really the result of the illness, which had progressed far enough to produce some of its most famous and sinister hallmarks: confusion, failure of mental focus and lapse of memory.... It must have been during the previous evening's murky distractedness that I made the luncheon date with Françoise Gallimard, forgetting my del Duca obligations. (14–15)

While Styron the award-winning novelist would never have committed such a faux pas as to insult the foundation honoring his work, Styron the depressive could not keep track of his dates, times, and obligations. "Dominated" by the illness and its "sinister hallmarks," the organized and socially reliable novelist finds that depression, in his words, "completely master[ed] my thinking, creating in me such obstinate determination that now I was able to blandly insult the worthy Simone del Duca." As Styron remembers, he came to his senses, "flabbergasted, stunned with horror at what I had done . . . [and] fantasized a table at which sat the hostess and the *Académie Française*, the guest of honor at *La Coupole*" (15). Like Primo Levi, about whose suicide even his friends feel such unwarranted shame and disappointment, Styron cannot control his irrational behavior; he is "mastered" by the depression that overcame him. When he insults the "worthy Simone del Duca," he is not himself.

Under this theory, then — arguably the most common in current circulation — depression is an illness that interferes with the capacity of the self to be itself. Thus, the person who killed Primo Levi was in some fundamental respect not Levi, and to blame him is to mischaracterize depression's mastery. Styron thus provides a strictly functional account: certain individuals have a condition that prevents them from being themselves; one must correct this condition to enable full selfhood. As Styron describes his gradual recovery, he "felt himself no longer a husk but a body with some of the body's sweet juices stirring again," and — lest anyone confuse mere sexuality with full selfhood — his physical reawakening to the self accompanies a rediscovered interiority: he "had [his] first dream in many months, confused but to this day imperishable" (75).

If this account of depression-as-illness is correct, however, it is unclear why Styron alleges an identity between gay and depressed individuals. Despite widespread disagreement about the basis of homosexuality, there is general consensus among the psychiatric community that homosexuality neither prevents the individual from being herself nor represents an illness that can or should be cured. To the contrary, being gay is importantly understood as self-constitutive, as Sontag's own discussion makes clear. In comparison to the afflicted, about whom there can be no accurate "national stereotypes," Sontag observes that "in the 1970s . . . many male homosexuals reconstituted themselves as something like an ethnic group, one whose distinctive folkloric custom was sexual voracity" (AIDS 164). When HIV entered the gay community, it may have flushed "out an identity that might have remained hidden" and proved an important "creator of community," but that emerging community importantly defined itself around being gay, not around being sick (AIDS 113).

The source of Styron's analogy between depression and homosexuality would rather seem to be the underserved shame historically allotted to both communities. But the analogy is taken further by Styron's own profound pessimism about the possibility of a lasting cure for depressive individuals. Writing before the SSRI revolution, Styron despairs of the then-current forms of therapy, commenting upon "the inexplicable nature of depression and the difficulty of its treatment" (11). The implication of the comparison is that depression is in some way a permanent condition that defines even asymptomatic intervals. By this account, depression might operate not unlike alcoholism as understood by Alcoholics Anonymous, in which the afflicted may successfully control the disease by avoiding liquor but must always understand himself to be an alcoholic — even in the absence of alcoholic behaviors. Caroline Knapp writes of alcoholism that "you wake up one morning and some indefinable tide has turned forever and you can't go back. You *need* it; it's a central part of who you are. . . . a slow, gradual, insidious elusive *becoming*" (6, 8, emphasis in original). That "becoming" is crucially irrevocable; at her core Knapp understands "alcoholism is a part of me, a reality I am learning to live with" (270). But is this the condition of the depressive? In the same way that Knapp comprehends herself to be crucially defined by her dependence on alcohol, a formerly depressive self could potentially operate as a self defined in opposition, or a self under siege. Such a self must always fight to be itself. But against what does the former depressive fight? An alcoholic might spend every day battling the temptations of alcohol, but, by Styron's own account, neither a depressive's behavior nor his character caused his depression. By extension, then, a former depressive's behavior and character should not be able to cause a recurrence. Eternal vigilance does not guarantee freedom from relapse. What is the content of depression in remission, in the absence of actual depressive symptoms?

The emergence of Prozac — and of the fantasy of a depression-free population that its appearance engendered — arguably enabled the answer to such questions. Yet the possibility of a cure, instead of eradicating depression by promising to alleviate its symptoms, succeeded only in divorcing the former from the latter.[20] No longer understood as a collection of characteristics — a set of symptoms that, taken together, are identified as a illness — depression after Prozac is imagined as a state of being, an identity in its own right independent from any particular characteristics or behaviors. In this sense the post-Prozac memoir, like Elizabeth Wurtzel's *Prozac Nation*, resolves the ambiguity inherent in Styron's text by establishing depression as a version of the type of alternative selfhood imagined by R. D. Laing, Sylvia Plath, Michel Foucault, and other members of the movement for anti-institutionalization. Yet it does so *through* biological definitions of insanity, rather than in opposition to them.

In the epilogue to her memoir, the best-selling account of America's newest lost generation, Wurtzel describes her reaction to the information that "six million Americans had taken Prozac" as "one of the creepiest moments" of her experience of depression (341). The explanation she offers, while nominally accounting for the "creepiness," itself raises a number of other questions: "As a Jew," Wurtzel explains, "I had always associated that precise number with something else entirely. How would I come to reinterpret six million, to associate it with something quite different, a statistic that ought to be frightening but instead starts to seem rather ridiculous?" (341–42). The analogy Wurtzel draws hinges on the reappearance of the number six million as a significant quantity, but why those two quantities — six million Jews and six million Prozac takers (or six million former depressives) — should be related through anything other than coincidence is not immediately apparent. As I suggest above, Percy would consider the indiscriminate use of Prozac as a type of holocaust, but (from Percy's perspective) where Na-24 created identities by killing selves — by rendering individuals nothing more than their identities — the Nazi genocide inadvertently created authentic selves by killing identities. That is, the Jews were targeted for their identity as Jews, but their capacity to survive such devastation ultimately established their status as authentic in *The Thanatos Syndrome* — albeit at an unendurable cost. In any event, if Wurtzel finds the coincidence so disturbing, she herself argues she only need wait a while; both Wurtzel and Kramer predict that the number of people taking Prozac will rise.[21]

Of course, the way in which they correlate, and hence their true "creepiness," resides in Wurtzel's relationship to the two numbers. That she understands the coincidence's significance depends upon her considering herself to have a similar relation to both quantities, to be a member of both groups. Furthermore, she considers the two memberships comparable in a crucial way: being Jewish and being depressed are both understood by Wurtzel as identities — modes of being rather than modes of behaving. The Jews killed in the Holocaust died for being Jews, not for acting Jewish. Under Nazi racial theories, an individual's Jewishness was determined biologically, not behaviorally; the actual practice of Judaism was irrelevant. Similarly, Wurtzel maintains not that she acts depressed but that she is depressed. It is one of the first facts she realized as an eleven-year-old, and, she explains, she "thought this alternative persona that [she] adopted was just that: a put on, a way of getting attention. . . . But after a while, the alternative me was really just me" (45). Later, she observes that the frightening aspect of starting psychopharmacological treatment resided in "[t]he idea of throwing away my depression, of having to create a whole new personality" (327).[22] Her reaction was not unlike, one might hypothesize, a self-identified Jew might feel should she learn that taking a pill would remove her Jewish identity.[23]

Needless to say, Wurtzel's analogy is not very precise, but the rough correlation that she draws is telling in comparison to both Styron's and Percy's ontology of depression, offering yet a third account of what depression properly is. One sees in *Darkness Visible* that Styron views depression as an illness that needs to be cured before the self can truly be itself; in his model of persons, depression is an obstacle to be overcome. By comparison Percy, in *The Thanatos Syndrome* and throughout his career, imagines depression as a technology, a means whereby the individual is summoned to the search for authenticity. Under this account, depression is not the self but brings one to it; it is the vehicle through which authentic selfhood is achieved. Wurtzel's analysis, however, differs from both of these models. She imagines that depression is the self—fundamentally and essentially. Neither a condition to be cleared up nor a means to be employed, depression is and always will be a constitutive part of who she is. And Prozac itself enables this discovery. Wurtzel explains that "there isn't any reason to draw the symptoms of depression into a particular category unless a therapist is about to prescribe an antidepressant. . . . Rather than defining my disease as a way to lead us to [Prozac], the invention of this drug has brought us to my disease" (301). It is only once the symptoms are cured that the disease is finally determined, becoming an identity independent of any biological or behavioral indicators.

Wurtzel herself does not seem entirely happy with this conclusion: if Jewishness and depression are understood to be comparable, the "creepy" part of the analogy lies in the fact that Wurtzel is quite comfortable proclaiming herself a Jew—"As a Jew" operates here as a strong statement of identity—but worries that it is ridiculous to identify herself among the legion of the depressed. The problem is not that Wurtzel is uneasy with her own depression, however; if she were, she would hardly be writing a memoir of it, let alone one filled with revealing anecdotes. Rather Wurtzel feels uncomfortable being identified with the other depressives, those open to accusations of "cosmetic psychopharmacology" who are trivializing the disease. She confesses, "Every so often, I find myself with the urge to make sure people know that I am not just on Prozac but on lithium too, that I am a real sicko, a depressive of a much higher order," and admits she cannot decide whether "to be dismayed by my need for Prozac one-upmanship, or by the fact that it isn't entirely unwarranted" (342). Thus Wurtzel feels comfortable identifying with Kurt Cobain and her friend Olivia, but balks at identifying with the taxi driver who "confesses he tried to kill himself with one hundred valium pills and a whiskey chaser" (338) or Olivia's cat, who suffered from "excessive grooming disorder, which meant that the cat had grown depressed and self-absorbed, perhaps because Olivia's boyfriend had moved out of the apartment" and receives a "feline-sized prescription" every day (333).

There is a certain irony in the fact that Wurtzel is untroubled about identifying with an event — the Holocaust — that she never personally underwent, making herself part of a community that understands itself to hold in common an experience never actually endured by the majority of its members; but hesitates to identify with a group of people — the Prozac Nation of her title — with whom she shares something extremely concrete, even if it is limited to the daily ritual of swallowing a pill. The problem is not a failure to identify. One could imagine an individual refusing to join the Prozac Nation because she refuses to view Prozac taking as in any way constitutive of self. To the contrary, the book is devoted to emphasizing Wurtzel's investment in depression as an integral part of who she is. Rather, Wurtzel's discomfort in imagining an essential connection between herself and Olivia's cat is comparable to that of, say, an Orthodox Jew who views Reform Judaism as insufficiently Jewish. Wurtzel implies that there are people on Prozac, and there are people on Prozac who are *really* depressed — the others are phonies, posers, wannabes, with no business claiming to be depressed at all. The category of the authentic, so crucial to the existentialist construction of the individual self, becomes a criterion of group identity, with real Jews and phony Jews, real depressives and phony depressives, debating standards of belonging.

Wurtzel claims that despite Prozac, she is still depressed, not because there are residual symptoms that Prozac is unable to treat (although there certainly are, as many a depressive was discouraged to find out once the media furor died off), but because in an important way depression has nothing to do with its symptoms. Wurtzel herself declines to elaborate on what, if not its symptoms, depression does have to do with — that is, what the content of depressive identity after Prozac might be — but her refusal to identify with the taxi driver (not to mention the cat) raises important questions about the various other identities that intersect with and are implicated in the category of the authentically depressed. Certainly it is easier for a white, upper-middle-class, well-educated woman to lay claim to the benefits of depressive identity (book contracts and the like) than a taxi driver. The point here, however, is not to insist that depression-as-identity ought be made available to all — though insofar as benefits do ensue from it, it certainly ought to be — but rather to ask whether depression-as-identity in and of itself makes any sense. Certainly, this is not what Walker Percy had in mind. By Percy's account, it is no better to be restricted to depressive identity than to any other, ethnic or not. Had he written *The Thanatos Syndrome* ten years later, the word "depressed" — like "Irish" or "Negro" — might have appeared in Father Smith's word association test, constituting yet another word deprived of its capacity to mean "something real." If depression remains a site for theorizing the self in all its complexity, the conclusions drawn in the 1950s versus the 1990s could not look much different.

Wurtzel's depiction of depression-as-identity, however, does makes sense in the context of the confusion in *Darkness Visible* of metaphors discussed in the opening of this section. Is depression more like cancer or homosexuality, like an illness or an identity? While Styron literally argues the former position — depression as a hindrance to selfhood — his metaphors figuratively foreshadow the latter — depression as a type of selfhood. In this sense *Darkness Visible*, published in 1990 but based on events from the mid-1980s and written by an author whose career spans the entire postwar period (from 1952 to the present), itself embodies the evolution from the positions of Percy and Wurtzel, between the existentialist and the identic points of view. Thus, Styron, who by chronology and bibliography might be thought an existentialist, can be seen debating the term "depression" with all the seriousness of the black intelligentsia arguing about the relative value of the designation "black" versus "Afro-American" and "African American"; he argues that "depression" is "a noun with a bland tonality and lack[s] any magisterial presence, used indifferently to describe an economic decline or a rut in the ground, a true wimp of a word for such a major illness" (37).

At the end of *Darkness Visible*, Styron explains that he was able to write about the experiences of an African American slave (in *The Confessions of Nat Turner* [1967]) or a Polish female Holocaust survivor (in *Sophie's Choice* [1979]) because all of these characters, despite their diverse backgrounds, were at their core just like him: they were depressed. He observes,

> after I had returned to health and was able to reflect on the past in light of my ordeal, I began to see clearly how depression had clung close to the outer edges of my life for many years. Suicide has been a persistent theme in my books — three of my major characters killed themselves. In rereading, for the first time in years, sequences from my novels — passages where my heroines have lurched down pathways toward doom — I was stunned to perceive how accurately I had created the landscape of depression in the minds of these young women, describing with what could only be instinct, out of a subconscious already roiled by disturbances of mood, the psychic imbalance that led them to destruction. Thus depression, when it finally came to me, was in fact no stranger, not even a visitor totally unannounced; it had been tapping at my door for decades. (78–79)

Styron here suggests that he could write of experiences far removed from his own not because all human experience is essentially universal (as Lynne Cheney might maintain), not because it is the power of the imagination to understand and empathize with experiences beyond its own, but because being depressed creates an identic link more powerful than the differences afforded by race, gender, or ethnicity. Disregarding liberal arguments that favor ubiquitous as opposed to dissimilar human traits, and existentialist arguments that view the self as a dynamic rather than substantive entity — as inevitably more than an identity — Styron implies here that identity does exist and in fact does matter. Only the difference is that he possesses the identity in question as if by "instinct" — the identity of the depressed. The differences between Styron and Sophie are thus rendered moot by the similarities of having "lurched down pathways toward doom."

At the time of its writing, *The Confessions of Nat Turner* garnered an enormous amount of criticism from various intellectuals, black and white, who claimed that Styron lacked the necessary knowledge to write the experiences of a black slave. Arguing that the novel would best be titled "The Imaginations of William Styron" for its exposure of the author as "a southern white man who has been raised in a racist society and is not free from the impact of its teachings" (Poussaint 17), these writers maintain that "Nat Turner does not speak in William Styron's *Confessions*. The voice in this confession is the voice of William Styron. The images are the images of William Styron. The confession is the confession of William Styron" (Bennett 4). This may be true. But their two voices need not be understood as so dissimilar if one accepts the implications of the depressive identity. Styron can write a novel with characters of other identities not because he is a good liberal, able to identify with black men, Holocaust survivors, and white women, but because he is an authentic depressive, and that depression-as-identity trumps race-as-identity, gender-as-identity, and ethnicity-as-identity. In many ways, this constitutes the perfect response to the liberal dilemma of the general / individual, for depression requires not assertions of universality but rather opens up a whole new way to join the particular. In fairness to Styron, he never claims that *The Confessions of Nat Turner* was anything more than his imagining, nor that Nat is one of the characters whose "psychic imbalance" he shared, claiming only that he felt "an early fascination with Nat Turner," having grown up in that region of Virginia and that interest inevitably led to the novel ("Nat" 438). Nevertheless it is a conclusion rooted in the logic of his account, a logic that to the list of American identities — gays, straights, Jewish Americans, African Americans — adds a new identity group: the Prozac Americans.

The idea of the Prozac Americans, while obviously facetious, suggests how far the idea of insanity, madness, or mental illness has traveled since the 1950s. Mid-century writers like Sylvia Plath, Thomas Szasz, R. D. Laing, and Michel Foucault saw in the medicalization of madness the death of an alternative way of being — a form of self victimized by the coercive expectations of normalcy. Its treatment is figured as a technology for the production of real phonies; doll-like individuals with "uniformity to their faces, as if they had lain for a long time on a shelf" (Plath 141). In such figuration, authenticity and mental illness are imagined as comparable states—qualities that separate the self from its social and institutional contexts and in which authenticity becomes an index to one's alterity. Yet as the ending of *The Bell Jar* suggests, such radical alterity cannot ultimately be sustained; the most Esther can hope for is "the attitude" (Menand 84) that helps her maintain a distance from her cultural context even as she exists within its boundaries. By comparison, writers from the end of the century, like Peter Kramer, Elizabeth Wurtzel, and William Styron, suggest that biological definitions of mental illness do little to limit its power as a form of identity, if not of selfhood. To the contrary, classifying these conditions as mental illness frees them to operate as entirely metaphysical categories. The medicalization of mental illness does not conscribe the discursive power of madness as Foucault and Szasz feared; instead, it legitimates and instantiates it as an identic category. That it does so at the precise moment when that category has lost much of its meaning through its (ostensible) cure makes it even more appropriate as a potential identity. As other forms of difference are reduced to their least objectionable components—hairstyles, food choices, religious beliefs held moderately—so too the Prozac Americans are defined by only the most innocuous of characteristics: a mild but pervasive sexual dysfunction that (while no doubt frustrating to those who experience it) places little burden of difference on the community overall.

The distance from madness to the Prozac Americans thus illuminates a fundamental shift in popular understanding of how the self or subject is constituted, and what role biological or cultural influences play in that constitution. As self- or subjecthood becomes identity, it turns from a quality that separates the individual from his cultural context to one that marks his overall belonging within larger groupings defined ethnically, racially, religiously, and so on. Walker Percy's *The Thanatos Syndrome* uses the debates between mental illness and madness to illustrate what it sees as the consequences of giving up the mid-century's existentialist models of the self. Satirizing both biological and cultural constructivism in the widespread medication of the depressed, the novel suggests that, in imagining depression as solely an illness, one overlooks its function as a technology of realizing an authenticity related to, but not conscribed by, cultural contexts. Instead, as existentialism retreated before poststructuralist and multicultural models of persons that privilege culturally based characteristics, so depression shifted from an instrument to an identity: from a technology to realize authentic being, to a way of being in and of itself.

3 "THEY DIDN'T DO IT FOR THRILLS"

Serial Killing and the Problem of Motive

WHEN DR. HANNIBAL LECTER, Thomas Harris's infamous serial-killing psychiatrist, consults with FBI agents Will Graham and Clarice Starling, he provides them with widely disparate advice on how to capture serial murderers. To Graham, the agent pursuing the so-called Tooth Fairy in *Red Dragon* (1981), Lecter suggests the solution lies in identifying with the killer. He claims that this is how Graham recognized him as the murderer of nine people. "Do you know how you caught me, Will?" he asks: "The reason you caught me is that we're *just alike*" (67).[1] Although Graham does not admit it, Lecter is correct; Graham visits him in the Baltimore Hospital for the Criminally Insane because there is "a mindset he had to recover after his warm round years in the [Florida] Keys" (57), without which he will be less successful investigating this new series of murders. In *The Silence of the Lambs* (1988), however, Lecter recommends Starling consider the teachings of the Emperor Marcus Aurelius in her pursuit of the serial killer nicknamed Buffalo Bill. "The Emperor counsels simplicity. First principles," Lecter explains. "Of each particular thing, ask: what is it in itself, in its own constitution? What is its causal nature?" (227). Where the first method posits a commonality between serial murderers and the general population—that repeat killers and their investigators can be "*just alike*"—the second postulates a fundamental schism between them. To identify the perpetrator, Starling must investigate "in itself" a "causal nature" significantly different from her own.

Part of this variance in methodology can be attributed to differences in the investigators. Graham, the reader is continually reminded, is an "*eideteker*"—a person with an unusually precise visual memory—who possesses "pure empathy and projection." In the words of forensic psychiatrist Dr. Alan Bloom, "he can assume your point of view, or mine — and maybe some other points of view that scare and sicken him" (*Red* 152). This outsized capacity for identification distinguishes Graham from the average investigator; Starling is merely an FBI trainee, albeit a very good one. Traditional assumptions about gender identification also play a role. Where Graham's success in locating the Tooth Fairy stems from his ability to identify with a male serial killer, Starling's capture of Buffalo Bill is based on her affinity with his female victims, having grown up in similar communities and in similar poverty. Her success results from her willingness to be sexual bait for Lecter to engage him with the investigation, and because at a crucial moment she recognizes a sewing pattern in a victim's closet.[2] Despite these obvious differences in gender and experience, however, both novels suggest that the primary reason Graham and Starling approach these cases differently is because of a disparity between the killers themselves, indicating a significant shift in Harris's understanding of serial murder between 1981 and 1988.

This shift is most evident in the contrasting motives the novels assign to each of the murderers. In *Red Dragon*, the Tooth Fairy (whose real name is Francis Dolarhyde) believes the murders of whole families provide the medium of his "Becoming." He bears their screams, the narrator claims, "as a sculptor bears dust from the beaten stone." His victims are "more important for the changing" that they make possible in him "than [for] the lives they scrabble after" (96). The novel implies that, for Dolarhyde, serial killing operates as a technology of self-actualization, where the murders are not an end in and of themselves (murder for murder's sake) but rather the vehicle through which he leaves behind the man who "for years had taken shit unlimited from people" (165) and becomes his "higher self": the Red Dragon, a figure taken from a William Blake watercolor (75). Harris in *The Silence of the Lambs* likewise suggests that Buffalo Bill is obsessed with his own transformation. As Lecter explains, "Billy thinks he wants to change" and is "making himself a girl suit out of real girls" to do it (163). Yet the novel goes to great lengths to emphasize that, in fact, "Billy's not a real transsexual." He only "thinks he is, he tries to be" (165). Though Buffalo Bill, like Francis Dolarhyde, believes he kills to enable a self-transformation, the impossibility of that change is continually emphasized in *The Silence of the*

Lambs.³ The crimes that Jame Gumb (Buffalo Bill's real name) believes reveal him as a woman in fact only manifest his actual essence. The "nature" represented by the murders posits a person "one thousand times more savage and more terrifying" than even Gumb himself recognizes.⁴

The novels thus provide two alternative explanations for the phenomenon of serial killing; more specifically, they suggest two alternative accounts of the connection between the act of serial murder and the person of the murderer. In *Red Dragon*, a serial killer creates himself through action. The suggestion is that who people are is a function of what people do. Yet in *The Silence of the Lambs*, the serial murderer illustrates himself in action, and those actions express, rather than constitute, the subject. To put this slightly differently, if for Francis Dolarhyde repetitive violence provides a medium of self-transformation, for Jame Gumb it constitutes a means of self-representation, revealing the self as it is instead of enabling the self to become.

The difference between these two imaginings of serial murder demonstrates more than just a change in Thomas Harris's thinking about serial killers over the course of his career. It illustrates in miniature two much larger and related transformations that occurred in the second half of the twentieth century. The first is an evolution in the popular understanding of the ontology of the serial murderer. The second is a change in the way writers and scholars have imagined the relation between the self and its behaviors—between whom one is and what one does—with profound consequences for the way authenticity is imagined by writers, cultural critics, and filmmakers during this period.

This chapter investigates the details of that first evolution to explore the fundamental consequences of the second. Examining serial-killing novels from Jim Thompson's *The Killer inside Me* (1952) and Patricia Highsmith's *The Talented Mr. Ripley* (1955) to Don DeLillo's *The Names* (1982) and Harris's Hannibal Lecter novels, this chapter considers the ways in which these authors imagine the phenomenon of repetitive murder in relation to self- or subjecthood. These novels ask: how does the act of multiple murders relate to the person of the murderer? As an authentic expression of a hidden self (Thompson), as a form of self-creation (Highsmith, Harris) or self-repair (DeLillo), or as a compulsive gesture of self-expression (Harris)? The variety of ways that the relation between a killer and his crimes are conceived in these novels render them crucial sites for the consideration of the connection between individuals and their actions. As important, they illustrate how that connection has evolved during the last half century.

That novels about serial killing should have something to say about this connection may not be immediately obvious. As the above examples from *Red Dragon* and *The Silence of the Lambs* demonstrate, however, the relevance of such considerations to this most mainstream of genres stems from the critical role that motive plays in these texts. Assessment of motive has a key narrative function in crime fiction generally, and in serial-killing fiction in particular. It constitutes the link through which individual actions (in this case, murders) are aligned with specific persons (serial killers) who might then be held accountable for them. Discovering motive is thus central to the project of the serial-killing novel: it operates as the narrative core around which the plot revolves, and through which both the killer and the crime are rendered intelligible (and therefore understandable) to the reader. Motives make individuals legible by recourse to their actions, by explaining how those actions constitute or represent them.

For example, the reader believes he understands something about Francis Dolarhyde by imagining that his crimes tell us about his psychology, his history, his biology, and so on. Yet they also make actions legible by recourse to their instigators, establishing a casual relationship between an individual and his behavior. The fictional murder of a suburban family becomes comprehensible when the reader understands the specific pathology that motivated Dolarhyde's conduct. Motive in serial-killing narratives may operate existentially, as a means to self-actualization; psychoanalytically, by reference to formative environments; biologically, in the mechanics of brain functioning; or spiritually, in theories of possession and supernatural beings. In any case, by assigning motives, these novels inevitably theorize a connection between the self/subject and his behavior.

That these narratives address the relation between persons and actions may explain their dramatic rise in popularity over the past four decades. This period saw a significant increase in cultural interest in serial murder. Sociologist Philip Jenkins reports, "Between 1977 and 1982, multiple homicide had come to be a well-known phenomenon in the mass media" (55) after the well-publicized arrests and trials of killers such as David Berkowitz, Ted Bundy, and John Wayne Gacy.[5] Citing data from "three apparently independent sources: the law enforcement bureaucracy, the news media, and popular culture" (223), Jenkins argues that by "the 1980s, the issue of serial murder was established as a major social problem," and that "the stereotypical serial killer [had] became one of the best known and most widely feared social enemies" (211). This dramatic proliferation of interest produced three widely disputed claims: first, that the number of serial killers in the United States has risen steadily since the 1950s; second, that this rise correlates with the proliferation of sophisticated media technologies (film, television, and, more recently, video games and the Internet) that could potentially influence behavior; and third, that because these technologies increasingly transmit images of violence, "America produces proportionately more of these killers than any other nation on earth" (Leyton xiv).[6] Serial murderers are now frequently considered to be indigenous to the United States, the inevitable progeny of a culture addicted to violent images, and enabled by a technology (the mass media) powerful enough to impact individuals' conduct.

Jenkins's exhaustive documentation of the uses to which serial murder is put by competing governmental agencies, interest groups, and media outlets does much to suggest that the perceived serial-killing epidemic of the past half century was largely illusory. This chapter engages less with the reality of serial murder than with the nature of its fictional representations.[7] If the late twentieth century has seen an ever-increasing fascination with America's "best known and most widely feared social enemies" (Jenkins 211), the depictions of those enemies have themselves undergone significant transformations. As a distinct mythos in the American cultural landscape, representations of serial killing are far from uniform. Jenkins notes, for example, that the years between 1983 and 1993 had "substantially reshape[d] perceptions of serial murder" (74) — and suggest an evolution that is frequently elided in contemporary critical accounts. Patricia Highsmith's Tom Ripley, who first appeared in 1955, bears only a passing resemblance to Thomas Harris's Jame Gumb and other killers from the end of the century; the differences between them provide a valuable index to recent changes in the constitution of the self.[8]

This "reshaping of perceptions" provides the focus for this chapter. Beginning with the premise that changes in the way one describes serial murderers has something to tell us about changes in the way one describes persons, the chapter traces the genealogy of serial killing from Tom Ripley to Jame Gumb — from the multiple murderers of 1950s' suspense fiction to the literary and cinematic serial killers of the 1980s and 1990s — through changes in the imagined relation between the act of murder and the murderer. That the relation between individuals and actions — between beings and behaviors — has something to say about authenticity has appeared in various places throughout this study. For Holden Caulfield, the idea that his behavior might not accurately reflect who he is produces a fear of the developing self. In a world where only partial self-knowledge is possible, Holden fears he cannot guarantee the authenticity of his conduct. His (fantasized) solution is never to behave: to maintain an ideal of stasis embodied by the panoramas at the Museum of Natural History. For Walker Percy, the rejection of social-constructionist and identity-based views of selfhood is premised on the idea that the self continually re-creates itself through transcendent action. The self "can only prove true to itself by seeing the human existent for what, at its minimum reach, it really is — not a quantifiable integer, a receptacle of biological needs and so susceptible to fixed inductions, but a transcending reality" ("Symbol" 286–87). In both cases, the commitment to action as a fundamental determinant of individual authenticity is itself an outgrowth of the mid-century's commitment to existentialist modes of being.

The chapter begins with novels about repeat killers from the 1950s, a period marked by interest in the twinned concepts of authenticity and existentialism. Both Jim Thompson's *The Killer inside Me* (1952) and Patricia Highsmith's *The Talented Mr. Ripley* (1955) are crucially interested in the putative inauthenticity of their murderers, yet that interest takes notably different forms. Thompson's sadistic Deputy Lou Ford appears in some respects as a prototypical Caulfieldian phony; as the novel's title suggests, Ford hides his ostensibly true nature behind a façade of inauthentic behaviors. A more accurate description might understand Ford less as a phony than as a real phony of the type Holly Golightly embodies. Despite its title, the novel asks whether there is a unique, individual self residing behind the façade of "dumb old Lou from Kalamazoo" (66), or whether Lou, like Holly, might have been "given [his] character too soon" (Capote 55). Though Lou Ford experiences himself as real, perhaps there is another real that is more real that Lou is supposed to be? By comparison, Highsmith's protean Thomas Ripley suggests a different relation, one in which the self emerges as the product, rather than the instigator, of his behaviors. Ultimately, these novels seek to answer the question: how does what a murderer does relate to who a murderer is? To put it slightly differently, does the act of murder produce or reflect the person of the murderer?

The chapter then examines Don DeLillo's novel *The Names* (1982) to consider how the rise of poststructuralist ideas about the subject influence that relation. How does one get from Thomas Ripley to Avtar Singh, from murder as a form of self-creation to murder as a (futile) gesture at self-repair? Refuting the existential freedom explored in *The Talented Mr. Ripley*, *The Names* rewrites Ripley's success as an inevitable but doomed attempt at self-realization: inevitable because the self experiences itself as an autonomous, self-determining subject; and doomed because that experience is an illusion. The subject is always already constituted within the structure of language. What is imagined in *The Names* as the futile act of the conscripted subject, however, is barely recognized in *The Silence of the Lambs* as action at all. In concluding, I consider the consequences of a commitment to identity-based models of the self or subject for the way contemporary literary and popular discourse think about individual conduct. Jame Gumb's murders are illustrations, compulsive gestures of self-representation, with an expressive as opposed to instrumental content. As such, his murders start to look like hate crimes — a category of criminal offense purposefully defined to account for the expressive or representative capacity of behavior. In hate-crime litigation — as in serial-killing investigations — the relevant question is not only what one did, but also what one was trying to say when one did it. Overall, these novels illustrate how as ideas about the subject turned from an existentialist ontology to a poststructuralist account, and then to an identitarian model, individual behavior shifted from an act to an art, from a method of self-realization to a form of self-representation.

The Killer inside Me, *The Talented Mr. Ripley*, and the Real Phony Serial Killer

The question of what constitutes a serial murderer is itself logically separable from questions of motive. One would expect that the crimes themselves, not the reasons the crimes were committed, would serve to categorize a perpetrator as such. The fact that Ted Bundy murdered approximately thirty-six young women as opposed to his reason for doing so should qualify him as a serial killer.[9] It should matter little if he were retaliating for an earlier breakup, revenging himself against his mother, or being possessed by the devil. Yet motive and its ostensible absence play a significant role in the categorization of serial murderers. One would not, for example, necessarily characterize an assassin for an organized-crime operation or a terrorist fighting a guerrilla war as a serial killer. The behavior may be the same in all cases — "the killing of three or more people over a period of more than thirty days, with a significant cooling-off period between the killings" (Holmes and Holmes 18)[10] — but the assassin and the guerrilla behave within a normative range of criminal behavior. While their acts may or may not be legally sanctioned, one could imagine another person behaving similarly.

Serial killing, by comparison, implies a certain opacity operating at the level of motive. Serial killers do not murder for money, out of a victim-specific rage (at a husband or wife), or to reduce market competition (as in the drug trade). They possess reasons for their crimes, but the alignment of their motives and the methods by which they seek to achieve them remains logically incoherent to others. For example, it is understandable to have a grudge against a former girlfriend (as is speculated about Ted Bundy), and it is conceivable (if abhorrent) to kill her in a rage, but not to murder in her place thirty-six unknown women with long dark hair parted in the middle.[11] In the latter situation, Bundy's motives (revenge against a specific person) and his methods (the murders of unrelated strangers) bear little relation to one another. The result, from the perspective of a detective investigating a victim-specific murder, is a motiveless crime.

Of course, this account suggests that the serial killer is not in fact motiveless; rather, his motives are entirely contingent and not reducible to a normative scale of criminal behavior. Will Graham observes that newspapers use the terms "random selection of victims" and "no apparent motive" (*Red* 78); but "'Random' wasn't accurate. . . . Mass murderers and serial murderers do not select their victims at random. . . . He chose them because something in them spoke to him" (80). Because of this, it is theorized that this contingent motive provides the strongest clues to the killer's identity. John Douglas, formerly the FBI's leading expert on criminal-personality profiling and the consultant to the film version of *The Silence of the Lambs,* explains: "Every crime has a motive. It's our job to learn enough about what goes on inside the heads of the men who commit these types of crimes so that the *why?* is clear enough to lead us to the *who?*" (Douglas and Olshaker 46).[12] Douglas (who may well have had a greater impact on contemporary fiction writers and filmmakers than on the criminal justice system) acknowledges that the collapse of the "*why?*" into the "*who?*" is as much the material of fiction as of crime fighting: "these are the questions pursued by novelists and psychiatrists, by Dostoyevsky and Freud, the stuff both of *Crime and Punishment* and *Beyond the Pleasure Principle*" (26). As Graham himself observes to his girlfriend Molly: "an intelligent psychopath—particularly a sadist—is hard to catch.... So you have to take whatever evidence you have and try to extrapolate. You try to reconstruct his thinking. You try to find patterns" (*Red* 6–7).

This commonplace of the detective novel, that motive constitutes identity, is explored at length in both *The Killer inside Me* and *The Talented Mr. Ripley*, in which ostensibly unmotivated murders provide the opportunity for an extended thought experiment on the relation of action to selfhood.[13] But where *The Killer inside Me* evokes but ultimately cannot sustain what is the mid-century's standard account of the phony—the individual who consciously adopts accepted behaviors for social advancement—*The Talented Mr. Ripley* suggests a different ontology. Of course, *The Killer inside Me* is not precisely a detective novel; as with much of Thompson's crime fiction, the novel is narrated by its criminal at the moment of his death, which makes discovering the identity of its killer a moot point. But the novel still concerns itself with identity and motive insofar as it attempts to determine *why* Sheriff's Deputy Lou Ford commits murder. Even as he plots his crimes, Ford also investigates those crimes in an effort to understand himself.

At first glance, Ford looks like an archetypal phony of the Caulfieldian type. Like Holden's representative headmaster, Mr. Haas, Ford conceals his true or actual self within a carefully maintained social exterior. "Lean and wiry," with "a mouth that looked all set to drawl," Ford looks and acts like a "typical Western-county peace officer... Maybe a little cleaner cut. But on the whole typical" (28). But when he metaphorically "[comes] out of the place [he] was hiding in," he acknowledges that he is a sexually violent murderer who at the age of fourteen victimized "a girl less than three years old" (19). The novel purports to reveal the authentic Lou Ford beneath this phony exterior by foregrounding the difference between what Ford thinks and what he says, what he says and what he does. In a discussion of this earlier crime, for example, the novel intersperses Ford's spoken comments to a fellow character—"Dad and I knew Mike hadn't done it. . . . knowing Mike, we were sure he couldn't be guilty"—with his thoughts set off in italics: *"Because I was. [He] had taken the blame for me"* (20). Furthermore, the novel has Ford himself theorize the logic behind such behavior, making deliberate conformity sound like a necessary part of western culture more generally. In the West, "a man had to be doggoned careful of the way he acted or he'd be marked for life. I mean, there wasn't any crowd for him to sink into" (67). *The Killer inside Me* thus suggests at first a model of the self that is fundamentally divided and represented through metaphors of depth: there is an exterior, performative self that conforms to social standards of correct behavior, and a hidden, interior self that recognizes its own deviation from those standards and protects itself from exposure.

Of course, this is precisely the mid-century's conventional account of the phony as well. Lou Ford emerges in the novel as Holden Caulfield's worst nightmare; not only does he appear to hide his true self behind the mask of a "dull good-natured guy who couldn't do anything bad if he tried" (92), but he does so deliberately—not because he lacks sufficient self-knowledge, but because it gives him pleasure. He enjoys convincing others that he's just "dumb old Lou from Kalamazoo" (66). This pleasure takes a very particular form. Ford likes to repeat clichés "in that deadpan way" (13) and then watch people "squirm" (4). In a notable conversation with Max, the local café owner, Lou comments that he "should have been a college professor or something like that" because he realized that "a lot of people think it is the heat that makes it so hot" when "It's not the heat, but the humidity." As Max "fidget[s]" (4) and "mutter[s] something about being wanted in the kitchen," Ford vocalizes Max's predicament for the reader: "If there's anything worse than a bore, it's a corny bore, but how can you brush off a nice friendly fellow who'd give you his shirt if you asked for it?" (4–5). What Ford enjoys in these moments is not only his own phoniness, his own pretense of social acceptability, but also the phoniness of others. Social standards of politeness require that Max not "brush off a nice friendly fellow," even when that fellow is unbearably tedious. Furthermore, the pleasure that Ford derives from this exposure — from forcing the phoniness of others out in the open — is itself similar to the pleasure found in the killings in which he engages. He confesses to the reader that "[s]triking at people that way [through the use of clichés] is almost as good as the other, the real way" (5). Prefiguring the connection between language and violence that will be a key aspect of poststructuralist analyses of the subject, the novel analogizes the use of clichés with murder, as part of a larger continuum of asocial behavior.

Ford's own phoniness thus works to uncover a broader phoniness in the social realm, and he repeatedly draws the readers' attention to it. The county attorney, Hendricks, "knew how things stood, but was too much of a phoney [sic] to admit it" (72); the doctor they send to investigate him "turned out to be phoney" (169); and most people would commit murder themselves if they were not "too nicey-nice and pretendsy to do anything really hard" (187). In emphasizing, first, the similarities between Ford and the fellow citizens of Central City (everyone is phony) and, second, the similarities between speaking clichés and killing people (it is "almost as good"), *The Killer inside Me* positions Lou Ford as simultaneously representative and deviant, as both the inevitable product of and profoundly other to the mainstream. On the one hand, he is just like everyone else; but on the other hand, he is a homicidal maniac. Ford thus operates as both Holden Caulfield's phony and also a version of Holden himself, exposing and commenting on contemporary social hypocrisy. As he investigates his own, ostensibly individual motivations, he is inevitably and unsurprisingly led back to the general culture of phoniness that surrounds him.

As Mark Seltzer notes, this positioning produces Lou Ford as "the Model-T, mass reproducible person, the hyper-typical deputy sheriff living in the hyper-typical American place, Central City," and evokes a common ontology of the serial killer: "the criminal's interior . . . not as *anti*-social but rather as *directly* socialized" (160, emphasis in original), determined by the culture that produced him. Though *The Killer inside Me* begins by implying that Ford possesses the "psycho-killer's chameleon[-]like capacity to simulate normality" (Seltzer 160–61), in fact the text is committed to differentiating between simulation and dissimulation—copying and deceiving. Ford simulates but he does not dissimulate; he has no self (or subject) that is hidden beneath his pretense of normality. There is, in Seltzer's words, no "real of the subject [that] resides somewhere within ... anterior to and apart from its social being in context" (163). Figuring Ford's interior as "*directly* socialized," the novel suggests that the problem Ford confronts is not conformity but rather uniformity. Ford is not pretending to be the same as everyone else; he *is* the same as everyone else—except, of course, for his murders. Understanding where those murders come from is part of his overall project. For much of the novel, Ford has no idea why he does what he does. He is continually "wondering about [him]self" (37, 57) and "thinking about [him]self" (82). Yet among the behaviors that seem to concern him most are those that actually *are* socially sanctioned—those in which he engages without consciously having to conform. Helping out a teenager in trouble with the law, Ford notes that "I hadn't put on an act. I *was* concerned and worried about the kid" (57).[14] Imagining his role as the western county peace officer, "[he] doubted if [he] could change. [He'd] pretended so long that [he] no longer had to" (28). And his worry about a fellow officer surprises him: "he was just one of hundreds of people I knew and was friendly with," Ford explains, "And yet here I was, fretting about his problems instead of my own" (82). In these moments, Ford is surprised that he would act like others as a matter of course—that what he wants to do and what he should do (socially speaking) happen to be the same. *The Killer inside Me* presents its narrator as baffled that, given choices, individuals might just choose to act the same.

Most concerning, of course, are the murders he commits. Yet even these actions turn out to be more typical—more uniform—than the reader might expect. Furthermore, they are not precisely a product of his own deviant psychology, but were "put upon [him]" (215) by the "hypocritical" behavior (107) of the larger culture. Ford describes his murderous impulses as "*the sickness*" (11) and notes that

> In a lot of books I've read, the writer seems to go haywire every time he reaches a high point. He'll start leaving out punctuation and running his words together and babble about stars flashing and sinking into a deep dreamless sea. . . . I guess that kind of crap is supposed to be pretty deep stuff—a lot of the book reviewers eat it up, I notice. But the way I see it is,

> the writer is just too goddamn lazy to do his job. And I'm not lazy, whatever else I am. I'll tell you everything.
> But I want to get everything in the right order.
> I want you to understand how it was. (179–80)

Thompson is satirizing the modernist reliance on stream of consciousness as a vehicle for representing a unique subjectivity, a technique that purports to provide an unmediated experience of another's consciousness and which is not without precedent in the genre of hard-boiled crime fiction. One possible reference is to James M. Cain's *Double Indemnity* (1936), which, like *The Killer inside Me*, is narrated in the first person by its dying criminal, takes multiple murder as its plot, and likewise addresses the question of motivation — the relation between individuals and actions. An insurance investigator who "didn't spend all this time in [the] business for nothing" (22), narrator Walter Huff plots with Phyllis Nirdlinger (who at the end of the novel is herself revealed to be a probable serial killer) to murder her husband and collect the insurance. His scam depends upon General Fidelity of California's reliance on actuarial tables as a guide to human behavior across populations. With a large enough sample, the tables indicate the probability of certain events (for example, suicide) without requiring any information about any *particular* individual's psyche or motivation. As such, actuarial tables are a testimony to a basic uniformity in human behavior. Given a broad enough population, human behavior will all start to be predictable. Thus the tables tell what people will do (x number of individuals in a population of a certain size will commit suicide), but not why they do it. And neither can Huff—even when he speaks about himself. He repeatedly foregrounds his inability either to control his actions or to account for them retrospectively.[15] For example, remembering how he "was going to get out of there, and drop ... her like a red-hot poker," Huff then admits, "But I didn't do it" (13) and explains himself by reference to a version of Poe's Imp of the Perverse: "I knew where I was at, of course. I was standing right on the deep end, looking over the edge ... and all the time I was trying to pull away from it, there was something in me that kept edging a little closer" (14).[16]

Double Indemnity ends with both Phyllis and Huff preparing to drown and relies on a near stream of consciousness to convey their suicides. Phyllis admits death is her "bridegroom. The only one I ever loved" and imagines feeling "his icy fingers creeping into [her] heart"; Huff promises to "give her away" to death. The shark that follows their ship is "a flash of dirty white down in the green" and a "black fin. Cutting the water in the moonlight" (114). In the final moments, Huff claims Phyllis is "beside me now while I'm writing. I can feel her," and the novel's last sentence is simply "The moon" (115). This turn to the ostensibly direct experience of consciousness to explain the interiority of the murderer is understood as a corrective to insurance investigator Keyes's reliance on "highbrow" "modern psychology" to account for "pathological case[s]." While Keyes "find[s] it helpful" as "the only thing that explains what [repeat killers] do" (105), the novel itself disdains rational explanations and mystifies its narrator's motivations. It prefers instead, in Ford's words, to "babble about stars flashing and sinking into a deep dreamless sea" (Thompson, *The Killer inside Me* 180).

The novels thus offer precisely different versions of how to account for the motivations of the multiple murderer. Where *Double Indemnity* disdains psychological accounts and relies on figurative language as a mimetic tool, *The Killer inside Me* dismisses figuration — supposedly "pretty deep stuff" — in favor of a realist account of events, "tell[ing] . . . everything. . . in the right order" so that the reader can "understand how it was" (180). Referencing the "endless files of psychiatric literature . . . Krafft-Ebbing, Jung, Freud, Bleuler, Adolf Meyer, Kretschmer, Kraepelin" that he has read, Ford claims "all the answers were here, out in the open where you could look at them" (27). The novel thus highlights the comprehensibility — and even the *typicality* — of such behaviors. Not the product of a highly contingent, individuated psychology, multiple murder appears instead as a predictable response to a particular set of circumstances: in similar circumstances, anyone might behave the same.

The novel itself offers a familiar Oedipal narrative of abuse to account for Ford's pathology. When he finds a photograph of the scarred backside of Helene (a former housekeeper and his father's mistress), Ford remembers being seduced and initiated into violent sexual practices as an adolescent. "I'd forgotten about it," he realizes, "now I forgot it again. There are things that have to be forgotten if you want to go on living" (108). The moment is presented as a version of the primal scene — the original horror that leads to all other horrors — but the problem is not the violence as such. It is his father's reaction to it. Ford describes "aching with the first and only whipping in my life; listening to the low angry voices" (106) and then recounts the conversation, in which Helene calls his father a "hypocritical son of a bitch" and announces "this didn't need to mean a thing. Absolutely nothing. But now it will. You've handled it in the worst possible way" (107). By being "made to feel that I'd done something that couldn't ever be forgiven," Ford reasons, "I had a burden of fear and shame put on me that I could never get shed of"; and since he "couldn't strike back at [Helene]," he began striking back at "any female." He explains, "Any woman who'd done what she had would be *her*" (215–16). Like Holly Golightly, whose character is "given too soon" (Capote 55) and produces her real phoniness, Lou Ford has his obsession with violent sexuality "put on [him]" because of his father's own hypocritical need to conform to sexual norms. The crimes that Ford commits are both him and not really him, a consequence of the dangerous interaction between himself, his father, and the expectations of the larger culture.

Lou Ford is thus a real phony: he experiences his need to murder these women as his own, but in fact this need comes from outside himself and is not genuinely his. Alone among the texts this study examines, *The Killer inside Me* seeks to represent the consciousness of the real phony. Unlike Capote and Herman Wouk (discussed in chap. 4), Thompson takes on the challenge of imagining the interiority of someone who is not supposed to have an interior that is individual and unique. This requirement explains Ford's turn to the literature of mental illness to account for himself. Even when representing the ostensibly personal psyche of a distinctive individual, the novel relies upon the language of generality and types. At the end of the novel, Ford quotes from a medical definition of schizophrenia: "the subject suffers from strong feelings of guilt . . . combined with a sense of frustration and persecution . . . yet there are rarely if ever any surface signs of . . . disturbance. On the contrary, his behavior appears to be entirely logical. He reasons soundly, even shrewdly" (218, ellipses in original). The novel then broadens its scope to include the reader in that definition, completing its critique of an omnipresent and deforming social influence and hypocrisy: "It was written, you might say, about—but I reckon you know, don't you?" (219). By leaving open the possibility that the reader might answer "myself" to the question, the novel suggests that schizophrenia could be the inevitable result of growing up in what Ford describes as "a peculiar civilization [where] [t]he police are playing crooks . . . and the crooks are doing police duty. The politicians are preachers, and the preachers are politicians" (118). Critics have read the novel's use of schizophrenia to explain Lou Ford as emblematic of "the crime fiction of the period," which "often featured protagonists in conflict with the consensus culture and whose opposition is externalized into a psychiatric state denoted explicitly or implicitly as 'schizophrenia'" (Payne 250). What starts out as an exploration of an individual's deviant psychology thus ends up as a narrative of legitimization, in which Ford becomes as much victim as victimizer, the inevitable product of the hypocrisy that he then critiques. Ford ends his story with a plea for greater tolerance — hardly what one would expect from the murderer of five people — that places his victims and himself on the same level. Listing the names of those he killed, he fantasizes that "Our kind" might "[get] another chance in the Next Place": "All of us that started the game with a crooked cue, that wanted so much and got so little, that meant so good and did so bad. All us folks . . . All of us. All of us" (244).

The Killer inside Me thus presents multiple murder as both comprehensible and socially produced, and the multiple murderer as simultaneously the product and the critic of social mores. Multiple murder by this account looks something like Holly Golightly's mean reds: the sign that being "*directly* socialized," to use Seltzer's term (160), is on some level unsupportable to the self that experiences it. There is inevitably some reaction against overwhelming social construction. Yet the novel's account of Ford's psychology feels unsatisfactory: among other things, can real phonies (or, for that matter, schizophrenics) successfully self-diagnose? At one point, Ford's lawyer offers a "definition . . . right out of the agronomy books" to explain his approach to understanding other people, and declares: "'A weed is a plant out of place.' I find a hollyhock in my cornfield, and it's a weed. I find it in my yard, and it's a flower" (236). Are multiple murderers really just misplaced hollyhocks? The dramatic failure of the novel to account adequately for the relation between who Ford is (a victim of sexual abuse) and what Ford does (murder five people) by way of his past victimization suggests that this failure is potentially deliberate, a refusal of easy causality on the part of the novel.

A different ontology of the multiple murderer is explored in Patricia

Highsmith's *The Talented Mr. Ripley*, in which a gratuitous murder provides the opportunity for an extended thought experiment on the relation of action to selfhood. The title character, Tom Ripley, is hired by Richard Greenleaf Sr. to befriend his expatriated son Dickie in the hopes of luring Dickie back to New York. Like Lou Ford, Tom Ripley appears in some ways like a prototypical phony.[17] This phoniness operates as both a structural and an actual condition: he is structurally phony in his position as the representative of parental authority, but not its actual embodiment; he is literally phony because he has no intention of convincing Dickie to go home, planning instead to use him to see Europe. But is he really phony in a Caulfieldian sense of the term? Holden's phonies are defined by their "phony smile[s]" (Salinger 13) — by their attempts to conceal an actual dislike behind a pretense of liking, to represent socially acceptable behaviors when, in actuality, they themselves are not socially acceptable. A closer examination of *The Talented Mr. Ripley* suggests that Highsmith imagines Tom Ripley in different terms.

The reader begins to see the novel's interest in self and action in its description of Dickie's murder. On a visit he and Dickie make to San Remo, Ripley impulsively bludgeons Dickie to death and buries his body at sea. The account makes literal the notion that to discover the killer's motive is to discover his identity, for Ripley's motive is identity itself. Highsmith describes the action as the result of Ripley's having "just thought of something brilliant: he could become Dickie Greenleaf" (100). Yet even though motive literally equals identity in the novel, this impulsive and ill-considered action belies the substantive connection between motive and self on which detective fiction customarily turns.[18] Ripley considers killing Dickie rather as someone else might imagine eating a doughnut — as a passing fancy, rather than as a deeply held wish or desire. Likewise, narrative agency in the sentences preceding Dickie's murder shifts away from Ripley and toward the acts he ostensibly will commit, suggesting that the action is in some way producing the self, rather than the self producing the action. The narrator states:

> [Tom] could have hit Dickie, sprung on him, or kissed him, or thrown him overboard, and nobody could have seen him at this distance. Tom was sweating, hot under his clothes, cold on his forehead. He felt afraid, but it

was not of the water, it was of Dickie. He knew that he was going to do it, that he would not stop himself now, maybe *couldn't* stop himself, and that he might not succeed. (103)[19]

Out on the water, Ripley can do whatever he desires, and yet the list of possible actions available to him (violence, sex, or murder) imply not so much that he wavers in his decision to murder (the following statement "he would not stop himself now" negates that possibility), but rather that the act exists independently of Ripley in some fundamental sense, and that Ripley will not know what has occurred until after it has taken place.[20] At some point during the moments leading up to the murder, Ripley becomes the object and not the subject of his actions; his fear is as much of a self produced in retrospect, a self that "*couldn't* stop himself," as it is of Dickie. Furthermore, that this self will also be called Dickie Greenleaf renders ambiguous the referent to Ripley's stated fear "of Dickie"; he refers not only to the man who sits across from him but also to the man he is about to become.

Of course, it is one thing to commit a murder and entirely another to assume the life as one's victim. The list of tasks that Ripley imagines are required to "step right into Dickie's shoes" — to "go back to Mongibello first and collect Dickie's things, tell Marge [Dickie's sometime girlfriend] any damned story, set up an apartment in Rome or Paris, receive Dickie's cheque every month and forge Dickie's signature on it" (100) — seem from an outside perspective to be naïve. One would suspect there is more to assuming the identity of another person than just getting an apartment, forging a signature, and avoiding known acquaintances. But *The Talented Mr. Ripley* proves such a suspicion to be wrong on the philosophical, if not the practical, level. The suspense of the novel lies in a series of near misses and close calls that require two more murders: the literal murder of Freddie Miles, a friend of Dickie's who tracks Ripley down at Dickie's apartment and suspects his secret, and the figurative *remurder* of Dickie, whose suicide Ripley fakes in order to inherit Dickie's trust fund (through the use of a forged will). But this suspense is only concerned with the quotidian negotiation of a world in which identity is fixed and determined through a series of presumably infallible markers: a signature, fingerprints on a package, a passport photograph. How does one forge a signature convincingly?

Avoid Dickie's friends and acquaintances? Answer the police after Freddie's murder? And, after Ripley resumes life as an amalgamation of Thomas Ripley and Dickie Greenleaf, convince everyone that Dickie killed himself? The metaphysical questions about selfhood that such a substitution of one person for another should raise retreat to the background when the reader begins to recognize an unavoidable fact about the novel. It is surprisingly easy for Ripley to become someone else.

This facility might first be attributed to Ripley's talent as an actor. He acknowledges early in the novel that he can "impersonate practically anybody" (58). Yet Highsmith suggests Ripley's "impersonations" generate effects far exceeding what one might expect. These effects, furthermore, throw into disarray the earlier understanding of Ripley as a phony. If "[t]he main thing about impersonation," as Ripley explains, is to "maintain the mood and the temperament of the person . . . and to assume the facial expressions that went with them" (131), Ripley's method produces unprecedented results. Practicing Dickie's "facial expressions" and "danc[ing] as [Dickie] would have" (122) — styles of behavior usually associated with a distinct, individual self — both produce internal changes in Ripley. The novel suggests that Ripley is convinced by his own actions. "His stories were good," the narrator argues, "because he imagined them intensely, so intensely that he came to believe them" (253). As the moment in the boat crystallized, acting like Dickie produces Ripley-as-Dickie retrospectively, as the product rather than the motivator of his behavior. Albert Camus, characterizing the actor as existentialist in "The Myth of Sisyphus" (published in the United States in the same year as *The Talented Mr. Ripley*), provides a description that fits Ripley remarkably well: "he abundantly illustrates every month or every day that so suggestive truth that there is no frontier between what a man wants to be and what he is. Always concerned with better representing, he demonstrates to what a degree appearing creates being. For that is his art — to simulate absolutely, to project himself as deeply as possible into lives that are not his own" (79).[21]

Thus, in an important sense, Ripley is not a phony because his "appearing" does not mask his actual self, as the "phony smile" Holden condemns might be said to do. By murdering Dickie, Ripley neither reveals nor betrays his true self and is shown as neither authentic nor inauthentic. Instead, he becomes a different person. Killing thus operates as a technology of self-transformation for Ripley, and suggests much about Highsmith's ontology of the self in which actions produce the states of being that are ostensibly caused by them. Reflecting on what "he learned . . . from these last months" as Dickie Greenleaf, Ripley produces a theory of existence that encapsulates the philosophy of the novel as a whole: "If you wanted to be cheerful, or melancholic, or wishful, or thoughtful, or courteous, you simply had to *act* those things with every gesture" (193). One's being inevitably follows. Thus Ripley, who has no individuating past — he has no family (an orphan), no earlier jobs, no cultural history, no stories of his life in America to recount, and indeed no character in the positive sense of the term — appears as the Sartrean existentialist par excellence, continually choosing his being through a series of actions that produce character retrospectively. Ripley's lack of a positive self is evident throughout the novel. Long before he meets Dickie, Tom understood his existence as a series of roles: that of an "intelligent, level-headed, scrupulously honest" young man at a cocktail party (6); "a young man who [wouldn't] throw money down the drain" with Mr. Greenleaf (22); and "a serious young man with a serious job ahead of him" on board the ship to Europe (34), suggesting the existentialist belief that the essential self does not exist as anything other than a sentimental fantasy. As Russell Harrison observes, "much that goes to form a personality is omitted in a Highsmith novel. . . . they are, in one sense, anti-*bildungsromans*" (22). Yet unlike *The Catcher in the Rye*, whose recasting of the genre involved imagining a self that did not change, *The Talented Mr. Ripley* imagines the self as constantly changing, and therefore incapable of the kind of moral or ethical development that the *bildungsroman* takes as constitutive.

This ontology is symbolized in a crucial moment of recognition: having resumed life as Thomas Ripley, he is interrogated by the same officers who questioned him as Dickie Greenleaf. Ripley panics when he thinks one officer "was staring at [his] hands . . . did the [policeman] possibly notice some resemblance?" (209). In *The Talented Mr. Ripley* it is the hands, not the face, that provide the distinguishing characteristic of the individual. While the face proves unrecognizable by wearing different expressions, the hands, a symbol of acts as opposed to essences, risk giving Ripley away.[22]

Yet Highsmith's interpretation of the existentialist ontology of self that girds *The Talented Mr. Ripley* suggests as much a critique as an endorsement of existentialist philosophy. If the existentialist argues that one can, and indeed must, choose one's existence, Highsmith asks: what if the existentialist (in Camus' phrase) "projects himself into lives" (79) that are currently occupied? What if the self one chooses to become already exists as somebody else? To put the question slightly differently: if behaviors produce being as existentialism asserts, why did Ripley need to murder Dickie? Why not become just like Dickie in every way? That to be *just alike* (for Ripley the condition of phoniness), as opposed to *just be* (the state of authenticity), proves unsatisfactory is illustrated early in the novel when Ripley and Dickie decide to spend the money Mr. Greenleaf gave Ripley on a trip to Rome. The narrator states:

> They sat slumped in the carrozza, each with a sandalled foot propped on a knee, and it seemed to Tom that he was looking in a mirror when he looked at Dickie's leg and his propped foot beside him. They were the same height and very much the same weight, Dickie perhaps a bit heavier, and they wore the same size bathrobe, socks, and probably shirts.
> Dickie even said, "Thank you Mr. Greenleaf," when Tom paid the carrozza driver. Tom felt a little weird. (67)

Dickie refers to his father, whose money they are spending, when he says "Thank you Mr. Greenleaf." The lack of a present, embodied referent for the name, however, opens the possibility that Dickie refers to Tom not as Mr. Greenleaf's "ambassador" or "stand-in," the alleged representative of his interests, but rather as Mr. Greenleaf himself. The ambiguity of the signifier "Mr. Greenleaf" makes visible a possible collapse in the structural difference that the role of "emissary" requires. Furthermore, the exchangeability of Dickie and his father at the level of the name (both were named Richard Greenleaf) juxtaposed against Tom's recognition of his and Dickie's physical similarity implies a further substitution: that of Tom for Dickie. A harmless joke thus illustrates simultaneously the likeness of Tom to both Dickie and his father, and his inevitable and interminable difference from them. What Tom senses in the carrozza is that he is both Mr. Greenleaf's representative and yet crucially not Mr. Greenleaf, that he is Dickie's "mirror" image and yet crucially not Dickie.

What this moment suggests, though not yet to Tom himself, is the irreducible fact of *difference*, irrespective of whether those differences can be said to matter. If one is the mirror image of someone — if Tom looks like Dickie, speaks Italian like Dickie, dances like Dickie — one still is not that someone, regardless of how inconsequential those remaining differences are. While this formulation opens the entirely reasonable question, "If those residual differences do not matter, why worry about them?" it also suggests a possible answer to why Tom needs to murder Dickie: if difference in and of itself is understood as a problem, murder provides the only solution, the only way in which Tom might become Dickie himself rather than his facsimile. Otherwise, Tom remains doomed to live a horrible truth, "true for all time," that in every friendship "there would always be an illusion . . . that he and they were completely in harmony and alike" when in fact Tom remains isolated by "the foreignness around him" (89).

The Names, Of Grammatology, and Linguistic Violence

The differences between Ripley and Dickie that are in and of themselves problems are also easily eradicated, as Tom's ultimate success at living life first as Dickie, then again as Tom attests. The novel does nothing if not endorse the idea that it is within the self's power to re-create oneself. That this self-creation must necessarily be understood as violent is also taken for granted, not just in *The Talented Mr. Ripley* but also in the poststructuralist criticism that made the intractability of difference the focus of its analysis. Highsmith's evocation of and interest in difference qua difference appears from this perspective as surprisingly prescient, foreshadowing the terms in which the primary critique of the existentialist subject would appear. In the introductory essay to their collection *The Violence of Representation: Literature and the History of Violence*, Nancy Armstrong and Leonard Tennenhouse discuss the composition of the novel *Jane Eyre* in terms particularly helpful to this project; they state, "Charlotte [Brontë] decided to outdo her sisters . . . by making something out of nothing at all — that is to say, making a self out of itself. In such a project, violence is an essential element" (6). Yet Jane, unlike Ripley, is not making herself into someone who already exists and must be gotten out of the way. The differences Jane encounters, and the violence that results, revolve around the medium through which such self-making occurs: the words in and through which her self comes "bursting forth." The authors explain, "The point of this discourse is to suggest that there is always more than discourse expresses, a self on the other side of words, bursting forth in words, only to find itself falsified and diminished because standardized and contained with the categories composing the aggregate of 'society'" (7).

The experience of this "standardized and contained" subject — who is simultaneously enabled and enfeebled by the words through which the self is built — forms the focus of Don DeLillo's *The Names*. James Ashton, the narrator of the novel, differentiates between the late-twentieth-century American serial killer — "the stocking strangler, the gunman with sleepy eyes, the killer of women, the killer of vagrant old men, the killer of blacks" (171) — and the murderous cult he, his wife, Katherine, and their friend Owen Brandemas discover while living in Greece. The sect's ostensible purpose is the worship of language and, more specifically, "[t]he alphabet itself. They were interested in letters, written symbols, fixed in sequence" (30). It becomes clear that this worship has included a series of seemingly motiveless murders throughout the Near and Middle East, yet James resists categorizing the cult's killings with the "ghastly and sick" murders of the so-called Manson family (202).[23] Unlike the "mass murderers" who commit murders that are "a product of [his] own reverie" (170–71), James argues, the cult's action suggests "a different signature . . . a deeper and austere calculation" (171) that evokes not the private motives of an isolated subjectivity but rather an intuitive impulse based in the universal dependence upon language. As one of the members observes to James, "Something in our method finds a home in your unconscious mind. A recognition . . . Our program evokes something that you seem to understand and find familiar, something you cannot analyze" (208).

James objects to correlating the cult's crimes with the Manson murders not because the crimes themselves are all that different; the cult's behavior certainly conforms to the operating definition of killings "spread over months or years, with a cooling-off period intervening" (Jenkins 21). Nor does he object because the purposes of the crimes vary all that much from those of, say, Francis Dolarhyde; the members seek and experience precisely the self-realization for which Ripley's murder of Dickie provides a model. The "terrible and definitive thing" that makes it right "to shatter [the victim's] skull, kill him, smash his brains" (209), in the words of one member, is the "frenzy" that the murder inspires, "a frenzy of knowing, of terrible confirmation. Yes, we are here, we are actually killing, we are doing it.... We had our proof" (211). In a sense, the murders instantiate the existentialist moment par excellence ("Yes, we are here ... we are doing it"), functioning as an epistemological tool to realize an ontological reality; the self's existence and, equally importantly, presence to itself. Even as murder supplies a vehicle of "proof," however, it creates the ontological reality it works to verify. Avtar Singh, the leader of an Indian sect of the cult (and whose name, with its aspirated "h," is an obvious stand-in for "sign"), "seemed to look different every time Owen saw him," James reports. This transformation is not only because he is "an impressive mimic" (or in Tom Ripley's words, talented at "impersonation") but rather because "his physiognomy changed, his features as aspect and character" (290). Absent of an innate or essential self, Singh uses the killings as "the philosophical base he relies upon for his sense of self." In the narrator's words, "They are what he uses to live" (291).

What DeLillo makes clear is that James objects to the cult/Manson family equivalence because the *motives* are different. In James's view the crimes betray none of the contingent subjectivity one associates with serial murder. Rather than the consequences (a dead body), it is the "program," in the words of one cult member, that "reaches something in us" (208). But the "program," not the product, is of value to more prototypical fictional serial murderers as well. The highly ritualized form of the crimes, the tableaux-like murder scene that needs to be "read" or interpreted for clues, and the development of "signature" elements are all standards of the genre and suggest that whatever the killer gets out of his crimes, the actual death of his victim is the least of it. In *The Names*, the insistence that such murders stem from and speak to something essential in human nature suggests that DeLillo offers the cult's crimes as the prototype of all serial killing—the *ur*-murders on which all serial murders are based.

Indeed Owen's recognition that "[i]t wasn't casual. They didn't do it for thrills" (81) wants to place these murders outside of the category of serial killing, suggesting the cult possesses an objectively comprehensible motive/method that separates them from the average serial killer. In other words, if one of the definitions of serial murder is its opacity of motive, then Owen's efforts to make the cult's actions part of an innate human desire works against this categorization. What James learns is that the victim is chosen on the basis of a coincidence of language: the initials of the victim's name match the initials of the place name where the murder is committed. First reducing names to a letter, the smallest element within a written linguistic system, the cult then murders a pre-chosen victim at the moment he enters a region whose name begins with the same letter, forcing a chance event within a system to carry an annihilating force, as if the coincidence of letters, names, and the objects they represent were anything other than arbitrary.

This effort is of a piece with Owen's and James's own desires for an essential relationship between the signifier and its signifieds, though they do not go quite to the same extremes. James, who regularly lies to his doorman about his travels, claiming he goes to Jordan when in fact he travels to Turkey, both worries and hopes that the "discrepancy between [his] uttered journey and the actual movements he made" will not cause "an air crash . . . or an earthquake" (103). Similarly, Owen, an archaeologist whose "first and current love" is "epigraphy . . . the study of inscriptions" (29), believes there is "a mysterious importance in the letters as such, the blocks of characters" he finds in the ancient ruins (35). If the cult's interest in language is unremarkable in the novel, however, the uses to which the alphabet is put (as a vehicle for victim choice) and its collation of language with murder renders explicit an implicit connection between language, writing, and violence operating symbolically throughout *The Names* and deconstructive theory more generally.[24]

In this way, DeLillo's cult renders literal a violence figured as implicit in the act of naming as such, translating the metaphoric violence attributed to language by poststructuralist literary criticism into an explicitly violent act. If, as Derrida asserts, violence "*does not supervene* from without upon an innocent language in order to surprise it," and instead posits "the unity of violence and writing" (*Grammatology* 106), then the cult's murders and *The Names* both represent and comment upon such assertions. Describing a by-now infamous scene in *Tristes Tropiques*, in which Lévi-Strauss capitalizes on the petty rivalries of a group of children in order to ascertain the unspoken names of the tribal members, Derrida comments upon Lévi-Strauss's assertion that the arrival of the archaeologist has introduced violence "upon a terrain of innocence, in a 'state of culture' whose *natural* goodness has not been degraded" (*Grammatology* 112). To imagine such innocence is, by Derrida's account, foolish romanticism. Any "state of culture" that possesses a system of naming already knows of violence, for the act of naming (even proper names, names that purportedly aspire to an essential relation with the self) requires inscribing the unique within a system, where it is "classified and is obliterated in *being named*" (109). As Derrida explains,

> To think the unique *within* the system, to inscribe it there, such is the gesture of the arche-writing: arche-violence, loss of the proper, of absolute proximity, of self-presence, in truth the loss of what has never taken place, of a self-presence which has never been given but only dreamed of and always already split, repeated, incapable of appearing to itself except in its own disappearance. (112)

By Derrida's account, the act of naming constitutes the loss of self-presence, the moment when the Derridean concept of *différance* is inscribed into being. "The first nomination," he explains, "was already an expropriation" (112). To have a name that is simultaneously oneself and not oneself—it represents the subject but is not the subject, stands in for the subject but cannot be the subject—annihilates the fantasy of self-presence, of an unmediated experience of the self. It is the same difference (or *différance*) that plagued Tom in the carrozza, when he both represents Mr. Greenleaf but is not Mr. Greenleaf, stands in for Dickie but can never be Dickie (or at least as long as Dickie is alive). Furthermore, to name is to force that which is experienced as unprecedented, individual, and unique (the self) to exist within a system that inherently allows for its replication (the number of Davids in any college classroom): the evolution of the definite into an indefinite article. Derrida is quick to observe that this loss is entirely symbolic. The subject loses what he never had, and thus loses, from a practical perspective, nothing at all. But this does not prevent that loss from inspiring a pathos immediately felt toward the children tricked into exposing their parents' names, but rapidly expanding to include the human condition in its entirety, the inevitable victim of language.

From this perspective, the cult's repeated murders look less like contingent acts of violence than deeply human, if doomed, existential acts of self-assertion against a totalizing system whose omnipresence allows for no possibility of escape, no exterior from which the individual might know himself outside of the systemic whole. Translating the violence hiding within language into a tool whereby language hides in violence, the cult seeks to rectify the inaugural act of inscription, to repair the original "classification and obliteration in being named" with its own tools. The novel thus illustrates the split between the phenomenological experience of the self as unique and its ontological reality as a construction within a system based in *différance*. This is of a piece with DeLillo's work more generally, which continually revisits the epistemological and phenomenological question of what can be known, and what counts as knowledge, in a system too expansive for individual comprehension. If the world systems (language, multinational capitalism, and intelligence networks, among others the novel addresses) exceed the capacities of the individual to comprehend, then what will constitute knowledge of the self or anything else? Language thus stands in as one of many possible systems whose dominion is total and whose outside is unattainable.[25] Indeed, Frederic Jameson claims that language is something of a blind in *The Names*, hiding the larger questions about multinational capitalism. He argues that "the motif of Language has here been reified, turned into a pseudo-concept; one which is supposed to send religious vibrations through one if one is a believing post-structuralist" (120).[26] What crucially matters here is the extent to which Ripley's existentialist conviction that "to be" the person to whom one aspires, "you simply had to *act* those things with every gesture" (*Talented* 193), is rewritten through a poststructuralist lens as a doomed endeavor, a useless attempt at self-definition in a world in which the subject is inevitably already constituted through *différance*, itself the condition of signification.

Thus, the violence that appears so oddly unnecessary in *The Talented Mr. Ripley*, when Ripley might have been satisfied with being Dickie's mirror image instead of Dickie himself, is accounted for in *The Names* by being always already present, always already a part of a world in which difference is both inevitable and insupportable. The world of the novel is one in which the first blow has always already been given, in which any retaliatory gesture looks quite literally like *self*-defense. In the logic of *The Names*, then, Ripley's violence looks less like the existentialist's desire for self-creation than a Derridean reassertion of presence rewritten for two characters, in which the self seeks an illusory wholeness, not with its unmediated self but with another person. Or to put it slightly differently, the difference Ripley seeks to eradicate *between* Dickie and himself—becoming not the emissary but the sovereign, not the facsimile but the real—in fact resides *within* Ripley proper, dooming his efforts. Both Owen and James come to this realization, though the cult does not. Explaining why he did not join the cult in India, Owen declares, "These killings mock us. They mock our need to structure and classify, to build a system against terror in our souls. They make the system equal to the terror" (308). Language is both the source of and the solution to "loss of the proper ... of self-presence" (*Grammatology* 112), to use Derrida's phrase; while the cult stones an old man to death, Owen "repair[s his] present condition" by recalling his childhood among evangelical Christians in Kansas (DeLillo, *Names* 304). "These early memories were a fiction" (305), James admits to the reader, and in Owen's own memory Owen is merely "a character in a story" (304), but "how else could men love themselves but in memory, knowing what they know?" (305). It is the fiction of a unified self, both necessitated by and constructed in language, that makes the present bearable.

Hate Crime and the Representation of Self

When Francis Dolarhyde falls in love with his colleague Reba McClane, he undergoes a version of the crisis that Tom Ripley experienced in the back of the carrozza: what the narrator terms "the new fright of being Two" (Harris, *Red* 265). Originally, "he and the Dragon had been One"; "[Dolarhyde] was Becoming and the Dragon was his higher self." His love for Reba, however, has severed his and the Dragon's desires. "Their bodies, voices, wills," are no longer the same (276). What Dolarhyde wants now "is to be able to Choose" (281) oneness with Reba instead of the Dragon, and to choose not to murder his next victims despite the Dragon's insistence. In frenzy he breaks into the Brooklyn Museum and eats the original Blake painting, thereby eradicating this newly experienced self-difference. Murdering the Dragon grants Dolarhyde self-presence—as murdering Dickie does for Tom (eradicating the difference between persons) and murdering strangers does for the cult (eradicating the difference between the self and the name)—and, by extension, control over his own becoming. Once the Dragon is quite literally within him, the narrator asserts, "He could choose anything" (299).

Harris here endorses the existentialist view that the ability to choose defines the active subject, and that the self is determined not by what one has done but rather by what one *does*. Under an existential ontology of person, Dolarhyde may have committed serial murders (or, more accurately, murders serially), but these acts do not define him as a serial murderer as such. As with Ripley, "the past is without force to constitute the present and to sketch out the future" (Sartre, *Being* 637) for Dolarhyde. There is no theoretical reason that he should not stop killing, settle down with Reba, and live out his life in quiet obscurity. Under this model of person, serial murder means nothing more than murder committed more than once; ontologically speaking, there is no reason to believe that just because Dolarhyde has killed three whole families (or Ripley has killed Dickie and Dickie's friend), he is a murderer, let alone a serial one. The existentialist power of choice means that at any moment, either man might transcend his former actions and become a different self.

Unfortunately for Dolarhyde it is too late for re-creating the self; Will Graham and the FBI have traced him to St. Louis. Though the past has no substantive claim on the present self, it does retain a legal prerogative. There are a host of reasons, not the least of which involves considerations of responsibility, why the law holds a present self accountable for any previous actions. Yet, as Will Graham explains to Reba after Dolarhyde's death, such legal considerations say nothing about the nature of that self.[27] "He was trying to stop," Graham declares. "You didn't draw a freak. You drew a man with a freak on his back" (Harris, *Red* 333).

That Dolarhyde is fundamentally a man and only secondarily "a man with a freak on his back" is embedded in Harris's narrative strategy for *Red Dragon*. It grounds Graham's investigative technique, based in identification and self-projection, and explains the novel's extended flashback to Dolarhyde's childhood of extreme abuse. This causal narrative, in combination with sections written from Dolarhyde's perspective, suggests that serial killers are made, not born, that Dr. Bloom is not entirely wrong when he describes Dolarhyde with "compassion" as "the child of a nightmare" (159). By comparison, Jame Gumb in Harris's *The Silence of the Lambs* is granted no such explanation. The novel provides few facts about his childhood, and the scenes told from his point of view contain only mocking descriptions of his homosexual affect. Indeed, Dr. Lecter ridicules Starling for her efforts to determine "a set of influences" responsible for Jame Gumb, accusing her of "giving up good and evil for behaviorism" (*Silence* 21). Working from the teachings of Marcus Aurelius—"of each particular thing, ask: What is it in itself, in its own constitution? What is its causal nature?"—Lecter explains "it's [Jame Gumb's] nature to covet. . . . he covets *being* the very thing you are" (227).[28] The movement from a causal narrative in the case of Dolarhyde to a causal nature in the case of Gumb epitomizes the differences in their ontological construction, as does Lecter's use of the verb "being" as opposed to "Becoming," Dolarhyde's own word for his transformation. If for Francis Dolarhyde serial murder enables him to become his higher self, for Gumb it constitutes who he already is.

But who is Gumb, exactly? His motive for murder is to simulate sex reassignment, which suggests he considers himself a woman. Yet Harris makes it clear that Gumb is mistaken in this motive, not because he believes in an essential as opposed to an action-based account of self but because he does not know what his self is. Forming "a costume of womanness to clothe his own body," Gumb invokes what Jay Prosser calls "the formula for transsexual ontology: the subject trapped in—and trying to escape—the wrong (sexed) body" (67). The male-to-female transsexual does not become a different sex; rather he changes his sex to match the gender he has always been, eliminating an experienced difference between the inside and the outside, the self and itself. Prosser explains: "For transsexuals surgery is a fantasy of restoring the body to the self. . . . 'It is like shedding an annoying and uncomfortable garment and being back in [one's] own self'" (82).[29] Crucially, to restore is not the same as to become; Gumb's motive, presented as the reparation rather than the transformation of the self, indicates a prior assumption of identity between Gumb and the women whose bodies he covets. What Gumb seeks is the body that properly goes with the self he already possesses, even as an adopted Jewish American might adopt the cultural customs (as opposed to the religion) of Judaism to correspond with his Jewish genealogy. But the only way that Gumb can know that a woman's body is properly his is by knowing he is a woman *despite* his body, just as the only way a Jewish American can know the customs of Judaism are his is by knowing he is Jewish despite his customs.

From Jame Gumb's perspective, then, he is not becoming a woman; he *is* a woman and always has been.[30] The second skin he sews for himself will illustrate, not create, his authentic selfhood. Of course Gumb is wrong; the FBI goes to great lengths to explain to Dr. Danielson, the head of the Gender Identity Clinic at Johns Hopkins, that "the [serial killer] we want is *not your patient*. . . . [he is] someone you *refused* because you recognized he was *not a transsexual*" (Harris, *Silence* 181). While Gumb certainly illustrates his selfhood through his crimes, that self is not female (as he believes) or even transsexual, as Dr. Danielson fears, but rather murderous. As Starling discovers during a victim's autopsy, "[s]ometimes the family of man produces, behind a human face, a mind whose pleasure is what lay on the porcelain table" (116–17). Jame Gumb's motive is to illustrate his authentic nature with his crimes, and he does precisely that. He just does not know what that authentic nature is. He is not a woman. He is a serial killer.

The model of selfhood that Harris replicates in his account of Jame Gumb — a model in which serial killing operates like a racial, ethnic, gender- or sexuality-based identity, an aspect of who one is rather than what one does — results in some peculiar consequences for the phenomenon of serial killing as a whole, consequences that appear at the very least counterintuitive. One concerns the very *seriality* of serial killing, which starts to look less like the necessary precondition for characterization as a serial murderer than merely its extrinsic manifestation. Under Harris's identic model, serial killers might be described as such despite the fact that they had never killed or had only killed once. (In fact, many discussions of frequency mention that current statistics are probably low since they do not allow for serial killers who were apprehended after only one murder and remain in jail.[31]) Similarly, serial killers might be understood as "passing" for identities other than their own, or there could be nonpracticing serial killers, just as there are nonpracticing Christians or Jews, and nonpracticing homosexuals.[32] Another repercussion arises from the fact that one could argue that serial killers are punished as much for whom they are as what they've done — logic with disturbing legal implications. At its most extreme, one could imagine a movement that would advocate equal rights for serial killers based on the argument that their behaviors should be protected, even as homosexual behavior is understood as inseparable from and a legitimate expression of gay identity.[33]

Clearly, this movement would never succeed, and even to equate serial killing with homosexual sex constitutes a gross injustice to the latter. But its logical possibility despite its patent absurdity illustrates the particularly legal difficulties posed by a model that locates selfhood in an intangible complex of motive and act. That selfhood is a legal in addition to an ontological consideration is most aptly illustrated by one of the numerous debates over the constitutionality of the various forms of hate crime legislation. As James B. Jacobs and Kimberly Potter explain, "Typically, [hate crime laws] bump up the penalty for a particular crime when the offender's motivation is an officially designated prejudice" (29).[34] This is not in itself so surprising: evaluating motive during sentencing is itself a commonplace of the judicial system. In Chief Justice Rehnquist's decision to uphold the constitutionality of hate-crime statutes in *Wisconsin v. Mitchell* (1993), he explains, "Traditionally, sentencing judges have considered a wide variety of factors in addition to evidence bearing on guilt in determining what sentence to impose.... The defendant's motive for committing the offense is one important factor" (2199). The operative theory is that the state is justified in punishing perpetrators who murder out of racial hatred more harshly than those who murder for money as long as there is a convincing reason to think that an extreme animosity toward strangers based upon their perceived group affiliation is more dangerous to society than greed.

Yet the centrality of motive in hate-crime adjudication suggests the way in which serial killing might operate as a telling example of a hate crime, not because the crimes are usually racially motivated (they rarely are), but because as crimes they are by definition understood to be outside the realm of normative criminal motive and to require particular consideration because of this fact.[35] Using the definition put forth above, Ted Bundy thus becomes the hate-crime perpetrator whose motive reveals a prejudice against women-with-long-hair-parted-in-the-middle-who-look-like-an-ex-girlfriend; John Wayne Gacy would be the hate-crime convict whose motive illustrates a prejudice against gay-street-prostitutes-who-ask-for-more-money-after-sex. It is only because no one understands those groups as categories deserving special protection that Bundy's and Gacy's motives do not qualify their crimes as hate crimes. The extreme animosity toward strangers based upon a presupposed group affiliation is the same.[36] Needless to say, their motives are not likely to constitute "officially designated prejudices" any time soon.[37] In any event, it is hard to imagine how

Bundy's and Gacy's punishments might be enhanced. Both received the death penalty many times over for their crimes.

Of course, the fact that Bundy and Gacy are not considered to have committed hate crimes is not an argument for or against hate crimes as such. One need only argue that prejudices against racial or ethnic groups are more dangerous than prejudices against "women-with-long-hair" or "gay-street-prostitutes" and still remain within the *Wisconsin v. Mitchell* finding that allows for differently motivated crimes to produce different harms. That is, as the state might argue that stranger hatred is more dangerous than greed, it could also argue that stranger hatred based on race is more dangerous than that based on hair length. The latter example serves only to show the logic that informs such categorizations. A more substantive attack on hate-crime legislation concerns its possible encroachment upon First Amendment freedoms, and in this way questions about the relation between motive, act, and identity inevitably surface. Curiously enough, the identity of the criminal and not the victim makes the crucial difference in hate-crime sentencing. Common perceptions of hate crimes view the status of the victim to be the fundamental issue, so that interracial crimes (where the victim and the perpetrator have different racial or ethnic affiliations) are punished more severely than intraracial crimes (where the perpetrator and victim are of the same race/ethnicity). If the perpetrator were to have chosen a different victim, the crime would be reclassified. This is superficially true, but in fact the racial or ethnic categorization of the victim plays only a supporting role. The constitutionality of these laws hinges on the relation between the motive and the act of the perpetrator.

One of the arguments for the unconstitutionality of these laws is as follows: "Generic criminal laws already punish injurious conduct; so recriminalization or sentence enhancement for the same injurious conduct when it is motivated by prejudice amounts to extra punishment for values, beliefs, and opinions that the state deems abhorrent" (Jacobs and Potter 121). If the motive for a particular crime is understood to contain both an instrumental and an expressive content, then that expressive content cannot itself be the basis for further punishment.[38] Parsing out the differences in these two understandings of motive, constitutional scholar Lawrence H. Tribe explains: "this is just the familiar distinction between motive in the more-or-less superficial, external sense corresponding to the classic criminal law notion of intent or of *mens rea*, and motive in a deeper, more attitudinal or expressive sense—a sense that evokes the First Amendment norm that people should not be penalized for the views, ideas or opinions they hold" (11). Thus, for hate-crime statutes to be constitutional, they can only punish those persons who choose their victims on the basis of race (or ethnicity, or sexual orientation), not because of any strongly held beliefs about race (or ethnicity, or sexual orientation). The minute the perpetrator's motives start to look like strongly held beliefs is the minute that hate-crime legislation might run afoul of the First Amendment.

Yet serial killing illustrates that, under an identitarian model of selfhood, *any* action can be said to contain such expressive content: the illustration of who a serial killer, or for that matter, a racist, is.[39] And this is not only a theoretical problem. The individuals most expected to commit hate crimes—the members of various radical organizations such as the Ku Klux Klan, the White Aryan Resistance (WAR), and the World Church of the Creator (WCOTC)—are described as understanding race crimes not only as the product of strongly held beliefs but also as expressions of their specifically racial—which is to say, specifically essential—identity. In his analysis of skinhead culture, for example, Mark Hamm explains, "Neonazi skinheads are violent because violence is a part of their subcultural heritage" (72): "violence is their signature trademark" (62), even as flaying women constituted Jame Gumb's "signature." This violence "operates as a language" (127), not a tool; it represents and expresses rather than executes or accomplishes. Furthermore, this violence is believed to be not only the cultural heritage into which skinheads are indoctrinated but also the racial heritage into which they are born. The quasi-religious movement known as Identity Christianity that forms the basis of many such racialist organizations believes that "God had commissioned individuals in different ages to use violence to preserve racial purity" (Barkun 280), and a predilection to such violence illustrates one's membership in this select group. As the oath taken by members of *Bruders Schweigen* (the Silent Brotherhood, also called The Order) attests: "I, as a free Aryan man . . . have a sacred duty to do whatever is necessary to deliver our people from the Jew and bring total victory to the Aryan race" (229).[40]

In a sense then, the primary argument against hate-crime legislation—that one punishes racists for who they are rather than what they do — is counterintuitively reinforced by the logic behind hate-crime legislation, which perhaps inadvertently implies that hating some types of persons is more damaging to society than hating others.[41] Of course, skinheads and other white supremacists rarely speak so eloquently about their motives. The identic language categorizing their behaviors may itself be attributed more to the social scientists who study such groups than the members themselves. Likewise, just because white supremacists claim that their motives are inseparable from their identities does not mean the state has to agree with them. The state might argue that prejudice can never be "motive in [the] deeper, more expressive sense" (Tribe 11) that would guarantee it First Amendment protection.

Tribe himself circumvents the First Amendment conflict outlined above by arguing that as long as the laws are "content-neutral," they cannot be accused of favoring one position over another. By this logic the mere existence of expressive content does not matter as long as the laws are neutral with respect to what that content is. Tribe explains: "on their face, such statutes ordinarily address the defendant's motive for committing the crime (i.e., the reason for selecting the victim), not the message communicated by the crime" (10). On this account, both the man who assaults Asian American women because he hates them and the man who assaults Asian American women because he loves them (and erroneously believes that assault is the appropriate way to show his affection) would be subject to sentence enhancement, despite the fact that the latter crime does not involve hate at all. In cases like the preceding, Tribe argues, "it is completely irrelevant *why* an attacker is targeting a victim on the basis of the victim's race, so long as that attacker's conduct is indeed triggered by an awareness of the victim's race" (8, emphasis in original). Though statistically those crimes in which the conduct is triggered by an awareness of race that does not involve racial bigotry are few and far between, this does not in and of itself invalidate the content-neutrality of the laws; for such laws to be constitutional, they need be neutral only in theory, not in the resulting practice.

But by claiming that bigotry is not necessary for hate-crime laws to be enacted, Tribe does not in fact remove content from these laws; he merely relocates that content outside of an evaluation of the relative worth of different races — are, say, Asian Americans better or worse than European

Americans? — and within the notion that racial (or cultural or sexual) identities are viable categories on which such evaluations can be made. The content no longer concerns the positive or negative value of a particular race (or ethnicity) and instead addresses the positive or negative value of racial (or ethnic) categories as such, thereby instantiating the notion that the self is essentially composed by such categories. This is an argument with which all serial killers would seem to agree; what made Ted Bundy's victims *victims*, after all, was his conviction that the fundamental category of person was one of gender and hair length. Other considerations (who she was, how she lived, what she believed in) were merely contingent. By reifying identic categories, hate-crime laws validate the logic of racist and serial killer alike; they might be ontologically different, but they still think a lot like everyone else.

4 ASSIMILATION, AUTHENTICITY, AND "NATURAL JEWISHNESS"

WRITING IN *Commentary* magazine in 1961, Daniel Bell analyzes the then current "crisis of identity" that defined contemporary Jewish experience. For mid-century Americans in general, he explains, "sensibility and experience rather than revealed utterances, tradition, authority, and even reason, have become the sources of understanding and of identity. One stakes out one's position and it is confirmed by others who accept the sign" (471). His account of this generation evokes both existentialism and David Riesman's theories of other-direction to describe a comprehensive break with the past and reorientation toward the immediate community of one's peers. Members of his generation feel kinship with those who share contemporary experience, not individuals who have gone before. This is a fact of modern existence for Bell, and "Few of us can escape this mark" (471). And it is especially true for Jews, since life lived in "*galut*" (exile) means that many of the ties with the past are already broken. But as a Jew, he asks, "how can one reject the God of Abraham, Isaac, and Jacob — without rejecting oneself? How then does a modern Jew continue to identify with the Jewish fate? And if such an identification is made and conditioned largely by experience, by a generational experience at that, what must be the consequences?" (472). Identifying memory as the primary link between modern Jews and the Jewish tradition, Bell represents this memory through the meaning of the *yizkor* — the prayers for the dead said communally on four major holidays, but within which each participant inserts the name of his own deceased parent. In its shared and individual aspects, the *yizkor* becomes for Bell a technology through which the individual joins the community and the community recognizes the individual.

Yet mere memory appears a frail thread from which to hang the future of American Jewishness. Memory, Bell argues, "has its risks" (474) — risks of sentimentality (in the romanticization of the shtetl), of accommodation and institutionalization (through the *"embourgeoisement"* of Jewish life in fund-raisers and memberships), of repression and alienation (the self-hating Jew), and ultimately of attrition, "a wasting away" in which "there is the word, Jew, but no feeling" (475). Identifying himself as "one who has not faith but memory," Bell describes his own life amid such risks, accepting the "double burden and double pleasure of my self-consciousness, the outward life of an American and the inward secret of the Jew" (477). With this description, Bell represents himself as hidden in his daily interactions; the individual who has a "secret" that goes unrevealed, who presents one identity externally but recognizes another within himself. Of course, this secret is hardly well concealed. Bell writes this essay in a national magazine, albeit one that ostensibly directs itself toward the Jewish community. And contrary to expectation given the mid-century's preoccupation with phoniness, he expresses no embarrassment at the purported disparity between his inner reality and his outer façade. "I walk with this sign as a frontlet between my eyes," he continues, "and it is as visible to some secret others as their sign is to me" (477). Like members of a covert society, mid-century Jews read each other's signs in a discourse operating below that of mainstream American culture.

Bell's interest in the problems of Jewish identity and Jewish assimilation was well shared during the postwar period, when Jewish American life after World War II and the Holocaust was the subject of much intellectual and popular interest. In various formats, writers such as Leslie Fiedler, Elliott E. Cohen, Harold Rosenberg, Saul Bellow, Herman Wouk, and Will Herberg, to name only a few, examined the complexities of a particularly American Jewish selfhood. These included competing ideas of how Jewishness should be defined; the consideration of the benefits of the mid-century's trend towards emphasizing human universality (as exemplified in Steichen's "The Family of Man" exhibit and book from 1955) against the possible disadvantages of a decreased emphasis on ethnic particularity; and the ambiguities and ambivalences of class mobility and Jewish assimilation, as manifested through the gradual but evident disappearance of Yiddishkeit — the collection of beliefs and traditions that had defined Eastern European Jewish culture and which immigration brought to the United States during the late nineteenth and early twentieth centuries. The changes in Jewish life that began with the large-scale emigration from Eastern Europe, and which intensified with the destruction of European Jewry during the Holocaust, created fruitful ground for the discussion of Jewish existence in America.

Historians like Peter Novick (1999) have argued convincingly that the immediate postwar period did not see many writers openly addressing the Holocaust, perhaps because "silence was a manifestation of repression" (3); or because people feared conversation about the Holocaust could perpetuate stereotypes of Jewish victimhood; or, as Novick himself argues, because there had been "revolutionary changes in world alignments" (85) that made discussion of the Holocaust impolitic during the politically volatile Cold War.[1] In Novick's analysis, the emergence of the Holocaust as the defining event of Jewish American identity does not fully happen until after the 1973 Arab-Israeli War, when Israeli vulnerability in the early days of the conflict underscored fears that the Holocaust was not a historically isolated event, and raised the specter that a mass annihilation of the Jews might again occur.[2]

That hesitancy of discussion did not extend to considerations of the future of a specifically American Jewry. In 1945, in the inaugural issue of *Commentary* (the official publication of the American Jewish Committee), editor Elliot E. Cohen wrote that "[w]ith Europe devastated, there falls upon us here in the United States a far greater share of the responsibility for carrying forward, in a creative way, our common Jewish and spiritual heritage" ("Act" 2). What that "creative way" of moving forward was to look like was a source of contention in a number of essays published in the magazine before 1950. Cohen's "Jewish Culture in America" (1947) and "The Intellectuals and the Jewish Community" (1949), Israel Knox's "Is America Exile or Home?" (1947), and Meyer Levin's "The Writer and the Jewish Community" (1947), are only a few examples. Once the 1950s began — and in keeping with the larger trend toward the hybridization of psychology and sociology — *Commentary* ran articles by such well-known sociologists as David Riesman, Nathan Glazer, and Herbert J. Gans, among others, who began to examine Jewish existence in postwar America. In essays like "The New Suburbanites of the 50s: Jewish Division" (Gersh 1954), the two-part series "The Jewish Revival in America" (Glazer 1955/1956), and "The 'Triple Melting Pot'" (Herberg 1955), these writers attempted to understand the transformations taking place within the American Jewish community. "Before the war, most Jews, like most other Americans, were part of the working class, defined in terms of occupation, education and income. Already upwardly mobile before the war relative to other immigrants, Jews floated high on the rising economic tide, and most of them entered the middle class" (Brodkin 42). Being middle class in the 1950s increasingly meant being suburban. Catherine Jurca explains, "In the postwar period, mass production, along with cheap and accessible land, financial incentives for veterans and builders, and high wages meant that suburban house ownership became available to most white middle-class and many working-class families for the first time in American history" (134). Jews were included among this relocation from the cities to the suburbs, and likewise included in the debates over whether the suburbs were the mechanization through which a stultifying middle-class homogeny would be produced.[3] Yet for Jews in suburbia, those debates took on the added question of what this suburban exodus would mean for the Jewishness of American Jews.

Enfolded within these debates — sometimes explicitly and sometimes only implicitly — was the question of whether there was any relation between Jewishness and authenticity. Part of this discussion concerned the role of religion in postwar American culture more generally, in which Judaism was included alongside Protestantism and Catholicism as one of the three dominant American faiths. Specifically, sociologists wondered what if any role organized religion played in the perceived uniformity of American life. In a telling instance, the well-known religious sociologist and social philosopher Will Herberg argued in *Protestant–Catholic–Jew* that the simultaneous increase in religious affiliation on the one hand, and secularism on the other, implied that a new era in American religiosity was occurring. That era was based on the potentially paradoxical "'strengthening of the religious structure in spite of increasing secularization'" (2, quoted from Sklare). Religion, Herberg claimed, was becoming increasingly structured and organized; Protestantism, Catholicism, and Judaism were not disappearing in the suburbs. To the contrary, more and more people were affiliating with their local churches and synagogues, taking part in events targeted at specific religious communities, and making a church- or synagogue-based sociality part of their lives. But whether these religious organizations supported the authenticity of their congregants was open to question. As bestselling novelist Herman Wouk remembers of this period, "Judaism meant ritualism, and ritualism meant conformity" (*My God* 30). Equally contentious was the question of whether the religion practiced in such settings was itself authentic. Institutionalization inspired a widespread apprehension that "the religion which actually prevails among Americans today has lost much of its authentic Christian (or Jewish) content" (Herberg 3). As Herberg's parenthesis indicates, Jewish authenticity is considered here as only part of a larger concern with contemporary religion and its effect on the American character more generally.

That larger concern stemmed from the possibility that suburban religious "identification, affiliation, and membership" was less about faith and more about "the social necessity of 'belonging'" (Herberg 41). Herberg understands such trends in terms by now very familiar to readers of this volume. "[I]t is not difficult to see the current turn to religion and the church as, in part at least, a reflection of the growing other-directedness of our middle-class culture," he argues. Once again, Riesman's theories of the mid-century, middle-class, American character are deployed to account for the evolution of American religious selfhood: "To identify and locate oneself in the social context is a requirement under all conditions; it becomes particularly pressing and urgent under conditions of other-direction, since other-direction craves conformity and adjustment" (59). Congregants may believe that they are engaging in genuine religious experiences, but in fact they are merely acting on their social radar, which directs them to be like everyone else. He argues that "[t]he vogue of Van Gogh and Renoir reproductions in the suburban home and the rising church affiliation of the suburban community may not be totally unconnected" (59). It is just another way of aligning oneself in relation to one's community. But crucially, "[t]hose who identify themselves religiously and join churches as a way of naming and locating themselves socially are not cynical unbelievers shrewdly manipulating false labels." That is to say, they are not phonies in the Caulfieldian sense of the term. Neither are they exactly authentic, however. "They mean what they say" — or like Holly Golightly, believe what they believe — but "there may well be other factors more authentically religious in the theological sense" (41) that they do not possess. The suburban Protestants, Catholics, and Jews may in fact be real phonies.

Yet Herberg's analysis illustrates that the question of a Jewishness and authenticity cannot, for two reasons, be entirely subsumed within these more general questions about religious affiliation as a part of the tendency toward uniformity of mid-century American culture. The first reason is that the Jewish experience is itself thought to be universal — "the Jews . . . reveal[ed] themselves as paradoxically the most 'American' of all the ethnic groups that went into the making of modern America" (10). In this sense the Jews were thought to stand in for Americans in their entirety, rather than to be absorbed within the larger category of "American." "Nothing is more characteristically American than the historical evolution of American Jewry" (172), Herberg maintains. At the same time, of all the groups Herberg discusses, only the Jews are imagined to possess something like Holly Golightly's "mean reds" — the angst imagined to stem from a self constructed entirely within cultural forms. At the end of the chapter titled "Judaism in America," Herberg describes the suburban Jew's "perplexity and restlessness" about contemporary Jewishness. It is Jews — not Protestants or Catholics — who are prone to ask, "Was this all there was to Judaism after all? Had it no higher purpose or destiny?" (198). Such questioning mirrors the "Reflections" of Daniel Bell with which this chapter began, who notices that "[i]n suburbia, one sees the signs of the false parochialism, the thin veneer of identity which rubs off at the first contact of the world" (477). For a complex of reasons, Jewishness was seen as the most essential of religious identities — in that it revealed not just faith, but also cultural and historical distinctiveness, and a potentially racial definition of self.

In this sense, Bell's reflections represent a personal and experiential version of what Herberg here identifies as a particularly Jewish phenomenon in the mid-1950s.[4] Yet Bell's article registers a subtle but crucially important shift in the ground on which authenticity is conceived. This shift both illustrates the particular way in which authenticity is understood during the postwar period, and also significantly foreshadows the central role that institutions and cultures are going to play in the production of authenticity toward the end of the century. On the one hand, Daniel Bell's description of the disjunction between "the outward life of an American and the inward secret of the Jew" (477) cannot but help to evoke the definition of phoniness that began this volume, in which the self is imagined to possess a façade that may, but also may not, align with an interior imagined to be authentic. For example, it is easy enough to deduce Holden Caulfield's reaction to Bell's self-description. While Bell might feel no shame in wearing a "sign as a frontlet between my eyes" visible to "some secret others" (477), it does not take much imagination to predict what Holden Caulfield might say, provided, of course, that he were able to see the sign in the first place. In this sense, Bell's admission about his outer and inner selves—about selves that are easily visible versus those that are inevitably coded—looks like the type of concerns that *anyone* might have during a time in which authenticity was of such paramount cultural interest. Bell is more sanguine about the inevitability of some phoniness than Holden might be, but their concerns are not so far apart. Both wonder about the implications for authenticity of difference in the self.

On the other hand, by imagining his "inward secret" as specifically Jewish, Bell shifts the discourse of authenticity into another register. The phony, and particularly the real phony, illustrate how authenticity is conceived as that which separates the individual from the group. This distinction is what makes it possible for Holly Golightly to be simultaneously real and fake: her realness comes from her own belief in her authenticity; her falsity from the fact that her character was constructed entirely within the social realm. By suggesting that Jewishness itself might define the "inward secret," Bell imagines an authenticity that might be shared among a group—or even might find its root in practices begun outside the self and later internalized. This authenticity would operate racially or ethnically; it is not dependent upon a group (a Jew is still a Jew even if he is the only one), but nevertheless is not *essentially* individual. Nor is it a priori hostile to the possibility that authenticity might align one with others. In this register, Bell's account of the "inward secret" looks like nothing so much as a technology of passing, most frequently associated in the United States with African or mixed-race Americans, and highly dependent on tropes of visibility and invisibility for its articulation.

This chapter considers the implications of this shifting register along a spectrum of approaches to the question of Jewish passing or assimilation from the late 1940s to the early 1960s. In this period of time, one might begin to comprehend how authenticity would be fundamentally transformed by the end of the twentieth century. This trajectory begins with the existentialist model of self, whose central importance for mid-century accounts of authenticity the first chapter elaborated. The opening section of this chapter thus takes seriously Bell's proposition that Jewishness might be an inward secret by examining the question of Jewish passing and the purported visibility of identity. It compares Elia Kazan's 1947 film *Gentleman's Agreement*, in which a gentile pretends to be Jewish, with his 1949 film of black/white passing, *Pinky* (1949). Yet where *Pinky* remains committed to an internal blackness that transcends skin color—and which Pinky finally embraces in a gesture of authenticity—*Gentleman's Agreement* rejects the possibility of a Jewish essence, of an "inward secret of the Jew" (Bell 477). *Gentleman's Agreement* does so, furthermore, not by merely deracinating "Jewishness" (producing it as a religious and ethnic rather than a racial category), but rather by emptying the category of all content, so that "there is the word, Jew, but no feeling" (Bell 475)—and, as a result, no actual Jews. The film thus anticipates the collective "whitening" of Jews as they joined the middle class during the 1950s. As literary critic Andrew Hoberek asserts, "the transformation of Jews from whites to nonwhites depended upon their transformation from workers and small businessmen (think Leo Minch) into members of the white collar middle class" (71). The film likewise illustrates why that "whitening" might be viewed as potentially threatening to Jewishness as a category of being, by suggesting that Jewish deracination might mean as well the emptying of all Jewishness as such.

In this sense, the film emerges as the fictional counterpart to Jean-Paul Sartre's treatise on authentic living, *Anti-Semite and Jew*, which was discussed at length in the first chapter. Sartre's Jews "have neither community of interests nor community of beliefs. They do not have the same fatherland; they have no history. The sole tie that binds them is the hostility and disdain of the societies which surround them" (91). Only the look of the anti-Semite constitutes them as Jews. In important respects, *Gentleman's Agreement* thus emerges as a narrativization of Sartre's project. But rather than seeing the film as a watered-down version of existentialist philosophy, one might instead imagine it as a perfecting of it. Foregrounding a non-Jew who pretends to be Jewish, *Gentleman's Agreement* enacts precisely the scenario that Sartre imagines: a world in which *all* Jews are not actually Jewish, in which *any* Jew is inevitably only pretending. From the existentialist perspective (if no other), the film's commitment to imagining a world without Jews looks like the solution to anti-Semitism rather than its desired culmination. In attempting to make the world safe for Jews, the category of Jewishness itself loses all meaning.

Once Jewishness has been dismissed as a racial category, passing itself can no longer exist; it must itself become assimilation, the abandonment of ethnic or religious beliefs and practices in favor of the dominant cultural traditions. The chapter thus turns to one of the high canonical works of mid-century Jewish and American literature, Saul Bellow's *Seize the Day* (1956), which explores the existentialist, inner-directed, and other-directed models of self in terms of the question of Jewish assimilation. Taking place over the course of one day, the novel stages a generational conflict between a son and a father as the conflict between other- and inner-directed character types that David Riesman postulated and Daniel Bell perceived as a threat to Jewish identity. With such models of self in operation, the novel could potentially be about any generational conflict. That the lead characters are Jewish might appear only an incidental fact of their composition. The apparent endorsement in *Seize the Day* of an existentialist model of self at the expense of those based in history and culture (inner-direction) or shared experiences among a generation (other-direction) would seem to support this conclusion. But if the existentialist model put forth by *Gentleman's Agreement* imagines that Jewish assimilation is inevitable, *Seize the Day* provides an alternative way for its lead character to be Jewish, by representing the "nerve of failure"—the privileged role that Jews were theorized to play within American culture. The generational conflicts within the text are mapped against a backdrop of profound material and social disappointment. In the terms through which that failure is understood, and the sacrificial role that failure is imagined to play within the larger community of postwar Americans, authenticity and Jewishness are imagined in *Seize the Day* as comparable terms.

Of course, as the significant class movement of the Jewish population might suggest, the failure represented in *Seize the Day* was not shared by the majority of American Jews during the 1950s. This chapter thus concludes with an analysis of that most popular of Jewish success stories, Herman Wouk's best-selling novel *Marjorie Morningstar* (1955), whose eponymous lead character famously appeared beside her creator on the front cover of *Time* magazine in September 1955. In Marjorie Morningstar's concluding *embourgeoisement* (to use Daniel Bell's word) within the Jewish suburbs, one can see the concern for the authenticity of the mid-century Jew, whose Jewishness was thought to be more about "belonging" (Herberg 41) than genuine religious feeling. The novel asks in its conclusion whether the reader is to understand Marjorie as, at core, a real phony. Yet the story told in *Marjorie Morningstar* unexpectedly foretells the crucial role that institutions will play in late-twentieth-century theories of authenticity. It imagines religious institutionalization not as the death of authentic Jewishness but rather as a technology for its creation. The coffee klatches, book groups and community centers appear at the end of the novel as a means of offsetting Jewish attrition — that "wasting away" (475) that Daniel Bell feared — by producing through a mystified mechanism that rarest of all mid-century character types: the natural Jew.

Mid-Century Jewish Passing: *Gentleman's Agreement* and *Anti-Semite and Jew*

First published in 1947, Laura Hobson's novel *Gentleman's Agreement* reached the top spot on the *New York Times* best-seller list and sold 1.6 million copies (McFadden). Elia Kazan's film of the same name was the 1947 winner of the Academy Award for Best Motion Picture. The film tells the story of Philip Schuyler Green (Gregory Peck), who has moved to New York City from California to take a job at the liberal magazine *Smith's Weekly*. His first assignment is to write a series on anti-Semitism — to "break it wide open," as his editor confidently declares. The film's most explicit articulation of the problem of anti-Semitism is given from a minor character whom Phil and his fiancée Kathy (Dorothy Maguire) meet at a party. Phil is introduced to the "the world-renowned physicist" Professor Lieberman (Sam Jaffe), a European immigrant and self-professed "man of science," so that they might "hash over some ideas . . . Palestine, Zionism." Professor Lieberman responds to Phil's request for his insights with a description of his newest "crusade":

> I have no religion, so I am not Jewish by religion. Further I am a scientist, so I must rely on science which tells me I am not Jewish by race, since there is no such thing as a distinct Jewish race. . . . [Therefore] I will simply go forth and state frankly, "I am not a Jew." Well with my face, that becomes not an

evasion but a new principle.... There must be millions of people nowadays who are religious in only the vaguest sense. I have often wondered why the Jewish ones among them still go on calling themselves Jews. Can you guess why? Because the world still makes it an advantage not to be one.... So you see, I will have to abandon my crusade before it begins. Only if there were no anti-Semites could I go on with it.

Professor Lieberman's observation that his face is what elevates an evasion (he was, in fact, born to Jewish parents) to the level of principle (if he is not Jewish, then Jewishness must not be biological) speaks to three crucial points about the immediate postwar period. First, it illustrates that the popular definition of Jewishness in the late 1940s was specifically racial — Jews were Jewish because of their faces (that is, their physiognomy), regardless of whether they actually practiced the Jewish religion. Professor Lieberman does not speak about individuals who worship as Jews; whether they do or do not is irrelevant to the discussion. Even "men of science" like Professor Lieberman, fully assimilated into rational Enlightenment culture, count as Jews. Second, his observation establishes the importance of visibility — and, indirectly, the look of other people which evaluates that visibility — as a crucial component of determining the existence of any individual Jew. *Gentleman's Agreement* plays with the erroneous assumption that Jewishness can be located in facial physiognomy, a fact discussed shortly. Finally, and most important, Lieberman's speech proposes a significantly different position — that it is only the beliefs of others that define the Jew as such. In so arguing, Lieberman evacuates Jewishness of any cultural or ethical content — a point that, needless to say, was the source of controversy.

The differences between a specifically racial definition of Jewishness and one based on the perception of others go beyond merely the correct attribution of Jewishness, however. They speak to a fundamentally different understanding of the self's relationship to the context in which it is situated. The former version argues for the self's construction outside of and with no regard to context. In a racial account, the Jew is Jewish even if he is the last Jew on earth and has never attended a synagogue, participated in a Bar or Bat Mitzvah or Seder, and so on. By comparison, the latter position views the self (or at the very least, the particulars of selfhood) as dependent on the existence of others. By Professor Lieberman's account, if a Jew were alone in the forest, he would not be a Jew. What *Gentleman's Agreement* illustrates is that ultimately what matters is not what one is, but rather what one is taken to be.

Thus, Professor Lieberman's claim that "only if there were no anti-Semites" could a Jew no longer be a Jew exactly mirrors Sartre's assertion from *Anti-Semite and Jew* that "It is society, not the decree of God, that has made him a Jew and brought the Jewish problem into being" (134). For Sartre, "man is defined first of all as a being 'in a situation'. . . . it forms him and decides his possibilities" (59–60). As the first chapter of this work discussed, Sartrean existentialism asserts that individuals are not definable by a racial, economic, religious, national, or cultural background: human reality "in and through its very upsurge decides to define its own being by its ends. . . . And this thrust is an *existence*; it has nothing to do with an essence or with a property of being" (*Being* 572). Though the anti-Semite "presupposes that the Jew is an indivisible totality," Sartre argues instead that the Jew is "a mosaic in which each element is a pebble that we can take out and place in another pattern" (*Anti-Semite* 62). Like Professor Lieberman, the Jews that Sartre describes "have only a ceremonial and polite contact with their religion" (65). The version of Jewishness that Sartre imagines is one in which the traditions, rituals, beliefs, and practices have no meaning for individual Jews — a point discussed at length in this chapter. Crucially for Sartre, the only thing that defines Jews as Jews is that "they have in common the situation of the Jews, that is, they live in a community that takes them for Jews" (67). Though any given individual may experience no connection with his or her Jewish ancestry, the power of the anti-Semite is to make the Jew "a Jew in spite of himself" (137) by so categorizing and containing him.

This power is itself expressed in *Being and Nothingness* through the concept of the look; the capacity of others to see the self, which structures the relation between any two encountering individuals. Another person's ability to gaze upon oneself produces that person as more than just another object in a world of objects. As Sartre explains, "my apprehension of the other in the world as *probably being* a man refers to my permanent possibility of *being-seen-by-him*; that is, to the permanent possibility that a subject who sees me may be substituted for the object seen by me. 'Being-seen-by-the-Other' is the *truth* of 'seeing-the-Other' (*Being* 345). Using an example of a man who, "moved by jealousy, curiosity, or vice" (347), peers through a keyhole to observe a private conversation, Sartre describes the eavesdropper's consciousness while absorbed in his task. When the eavesdropper hears footsteps in the hall and realizes "Someone is looking at me!" (349), that pure consciousness lost in its acts is instantly suffused with shame at being available to someone else's judgmental gaze. The Other's look has the power to reduce the self to its objectivity or facticity. In Sartre's account, "the Other is first the being for whom I am an object; that is, the being *through whom* I gain my objectness" (361). Though the eavesdropper had previously "no self to inhabit [his] consciousness . . . [he is] a pure consciousness of things" (347), once the Other appears, he is "*seated* as this inkwell *is on* the table; for the Other *[he is] leaning over* the keyhole as this tree *is bent* by the wind" (352). Caught in a particularly humiliating situation—spying on a private conversation—the eavesdropper is transfixed by the look into an object for the Other's use: his judgment, his ridicule, and his pleasure.

The solution is to look back. Sartre claims that the "defensive reaction" of the gazed-upon self causes "the Other to appear before me in the capacity of *this* or *that object*. As such, he will appear to me as a 'this one'; that is, his subjective quasi-totality is degraded and becomes a totality-as-object co-extensive with the totality of the World" (393). Further, "from the moment when the Other appears to me as an object, his subjectivity becomes a simple *property* of the object considered. . . . [He] 'has' a subjectivity as this hollow box has 'an inside.'" Since one cannot be "*an object for an object*" (384), gazing back allows the self to recover its subjectivity. The possibility that the Other then may look again and produce himself again as the subject—and with the self as an object—creates a potentially infinite exchange of looks, in which the relative positions of subject and object are continually exchanged between look-er and look-ee; the self is "referred from transfiguration to degradation and from degradation to transfiguration without ever being able either to get a total view of the ensemble of these two modes of being" (394). Neither participant has a clear means to emerge from a seemingly endless rotation of subjectivity and objectification.

Of course, in the above cycle of looking—with the individual continually giving and receiving gazes—the effects of the look of the other are purely phenomenological. The actual ontology of the self as a being in a situation remains the same. Though the act of being looked at reveals "the pure probability that I am at present this concrete *this*" (374), it cannot change the ontological fact that the self is continually recreating itself through its choices. As Sartre insists, "there is no character; there is only a project of oneself" (705). But each look does "prove concretely — and in the indubitable certainty of the *cogito* — that we exist for all living men; that is, that there are (some) consciousnesses for whom I exist" (374). Our lives become a version of the man who appears in public to give a lecture or perform in a play: "we never lose sight of the fact that we are looked at, and we execute the ensemble of acts which we have come to perform *in the presence of* the look; better yet, we attempt to constitute a being and an ensemble of objects *for* this look" (375). If the self is inevitably a being in a situation, which decides its possibilities, it is also a being aware of a situation, on some level inevitably performative.

This fundamentally performative aspect of the self is something of which Phil Green in *Gentleman's Agreement* takes advantage. Stumped on what to say in his article on anti-Semitism, beyond the "same old drool of statistics and protests," Phil recognizes he has "facts and evidence," but has "ignored feelings." He considers asking his childhood friend Dave Goldman how "he feels about this thing" — Phil seeks to discover "what must a Jew feel" — but abandons the plan when he realizes "there is not any way you can tear open the secret heart of another human being." Perhaps not: subjectivity, after all, is subjectivity. But Phil imagines he's found the next best thing. He decides to *pretend* to "be Jewish," realizing "nobody knows [him] around here" and — like Professor Lieberman — there is nothing in his face to argue against it. This plan has worked well before. "On the coal mine series," Phil remembers, he did not "tap some poor, grimy, guy on the shoulder and make him talk." He got a mining job, "went down in the dark . . . [and] slept in a shack." He "*was* a miner" (emphasis mine) and "found the answers in [his] own guts." "Concentrating a lifetime into a few weeks," Phil experiences for himself anti-Semitism in everyday life: at the workplace, in restaurants, among his son's friends, and at a restricted hotel. In so doing, he discovers not only "how must a fellow like Dave feel," but also the covert racism hidden among "the good people, the nice people," with whom he shares his life.

4. Phil Green looks at his face in the mirror. *Gentleman's Agreement* (1947). Twentieth Century Fox.

Phil's project works because the world of the film ascribes to a logic of racial passing—a logic that maintains that whatever defines a race, it is not its external manifestation. Thus, all Phil needs to do to convince people of his Jewishness is tell them it is so. The film emphasizes the importance of the look (or as film studies would come to call it in the 1970s, the gaze) in constructing what is seen—in this case, a Jew where none actually exists. *Gentleman's Agreement* plays with the looks that characters give one another, and the ways in which the audience can be made—or, more often, prevented—from sharing a character's point of view. In the scene when Phil first conceives of his performance, the film presents him looking at himself in the mirror as he catalogues his physical characteristics in comparison to Dave's. Phil notes he's got "dark hair, dark eyes, so's Dave, so've a lot of guys who aren't Jewish. No accent, no mannerisms, neither has Dave." He renames himself, "Phil Green, skip the Schuyler, might be anything." Yet crucially in this moment, Phil's reflection in the mirror is not prevented from Phil's own point of view. The audience is not sharing Phil's look when he gazes at himself; one cannot see what Phil sees.

This technique becomes more compelling when one realizes that there are no point-of-view shots at any point in the movie.[5] In the shot/reverse-shot sequences of conversation, for example, the shoulder of the nonspeaking character is carefully left in the frame that primarily focuses on the speaking character. In a representative instance, Phil speaks with his secretary, Estelle Wales, and she admits to him that she too is Jewish, and that she changed her name from Walovsky to get her job. During the exchange, the left and back side of Phil's shoulder and face are visible when

5. Estelle Wales in conversation with her employer Phil Green. *Gentleman's Agreement* (1947). Twentieth Century Fox.

the camera focuses on Estelle, and the right and back side of her shoulder are apparent when the shot focuses on Phil, appearing prominently along the edge of the frame. The composition is awkward, but it has the advantage of never allowing the audience to imagine that they see precisely what a given character sees, or that any individual look can be shared between two people. In those instances where the characters are too far apart to be contained in a single frame, the movie employs eyeline matches — shots that reveal what the character is seeing, but *not* from that character's point of view.

The importance of this technique becomes clear when one realizes that the director of *Gentleman's Agreement* specifically does not want the audience to see what Miss Wales or any of the other characters see when they look at Phil: namely, a Jew. The audience knows that Phil is not really Jewish. They are privy to his experiment in anti-Semitism from the beginning. This knowledge prevents us from seeing what Miss Wales sees — or imagines she sees — when she gazes upon her boss. This failure of identification is then rendered literally in the film's rejection of point-of-view shots. Refraining from shooting through the eyes of any of the characters, even Phil's, *Gentleman's Agreement* disallows the easy identification afforded by sharing someone's gaze.

Further, the film uses the looks that characters give one another as a force for objectification, much in Sartrean terms. Though this objectification must take place whenever any character looks at any other, it becomes most apparent in those moments when Phil encounters the anti-Semitism it is his mission to experience. Insisting that he "wants to make [the

6. Phil Green converses with his secretary, Estelle Wales. *Gentleman's Agreement* (1947). Twentieth Century Fox.

management] look me in the eye," Phil travels to the restricted Flume Inn and provokes a conflict by announcing he is Jewish and goading the manager to admit that Jews are not permitted in the hotel. The film presents the confrontation between Phil and the manager by using first the same shot/reverse-shot technique that marks his filming of any conversation, leaving the shoulder of the listener in the frame while the other character speaks. Cutting then to a two-shot in which two bellboys can be seen in the background, the manager spins the registration cards to illustrate that there are no free rooms, while the bellboys themselves stare openly at Phil. While an older couple moves into the frame, Phil announces that he is Jewish; the couple then covertly (and not so covertly) stare at Phil out of the corner of their eyes. After the manager refuses Phil a room, we see Phil staring impotently at the closed door to the manager's office, with the hotel guests staring at him in the background. In each of these three shots, the actors in the background emphasize the act of looking and its effect upon Phil as he is objectified as a Jew.

One can compare how the problems of passing are negotiated in *Gentleman's Agreement* with Kazan's other passing movie of the immediate postwar period, *Pinky* (1949). The character of Pinky is a young, mixed-race woman (played by Jeanne Crain), who has been living as white in the North while she completed her nurse's training. There, she fell in love with a white doctor at the hospital, whom she has not told about her biracial parentage. At the start of the movie she returns to her southern home to be reunited with her grandmother, called Aunt Dicey (Ethel Waters) by the community. While there, Pinky nurses Miss Em (Ethel Barrymore),

7. The bellboys stare at Phil Green trying to check in to the Flume Hotel. *Gentleman's Agreement* (1947). Twentieth Century Fox.

8. The older couple sneaks covert glances at Phil Green. *Gentleman's Agreement* (1947). Twentieth Century Fox.

the white matriarch of the community and her grandmother's employer, who lives in the former plantation house — "slave built, slave run, and run-down ever since." Her fiancé, Tom (William Lundigan), follows her and discovers her secret. When Miss Em dies, she surprises the town by leaving her house and land to Pinky, challenging the state's traditions against the black inheritance of white property. The questions of the film center on Pinky's future. Will she to return to the North and her white fiancé to live as white? Or will she fight to inherit Miss Em's property and stay in the South, working in the African American community, as both her grandmother and Miss Em desire? Not surprisingly, these questions are finally about the concept of black/white passing itself, asking the now-familiar question for studies of culture and race in the United States: is there an innate blackness that triumphs over its lack of physiological manifestation?

This question is complicated by the casting of a white actress in the part of Pinky. As Charlene Regester explains, "When a white actress assumes

9. The hotel guests all stare at Phil Green. *Gentleman's Agreement* (1947). Twentieth Century Fox.

the mulatto role, the way in which the cinema industry visibly constructs race is still at issue, and if the construct that is provided is an artificial construct, then can race be visibly represented?" (72). Where in *Gentleman's Agreement*, the film's task is to prevent audiences from seeing Phil Green as a Jew, even when the other characters do, in *Pinky*, audiences must be convinced to see a mixed-race character where none actually exists. Once again, the point-of-view shot is rendered problematic. To explore fully the putative ambiguity of her situation, Pinky cannot be shown through southern eyes, which would view her as uncomplicatedly black. Nor can she be presented from the northern perspective of Tom, who sees only white and actively works to deny the connections Pinky feels for the African American community. Instead, the film carefully manipulates the *mise en scène* to produce Pinky in racialized terms. Susan Courtney (2005) provides an extended analysis of the first five scenes, which are designed to establish the audience's immediate impression of Pinky as white and then rewrite that impression through the careful manipulation of cinematic space and shadow. Moving Pinky through a series of spaces whose racial coding is gradually revealed, the film undermines the audience's initial, easy assumption of Pinky's whiteness — enabled by Crain's own pale skin — and produces her instead as African American.

This spatial positioning plays alongside a series of interpellations by the community, many of which foreground the look — and then the look again — of the other characters as they recognize Pinky first as white and then as black. When Pinky first approaches her grandmother, Aunt Dicey takes her for a white woman, calling out "Good morning, ma'am" as she

10. Aunt Dicey smiles at Pinky thinking she is a white woman. *Pinky* (1949). Twentieth Century Fox.

11. Aunt Dicey looks again and realizes the white woman before her is her granddaughter Pinky. *Pinky* (1949). Twentieth Century Fox.

hangs the washing. The shot catches first Dicey's smile for a white stranger, and then lingers on her face as her expression changes to a look first of shock and then of sorrow as she recognizes her granddaughter and realizes that she most probably has been passing. The sequence of double-takes is repeated when Pinky is stopped while walking in the black section of town by two drunken white men who protest that they can't "let no white girl walk by herself through this here nigger section." When Pinky announces "I live in this section," they take this as permission to assault her, forcibly holding up her face to the light to examine its color. Finally, in one of the most explicit representations of the power of the look to objectify, after Pinky wins her court case and inherits Miss Em's house and land the camera reveals her walking the gauntlet of white and predominantly male gazes as she exits the courtroom.

The film thus foregrounds the same emphasis on looking as *Gentleman's Agreement*, but with a difference. If *Pinky* encourages the audience to see

12. Aunt Dicey registers her sorrow when she realizes that Pinky has been passing for white in the North. *Pinky* (1949). Twentieth Century Fox.

what is not there—and thus believe there is a content to race beyond its visual manifestation—*Gentleman's Agreement* actively tries to prevent the audience from seeing the Jew, and encourages it to judge those who do. When Phil and his secretary discuss a job advertisement that states "Religion is a matter of indifference," Miss Wales disagrees with the policy. She comments, "It's no fun being the fall guy for the kikey ones. . . . You know the sort that starts trouble in a place like this. And the sort that doesn't, like you or me." Phil, never one to miss an opportunity to chastise, finishes her sentence: "because we don't look especially Jewish. Because it can be kept nice and comfortable and quiet." Indeed, tall, blond Miss Wales contradicts the traditional stereotypes of Jewish appearance. Yet the final purpose of the movie is to suggest that passing is finally impossible, not because there are essential Jewish characteristics that cannot be hidden (if there are, Miss Wales has successfully disguised them), but rather because a Jew who is passing is fundamentally *not a Jew*. To be Jewish, the "situation" must include individuals who identify you as such. Without that, the category of "Jew" has no meaning.[6]

The script of *Gentlemen's Agreement*, as might Sartre himself, ignores the possibility that Miss Wales herself might give the category meaning by having more than a formal relationship to her Jewishness. The movie follows the lead established in *Anti-Semite and Jew* and assumes that the Jews under consideration are entirely assimilated into American culture. Obviously, this assimilation is one with which critics did not always agree. Harold Rosenberg, reviewing *Anti-Semite and Jew* in *Commentary* in 1949, underlies the similarities between *Gentleman's Agreement* and Sartre's text

13. The white men hold Pinky's face up to see its color. *Pinky* (1949). Twentieth Century Fox.

when he adopts the same rhetorical strategy (and mining example) that Phil employs when describing his journalistic methodology. Rosenberg argues that Sartre believes "human identity can be deduced from 'environment.' To know a Flemish miner [one] would study his work and conditions and the landscape in which he lives, etc.; the same for a Parisian novelist" (11). Rosenberg argues to the contrary that the Jew has a history ("the common story of the Jews" [13]) and a cultural tradition ("the 'Jewish intellectual'" [14]) that forms the content of Jewishness. "Since the Jew possesses a unique identity which springs from his origin and his story," he can suppress it or celebrate it as he chooses. For those who choose celebration, Rosenberg maintains, "the Jewish identity has a remarkable richness" (18).

The distinction between Rosenberg's understanding of the Jew — one rooted in cultural and historical circumstances — and Sartre's — one constituted in a continual and immediate present through the scrutiny of others — underscores why the Jew might emerge as an existential hero. That he is the hero from the film's perspective goes without saying. The publication of his article presents Phil as a hard-hitting investigative journalist, a crusader for the values enshrined in the U.S. Constitution, who rallies his readers behind the *anti*-anti-Semitic cause. Most notably, one of the people who Phil must rally is his own fiancée, Kathy, who according to Anne Dettrey (Celeste Holm), the fashion editor of Phil's magazine, "hasn't got the guts to take the step from talking to action. One little action on one little front." Kathy appears, in her own words, a "little too well bred, self-confident, artificial, a trifle absurd, and typical New York," and part

14. Pinky exits the courtroom under the gaze of the white community. *Pinky* (1949). Twentieth Century Fox.

of the project of the movie is to release her from the social breeding that dictates, when faced with anti-Semitism, that the best thing to do is to "just [sit] there" and pretend it does not exist. This conflict between manners and ethics is explicitly staged at the end of the movie after Phil and Kathy have broken their engagement. Kathy goes to Dave Goldman to ask if he thinks she "is anti-Semitic" (Phil has made it clear that he does), and then describes being "ill . . . sick with rage and shame" at hearing "a vicious little story" at a dinner party. Kathy's reluctance to repeat the joke — "I can take naughty words, you know," Dave assures her — encapsulates her overall commitment to overlooking "vulgar" anti-Semitism for the sake of manners. Dave observes, "I wonder if you'd feel so sick now, Kathy, if you had nailed him. There's a funny kind of elation about socking back. I learned that a long time ago." Her lesson is to discover that it would be more upper class to confront the man with his unacceptable beliefs than to ignore them.

Kathy's conversion is central to the project of the movie more generally, which is less to wipe out anti-Semitism than to recast it as a properly lower-class phenomenon. It is not as if Phil Green is masquerading as a Jew at a dinner party where Representative John Elliott Rankin is "call[ing] people kikes." The only openly anti-Semitic characters — other than secretary Estelle Wales — are a drunken couple with rough accents and without a reservation at an expensive restaurant where Dave, Ann, Phil, and Kathy are eating dinner. Rather, the movie targets the "gentlemen" of the title who have an unspoken pact not to rent their summer houses to Jews, not because they do not like them, but because they do not want to cause a scandal with the neighbors. In fact, when Kathy refers to this arrangement (she herself does not want to rent her summerhouse to Dave), Phil is most shocked to note that she would use the word "gentlemen" to describe such people at all. It is the fuss that Kathy herself objects to, not Jews per se (although they do "always make trouble for everybody! Even their friends. They force people to take sides"). She calls off her marriage to Phil because of the "hothead shoutings and nerves" that any discussion of Jews inspires. The point is that to be anti-Semitic is not ethically questionable, but rather vulgar and low class.

Yet Phil is the existentialist hero as well. Though pretending to be Jewish when one is not might be thought to constitute precisely the kind of inauthenticity against which Sartrean existentialism ostensibly rails, his final realization that behaviors rather than essences determine the individual qualifies him for heroic status. If a person "cannot be distinguished from his situation, for it forms him and decides his possibilities," it is still up to him "to give it meaning, by making his choices within it and by it" (Sartre, *Anti-Semite* 60). Evaluations of authenticity will be made on the basis of those choices as such, not on whether those choices align with a putative internal essence or being. The ethical centrality of choice makes sense when applied to Jews as Jews, particularly after the Holocaust. But it makes less sense in *Gentleman's Agreement*. How do you assert your claim as a Jew when you are not a Jew, as Phil does?

The parallels among the instances emerge only when one realizes that, in Sartre's analysis, any claim that the Jew might make is by definition as specious as Phil's claims to Jewishness. In Sartre's account, the sole determinant that makes a Jew Jewish is his situation: the fact that he cannot be but a Jew in the associations in which he finds himself. Thus, under Sartre's definitions, even religious Jews need to be understood as Jews first and religious afterward. For Sartre, what we might think of as behavioral Judaism—the actual religious or cultural practices—cannot be constitutive of Jewishness. The anti-Semite does not actually care about how Jews behave: he cares about who they are. Sartre maintains that this in and of itself is a mistake. There is nothing essential or intrinsic in which that Jewishness might lie. But by this account, for a Jew to choose to be authentic means she must choose to make the same mistake about herself that others make about her. As with Holden Caulfield, whose situation made him *feel* like a deaf-mute (neither speech nor audition seem to help him improve his lot), and thus made it theoretically possible to *become* a deaf-mute, so too the Jew must embrace his situation. To be authentic, each Jew must acknowledge that — even though there is no essential Jewish quality, even though there is nothing to the concept of the Jew (as opposed to the Jewish religion) beyond the error of the anti-Semite — I am, nevertheless, a Jew.

The result is that the only time Dave Goldman references his own Jewishness is in response to anti-Semitism: a reference he makes to his children's first encounter with schoolyard anti-Semites, his comment to Kathy about discovering the "funny kind of elation about socking back," and his decision literally to "sock" the drunk couple at the restaurant when they call him a "yid." Similarly, for Phil, it matters not that he is not Jewish but that everyone thinks he is, as is blatantly illustrated in the scene at the Flume Inn: "authenticity for him is to live to the full his condition as Jew; inauthenticity is to deny it or to attempt to escape from it" (Sartre, *Anti-Semite* 91). And what might emerge as one of the more problematic moments in the film — when the gentile lectures the Jew about anti-Semitism — instead represents the fulfillment of the existentialist project. The Jew is inevitably and always a gentile first.

From an existentialist perspective, then, one of the central critical complaints one could make about *Gentleman's Agreement* turns out not to be a fault at all. Critics have long observed that the film's engagement with anti-Semitism itself is at best toothless and at worst an evasion of the issue so explicit that even Professor Lieberman himself might be proud. By imagining its victims to be "some innocent gentile who by putting on glasses mysteriously came to look Jewish" — in the words of Leslie Fiedler, discussing Arthur Miller's novel *Focus*— "or some high-minded reporter only pretending to be a Jew," the movie (and the novel on which its based) reinforce that "sneaking suspicion that Jew-baiting is real but Jews are imaginary, just as, to the same mind, witch-hunting is real but witches are only fictions" ("Bellow" 112). For Fiedler, Rosenberg, or Bell, this entirely misses the point of both Jewishness and anti-Semitism; for the existentialist, this position would be correct.[7] Jews do not exist beyond the perceptions of others.

This fact explains why at the end of *Gentleman's Agreement*, Phil, like all the other real and ostensible Jews in the movie — Professor Lieberman, Estelle Wales, and even Dave Goldman — is perfectly happy to leave Jewishness behind and begin his life with Kathy.[8] By comparison, at the end of *Pinky*, Pinky sues the county for her inheritance from Miss Em, wins her case, and stays in the South to start a school on the old plantation for "her people." Tom challenges her on this identification; "They're not your people, Pat," he insists. "Not really. There'll be no Pinky Johnson after we're married. You'll be Mrs. Thomas Adams for the rest of your life." But Pinky responds: "Tom, you can change your name. But I wonder if you can change what you really are, inside." While it would be appealing to imagine that Pinky rejects Tom's sexism as much as anything else, the movie is profoundly committed to imagining a specifically black racial essence (be it genetic, historical, or cultural) that transcends the contingencies of facial pigmentation.

The Jews are never really Jews in *Gentleman's Agreement*, yet to live authentically they must pretend to be because of the objectifying look of the anti-Semite. By comparison, African Americans are always black in *Pinky*, despite the fact that to gaze upon them may reveal no identifying racial markers. The disparity between these representations of the lived condition of two racial or ethnic minorities in the United States provides a brief reminder of the differences facing blacks and Jews as they struggled across the second half of the twentieth century for full participation in American civic life. As Karen Brodkin demonstrates, it was far easier for the Jew to be deracinated than for African Americans.[9] It is worth noting, however, that in these films the differing representations of Jews and blacks correlate with divergent attitudes toward both recent and antebellum history. In keeping with the postwar tendency to avoid overt mention of the Holocaust, the script of *Gentleman's Agreement* never even mentions the destruction of European Jewry. Though one might assume that an interest in anti-Semitism in 1947 could not avoid referencing the Holocaust in the minds of the audience, none of the characters (not even Dave Goldman, authentic Jewish spokesperson) mention why an article on anti-Semitism seems so timely to the editors of *Smith's Weekly*. Slavery, too, goes virtually unmentioned in *Pinky*. The only explicit reference to slavery, mentioned earlier, occurs when Pinky describes the run-down plantation house that becomes her inheritance as "slave built, slave run, and rundown ever since."

But the mere presence of that house, and its prominent placement in the *mise en scène* of many shots, continually suggests the source of Pinky's light skin. So, too, the film's plot, with its emphasis on legal versus genetic inheritance, cannot help but allude to the history of slavery in the United States and the sexual exploitation and abuse of slaves by whites. Surely no one in Pinky's community—or, for that matter, no one in the audience—can miss the fact that Pinky and Miss Em are potentially genetically related, even if they do not share a socially and legally recognized family. Her eventual legal inheritance of the house thus renders explicit an implicit genetic relation, and suggests an effort on the part of the film at least to acknowledge, if not correct, the historical crimes of slavery.

The differing attitudes toward history suggested by these films help explain why the existentialist ontology of self, particularly as represented in *Anti-Semite and Jew*, might have been so appealing a way of accounting for Jewish selfhood in the postwar period. In the eternal present of existentialist existence, in which the self is continually made and made over by the choice of the individual in the face of a hostile and alien world, the fact of recent Jewish history can be overlooked. The competing claims of the present versus the past, as part of the dilemmas of Jewish selfhood, are taken up in the next section, in which the problem of authenticity is explicitly staged as a conflict between the present and the past, between the lived traditions of history and the possibility of self-creation.

Seize the Day and the Authenticity of Failure

Sartre's insistence that the Jew exists only in the eyes of the anti-Semite might have been philosophically provocative, but its endorsement in a film such as *Gentleman's Agreement* was not enough to convince the community of American Jews that they were gentiles first and foremost. Leslie Fiedler, after commenting that in texts like *Gentleman's Agreement* Jew-baiting is real but the Jews themselves seem imaginary, argues in 1957 that "the Jews for the first time [have] move[d] into the center of American culture"—a moment Fiedler marked by "the appearance of Marjorie Morningstar on the front cover of *Time*" ("Bellow" 109, 110). Like Will Herberg, who claimed nothing is more "characteristically American than the historical evolution of American Jewry" (172), Fiedler maintained that in every level of American society, Jews—far from becoming imaginary—were "in the process of being mythicized into the representative American[s]" (110).[10] Between 1947 and 1957, the Jew in this analysis went from being imaginary to being an American Everyman. Andrew Hoberek's analysis of the class mobility of mid-century American Jews illustrates that "[t]he period following World War II was the classic era of Jewish assimilation, or incorporation into the American mainstream. Jews entered this period as nonwhite outsiders associated with foreignness, the working class, and disreputably left-leaning politics, and left it as mainstream white middle-class Americans" (71). What was to happen to their Jewishness in this process of first deracination, then assimilation, was the subject of much interest during the period, and inevitably had to struggle with the implications of existentialist thinking on the idea of the Jewish self. But the choices among suppressing, surpassing, or celebrating Jewish identity that Harold Rosenberg offered in response to Sartre's thesis were hardly as clear-cut as either Sartre or Rosenberg himself would suggest.

In Saul Bellow's 1956 novel *Seize the Day*, the choice appears at first to suppress (or more accurately, ignore) the past. As Emily Miller Budick observes, "There are probably few more assimilated Jewish characters in American literature than Tommy Wilhelm" (93). Jewish by birth, his "mother had belonged to the Reform congregation" and his father, Dr. Adler, "had no religion" (82). He changed his name from Wilhelm Adler to Tommy Wilhelm when he moved from New York to California to pursue a career in acting that ultimately failed. Since returning to New York, he separated from his wife and moved into the same hotel as his father—the Hotel Gloriana, most of whose guests are "past the age of retirement" (1). His job as a children's furniture salesman, lost months earlier, brought him into contact with all kinds of people, but when asked if some of his potential clients "don't like Jews?" he responds only that he "'can't afford to notice" (77).[11] It is hard to imagine Phil Green taking such slights so casually.

The novel follows Wilhelm along the course of a day in which his fortunes, already falling when the novel opens, ultimately fail. Fired from his job and harassed by his wife for support payments, he invests his last seven hundred dollars in commodities futures at the advice of a fellow hotel guest, Dr. Tamkin. Tamkin is a self-described psychiatrist, poet, and spiritual counselor, "a scientific man," who may or may not be a con artist—

"a case for the district attorney's office to investigate" (54). By the conclusion of the novel, he appears to have fleeced Wilhelm of those final funds. As the day progresses, the novel presents numerous examples of Wilhelm's ill-fit with a world defined by material and financial success. It is a world in which "[e]veryone [is] supposed to have money" and "made it a shame not to have [it]" (27). It is populated by a "heartless, flaunting, boisterous business class" (60) that indulges in "the cynicism of successful people" (13). Wilhelm himself is "horrified" by cynicism, though he fears it is "necessary" for success. Constantly tired, he attributes his fatigue to that omnipresent "cynicism. Too much of the world's business done. Too much falsity." He repeatedly berates himself and the world both: "Chicken! Unclean! Congestion! . . . Rat Race! Phony! Murder! Play the Game! Buggers!" (13–14). He is the unclean chicken who cannot "play the game," but the world itself is populated by phonies and murderers.

Seize the Day is thus simultaneously an analysis of the particular place of failure during a historical moment marked by remarkable affluence, and of the relations among male generations—father, son, and "Machiavellian surrogate father" (Fiedler 114) in the form of Dr. Tamkin.[12] During a period in which prosperity more generally was reflected in the American Jews' "continued ascent en masse into the American middle class" (Shapiro 125), Bellow in *Seize the Day* portrays failure—economic, romantic, and familial—as the backdrop against which the generational conflicts of the novel play out. Like Holden Caulfield, whose own refusal to play the game on ethical grounds appeared only as an inability to succeed at it, Wilhelm's failure in the novel is represented as the most authentic thing about him. He refuses to succumb to the cynicism (or phoniness) that is necessary for success, despite his misery over his lost prospects. But as the novel illustrates, that which makes Wilhelm the most authentic is also what makes him the most Jewish—through the particular role that failure was imagined to play in reforming postwar American values. That failure is also the thing that makes his father most despise him, representing as it does an affront to Dr. Adler's sense of his own self-worth.

Wilhelm and his father appear oppositely in the novel. Dr. Adler "uphold[s] tradition" whereas Wilhelm is "for the new" (11). In keeping with the focus on the look in *Gentleman's Agreement*, the novel presents its respective characters highly visually—to the point where Cynthia Ozick observes of *Seize the Day* that Bellow has "invented a refreshed phrenology.... wherein higher consciousness can infiltrate portraiture" (xv–xvi). The older man, recently retired from his medical practice, is "idolized" for being "a fine old scientist, clean and immaculate," who "stands straight and understands everything you say" (Bellow, *Seize* 9). A "master of social behavior" (25), Dr. Alder literally and metaphorically "still has all his buttons" (9). His flawless self-presentation is indicative of the profound self-discipline that produced his considerable material success. That self-discipline likewise recoils from the requests for sympathy that Wilhelm solicits at every turn (8, 24, 42, 46, 50, and 106). He pleads to his father: "[i]t isn't all a question of money — there are other things a father can give to a son" (106). By comparison, Wilhelm — or Wilky, as his father calls him — was once a good-looking fellow who "could charm a bird out of a tree" (3). With the turn of his fortunes, however, he has grown "untidy" and "unrested," with "eyes red-rimmed from excessive smoking" (29). "A wide wrinkle like a comprehensive bracket sign was written upon his forehead, the point between his brows" (4) and "on his broad back, stooped with its own weight, its strength warped almost into deformity, the collar of his sports coat appeared anyway to be no wider than a ribbon" (13). Dr. Alder is "ashamed of" Wilhelm (11) for "let[ting] himself go and look[ing] like hell" (29); Wilhelm resents his father for being "a selfish old man" (23) who "behaved toward his son as he had formerly done toward his patients," without "family sense" (8).

The generational differences the novel charts are represented through an early miscommunication, when Wilhelm, his father, and Mr. Perls (a fellow German Jewish resident of the hotel) discuss Wilhelm's former job with the Rojax Corporation. Wilhelm explains that his employer "took a son-in-law into the business — a new fellow" on the pretense that Wilhelm's sales territory was too big for one person. In fact, Wilhelm explains, it was because he was in line to be made "an officer of the corporation. Vice President" (32), and the corporation did not want to give him that position:

> "I can't let them get away with it," he said. "It's also a question of morale."
> His father corrected him. "Don't you mean a moral question, Wilky?"
> "I mean that, too. I have to do something to protect myself. I was promised executive standing." Correction before a stranger mortified him, and

his dark-blond face changed color, more pale, then more dark. He went on talking to Perls, but his eyes spied on his father. "I was the one who opened the territory for them. I could go back for one of their competitors and take away their customers. *My* customers. Morale enters into it because they've tried to take away my confidence." (33–34)[13]

The moment embodies much of the distinction between Wilhelm's and Dr. Alder's outlook. Adopting the terms used by David Riesman to illustrate the generational shift from the inner- to the other-directed — "From Morality to Morale" (the title of a chapter in *The Lonely Crowd*) — the novel characterizes Wilhelm as other-directed, concerned with morale, hurt feelings, and his stolen confidence.[14] Any retaliation, even the ethically dubious action of stealing Rojax's customers — "*My* customers," Wilhelm corrects himself — is justified in the view of such an offense. Wilhelm's repeated and desperate pleas for his father's acceptance epitomize the other-directed belief that "[a]pproval itself, irrespective of content, [is] almost the only unequivocal good" (Riesman, *Lonely* 48). By comparison, for Dr. Alder the word "morale" has no meaning in these circumstances. Were the question genuinely about morality, he might have had sympathy. But the Rojax Corporation is well within its rights to bring in a son-in-law as a salesperson. Wilhelm's feelings are irrelevant to the situation at hand. Possessing the code of abstract values that defines inner direction, Dr. Adler — like inner-directed parents more generally — is able to "'love' only those children who made good in the outer world" (48). His strict adherence to deportment suggests this internalized morality, even as his disgust at his son's hygiene illustrates a larger abhorrence of his son's excessive regard for his own feelings. "[H]e may be trying to teach me that a grown man should be cured of such feeling" (53), Wilhelm realizes. But to be cured of feeling would mean succumbing to the cynicism so prevalent among his more successful peers.

Tracking the differences between Dr. Adler and Wilhelm — between the respect for tradition and the embrace of the new — in terms of Riesman's description of inner- and other-directed character, the novel represents two models of the self as determined by environment. Yet there is a third model that the novel puts forth: Dr. Tamkin's, whose existentialist mantra of "Seize the day" (62) is honored with the book's title. Dr. Tamkin operates as a surrogate father for Wilhelm; he "sympathizes with [him]" (8) and claims to have been "treating" (68) him without his knowledge. His putative psychiatric practice is about "[b]ringing people into the here-and-now ... The past is no good to us. The future is full of anxiety. Only the present is real" (62). He advocates "'here-and-now' mental exercises" to stop his patients from fixating on "the future and the past" (85): "'Here and now I see a man.' 'Here and now I see a man sitting on a chair.' ... Grasp the hour, the moment, the instant" (86). To account for the inconsistencies one finds in people, he theorizes, "In here, the human bosom ... there isn't just one soul. There's a lot of souls":

> But there are two main ones. The real soul and a pretender soul. Now! ... The interest of the pretender soul is the same as the interest of the social life, the society mechanism. This is the main tragedy of human life. Oh it is terrible! Terrible! You are not free. Your own betrayer is inside of you and sells you out. You have to obey him like a slave. He makes you work like a horse. And for what? For who? ... The purpose is to keep the whole thing going. The true soul is the one that pays the price. It suffers and gets sick and it realizes that the pretender can't be loved. Because the pretender is a lie. The true soul loves the truth. (66–67)

The "pretender soul," representing the "society mechanism," mimics precisely the model of phoniness described by Holden Caulfield and others. Compelling the "real soul" for the purposes of social advancement, the pretender soul embodies "the social life." It is the internalized social coercion that was imagined to be a particularly mid-century American malaise. The pretender soul betrays the authentic soul "to keep the whole thing going": the social and material world that values cynicism and monetary success above all else. And as with other discussions of phoniness, that oppression ultimately proves damaging to that "real soul," which grows sick and "feeble" under the pretender soul's parasitic control. Holden's original model of phoniness imagined a mutable exterior that could be falsified, and an authentic interior that represented the genuine self. Tamkin's model suggests each self is in fact two selves, one tuned to the impulse of social success, another representing the genuine person that is defeated in its inclination toward the truth.

Wilhelm finds comfort in Tamkin's philosophizing. "In Tommy he saw the pretender" (68) responsible for his impetuous decision to abandon his father's name and seek success as an actor in Hollywood. At the opening of the novel, he had understood the change of his name as "his bid for liberty. Adler being in his mind the title of the species, Tommy the freedom of the person." A man "[w]hen he's young and strong and impulsive and dissatisfied with the way things are" believes he can "rearrange things to assert his freedom." But, Wilhelm realized, "[i]n middle age you no longer thought such thoughts about free choice" (21). To imagine Tommy instead as a "pretender soul," rather than as a symbol of his failure at self-creation, leaves open the possibility for change, for the chance for the "real soul" to break free. Yet, as Wilhelm quickly realizes, "even Wilky might not be himself":

> Might the name of his true soul be the one by which his old grandfather had called him — Velvel? The name of a soul, however, must be only that — soul. What did it look like? Does my soul look like me? Is there a soul that looks like Dad? Like Tamkin? Where does the true soul get its strength? Why does it have to love truth? (68)

His movement through the various names available to him — from Tommy, the self-created actor; to Wilky, his father's nickname for him and connected to his patronymic Adler; and finally to the Yiddish Velvel — Wilhelm seeks an authentic self that might be divorced from the "society mechanism" that demands a phony self-presentation for success. Yet he likewise moves back through the recent generations of Jews. Tommy suggests the fully assimilated, American Jew with no real contact to his faith, whereas the name Wilky Adler evokes the prewar German Jewish communities of his father, the inner-directed generation that internalized certain principles of the ethical and successful life, and then brought them to the United States. That community was known for its integration within German culture more broadly, and in the United States for its initial anxiety about later Jewish emigration from Eastern Europe, whose "crude religion [and] extreme radicalism" might undermine their assimilated middle- and upper-class status.[15] But the Yiddish nickname Velvel suggests a further retreat, to a time before assimilation, when Jewish culture was still a separate subcommunity within various national and linguistic communities. Wilhelm's initial fantasies of authenticity are likewise fantasies of increasing immersion in Yiddishkeit.

The rumination does not end with Velvel, however. If authenticity is based primarily in genetic and linguistic — which is to say, cultural — history, one could count back through the generations, and the languages in which they spoke, indefinitely. Wilhelm's movement through the previous three generations thus suggests the elusiveness of authenticity: at what point does one find the authentic name or the authentic self? When does one stop going back? As Wilhelm later recognizes, neither genealogy nor language and cultural history guarantees authenticity, or, for that matter, even connections among their speakers and members. The truth is "[e]very other man spoke a language entirely his own, which he had figured out by private thinking; he had his own ideas and peculiar ways." Language here shades into both thinking and ritualized behavior, through which culture is constituted. Wilhelm continues, "If you wanted to talk about a glass of water, you had to start back with God created the heaven and earth; the apple; Abraham; Moses and Jesus; Rome, the Middle Ages; gunpowder; the Revolution; back to Newton; up to Einstein; then war and Lenin and Hitler" (79). The relevant history is what might be thought of as mainstream American: Jewish and Christian (Moses and Jesus), with European roots (Rome, the Middle Ages), and American specificity (the Revolution). It is only after "reviewing this and getting it all straight again you could proceed to talk about a glass of water. 'I'm fainting, get me a little water.' You were lucky even then to make yourself understood" (79–80). The realization is one of profound alienation, in which shared cultural history guarantees nothing. It must be re-created exhaustively in each encounter between strangers.

Instead, the real or authentic soul is imagined to be prelinguistic and precultural. After rejecting Velvel as his authentic self, Wilhelm decides, "The name of a soul, however, must be only that — soul" (68). Like the individual who speaks his own language and performs his own "peculiar ways," the easy connections implied by shared names and shared culture are false — just part of the pretender soul's adherence to the society mechanism. In this way, living in Dr. Tamkin's continuous present seems to make sense. Con artist though he may be, Tamkin's idea of the self as existing only in the here-and-now fits not only with Wilhelm's prelinguistic soul, but also with Sartre's image of the Jew as only constituted through the gaze of the anti-Semite. Both share the idea that the social world — through the pretender soul's machinations or the look of the other — traps and falsifies the self.

This model of self is mirrored in Bellow's discussions of his own literary practice, in which he notoriously resisted any attempt to define him as primarily a Jewish writer. In a detailed analysis of Bellow's writings about his craft, Michael Kramer explains that for Bellow, "A true writer, committed to his art, cannot *by definition* be a Jewish writer in this sense. He cannot be defined by his roots" (9, emphasis in original). Bellow's Foreword to Allan Bloom's polemic against multiculturalism, *The Closing of the American Mind* (1987), addresses the problem. Published in the same year as *The Thanatos Syndrome*, Bellow's Foreword suggests a frustration, similar to Walker Percy's, with the idea that individuals are fundamentally constructed through their cultural, ethnic, or racial contexts. He argues that that "[t]he commonest teaching of the civilized world in our time can be stated simply: 'Tell me where you come from and I will tell you what you are'" (13). Bellow explains that "as a Midwesterner, the son of immigrant parents, I recognized at an early age that I was called upon to decide for myself to what extent my Jewish origins, my surroundings (the accidental circumstances of Chicago), my schooling, were to be allowed to determine the course of my life." His careful phrasing — these "accidental" and contingent factors either were or were not "*to be allowed* to determine" a life's course (emphasis added) — mimics the existentialist belief that ontological freedom demands one resist the temptation of mere facticity.[16] There can be "a free for-itself only as engaged in a resisting world" (Sartre, *Being* 621). Such phrasing likewise suggests the source of Bellow's own sense of superiority (apparent everywhere in the Foreword) in relation to the trend toward culturalist models of the self that Bloom's book excoriates. Some individuals might succumb to the constitutive influences of the environment, but Bellow would not permit himself "to be wholly dependent on history and culture" (Bellow, "Foreword" 13). Yet the conflict between a desire for self-creation that rejects "Jewish origins," and the inevitable "history of the collectivity of which he is a part" (Sartre, *Being* 619) which forms part of one situation, constitutes one of the central interests of *Seize the Day*.

In *Seize the Day*, one way in which this conflict appears is in the omnipresence of Jewish references through which all three of the models of self—generational (Wilhelm), cultural-historical (Dr. Adler), and existentialist (Tamkin)—are presented. As Gaye McCollum Simmons's work demonstrates, though the novel does not provide moments of a particularly Jewish self-identification, it does contain references to a Jewishness that—while not constitutive of the self—is nevertheless a persistent part of the cultural field against which the novel unfolds. When asked whether he has "reserved his seat in the synagogue for Yom Kippur," Wilhelm reflects that "he should say a prayer for Mother once and a while.... At the cemetery Wilhelm had paid a man to say a prayer for her." Though he does not attend services, Wilhelm "would occasionally perform certain devotions, according to his feelings. Now he reflected, in Dad's eyes I am the wrong kind of Jew. He doesn't like the way I act. Only he is the right kind of Jew" (82–83). The moment provides another version of the other- versus inner-directed divergence between Wilhelm and his father; Wilhelm prays according to "feeling" whereas Dr. Adler imagines as wrong a Jew who does not attend to a ritualized code. But crucially, Wilhelm is "the wrong *kind* of Jew" (emphasis added). He is still, however, a Jew. Such a formulation palpably demonstrates the difficulty of letting go of a Jewishness that is defined in cultural, historical, or racial terms.[17]

Yet there is another way in which Jewishness is figured in the text, one that avoids the ambiguities of the existential model and, as importantly, is consistent with the novel's interest in David Riesman's theories of character. Writing in 1948 Riesman provided an analysis of the importance of "the nerve of failure" for individuals, the Jewish community, and American culture more generally. "A Philosophy for 'Minority' Living: The Jewish Situation and the 'Nerve of Failure'" imagines the nerve of failure to be "the nerve to be oneself when that self is not approved of by the dominant ethic of a society" (413). To be willing to fail as a consequence of one's values is to "have the capacity to go it alone" (413) and define a private view of success, "to face [one's] situation realistically and yet be unshaken by what the majority considers 'failure'" (414). In this sense, the individual is to follow the guidance of his "true soul" and have faith in his own "peculiar ways"—to use Tamkin's phrase: "'to love the truth'" and avoid the "'pretender [which] is a lie'" (Bellow, *Seize* 67).

Riesman argues that the Jew's historical position of economic and social isolation uniquely situated him to possess the "nerve of failure." It granted him a particular "attitude" — to use Louis Menand's term — toward mainstream social and material success by positioning him outside of the customary routes to social and material power. Jews were thus uniquely positioned to see "'through' power by observing its blindness in comparison to the weak" ("Philosophy" 414). With immigration and assimilation, however, Jews forfeited this authenticating distance from mainstream culture "in return for a chance to participate in the wider world" (415). "The melting pot," which produces "'Americans all' of a starched uniformity, freed of all cultural coloring" (416), encouraged the Jewish immigrant "to discard his own values without assimilating prevailing values. As a result he often became a caricature of the American careerist" (417). Riesman's characterization of the Jew as a caricature here is telling: to be truly a careerist one would have to internalize the values that align success with material worth, whereas a caricature performs the role of the careerist, masking a cynicism "that seeks money and power without the conviction that they represent the fruits of virtue" (417). In this sense, the successful Jew is a phony. His traditional values teach him the paucity of material success as a guarantor of ethical superiority, but his contemporary setting encourages and rewards precisely that success. In the economic market, everyone must "'show one's stuff' . . . and one's stuff is one's 'personality,' an externalized part of the self." Prefiguring the terms of Dr. Tamkin's social critique, Riesman argues that it is "not the genuine self that is put on the market in the race for economic achievement but the 'cosmetic' self, which is as free of any aroma of personal, non-marketable idiosyncrasy as it is free of 'B.O.' or last year's waistline" ("Philosophy" 416). Substitute "cosmetic self" and "genuine self" for "pretender soul" and "real soul," and you have a version of Tamkin's philosophy.

The purpose of Riesman's analysis is less to argue that Jews inevitably will fail to embody fully the values of mainstream America — and thus fail to achieve an American success — as to assert how their willingness to redefine success through the nerve of failure might serve the needs of Americans more generally. As he notes, "it would be unfair to blame Jews for losing their traditional ethics in the melting pot, as to blame them for not emerging from it as Anglo-Saxon gentlemen" (420). The melting pot aims to produce a "starched uniformity," but it does not always succeed. What Riesman seeks is a reinterpretation of Jewish values so as "to foster a Jewish self-image independent of the majority ethic." He wants the Jewish community to be willing to risk failure on mainstream terms since "the experience of many Jews in America must be that this adherence [to mainstream values] is emotionally precarious, and that it easily becomes self-destructive once things do not go well for oneself or one's group" (422). The nerve of failure, with its goal of "independence from the majority," would produce gains "in the happier lives of Jews" and reduce "Jewish self-contempt" (422). As important, this redefinition might give majority American culture the opportunity to reevaluate and develop its own values. Formulating the belief that would appear in *The Lonely Crowd*, Riesman's conclusion returns his discussion to the individual to consider the particularly *social* importance of the self that "is not approved of by the dominant ethic of society" (413). It echoes an assertion from *The Lonely Crowd* that since "people may be compelled to behave in one way although their character structures them to behave in the opposite way . . . the disparity between socially required behavior and characterologically compatible behavior is one of the great levers of change" (29).[18] The minority group, in its inability to embody the "starched uniformity" of majority culture, shows that culture "our compelling need of the nerve of failure to defend an independent view of the self and of what life holds" ("Philosophy" 422).

Wilhelm's failure thus ends up being simultaneously the most authentic, and also the most Jewish, thing about him. Further, it suggests a larger purpose to his life. Twice the narrator suggests that he might play a symbolic role within a larger human context. While Wilhelm discusses his loss of morale with Dr. Adler and Mr. Perls, the narrator comments that "[t]he peculiar burden of his existence lay upon him. . . . he was apt to feel this mysterious weight, this growth or collection of nameless things which it was the business of his life to carry about" (35). Later, when Wilhelm sits with his father and resists—unsuccessfully, as it turns out—the temptation to seek sympathy, the narrator states:

> But at the same time, since there were depths in Wilhelm not unsuspected by himself, he received a suggestion from some remote element in his thoughts that the business of life, the real business—to carry his peculiar

burden, to feel shame and impotence, to taste these quelled tears — the only important business, the highest business was being done. Maybe the making of mistakes expressed the very purpose of his life and the essence of his being here. Maybe he was supposed to make them and suffer from them on this earth. (52)

Alluding to these "not unsuspected" depths, the narrator intimates that Wilhelm is correct to believe in his own importance with regard to "the business of life," the universal project on which life itself dwells. That twice-repeated phrase evokes the times when Wilhelm himself refers to "the world's business" (14, 32) as making money. However, its modification in this passage by the phrase "the real business" suggests its relative importance by comparison. Similarly, the use of the adjective "real" links "the business of life" with the authenticity of a "real soul," even as both uses of the adjective "peculiar" refer the reader to the "peculiar ways" (79) that are the individual's own and not part of any cultural past. The passages thus emphasize both Wilhelm's authentic individuation and his universal purpose. What that purpose might be remains suggested only through the series of active verbs that define the crowds on upper Broadway in the final pages of the novel, and suggest the type of immediacy, the here-and-now, that Dr. Tamkin puts forth: "And the great, great crowd, the inexhaustible current of millions of every race and kind pouring out, pressing round, of every age, of every genius, possessors of every human secret, antique and future, in every face the refinement of one particular motive or essence — *I labor, I spend, I strive, I design, I love, I cling, I uphold, I give way, I envy, I long, I scorn, I die, I hide, I want*" (111). For Wilhelm, that motive might be "*I bear*," or even "*I fail.*" If we take seriously Riesman's claim that failure has the purpose of modeling the reinterpretation of mainstream standards of success, then the failure of Wilhelm's "own values" of feeling rather than cynicism at the hand of the "stronger oppressive power" (Riesman, "Philosophy" 422) demonstrates one area in which that reinterpretation might begin.

In this sense, Wilhelm emerges as the type of model that Riesman suggests the Jewish minority as a whole might represent in American culture: the embodiment of a different value system — in this case, a system that puts "feelings" ahead of material gain and insists cynicism is too high a price to pay for material success. In the final moments of the novel, when Wilhelm weeps at the funeral of a stranger, the release of emotions takes him "past words, past reason, coherence" (113). The narrator says that he "alone of all the people in the chapel, was sobbing" (114). Wilhelm thus emerges as the chosen mourner, not only of the stranger but of himself and everyone else: "The source of all tears had suddenly sprung open within him, black, deep, and hot, and they were pouring out and convulsed his body. . . . The flowers and lights fused ecstatically in Wilhelm's blind, wet, eyes; the heavy sea-like music came up to his ears. It poured into him where he had hidden himself in the center of a crowd by the great and happy oblivion of tears. He heard it and sank deeper than sorrow, through torn sobs and cries toward the consummation of his heart's ultimate need" (113–14). At once he weeps for everyone, from "the source of all tears," and for himself, in response to an authentic "ultimate need." Yet in foregrounding the costs of such failure over the 115-odd pages of the novel itself, *Seize the Day* suggests the costs to the individual of such individuality, the psychic expenses in being one of Riesman's "great levers of change" (*Lonely* 29).

Marjorie Morningstar and Real Phony Jews

Herman Wouk's novel *Marjorie Morningstar* was a bestseller in 1955.[19] Set in 1930s New York City, the novel tells the story of Marjorie Morgenstern, a young Jewish woman whose parents have just moved from the Bronx to the Upper West Side. The story is of the successful Jews, the ones who assimilate and manage — unlike poor Tommy Wilhelm — to achieve middle-class respectability. Marjorie's father is not educated but does well as a manufacturer. Her mother is a repository of middle-class common sense who wants Marjorie to marry up, preferably to the heir of a major department store. Marjorie herself begins the novel as a freshman at Hunter College and wants to be an actress. Wouk portrays his female lead as continually negotiating the terms of her assimilation into mainstream American culture: she plots to change her name to Marjorie Morningstar for a stage career, endlessly debates whether to eat bacon and lobster, and is embarrassed by her *Yiddishkeit* relatives like her Uncle Samson-Aaron, who speaks with a heavy Eastern European accent, performs folk dances, and overeats at her brother's Bar Mitzvah. Edward S. Shapiro writes that the ostensible "theme of the novel is the conflict between Marjorie's two selves, the aspiring actress Marjorie Morningstar, who rejects Jewish middle-class values, and Marjorie Morgenstern, who wants to marry and have children" (157). But the novel is also the story of the clash between "the adolescent, the rebel . . . the Bohemian" and "the adult, the respectable—the Bourgeois" (Fitch 132). The Bohemian is represented by Noel Airman—né Saul Ehrmann—a Broadway librettist with a symbolically deformed arm. Noel longs to be Noel Coward, seduces Marjorie after they meet at a resort in the Catskills, strings her along for two years, and then abandons her for the decadence of prewar Montmartre. The bourgeois is Marjorie herself, who after pursuing Noel to Paris, decides he is not worth it and returns home to become Mrs. Milton Schwartz of Mamaroneck, New York. Though her premarital sexuality constitutes "a permanent crippling, like a crooked arm" (553), at the end of the novel she lives happily with her husband and children.

The novel was widely condemned by critics who denounced its tedious length and pedestrian writing. Most scathingly, Norman Podhoretz claimed that, in his efforts to render "the feel of an emotion or a mood or a conversation," Wouk "points vaguely into space like a blind man trying to locate an object in an unfamiliar room" (186). Yet in its conflict between the free-spirited and the respectable, critics like Podhoretz and Robert E. Fitch found something more substantial to dislike: namely, the way in which the novel appeared to celebrate a Jewish middle-class existence at the expense of quasi-nonconformist experimentation. In this reading, Marjorie's eventual life in Mamaroneck is the consequence not of her "unfortunate impulse to conform"—first to Noel's Greenwich Village philosophy and then to the conventionality of her upbringing—but of the novel's overall belief that it is a mistake to possess "an appetite for diverse areas of experience [and] an unwillingness to settle into the common routines." *Marjorie Morningstar* is thus an endorsement of American youth in general, who get married "so early," choose careers "so sagely," and face life "so soon with a sober countenance, a steady hand, and resigned knowledge of human limitation." It reveals not "the 'glorification' of bourgeois life but the *Weltanschauung* of America's young adults" (Podhoretz 187), who achieve respectability not because they actually *respect* respectability, but because of, as Riesman might have said, a "classical 'failure of nerve'" (Fitch 133). In this sense the novel becomes the anti–*Catcher in the Rye*. It, too, reconciles its heroine with the practical realities of adulthood, but unlike *Catcher*, it never suggests that adolescent rebellions might be useful as a technology of authenticity — a means of establishing a "modest degree of contempt" (Menand 84) for social norms that mark the adult's distance and autonomy from his social milieu. As the first chapter suggests, the absence of such distance equals the type of real phoniness to which Holly Golightly succumbs.

What upsets the critics the most, however, is the novel's putative assumption that the future of American Jewishness lies in what Daniel Bell referred to, as mentioned at the beginning of this chapter, as the "embourgeoisement" (474) of Jewish life. As Podhoretz demands, "Why is it that all the vulgarities and accidental accretions of American Jewish life are urged upon us as part of the burden a Jew must carry — as though weddings at the Pierre and catering by Lowenstein and the suburban kaffeeklatsch have achieved the status of the *mitzvot*?" (188). It is certainly true that the novel ends with Marjorie fully ensconced in the type of suburban institutional life that Daniel Bell fears, in which memory is satisfied, "when there is no faith, by 'good works'" (474). As rejected suitor Wally Wronken observes at the end of the novel, Marjorie in adulthood is "a regular synagogue goer, active in the Jewish organizations of the town . . . [and] rather strictly observant." When he tries to "pin her down on what she really believed," Marjorie makes no clear statement of faith: "She was curiously evasive" (Wouk, *Marjorie* 562). Yet for Podhoretz to say that the novel advocates this type of Jewishness is not precisely correct. In the conflict represented between Noel and Marjorie, the bohemian and the bourgeois, *Marjorie Morningstar* presents equal ambivalence about both lifestyles. The life that emerges as authentic is that of a relatively minor character — Michael Eden — who Marjorie meets on her way to Europe.

What is important for this study are the terms through which the novel's analysis of mid-century American Jews is rendered. As the bohemian, Noel Airman is an "egregious phony" (21), to quote William du Bois. The insubstantiality of Noel's iconoclastic philosophy is summed up through his ultimate lack of accomplishment. Nor does he achieve the symbolic failure of Wilhelm that establishes the latter's authenticity. Though he talks a good game, he never achieves any kind of success. His Broadway debut quickly closes, and the end of the novel finds him "a third-rate baldish television writer" (560) living off his wife. Wally describes him: "'he does a little of this and a little of that, a tune, a lyric, a piano solo, an orchestra arrangement... a conversation in French, a conversation in Spanish, an argument about Freud or Spengler, and that's Noel Airman, the beginning and end of him'" (218). This is to say, Airman is an "air man," a *luftmensch*, a dilettante without substance. By comparison, rejected Wally Wronken emerges as the more genuine version of the artist; he becomes a successful playwright and is granted the privilege of passing judgment on what Marjorie becomes. Yet much like Tamkin, whose status as the con artist cannot fully undermine the value of his thinking about the self, Noel's critique of Marjorie is ultimately borne out. After their first romantic encounter, Noel clarifies for Marjorie why they cannot be a couple. She is a "golden-haloed Shirley" (174), a type with whom Noel promised himself he would no longer engage. In college, he explains:

> I went out with Shirley after Shirley. It was uncanny. She was everywhere. I would hear about some wonderful new girl — Susan Fain, Helen Kaplan, Judy Morris, her name didn't matter. I'd telephone her, make a date, go up to the apartment, she'd open the door — and there would stand Shirley. In a different dress, a different body, looking at me out of different eyes, but with that one unchanging look, the look of Shirley. The respectable girl, the mother of the next generation, all tricked out to appear gay and girlish and carefree, but with a terrible threatening solid dullness jutting through, like the gray rocks under the spring grass in Central Park. (171–72)

Noel's scathing denunciation of middle-class respectability adopts an image of uniformity as the source of its critique. The numerous Shirleys replicate themselves across the Upper West Side, though they are not solely a Jewish phenomenon. Noel explains, "'It is a general problem, not a Jewish one.... Shirley Jones has the same nature as Shirley Cohn'" (174). A Shirley inevitably maintains that "she's going to *be* somebody. Not just a wife" — she inevitably plays the part of "Lady Brett Ashley with witty devil-may-care whimsy and shocking looseness" — but in these protestations she is false.[20] Her performance is a "'dismal caricature... and nothing but talk'" (173). In this sense Shirley is a phony, much as Noel himself is a phony. Both put on the trappings of bohemia with neither genuine conviction (in

Marjorie's case) nor genuine talent (in Noel's). In "talk[ing] Lady Brett and act[ing] Shirley" (173), Marjorie's exterior performance is a caricature, much as Riesman's successful Jew is "a caricature of the American careerist" ("Philosophy" 417) — roles put on for social advancement that conceal one's lack of conviction.

But if Marjorie as Shirley is a phony, she is also a real phony. Like Holly Golightly, she actually "believes all this crap she believes" (Capote 29). In protest against Noel's characterization, Marjorie insists she is "*going to be an actress*, not a fat dull housewife with a big engagement ring," but she is "increasingly uneasy at every word he was saying" (173). Astonished "when a shudder broke through her frame" (172), Marjorie registers somatically the truth of Noel's observations, even though she cannot or will not register it consciously. In a telling encounter, Marjorie's mother accuses her, "You told Papa that you don't want to marry Noel. Don't tell *me* such stories. . . . You think you're going to get this fellow to marry you, and steady down, and use his talents and become someone big." Not exactly adverse to the idea — "Listen, it's a very tough job, but it's possible" — her mother encourages Marjorie to leave the resort to make Noel miss her. Marjorie insists, "I'm not planning to marry him. I'm not planning anything. I'm just *enjoying* myself"; her mother replies, "All right. Marjorie remains Marjorie. Say what you please" (206). Her insistence on her own nonconformity is "Marjorie remain[ing] Marjorie," simultaneously an essential part of her identity and also not truly her. As was observed of Holly Golightly, even though Marjorie experiences herself as real, there is another real that is somehow more real that Marjorie is supposed to be.

Yet this movement from "Lady Brett Ashley," who is really Shirley playing a role, to Shirley herself seeking a husband, and then to Marjorie who was raised to be Shirley, inevitably raises the question of which part, if any, is supposed to be the ostensibly real Marjorie. Like Wilhelm Adler, traveling back through the names that may belong to his true soul, in Shirley, Marjorie, too, may have found just another pretender. The very use of the word "Shirley" as the label of a type rather than the name of an individual suggests as much. As Noel observes, Shirleys are created by a particular upbringing and social environment. The reason Shirley Jones and Shirley Cohn can be the same is because they are raised "in the same milieu" and are "in the same jam." They naturally "evolve[d] into the same creature"

(174). Noel insists, "I'm not blaming Shirley for anything" (173). Shirley is a product of her culture. Later, when Noel abandons Marjorie via letter for Paris, he elaborates, "It all goes much beyond your conscious intent. You can't help being what you are.... I could never work the slightest alteration in YOU. From the first moment I encountered you, you have never changed an iota, never deviated from your line by a hair. You were, you are, you always will be, SHIRLEY" (430). The product of her environment or "milieu," whatever "real soul" Marjorie might have possessed has disappeared in the miasma of familial and cultural influence.

Ironically, the one character on which the novel provides the imprimatur of authenticity is the one character who Holden Caulfield, in his superficial judgments, might have described as phony. Michael Eden is ostensibly a chemical salesman whom Marjorie meets while crossing the Atlantic after Noel in 1938. During this interlude, the tone of the novel shifts from melodrama to spy thriller, as Mike tells Marjorie mysterious details about himself that she does not know how to reconcile. He claims to be "just a Kiwanis Club boy," but as Marjorie observes, "Kiwanis Club boys don't usually know that they're just Kiwanis Club boys" (463). Of course, Marjorie's instincts are exactly right. With his American passport and non-Jewish sounding name, he is helping Jews to flee Germany in what the readers recognize as the spring before *Kristallnacht*. Like Phil Green, Mike Eden is passing, but also like Phil Green, he is passing for a good cause — to help the Jews. He describes his genesis as a spy in a suicidal depression that drove him to a renowned psychoanalyst in Berlin. He was cured, not by the analyst himself, but by spiriting the analyst out of Germany. At this point, the difference between a real problem (genocide and the lives of millions) and a phony problem (suicide and the life of one), is made clear. "Most of the ones I go after have little kids," he explains. "I'm happiest when there's a kid in the picture. Who knows which of those kids is going to be a Heine, or Disraeli, or Einstein, or Freud?" (510). Though Marjorie begs him to return with her to safety in the United States, Mike is the novel's martyr; he is sacrificed for European Jewry. More immediately, he is also sacrificed so that Marjorie will finally see through Noel, whose apolitical attitudes toward the worsening European situation — not to mention his love affair with his German landlady — make him naïve and foolish in Marjorie's eyes.

All of this places Marjorie's final embrace of her inner Shirley in an ambiguous light. The novel's conclusion jumps fifteen years forward to 1954 as Wally Wronken evaluates Marjorie's married life in Mamaroneck; like Holly Golightly, whose real phoniness prevents her from telling her own story, Marjorie's ending must be represented from another character's point of view for her suburban "*embourgeoisement*" to have any poignancy. As this book shows, the real phonies *always* think they are real—they always believe what they believe. It is outsiders who evaluate the putative appropriateness of those beliefs for the individuals that possess them. Wally describes his "shock when the gray-headed lady" sitting on the porch "turned out to be Marjorie." She looks, he claims, "very much like Mrs. Milton Schwartz and not much like the Marjorie Morgenstern I last saw at a much too plush wedding at the Pierre." "Contented she obviously is" (559), Wally claims. But "she is dull, dull as she can be, by any technical standard. You couldn't write a play about her that would run a week, or a novel that would sell a thousand copies" (562). Though the novel *Marjorie Morningstar* itself puts the lie to Wally's statement (it is unbelievably dull, but it certainly sold many more than a thousand copies), his condemnation evokes Noel's own complaint about the Shirleys: that they possess "a terrible threatening solid dullness" (172). Similarly, in her embrace of religious institutions and rituals, Marjorie looks not unlike the mid-century Americans Will Herberg describes as more socially than authentically Jewish. What is different about this case is that the real phony is not failing to live up to an authentic individuality that is exclusively hers; rather she is failing to live up to an authentic *group* identity. To put this in another way, Holly is a real phony because her consumption of popular culture distorted her inner authenticity. She thinks she's real, but the narrator knows that there is another real that is more real that she is supposed to be. Herberg's religious suburbanites, however, are real phonies because they consumed the wrong kind of Judaism (or Protestantism, or Catholicism): they too think they are real, but Herberg knows that there is another real—a *group* real—that they are supposed to be. The problem isn't that they are too like the group, as it is for Holly. It is that they are too like the *wrong* group, the group that treats religious affiliation like "the vogue of Van Gogh and Renoir reproductions" (59). Group affiliation in and of itself is not the problem.

Furthermore, this is why the depiction of Marjorie Morningstar itself seems nothing more than sorrowful about Marjorie's final real phony status. Reflecting back on his visit, Wally realizes that in "presenting [him]self to Marjorie, a successful playwright when she'd just be another suburban housewife gone to seed," he has made no real triumph over the beauty who spurned him: "she doesn't even remember herself as she was" (564). In the same way that Marjorie was "remain[ing] Marjorie" when she refused to acknowledge to her mother her own conventionality, so now Marjorie is remaining Marjorie in her refusal to see how far she has traveled from who she was. The final nostalgia that coats Wally's remembrances — "But one thing I know now I will never have — the triumph I once wanted above everything else on earth . . . I will never have that second kiss from Marjorie" (565) — is the nostalgia about a woman who was once individual and "unique" (Capote 84) enough to be loved, who became "just another suburban housewife" (Wouk, *Marjorie* 564).

Yet this is just Wally's condemnation. From Herman Wouk's perspective, though Marjorie might be a real phony, she also might be performing the same type of Jewish rescue for which Mike Eden is so fondly remembered. Wally himself is surprised when he first learns of Eden. He had thought Noel "was the big love of her life," but he thinks "in this man she met on the ship, was a missing piece of the jigsaw, possibly even the key piece" (561). The implication of "the key piece" suggests that it is Eden who brought her back to the form, if not necessarily the substance, of Jewish religious life, and in embracing that form, Marjorie, too, potentially becomes a saver of Jews.

Four years after *Marjorie Morningstar* appeared, Wouk wrote *This is My God* (1959), an account of the Jewish faith and his own orthodoxy, in response to a Jewish friend and "skeptic far removed from the practice of Judaism" (3). In it Wouk compares what he calls "natural Judaism" to the lived experience of Jews in the United States. Natural Judaism occurred when the "laws and ceremonies were as familiar [to a Jew] as American ways are to an American. . . . [T]hey had acquired the same invisibility, so to speak; had merged with everyday reality, and seemed natural." Wouk describes here a Jewishness that is lived authentically and unself-consciously. But in America "[s]uch a natural Judaism exists among few Jews today" (28). Part of the problem is conformity, "much the greatest threat to the survival of the Jews in the United States" (30). Observing that "[i]n the death camps of the Nazis, Jewish doctors, publishers, businessmen . . . sometimes took to reading the Bible, and even to painful mastering of the Hebrew alphabet, in an effort to learn, before the darkness closed in, who they really were":

> There will be no death camps in the United States that we live in. . . . The threat of Jewish obliteration in America is different. It is the threat of pleasantly vanishing down a broad highway at the wheel of a high-powered station wagon, with the golf clubs piled in the back. . . . "*Mr. Abramson left his home in the morning after a hearty breakfast, apparently in the best of health, and was not seen again. His last words were that he would get in a round before going to the office. . . .*" Of course Mr. Abramson will not die. When his amnesia clears, he will be Mr. Adamson, and his wife and children will join him, and all will be well. But the Jewish question will be over in the United States. (258)

As in *The Thanatos Syndrome*, which viewed the widespread use of psychotropic medication as a kind of holocaust, suburban assimilation is compared to "Jewish obliteration" of the death camps. And as with *The Thanatos Syndrome*, Wouk's comparison of suburban life to a concentration camp may seem in the poorest of taste. Though the Jewish question may end through assimilation, it will not end with the actual death of individuals. Mr. Adamson is still alive, and possibly even happy. Arguably, his assimilation was a choice, even if not the one Wouk would prefer for him. The use of amnesia as its technology signals Wouk's own choice to blur the question of individual volition in his analysis. It allows one to imagine that Mr. Adamson's choices may not have been choices at all.

At another point, Wouk recognizes the imprecision of his Holocaust analogy: assimilators are "lost from Judaism, that is all." They do not *die*; they just cease to be Jews. But, he argues, "from the viewpoint of an army, it makes little difference whether a division is exterminated or disperses into the hills and shucks off its uniforms" (*My God* 234). Perhaps—unless you think that an army would do well to acknowledge the difference between a rout and when its soldiers vote with their feet. What the comparison does provide is an explanation of how Marjorie Morgenstern, suburban real phony, might also be a hero. By preserving some form of Jewish life in the suburbs, she makes a gesture, however small (and Mike himself thought his gestures were small) to prevent the holocaust of assimilation. Wouk further elaborates, "[I]n the main the American Jewish revival of religion is so far a social change rather than a religious or intellectual one" (119). He here echoes Herberg's concern that "there may well be other factors more authentically religious in the theological sense" (41) than joining a Jewish book group. But Wouk continues, "[F]or those who want Judaism to live, a revival on any basis ought to be welcome to begin with. Presumably in time the substance can take the central place" (119). For all their real phoniness, the real phonies are providing a valuable service. Natural—which is to say, authentic—Judaism will return in time.

Wouk did not have long to wait. In a series of four articles published between 1954 and 1959, *Commentary* magazine channeled the suburban exodus of a New York family to a Jewish suburb of Boston. The author, Evelyn N. Rossman, used pseudonyms for herself and the town, Northrup, to protect her privacy and guarantee that her neighbors would behave authentically around her. The early columns (from 1954 and 1956) are full of the disparaging descriptions of suburban developments that one expects from the college educated in the 1950s. The author is continually negotiating her own expectations of Jewishness in comparison to her neighbors: "the older people worry about religion. The younger ones want good times," a neighbor explains: "fashion shows, skits, bingo nights, and penny auctions . . . book reviews, cooking classes, and musical programs" (Rossman 1954, 397). The Hadassah chapter has "only a few people . . . who were really concerned about Zionism . . . it was really a social club for women" (397). The rabbi is insistent that "the survival of Judaism depended upon an active, unified community. It was better for Jews to get together to play bridge or basketball than not to get together at all" (398). She laments "our kind of organized Jewish community provides no haven for serious people"; the rabbi, Hebrew school director, and other serious members (such as herself) "speak cynically to the few that understand about the loss of Jewish values, the disrespect for study, for social conscience, culture, and charity" but everyone "perforce accepts the mass values as the standard for the community and the culture" (404). Yet in an echo of Wouk's own concerns, the subtitle of the final article in the series (from 1959) is "Decade in Northrup: A Natural Jewishness Emerges." Natural Jewishness, according to Rossman, is a Jewishness "that is Jewish without drawing all of its definitions from the organizations" (214): that is, it implies a Jewishness that belongs more to the individual than the institution, that flourishes outside of purely institutional contexts. When a friend visiting from the city asks "Why do individuals like you stay here? . . . Do you need a temple, a community? Do you ever need to conform to a group?" Rossman responds, "I realized that the longer we lived in Northrup the less we conformed — the more we were ourselves" and admits, "we don't know whether we took, or were given permission, to be ourselves" (222). What she doesn't ask is whether the selves they are were grown through the Jewish institutionalization in which they lived for ten years.

5 "THE MAN HE ALMOST IS"

Performativity and the Corporate Narrative

AT A CRITICAL MOMENT in Sloan Wilson's *The Man in the Gray Flannel Suit* (1955), Tom Rath turns down what the novel describes as "a marvelous opportunity" (226). He has been offered a promotion to become the personal assistant for Ralph Hopkins, president of the United Broadcasting Corporation and "one of the few authentic business geniuses in New York" (36). After thinking about it, Tom admits,

> I don't think I'm the kind of guy who should try to be a big executive.... I'm not the kind of person who can get all wrapped up in a job — I can't get myself convinced that my work is the most important thing in the world. I've been through one war. Maybe another one's coming. If it is, I want to be able to look back and figure I spent the time between wars with my family.... And I know that to do the kind of job you want me to do, I'd have to be willing to bury myself in it, and, well, I just don't want to. (251–52)

Positioned between the United Broadcasting Corporation and his wife, Betsy, and their children, Tom is choosing between the institutions of corporate America and the nuclear family that forms their base. Deciding between them means figuring out what "kind of guy" Tom thinks he is. Is he the "kind of person" who can get "all wrapped up" in his work? The choice gains its ethical force through his evocation of time as a precious and diminishing commodity. Time has always been an issue for Tom. When he was in World War II, he lived "thinking each day was the last" (81) and counted each second "the way a miser might count his money" (239). While he works for Hopkins, "the big sweep hand on his wrist watch seemed to crawl with maddening slowness" (238). Time, which was wealth in World War II (seconds equal money), is not worth investing in a job that will earn actual money during the postwar era. The novel legitimizes this choice when Hopkins promises to find Tom a position at UBC more in line with his ambition, claiming, "We need men like you—I guess we need a few men who keep a sense of proportion" (253). In *The Man in the Gray Flannel Suit*, the decision not to be buried in one's professional life is a choice in favor of balance, domestic harmony, and most important, "honesty" or authenticity, rather than "cynicism" or phoniness.

The previous chapters have identified four locations where the questions of authenticity and its opposites were of paramount interest during the postwar period. Chapter 1 examined the emergent figure of the teenager to consider the problem of development—the idea that the self changes over time—for contemporaneous ideas about authenticity. In chapter 2, the theorization of mental illness is explored to investigate how the relation of the self to its body influences notions of the authentic self and how those notions have shifted with the introduction of identity politics at the end of the twentieth century. The correlation between the self and its actions provided the focus of chapter 3: Do one's actions produce or reflect the authentic self? Is action constitutive or representative of the self that engages in it? The answers to such questions prove crucial for not only textual but also legal understandings of the connection between individuals and their acts. Chapter 4 investigated narratives of postwar Jewish experience to trace the emergence of an early interest in the idea of group authenticity.

This chapter considers the literature, film, and theory of corporate life to examine the relation between the self and the institutions that surround it, from the anxiety about white-collar labor expressed in the 1950s to the emergence of performance theory at the end of the century. The fear that Tom Rath expresses—that he is not the "kind of person" who should be an executive, and that working for Ralph Hopkins will "bury" him—is itself representative of this larger anxiety, which is common both to novelists and sociologists from mid-century America. Further, it reappears in more contemporary discussions over the relation between the subject and its institutional contexts by theorists like Louis Althusser and Judith Butler. Sociological works such as C. Wright Mills's *White Collar* (1951), William Whyte's *The Organization Man* (1956), and Erving Goffman's *The*

Presentation of Self in Everyday Life (1958); narratives like *The Man in the Gray Flannel Suit*, Richard Yates's *Revolutionary Road* (1961), and more recently, Cameron Crowe's *Jerry Maguire* (1996); and theoretical analyses like Louis Althusser's "Ideology and Ideological State Apparatuses" (1970) and Judith Butler's *The Psychic Life of Power* (1997), all suggest the problems inherent in representing the link between the subject or self and larger economic, social, state, and familial structures. Do institutions inhibit or enable the self? Are they destructive or productive of authentic existence? Tom Rath imagines companies like UBC are turning him into a "cheap, cynical yes man" (Wilson, *Man* 186). In *Revolutionary Road* and *Jerry Maguire*, however, corporations — and the norming institutions that they represent — play a more ambiguous role in the formation of the individual. The diversity of responses to such questions across the past fifty years illustrates both their complication and their persistence. As important, those responses tell us much about the ways in which the self is imagined to be constituted, either in opposition to or enabled by the institutions that envelop it.

These competing representations of institutional influence — as regulating and limiting, or producing and enabling — are crucial for understanding the ways in which authenticity is understood during the second half of the twentieth century. Further, they suggest how contemporary performance theory, which is commonly thought to signal the *demise* of authenticity as an ideal, ultimately rehabilitates the concept by refiguring the terms. This chapter analyzes *The Man in the Gray Flannel Suit*, *Revolutionary Road*, and *Jerry Maguire* alongside contemporaneous theories of organizational life to consider how the self or subject is alternately formed or deformed by institutions. For *The Organization Man*, *The Man in the Gray Flannel Suit*, and *White Collar*, the corporation and the work that takes place within it appear as fundamentally inauthenticating — as a production line for real phonies. As Catherine Jurca explains, the new middle-class identity of the 1950s was "grounded in its resistance to the institutions that are so crucial to it" (138). Working from Jurca's analysis of middle-class resistance, this section demonstrates that uniformity, rather than conformity, is understood as the fundamental social problem. This produces the surprising result that phoniness as such (as opposed to its real version) unexpectedly emerges as a form of social good. Phonies, according to William Whyte, are not the hypocrites that Holden Caulfield imagined; they are just utilizing a form of "protective coloration" (Whyte 11) to shield themselves from the uniforming pressure of middle-class existence.

The second section of chapter 5 provides an extended reading of Richard Yates's *Revolutionary Road*, which differentiates itself from *The Man in the Gray Flannel Suit* by examining in close detail the ways in which the self is influenced by the organizations of corporate and suburban life. With characters that look not unlike the performative subjects imagined in the 1990s, *Revolutionary Road* provides a different part for the corporation to play in the production of the individual. The novel combines Mills's and Whyte's indictment of the inauthenticating forces of institutions with a model of selfhood reminiscent of Erving Goffman's analysis of mid-century role-playing, *The Presentation of Self in Everyday Life*. Continually portraying themselves to their friends, colleagues, and one another as the people they most wish to be, Frank and April Wheeler appear as less the essential selves of Holden Caulfield's fantasies than performative constructs, continually revised through their interactions with postwar American culture. Like William Whyte and C. Wright Mills, who argue that corporate life regulates "the intimate life-fate of the individual and the kind of personality he may develop and display" (Mills, *White* 184), *Revolutionary Road* figures institutions as asserting a fundamental influence over the performative self. In its portrayal of Frank and April Wheeler's "tragedy" (232), the novel suggests that resistance to these institutions — in the manner of a Tom Rath — is potentially just as dangerous as submitting to them. Unlike Tom Rath, who successfully avoids what the Wheelers imagine as institutional "contamination" (20), April and Frank's story ultimately ends in the twinned catastrophes of death and uniformity.

By figuring the self as primarily performative, *Revolutionary Road* thus distinguishes itself from other corporate narratives of the period and prefigures the terms in which debates about authenticity will take place toward the end of the twentieth century. The final section of this chapter considers a contemporary instance of the corporate narrative, Cameron Crowe's 1996 Oscar-nominated film *Jerry Maguire*. Jerry, like Frank and April, strives to become the man he wants to be "and almost is" (Crowe 137).[1] And like Frank and April, that transformation is understood in performative terms. *Jerry Maguire* is examined alongside Judith Butler's critique of Althusserian interpellation to examine how the performative subject is thought to be constituted through the institutions that surround him. For Althusser—and not unlike Whyte and Mills—institutions preclude the possibility of authenticity; the subject's constitution within the ideological state apparatus renders authenticity and its opposites fundamentally beside the point. Yet authenticity is given a new life through the notion of a performative agency that outruns the conditions of its emergence. Ultimately, such disparate texts as *Revolutionary Road*, *Jerry Maguire*, and Butler's *The Psychic Life of Power* evoke precisely similar ideas about agency and authenticity. Though Judith Butler speaks of the poststructuralist subject and *Jerry Maguire* evokes a pop-psychologized identity, both are fundamentally engaged in imagining ways that the subject or self might use institutions to become, as Jerry asserts, "the me I'd always wanted to be" (Crowe 38). Authenticity becomes not an interior state to be discovered and lived, but rather a potentiality that is made all the more desirable for being unobtainable. The result is that contemporary performance theory, often understood as the answer to questions of authenticity, instead only re-inscribes the very authenticity it purports to undermine.

The Man in the Gray Flannel Suit serves as an exemplary place to begin this discussion for two reasons. First, it represents narratively one of the key sociological questions that motivated works like C. Wright Mills's *White Collar* and David Riesman's *The Lonely Crowd* and that form the subject of this chapter: to quote Riesman, "What is the relation between social character and society? How is it that every society seems to get, more or less, the social character it 'needs'?" (5) Both writers consider the expanding white-collar world to be particularly "characteristic of twentieth-century existence" (Mills, *White* ix). "By examining White Collar Life," Mills argues, "it is possible to learn about what is becoming more typically 'American' than the frontier character probably ever was" (xv). If "[t]he first lesson of modern sociology is that the individual cannot understand his own experience or gage his own fate without locating himself within the trends of his epoch," then "[t]o understand white collar people in detail, it is necessary to draw at least a rough sketch of the social structure of which they are a part" (xx). To sketch that social structure means sketching the world of the corporation, the suburbs, and the family. It requires understanding what were viewed as the particularly coercive demands that such institutions placed on the individuals who lived within them. In a world in which "popular culture [is] used, often quite desperately, for training in group adjustment" (Riesman, *Lonely* 156–57), novels like *The Man in the Gray Flannel Suit* provided key evidence for sociologists who sought to delineate the inauthenticating pressures of contemporary life.

Second, the novel itself was identified, both at the time of its publication and in the decades that followed, as an accurate representation of everything that was thought wrong about the 1950s: consumerism, conformity, and complacency. As Sloan Wilson observes in his afterword from 1983, Tom Rath "was taken to be a typical advertising man, though in the book he had worked on a charitable foundation for mental health established by the president of a big broadcasting company. Intellectuals, hippies and flower children began to consider him not a protestor against conformity, but an arch example of it."[2] Whether Wilson is correct to characterize Tom as a "protestor" is open to some debate. For William H. Whyte, Tom Rath emerges as a prime example of the organization man his study derides. Published one year after *The Man in the Gray Flannel Suit*, *The Organization Man* views Tom's refusal of Hopkins's promotion, his overall lack of ambition, and his conviction that spending time with his family is worthwhile as emblematic of the new "Well-Rounded" employees (129) sought by human resource departments. Such employees have "implicit faith that The Organization will be as interested in making use of their best qualities as they are themselves, and . . . can entrust the resolution of their destiny to The Organization" (130). These young men believe that it is best for the organization "not to have people getting too involved in their jobs," since a well-rested man, "at peace with his environment," will be better positioned to handle the new science of human relations with "poise and understanding" (132).

The increasing ranks of these well-rounded employees illustrate a larger shift from the "Protestant Ethic" to the "Social Ethic" (6) that *The Organization Man* deplores. If the Protestant ethic "counseled struggle against one's environment — the kind of practical, here and now struggle that paid off in material rewards" (15), the social ethic "makes morally legitimate the pressures of society against the individual. Its major propositions are three: a belief in the group as the source of creativity; a belief in 'belongingness' as the ultimate need of the individual; and a belief in the application of science to achieve that belongingness" (7). Fundamentally, the social ethic imagines that there is no inherent discrepancy between the needs and desires of the organization and that of the individual. Its harmfulness lies in its "soft-minded denial that there is a conflict between the individual and society." Whyte argues that "there must always be, and it is the price of being an individual that he must face these conflicts. He cannot evade them, and in seeking an ethic that offers a spurious peace of mind, thus does he tyrannize himself" (13–14). Pretending that their own needs and those of their employers are the same, the organization men whom Tom Rath represents enslave themselves to the demands of their companies to the detriment of both.

Tom Rath — who actually refuses to turn his life over to his employer — thus seems to appear as a counterintuitive example of the white-collar drone. How Tom manages to exemplify the new white-collar worker is demonstrated below. For now it is important that, as with many of the sociologists analyzed thus far, Whyte's analysis bases itself in an a priori assumption of individuality in the strongest sense of the term. Anyone (organization man or otherwise) who does not experience him- or herself as continually embroiled in conflict with his or her environment reveals not a genuine compatibility with social beliefs and mores but rather "a lack of will or imagination" (Whyte 10). Furthermore, this commitment to individuality takes place at the expense of the organization man himself, who "cannot evade" a lifetime of "conflict between the individual and society" (14). As previously discussed, whether or not this struggle is in the best interests of the individual who engages in it is of little importance because the struggle carries an ethical imperative alongside its presumed inevitability. What first appears as a commitment to the individual turns out to be a commitment to individuality that occurs at the expense of the individual (who is obligated to struggle) and with the society as the presumed beneficiary. "The idea that in isolation from [the community] — or active rebellion against it — he might eventually discharge the greater service is little considered" (8) by those who adhere to the demands of the social ethic. *The Organization Man* thus echoes David Riesman's claim about the particularly social efficacy of individuality as such. Since "the disparity between socially required behavior and characterologically compatible behavior is one of the great levers of change" (Riesman, *Lonely* 29), the absence of such a disparity risks economic, cultural, and individual stagnation. True service lies in fighting with organizations, institutions, and society as a whole. How will these institutions improve if everyone merely submits to their injustices, subsuming the needs of the individual to the smooth running of the organization? Submission, from Whyte's perspective, has always been the easiest route. The social ethic makes it ethically justifiable as well.

Whyte thus concurs with Herbert Marcuse's belief that individuals cannot be genuinely the same as everyone else. Unlike Marcuse, however — whose conviction that the United States has "individuality . . . in name only" (103) is corroborated by the "private automobiles," "dozens of newspapers and magazines," and "huge refrigerators filled with frozen foods" (100) that pervade suburban homes — Whyte claims upfront that there will be "no strictures in [his] book against 'Mass Man.'" He professes no interest in "the surface uniformities of U.S. life" because "the spectacle of people following current custom for lack of will or imagination to do anything else is hardly a new failing" (10). Neither do these "surface uniformities" have much to do with the more pressing problem of individualism that he views as in decline. "The man who drives a Buick Special and lives in a ranch-type house just like hundreds of other ranch-type houses can assert himself as effectively as the bohemian against his particular society," Whyte declares. "He usually does not, it is true, but if he does, the surface uniformities can serve quite well as protective coloration." "Protective coloration" is a great tool for the organization men who want "to control their environment rather than be controlled by it." With surface uniformity, "[t]hey disarm society" (11). While Holden Caulfield and others like him might find phoniness ethically intolerable, in fact these corporate chameleons are America's best hope against the encroachments of the social ethic upon the individual.

Whyte, then, is less concerned with the possibility of phoniness than with the prospect of its absence. Surprisingly enough, he actually *admires* phonies. As long as these "surface uniformities" are only on the surface, he has no problem with them. In fact, they are reassuring since their superficiality promises a greater depth of character where an ostensibly genuine individuality might reside. Only when those uniformities become something more fundamental—something like a lack of individuality or imagination—does Whyte grow troubled. He explains, "To be aware of one's conformity is to be aware that there is some antithesis between oneself and the demands of the system. This does not itself stimulate independence, but it is a necessary condition of it; and contrasted with the wishful vision of total harmony now being touted, it demonstrates a pretty tough-minded grasp of reality" (156). True independence stems from the recognition that one is simultaneously influenced by one's context and, inevitably, in conflict with it. To believe there is no distinction between the institution and oneself, the surface and the depth, begins to suggest real phoniness, where the individual is imagined to be both in sync with the demands of the organization (the real part of the real phony), and yet fundamentally in conflict with it (the phony part). Whyte fears a type of person like Holly Golighty, who actually "believes all this crap she believes" (Capote 29). These individuals are the ones who do not "only work for The Organization. They . . . *belong* to it as well" (3, emphasis in original). In its open acceptance of surface uniformities—the kind of phoniness that makes Holden Caulfield crazy—*The Organization Man* comes closest to stating openly a key aspect of the mid-century's preoccupation with uniformity, rather than conformity. Superficial uniformity is only a problem when it is not merely "protective coloration." It is only a problem when it becomes *actual* uniformity—when it becomes real phoniness.

Tom Rath chooses not to devote himself to his work at the expense of his family, which makes him a surprising representative of the principles of belonging and togetherness in the workplace. His choice not "to bury [him]self in [his work]" (252) suggests he recognizes "antithesis between oneself and the demands of the system" (Whyte 156). From one perspective, Tom looks like precisely the tough-minded employee who knows how easy it is to be manipulated "into satisfying solidarity with the group so skillfully and unobtrusively that he will scarcely realize how the benefaction has been accomplished" (Whyte 36). For Whyte, *The Man in the Gray Flannel Suit* becomes a model of the social ethic less in Tom's attitude toward his work than in his boss's reaction to it. By implying that the United Broadcasting Corporation has no problem with Tom's antipathy to hard work, competition, and the need to subsume himself within the company, the novel makes an implicit promise to its readers that the individual's wishes — to be paid well without working too hard — and those of the organization — to make a profit — can coexist. *The Man in the Gray Flannel Suit* and other novels like it are "masterpiece[s] of the have-your-cake-and-eat-it finale" (Whyte 251), and operate as propaganda for those corporations who adhere to the principles of togetherness, belonging, and scientific rationality.

Wilson's novel operates as propaganda for the social ethic only in the novel's insistence on a happy ending in which the conflict between UBC and the Raths are resolved without Tom's termination. Overall, the novel's attitude toward the inauthenticating pressures of institutions bears far more resemblance than difference to the ideas expressed in *The Organization Man*. Like Holden Caulfield, for whom any contact with others risked inauthenticity, Tom Rath is continually aware of how his behavior is contaminated by the institutions with which he aligns himself. Withholding themselves psychically (if in no other way) from the institutions that embrace them, Tom and Betsy Rath embody what critic Catherine Jurca views as a key aspect of middle-class identity in the 1950s: they "repudiate their middle classness, in what becomes a dominant fictional paradigm of white middle class experience . . . Other people belong in the development, not us; everyone else is happy as a corporate drone, except for me." That very dissatisfaction "with the suburb and the corporation proves an engine of mobility that frees them from the constraints of each" (139). In these novels the suburbs are less a destination — a sign that one has made it beyond the confines of the lower-middle classes — than the impetus to further class striving for the better suburb, the classier development, and so on.

Jurca's analysis focuses on representations of the suburbs, and the "sanctimonious suburbanites" who populate them, to provide a forceful account of how Richard Wright's *Native Son*, James M. Cain's *Mildred Pierce*, and other novels of the first part of the twentieth century imagine suburban life. This chapter explores how texts like *The Man in the Gray Flannel Suit* enshrine "honesty" as the guarantor against phoniness, or what the novel calls "cynicism," instigated by the mid-century institutions of the suburb, the corporation, and so on. While Tom fears the professional costs of telling the truth to his boss — Hopkins may decide "he's a nice honest guy who just happens to be no use to him at all" — his wife Betsy worries that he's becoming "a cheap cynical yes-man" (186). With Betsy's encouragement, he tells Hopkins his opinion of a speech Hopkins is giving on mental health policy. Far from ending Tom's career, this honesty results in speech revisions that prevent Hopkins from seeming "phony" (202) to the doctors whose endorsement he needs to get his project off the ground. "I've been worrying too much about Hopkins's honesty and not enough about my own" (203), Tom admits. But worrying about his honesty *produces* Hopkins's by protecting his public image from charges of phoniness. Authenticity, it appears, is contagious.

All of this honesty, however, only serves to embed the Raths more thoroughly in the institutions from which they ostensibly sought to be alienated. "Absolute resistance to the suburb culminates in its reproduction" (Jurca 158), in the form of the new housing development the Raths decide to build with property Tom inherits from his grandmother. Their flight from the suburbs to the ancestral home paradoxically resituates them in a suburb they themselves create in order to *afford* that ancestral home — soon to be surrounded by eighty houses on quarter-acre lots (147–48). Fighting with the institutions that threaten authenticity only serves to replicate them. What is left is merely the conviction of one's own difference, an "attitude" (84), to quote Louis Menand's description of *The Catcher in the Rye*. As argued in chapter 1, that attitude, "a modest degree of contempt" (Menand 84) for the world of the corporation and the suburb, guarantees the individual a way to maintain distance from institutions even as they surround him. It promises that he does not "*belong*" (Whyte 3) to such organizations even as he enjoys their benefits. This attitude guarantees that one has not fully internalized the beliefs and values of mainstream culture. It is how one makes sure he is not, in fact, a real phony.

This indictment of the corporation and suburb is picked up in Richard Yates's account of Frank and April Wheeler's "tragedy" (232). In the section that follows, *Revolutionary Road* is analyzed in terms of the "contaminating" (20) effects of the office and suburb. Yet in many ways the novel goes further than *The Man in the Gray Flannel Suit* in its detailed examination of how, precisely, mid-century institutions influence their subjects. Adopting a model of self less essential than performative, the novel stages the mechanisms through which the corporation molds its workers, and thus prefigures the ideas of Althusserian interpellation and the performative self that prove so crucial to figurations of subject or selfhood at the end of the century.

New and Better People: *Revolutionary Road* and *The Presentation of Self in Everyday Life*

A third of the way through *Revolutionary Road*, April Wheeler confronts her husband, Frank, with a plan.[3] Speaking with an "odd, theatrical emphasis" (107), April proposes that the family move to Paris so that Frank can spend time "finding himself" (109). She will support them doing secretarial work for NATO, because "it's unrealistic for a man with a fine mind to go on working like a dog year after year at a job he can't stand, coming home to a house he can't stand in a place he can't stand either, to a wife who's equally unable to stand the same things" (110). In a "moment of self-abasement" (111), she takes responsibility for the suburban drudgery that their married life has become. As newlyweds, Frank and April had been living a mildly bohemian life in Greenwich Village. When she became pregnant, she proposed a do-it-yourself abortion that he interprets as evidence of her refusal to be "tamed" and "submissive" (50) before the institution of marriage. For Frank, the proposed abortion became a symbol of the way April "held herself poised for immediate flight; she had always been ready to take off the minute she happened to feel like it" (48). Six years later, in the suburbs of western Connecticut, April argues that by threatening to abort their unplanned first child and then allowing herself to be talked out of it, the child became "All [Frank's] Responsibility." Frank had to "turn [him]self inside out to provide" for the family and "give up any idea of being anything in the world but a father" (111–12). When Frank objects that he has no "definite, measurable, talent" to be anything else, she responds, "It's got nothing to do with definite, measurable, talents — it's your very *essence* that's being stifled here. It's what you *are* that's being denied and denied and denied in this kind of life" (115).[4] Her assertion separates who Frank is from what Frank does, imagining that his value lies not in talents his work life has failed to manifest, but rather in a mysterious essence irreducible to actual productivity.

But what is Frank exactly? What is the essence that has been stifled by corporate, parental, and suburban drudgery? According to April, he is "the most valuable and wonderful thing in the world." He is "a man" (115). The novel thus echoes the patriarchal ideology of mid-century culture that figured the American male as the central and dominant force and placed women in the secondary role of wife and lover.[5] By April's account, her unwillingness to submit to the institutions of marriage and motherhood — to accept her subordination to her husband and children — forced Frank to submit all the more completely to the institution of fatherhood and to the corollary institutions that submission required: Knox Business Machines, the corporation for which he works to support the family in the Connecticut suburbs, those "deadly dull homes" (20) in which that family would be raised. They surrendered to "the great sentimental lie of the suburbs," that "enormous, obscene delusion . . . that people have to resign from real life and 'settle down' when they have families" (112). "Of all the capitulations in his life," Frank realizes, "this was the one that seemed most like a victory." The moment when April yields to his superior masculine essence constitutes the moment when "[t]he past could dissolve at his will and so could the future; so could the walls of this house and the whole imprisoning wasteland beyond it." In Frank's fantasy, the house and the suburb, the past and the future, must "dissolve" at the force of his will through the submission of a woman, "the marvelous creature who opened and moved for him, tender and strong" (115).

Revolutionary Road's commitment to the convention of patriarchal gender relations, in which the man is the head of the family and the woman is the supportive helpmeet, suggests the novel's alignment with postwar American discourses that "transformed the identity of the (predominantly Anglo-) American male by manufacturing and containing his identity within the consumptive topography of suburbia" (Moreno 85).[6] Michael P. Moreno argues that, like Tom Rath, Frank Wheeler represents the organization man who suffers from "*white plight*, that inner struggle between conforming to the mores of the Cold War and escaping from them into a illusory wilderness of personalized possibilities" (88, emphasis in original). These discourses imagined masculinity in particular to be at risk in the new cultures of consumption; the newly domesticated male of the suburbs was considered at best a "degenerate" (Medevoi 21) version of the American soldier who fought on World War II battlefields. *Revolutionary*

Road participates in this rhetoric by figuring Frank's debased masculinity in comparison to his father's expertise in such manly pursuits as hunting and woodwork. Frank recalls his father's hands carrying a briefcase or working with tools: "it wasn't only their strength he envied; it was their sureness and sensitivity . . . the aura of mastery they imparted to everything Earl Wheeler used. . . . [Frank] continued to believe that something unique and splendid had lived in his father's hands" (36–37). Like *The Man in the Gray Flannel Suit*, the novel represents Frank and April as participating in an anti-institutional way of thinking that imagines that the organizations and conventions of postwar America erode the fundamental natures of the men and women who live within them.

For example, Frank consistently worries about the corrosive effect of corporate and suburban life on their essences. He observes that "[e]conomic circumstance might force you to live in [the suburban] environment, but the important thing was to keep from being contaminated. The important thing, always, was to remember who you were" (20). When they first visit their new house, he jokes that "one picture window [isn't] necessarily going to destroy our personalities" (29); and when he seeks a corporate job, his one requirement is that it "can't possibility touch [him]," so that he can "retain [his] own identity" (75). Yet unlike *The Man in the Gray Flannel Suit*, *Revolutionary Road* includes the family among those institutions. It is not a refuge from the inauthenticating forces of the corporation and the suburb. It represents another instantiation of them. Reading with his children, Frank feels "as if he [was] sinking helplessly into the cushions and the papers and the bodies of his children like a man in quicksand" (56). April asks the children questions "in a rush of ebullience," but her eyes "go out of focus during their replies, and a minute later she'd be saying 'Yes, darling, but don't talk *quite* so much, okay? Give Mommy a break'" (127). The Wheelers thus subscribe to a model of self based in elemental qualities that are continually in danger of "contamination" by external forces: the corporation, the suburbs, and even the family.

Frank and April Wheeler thus appear in the novel as adult Holden Caulfields, continually obsessed with the possibility that the world they inhabit inauthenticates them. Holden feared that if he became a lawyer he would constantly wonder about his motives for "saving guys' lives" — does he do it because he wants to save those lives or because he wants "to be a terrific lawyer, with everybody slapping you on the back and congratulating you in court" (Salinger 172)? He fears the seductions of professional life, which offer money and prestige hidden within ostensibly altruistic behaviors. Frank, confident that he does not "*belong*" (Whyte 3) to his employer, takes "a secret astringent delight" (Yates 76) in the fact that he has not surrendered to the mystique of corporate life. He loves "the absurd discrepancy between his own ideals and those of Knox Business Machines; the gulf between the amount of energy he was supposed to give at the company and the amount he actually gave" (77). This fear of "contamination" implies a commitment to a model of self that is simultaneously essential and at risk. It imagines that the self is influenced by the social world but still remains fundamentally in opposition to it.

In *The Catcher in the Rye*, this commitment to an essential model of the self is Holden's, but, importantly, not the novel's. Similarly, in *Revolutionary Road*, April and Frank may believe mysterious essences define them, but the novel as a whole evokes a model of self that is less fundamental than performative. The mocking tone of the narrative makes it impossible for the reader to subscribe fully to Frank and April's view of the self in which primary natures are polluted by a corrupt and decaying culture. In his Introduction, Richard Ford identifies this tone as part of what makes the novel so hard to characterize: is it realism, providing "the particulars of life-as-lived" (xxi)? Or is it "derision and satire," providing a "distance from which we can exercise judgment and be relieved that the Wheelers aren't us" (xxii–xxiii)? That distance between the narration and its subjects appears most vividly in the novel's treatment of the Wheelers' belief in essential natures. The idea of running away to Europe, where Frank might finally live up to the promise of his "first-rate, original mind" (Yates 113), is based in the fantasy that there is "nothing in the world [Frank] couldn't do or be if [he] only had a chance to find [him]self" (114). His fundamental nature only needs to be given a chance to emerge. Yet the novel suggests that such a fantasy is not about the people the Wheelers are, but rather about the people they most want to be.

Revolutionary Road signals the discrepancy between these two states—the persons the Wheelers are and the persons they want to be (and believe they are in spirit, if in no other way)—in the performances they stage for each other. The difference is marked in the "theatrical emphasis" (107) of

April's speech when she outlines her plans. She plays the part of the self-abasing and nurturing wife, and Frank quickly senses the role he must play for her in response. As she counters his protestations of ordinariness with evidence of Bill Croft's admiration for his brains, he is "afraid he could detect a note of honest doubt in her voice," which is "distressing" to him. In response, his own voice takes on "a resonance that [makes] it every bit as theatrical as hers. It [is] the voice of a hero, a voice befitting the kind of person Bill Croft could admire" (114–15). The play-acting in which April and Frank engage signal to the reader the divergence between the performance and the person, between whom they are and whom they want to be.

These are neither the first nor the last performances that April and Frank will stage for one another and the individuals around them. In college, Frank's marks "were seldom better than average," but "there was nothing average about his performance in the beery, all-night talks that . . . [ended] in a general murmur of agreement" (21). When he seduces Maureen Grube, a secretary at Knox, he projects "a portrait of himself as a decent but disillusioned young family man, sadly and bravely at war with his environment" (97). April's behavior after an argument "seemed determined to prove, with a new, flat-footed emphasis, that a sensible, middle-class housewife was all she had ever wanted to be" (43), and her voice, celebrating his birthday, has a "quality of play-acting, of slightly false intensity, a way of seeming to speak less to him than to some romantic abstraction" (103). Most important, after they agree to move to Paris, they repeatedly "take their places in the living room" to discuss their plans. At these moments, when April "tip[s] back her head to laugh or leans forward to reach out and tap the ash from her cigarette, she [makes] it a maneuver of classic beauty." Frank himself has "developed a new way of talking, slower and more deliberate than usual." Surreptitiously admiring "his walking reflection in the black picture window," he believes he can "see the brave beginnings of a personage" (126–27). Frank realizes in these conversations that "[t]he very substance of their talk . . . the message and the rhyme of it, whatever else they may be saying, was that they were going to be new and better people from now on" (126). The world of *Revolutionary Road* is one in which the Wheelers, their friends the Campbells (who "bring out the best in them" [57]), the real estate agent Mrs. Givings, and even the mistress, Maureen Grube—who with her roommate Norma "enjoy[s] classic roles of mentor and novice in an all-girl orthodoxy of fun" (95)—continually play the parts of the persons they hope to become.

Not surprisingly, however, *Revolutionary Road* displays the failure of these performances to sustain themselves. Yates's novel emphasizes the inability of its characters to keep those self-presentations going indefinitely, or to match the presentations with behaviors that would substantiate them. The eventuality of that failure is figured in the opening pages, which set the stage for the novel's interest in performativity more broadly. The book begins with the final dress rehearsal before the inaugural production of the Laurel Players, an amateur theatrical group that the Wheelers and the Campbells join in order to revitalize the culture of the suburbs. Their goal is to show their fellow suburbanites "a way of life beyond the commuting train and the Republican Party and the barbeque pit" (61). As important, they also seek to assure themselves that "they alone, the four of them, were painfully alive in this drugged and dying culture" (60). The novel opens with the director (imported from the city) addressing the cast after a dress rehearsal of *The Petrified Forest*. He admits "I'd more or less resigned myself not to expect too much," and states,

> "Maybe this sounds corny, but . . . [s]itting out there tonight, I suddenly knew, deep down, that you were all putting your hearts into your work for the first time." He let the fingers of one hand splay out across the pocket of his shirt to show what a simple, physical thing the heart was; then he made the same hand into a fist, which he shook slowly and wordlessly into a long dramatic pause, closing one eye and allowing his moist upper lip to curl out in a grimace of triumph and pride. "Do that tomorrow night," he said, "and we'll have one hell of a show." (3–4)

The moment takes its source from every clichéd account of the director's speech before opening night. The description, emphasizing the director's gestures timed to his words—"he let," "he made," "he shook"—and their particular effects—"slowly and wordlessly into a long dramatic pause," "a grimace of triumph and pride"—establishes for the reader that this speech is itself a performance. The director is playing the role of the director, providing the stock lecture that is necessary to guarantee a successful opening night. It works: the cast "could have wept with relief" (4). Yet this heartwarming moment cannot force its own reality on the production the Players stage the following evening, largely because the director himself cannot sustain his act. The leading man suddenly takes ill and the director stands in for him: "He was doing his fervent best and delivering each line with a high semi-professional finish, but there was no denying that he looked all wrong in the part of Alan Squires—squat and partly bald, and all but unable to see without his glasses, which he'd refused to wear onstage" (8). The director is unable to rise to his promise of the previous evening. Drawing on the same "contamination" that Frank feared from the suburbs more generally, the novel claims, "The virus of calamity, dormant and threatening all these weeks, had erupted now and spread from the helplessly vomiting man until it infected everyone in the cast" (8–9). Most important, it infects April Wheeler, playing the female lead, and ends her fantasy that she might have been "The Actress if she hadn't gotten married too young" and "spoiled" (112) her and Frank's life by carrying her first pregnancy to term.

The implication of these opening pages is that performances will not always be maintained; just because Frank, April, or the director might play the part of the successful father, the contented housewife, or the great director does not mean that those roles can be upheld indefinitely. Significantly, the novel figures the performance as failing because of *another* performance and not because there is an essential self that does not correspond to it. Instead of positing an authentic self that was in conflict with the director's self-presentation and that eventually made itself known, in *Revolutionary Road* the director's second performance merely rewrites and replaces his first. The novel thereby avoids answering the question of whether there is an essential or innate self altogether, separating its own views from those of its main characters. Since the failure of the Laurel Players "could hardly be fobbed off on Conformity or The Suburbs or American Society Today" (61), the usual culprits blamed for the dreariness of their existence, Frank and April must face for the first time the prospect that just acting like the persons they want to be will not necessarily make it so.

Revolutionary Road thus sets up from its beginning the ultimate failure of the performances in which Frank and April engage throughout the novel. More generally, the novel addresses the growing mid-century conviction that role-playing formed a crucial component of everyday business and social interaction. The possibility that corporate life at the very least requires a certain amount of play-acting is taken for granted in much of the postwar sociological literature. For example, William Whyte observes that top executives "have always had to play a role, but the difference between the role and reality is becoming increasingly difficult to resolve.... They applaud better human relations, permissive management, and the like"—the principles of the Social Ethic—"yet for them personally these same advances ask them to act out something of a denial of the kind of people they really are" (151). C. Wright Mills remarks that "[o]ne knows the salesclerk not as a person but as a commercial mask, a stereotyped greeting and appreciation for patronage" (*White* 182), which is the outward manifestation of the "difference between what they really think of the customer and how they must act" (*White* 183). For David Riesman, the other-directed businessman "handles all men as customers who are always right; but he must do this with the uneasy realization that, as Everett Hughes has put it, some are more right than others"; the result is that "the other-directed person tends to become merely his succession of roles and encounters and hence to doubt who he is or where he is going" (*Lonely* 139). Most explicitly, in *The Presentation of Self in Everyday Life* (1959), Erving Goffman notes that "executives often project an air of competency and general grasp of the situation, blinding themselves and others to the fact that they hold their jobs partly because they look like executives, not because they work like executives" (47). All of these studies imagine that, as for the Wheelers and their friends, performance forms a fundamental part of quotidian existence.

Of all of these texts, Goffman's *Presentation* takes that hypothesis to its logical extremes. Dividing all communication into two categories, "expressions given and expressions given off" (4), *The Presentation of Self in Everyday Life* focuses on the latter; it adopts metaphors of "theatrical performance," to "consider the way in which the individual . . . guides and controls the impression [others] form of him" (xi). It investigates the "dramaturgical problems of presenting [an] activity before others," arguing that "[t]he issues dealt with by stagecraft and stage management are sometimes trivial but they are quite general; they seem to occur everywhere in social life, proving a clear-cut dimension for formal sociological analysis" (15). Goffman thus considers not only the mechanics of actual performances — fronts, realizations, idealizations, expressive control, as well as problems of misrepresentation and of reality versus contrivance — but also the related phenomenon of team role-playing, in which two individuals conspire in a performance (think of Frank and April chatting in the living room); the differences in regional behaviors; and the problems of discrepant roles and communications that are out of character.

Goffman makes a number of observations that elucidate the particular ways that everyday performance is understood during the postwar period. He comments that "[a]s members of an audience it is natural for us to feel that the impression that the performer seeks to give us may be true or false, genuine or spurious, valid or 'phony'" (58). Yet he is quick to note that terms like "phoniness," at least as Holden Caulfield might have used it, do not necessarily apply to the types of play-acting that he describes. He identifies three different types of attitudes performers might have toward the roles they play. The first is the sincere attitude, in which "the performer can be fully taken in by his own act . . . and can be sincerely convinced that the impression of reality which he stages is the real reality" (17). The second is the "cynical" attitude, in which "the individual has no belief in his own act . . . the cynic, with all his professional disinvolvement, may obtain unprofessional pleasures from his masquerade" (18). Remove the unprofessional pleasure, and these cynics are the logical counterparts of those organization men whom Whyte admired for their "protective coloration" (11). The third type of performer fits most particularly with *Revolutionary Road* — the performer for whom the mask she wears represents "the conception we have formed of ourselves — the role we are striving to live up to — this mask is our truer self, the self we would like to be" (19, quoted from Robert Ezra Park). These individuals produce "idealized" or "socialized" performances. Quoting from Charles H. Cooley, Goffman observes, "If we never tried to seem a little better than we are, how could we improve or 'train ourselves from the outside inward?'" Operating before the gaze of others, these performers "tend to incorporate and exemplify the officially accredited values of the society, more so, in fact, than does his behavior as a whole" (35). Presenting idealized versions of oneself — not who one is, but who one most desperately wants to be — creates an expectation in the audience that then helps mold the performer into her best self.

In *The Presentation of Self in Everyday Life*, Goffman argues that performance structures the most mundane of human interactions. *Revolutionary Road* takes that analysis one step further to consider what happens when the performance cannot be sustained or, as Goffman puts it, when the "impressions fostered in everyday performances are subject to disruption" (66). In Goffman's text, such disruptions are of intellectual but not ethical interest since he is careful not to imagine any authentic reality against which such performances should be measured. He notes that when "we think of those who present a false front or 'only' a front, of those who dissemble, deceive and defraud, we think of a discrepancy between fostered appearances and reality" (59). In fact, "there is often no reason for claiming that the facts discrepant with the fostered impression are any more the real reality than is the fostered reality they embarrassed" (65). What Goffman seeks to avoid is establishing some sort of authentic self against whom any individual performance might be judged. Since all is presentation, to value one above the other would be spurious. While it is intellectually interesting to note the variety of responses people have to performances that fail, it is not of ethical importance. Instead, Goffman takes his cue from Jean-Paul Sartre — whose *Being and Nothingness* he cites three times — and imagines that ethical consequences only accrue to the *consequences* of such performances:

> A correctly staged and performed scene leads the audience to impute a self to a performed character, but this imputation — this self — is a *product* of a scene that comes off, and not a *cause* of it. The self, then, as a performed character, is not an organic thing that has a specific location, whose fundamental fate is to be born, to mature, and to die; it is a dramatic effect arising diffusely from a scene that is presented, and the characteristic issue, the crucial concern, is whether it will be credited or discredited. (252–53, emphasis in original)

Like Sartre, for whom every action, or performance, might be thought to constitute the self in retrospect (think of Holden Caulfield leaving the hospital, unsure of what he'll do until he does it), Goffman cares not whether a performance accurately reflects an authentic essence (which may well not exist anyway) but rather whether that performance can be sustained with a minimum of injury to those exposed to it. By this account, Holden's performances are fundamentally benign, for even when they fail, the consequences are only his embarrassment. On the other hand, Tom Ripley's performances would be an ethical catastrophe, since their consequences include murder.[7]

Goffman may not be interested in what happens when performers cannot maintain to their performances, but *Revolutionary Road* certainly addresses this point. Frank and April's plans to escape to Paris begin to crumble long before April discovers that she is pregnant again, but it is this third pregnancy that ultimately causes the catastrophe that defines the book's genre of "tragedy." The couple divides along the familiar lines. Frank once again wants the child, but he also desperately wants to avoid moving to Paris where, he fears, his vision "of [April] coming home from a day at the office — wearing a Parisian tailored suit, briskly pulling off her gloves — coming home and finding him hunched in an egg-stained bathrobe, on an unmade bed picking his nose" (109) would be realized. April again wants to implement the home abortion and save the Paris plans because "the whole *point* of going was to give [Frank] a chance to find [him]self" (207); but also because having another child will mean "Two years? Three years? Four?" before she "can take a full-time job" (207). More important (as she admits to Shep Campbell after a drunken tryst in a parking lot), she does not "know who [she] is" (262) and Paris might have been the place to find out. Neither Frank nor April speaks openly about his or her concerns; instead they argue in their roles of the self-sacrificing wife and the moral husband. Yet these performances do have real-world consequences of the type about which Goffman warns. April acquiesces to Frank's wishes, but this acquiescence lasts only long enough for her pregnancy to complete its first trimester — the time during which an at-home abortion might be the safest. She then changes her mind, writes Frank a note saying that "*whatever happens please don't blame yourself*" (310), and induces a miscarriage, from which she hemorrhages and dies. The novel observes, "The Revolutionary Hill Estates had not been designed to accommodate a tragedy. Even at night, as if on purpose, the development held no looming shadows and no gaunt silhouettes. It was invincibly cheerful, a toyland of white and pastel houses" (323). It is the wrong stage for the denouement of the Wheelers' play. The Revolutionary Hill Estates is designed for a situation comedy, that "television crap where every joke is built on the premise that daddy's an idiot and mother's always on to him" (129), and specifically not a tragedy.

At the very least, April's demise guarantees that writers like William Whyte will not dismiss the novel for its relentless cheeriness about corporate and suburban life. No one both has and eats his cake in *Revolutionary Road*. The important question becomes why April is the character whose performance cannot be sustained indefinitely? The answer lies in the central role that institutions are imagined to play in the production of those very performances. The idea that individuals use their self-presentation to produce the selves they want to be — to quote Goffman (quoting Cooley) that individuals are trained "from the outside inward" (35) — is endorsed by the novel, and institutions are granted an important role in such training. The difference between Frank and April, then, is not that Frank is better at sustaining those presentations than April is, but rather that Frank has outside help. He cannot withhold himself from social and corporate institutions in the same way that April can. To put it slightly differently, *Revolutionary Road* imagines along with C. Wright Mills that in white-collar work "one's personality and personal traits become part of the means of production" so that "a person instrumentalizes and externalizes intimate features of his person and disposition" (Mills, *White* 225). The difference between them is that for Mills, the indoctrination of the whole person to the needs of the corporate machine "has carried self and social alienation to explicit extremes" (225), whereas for Yates, it keeps one alive but at the cost of creating a stultifying uniformity.

This tendency to be trained "from the outside inward" by the institutions that surround him is explored in Frank Wheeler's own experiences at Knox Business Machines, suggesting a role for institutions to play in helping individuals "improve." As illustrated above, when Frank and April decide to make the transatlantic move, they begin the series of performances that convey to one another that "they were going to be new and better people from now on" (126). However, the changes that actually occur in Frank take place not in the living room, where he imagines he sees "the brave beginnings of a personage" (127), but rather at Knox, the very place where he hoped to "retain [his] own identity" (75). When he first takes the job, Frank is amused by the fact that he works for the same company where his father had been employed as a salesman; he loves the "joke" that the company where Earl Wheeler slaved is the same place where he expresses "a sleepy disdain of tension and hurry" (76). He feels a secret delight in the idea that he can give Knox a "nice college-boy smile for so many hours a day, in exchange for so many dollars," but beyond that he and the corporation will "leave each other strictly alone" (75). Yet the novel takes pains to point out that, six years later, Frank's "actions on entering the lobby were absent-mindedly expert: he obeyed the pointed finger of the elevator starter without quite being aware of it, nor did he notice which of the six elevator operators it was who sleepily made him welcome" (78). The white-collar workday has impressed itself upon him: despite his insistence that the corporation "can't possibly touch [him]" (75), he walks "into the Knox Building like an automaton" (78).

This automation was thought to be shared by the organization man more generally in the postwar era. As C. Wright Mills explains, "The alienating conditions of modern work now include the salaried employees as well as the wage workers"; as work "comes more fully under mechanization and centralized management, it levels men off again as automatons" (*White* 227). Thanks to the machines of the type that Knox itself churns out—like the "Knox '500' Electronic Computer . . . [which] could 'perform the lifetime work of a man with a desk calculator in thirty minutes'" (Yates 78)—"the number of routine jobs is increased, and consequently the proportion of 'positions requiring initiative' is decreased" (*White* 205) among white-collar labor. Like the white-collar worker for whom "work becomes a sacrifice of time, necessary to building a life outside it" (228), Frank has learned "new ways of spacing out the hours of the day—almost time to go down for coffee; almost time to go out for lunch; almost time to go home—and he [came] to rely on the desolate wastes of time that lay between these pleasures as an invalid comes to rely on the certainty of recurring pain. It was a part of him" (Yates 80). This kind of indoctrination is precisely what Frank imagines that he would be able to avoid by taking the job at Knox, yet the novel suggests that this internalization—or from Frank's perspective, contamination—is inevitable. Whether one likes it or not, the work one does day in and day out will become a "part of [you]."

Nor is this internalization only a bad thing—unless one considers institutional success as bad (which the novel seems to believe). The morning after Frank and April make the decision to move to Paris, Frank returns

"THE MAN HE ALMOST IS" 215

to the office confident that he will be leaving the job in just a few months. He discovers on his desk a project that has been plaguing him for eight weeks: a series of complaints from the branch manager in Toledo about the "many serious errors and misleading statements in SP-1109," the brochure and technical manual for the Knox "500" (87). As Frank sits before the Dictaphone, "he began to get ideas, and soon he was intoning one smooth sentence after another, pausing only to smile in satisfaction" (122). He creates a new sales brochure for the upcoming National Association of Production Executives conference titled *Speaking of Production Control* that, he promises, will "give the NAPE delegate nothing more or less than what he wants, colon: the facts" (123). When Frank plays it back, "[i]t sounded very authoritative": "No one could have told that he didn't know what he was talking about" (123–24). Dealing with this project encourages him "to tackle two or three other matters in the stack of things he couldn't face." He is a "demon of energy," and by the end of the day he realizes:

> It was because April had left a small pocket of guilt in his mind last night by saying that he'd "worked like a dog year after year." He had meant to point out that whatever it was he'd been doing here year after year, it could hardly be called working like a dog — but she hadn't given him a chance. And now, by trying to clear all the papers off his desk in one day, he guessed he was trying to make up for having misled her. (124–25)

As Frank notes, his productivity is inspired through guilt. When he is shamed by being told how hard he works, he actually bothers to work hard; the discrepancy between the work-driven husband that he presented to April and the clock-watcher he played at Knox compels him for once to try and match his actions to his performance. And unlike at home, where both his and April's efforts to be better spouses and better parents are inevitably thwarted by one another, Knox responds positively to Frank's efforts to "work like a dog," even if only for a day. His boss introduces him to Bart Pollack, the general sales manager for the electronics division, who tells him, "They're just tickled to death in Toledo" (174) over the new *Speaking of Production Control* brochure. They ask him to do "a whole series of the crazy things," he tells April: *Speaking of Inventory Control, Speaking of Sales Analysis, Speaking of Cost Accounting,* and so on (174). Bart takes him to lunch at the very restaurant where Frank and his father ate years earlier and produces a whole new role for him to play; he wants to send Frank "out to groups of people all over the country . . . [to] talk computers, chapter and verse" (203). Above all, Bart tells him, to take this promotion would be "a fine memorial tribute to your dad." Those "abysmally sentimental words," the novel informs us, "sent an instantaneous rush of blood to the walls of [Frank's] throat . . . for a minute he was afraid he might weep into his melting chocolate ice cream" (205).

It is clear that Frank wants to take the promotion and that April does not; his announcement of the possible promotion coincides with hers about the pregnancy, and the series of crises that structure the end of the novel begin to unfold. Frank's sudden success at Knox Business Machines—his ultimate submission to the corporate institution—is not matched by a corresponding submission on April's part to the institution of motherhood. Frank theorizes that it might have to do with her upbringing being shuttled back and forth between various aunts. In her reminiscences, April's parents appear to him "only as flickering caricatures of the twenties, the Playboy and the Flapper, mysteriously rich and careless and cruel . . . [and] divorced within a year of the birth of their only child" (38). "Wasn't it likely," he speculates, "that a girl who'd known nothing but parental rejection from the time of her birth might develop an abiding reluctance to bear children?" (224–25). The novel neither entirely supports nor rejects Frank's turn to Freudian accounts of the psyche to explain (or explain away) April's reluctance to continue their life as is. In the moments before her abortion/suicide, she remembers a disappointing childhood visit from her parents and observes of her family playing that "from a distance, all children's voices sound the same" (305). At the same time, the novel provides plenty of other reasons that April might not want to continue living the existence laid out before her. After all, in the 1950s, women did not have as many roles to choose from as their male counterparts; the institution of the family was virtually the only institution to which one was invited to submit. Published two years before *The Feminine Mystique* (1963), the novel only indirectly addresses the type of limitations imposed by the cult of femininity. Degraded masculinity is much more at issue for *Revolutionary Road*. Even so, for a novel not particularly concerned with the problem of female prospects as such, April's opportunities appear comparatively bleak. As she herself acknowledges, "in a sentimentally lonely time long ago, she had found it easy and agreeable to believe whatever this one particular boy felt like saying, and to repay him for that pleasure by telling easy agreeable lies of her own," until now she finds herself "working at life the way the Laurel Players worked at *The Petrified Forest* . . . and then [she was] face to face, in total darkness, with the knowledge that [she] didn't know who [she was]" (304–5).

It is not ultimately clear which of the two of them — April or Frank — has the (relatively) happier ending. It is difficult to imagine a less happy conclusion than a successful suicide. Frank's situation thus might seem more optimistic than April's death, but the terms through which his continued life is presented render that conclusion ambiguous at best. A year after "the time of the Laurel Players" (331), Shep Campbell recalls a visit Frank paid to him and Milly. Frank had taken the job with Bart Pollack, moved to the city, and sent his children to live with his brother's family in western Massachusetts, where he spends his weekends. The narration moves away from Frank's or April's point of view to provide an ostensibly outside perspective on the man that Frank has become. "He was so damned mild!" (330), Shep remembers:

> And it was even worse than that: he was boring. He must have spent at least an hour talking about his half-assed job, and God only knew how many other hours on his other favorite subject: "my analyst this"; "my analyst that" — he had turned into one of those people who want to tell you about their God damned analyst all the time. (331)

Frank has turned into the person he hoped never to be, and because the reader does not get this narration from his perspective, one cannot not know if he recognizes this fact, or how he feels about it. As with both Holly Golightly and Marjorie Morningstar, Frank's ending must be told from the point of view of someone else. Shep himself is appalled by the transformation in him. Frank had always claimed that the worst thing that could happen at a party would be for Shep to say "'How's the job going, Frank?' in dead earnest, just as if Frank hadn't made it clear, time and again, that his job was the least important part of his life" (65). Now it is he himself who can spend "at least an hour" talking about that "half-assed job" (331). Further, that indoctrination into the norms of white-collar labor has extended itself into his psyche. The institution of psychoanalysis — what

Frank once called "the new religion ... everybody's intellectual and spiritual sugar-tit" (65) — has him describing "getting down to some basic stuff; things [he'd] never really faced about [his] relationship with his father" (331). The implication is that Frank has at last fully succumbed to the institutions of the corporation, the suburbs, psychoanalysis, postwar masculinity, and so on. All that submission has made him predictable, or "boring"; no one would say that Frank does not *belong* (Whyte 3) to Bart Pollack Associates in a way he never wanted to belong to Knox Business Machines. He is *not* a "man who drives a Buick Special" as a form of "protective coloration" (Whyte 11). Rather Frank has become a real phony, a person who can no longer maintain the authenticating distance between himself and the institutions of middle-class adulthood that surround him. Shep, like Capote's narrator, and Wally Wronken, is positioned by the novel to inform the reader that there is another real that is more real that Frank is supposed to be. Like Riesman's adjusted characters, he "reflects his society ... with the least distortion," not because he "was made for it" (*Lonely* 242) but rather because it gradually modeled him in its own image. By comparison, if the mark of the autonomous individual, in Riesman's terms, was her ability to "choose whether to conform or not," then April *did* choose. She no longer believed in her own ability to maintain Menand's authenticating "attitude" from the institutions that enclosed her. Her ending in *Revolutionary Road* thus becomes the alternative end that Esther Greenwood avoids in *The Bell Jar*.

Jerry Maguire, Judith Butler, and the Personal Brand

When Jerry Maguire (Tom Cruise), the leading character of the eponymously titled film, describes in retrospect the events that led to his "breakdown" — or "*breakthrough*" as he prefers to call it — he emphasizes the role played by conscience (Crowe 37).[8] Why did he lose his job as a sports agent, start his own company, get married, get separated, and finally reach a state of "complet[ion]" (177), both professionally and personally? Because, he explains, "A hockey player's kid made me feel like a superficial jerk, I ate two slices of bad pizza, went to bed, [and] grew a conscience" (106). This newly grown conscience compels Jerry to write an admittedly "'touchy-feely'" (38) mission statement — one that proposes a sports agency founded on "fewer clients, less money, more attention, caring for them, caring for ourselves"[9] — describing not only the business Jerry wants to create but also "the me I'd always wanted to be" (38). There is no difference between founding a company and forging a self in *Jerry Maguire*. Professionally, Jerry creates an agency to help his clients realize not only their professional ambitions but also the "love, respect, community . . . and the dollars too" (120) that are the apotheosis of celebrity culture. Personally, Jerry struggles to achieve "intimacy" (163), to "talk, really talk" (113), and to become, in his wife Dorothy's terms, "the man he wants to be . . . and the man he almost is."[10]

As with *Revolutionary Road*, *Jerry Maguire* tells the story of someone who wants to change. How this transformation takes place forms part of the subject of this section of the chapter. In many respects, the similarities between *Jerry Maguire* and *Revolutionary Road* belie the thirty-five years that separate them. Both works imagine the process of individual evolution (for good or bad) to be crucially dependent on the institutions that surround that self or subject. Yet the remainder of this discussion focuses on what *Jerry Maguire* renders visible in and about recent American culture more generally — namely, its tendency to offer competing accounts of the self as either a process or a project. When *Jerry Maguire* was released in 1996, the idea of the self as project was a commonplace one. It has long been the enabling belief of the self-help industry, whose narratives of decline, crisis and epiphany, and self-conscious transformation provide the obvious referent for the film's opening monologue and montage. Like an addict testifying at a meeting, Jerry describes the heady world of professional sports, his gradual realization that "in the quest for the big dollars, a lot of the little things were going wrong" (34), and then, the crisis: leaving the bedside of an injured hockey player, Jerry hears the player's son call out, "Hey! Mr. Maguire!" and he turns. In the moments that follow, his opening assertion that "I am the sports agent. . . . It's what I do" (33)[11], in which being and doing are understood to coexist without conflict, is replaced with existential doubt expressed in voiceover: "Who had I become? Just another shark in a suit?" (36). The mission statement that follows from the incident constitutes a blueprint for both a new profession and a new person.

Jerry's efforts to make a project of himself thus represent a recognizable

15. The hockey player's son calls out to Jerry Maguire. *Jerry Maguire* (1996). Sony Pictures.

construct in mainstream American culture at least as old as *Revolutionary Road*, in which Frank and April promise one another they will be "new and better people from now on" (126). However, it is less familiar in contemporary critical discourse, in which the self as a process has emerged as by far the more familiar paradigm. As often as mainstream American texts have celebrated the prospect of self-transformation, poststructuralist critical writing has as often doubted its possibility. Yet in inadvertent homage to one of that paradigm's central theorists, the idea of the self as process is also evoked by *Jerry Maguire*'s opening sequence. Put the hockey player's son in a policeman's uniform, and the moment inadvertently reenacts Louis Althusser's most famous example of interpellation, in which the policeman's hail of "Hey! You there!" (Althusser 174) constitutes the subject within the realm of state authority. What is important, though, is that the similarities between the two moments begin and end there. For Althusser, the policeman's summons represents an inevitable procedure, the moment when the state "'recruits' subjects among individuals (it recruits them all), or 'transforms' individuals into subjects (it transforms them all)" (174); in *Jerry Maguire*, the child's call is figured as an opportunity.[12] The hail that the hockey player's son embodies operates less as conscription than an invitation, a chance for self-examination and ideally self-revision. Like Althusser's representative French citizen, Jerry recognizes himself in the call to "Mr. Maguire" but, in turning, finds he does not like the identity proffered, that of "a shark in a suit" (36). But unlike the French subject, whose affective relationship to interpellation is fundamentally beside the point, in *Jerry Maguire* whether or not one likes one's hailing is of paramount concern.

To put this somewhat differently, if, as Judith Butler observes of interpellation, "the turn toward the law is not necessitated by the hailing; it

16. Jerry turns to face the hockey player's son. *Jerry Maguire* (1996). Sony Pictures.

is compelling, in a less than logical sense, because it promises identity" (*Psychic Life* 108), then what *Jerry Maguire* suggests is that the identity conferred is potentially open to modification. Furthermore, this is a suggestion with which Butler would seem to agree, implying an unexpected convergence of mainstream and critical perspectives in the last fifteen years. In *The Psychic Life of Power* (1997), Butler recounts the means whereby Althusser's Ideological State Apparatus produces the "subjected being, who submits to a higher authority, and is therefore stripped of all freedom except that of freely accepting his submission" (Althusser 182). As a procedure, it is inevitable and total. The subject in Althusser is only interpellated as "a (free) subject . . . in order that he shall (freely) accept his subjection . . . in order that he shall make the gestures and actions of his subjection 'all by himself'" (Althusser 182). Yet for Butler, the process of subjection is invariably incomplete and the failure of interpellation "to determine the constitutive field of the human" (*Psychic Life* 129) provides the space for "an agency that outruns and counters the condition of its emergence" (*Psychic Life* 130). This agency enables the political resignification of identity categories; in Butler's most famous instance, it makes possible the "resignifying practice in which the desanctioning power of the name 'queer' is reversed" (*Bodies* 232) and constitutes the subject's capacity to reconfigure the terms that enabled his emergence. Where for Jerry the hail invites us to "start our lives" (38), for Butler it makes visible a "potentiality . . . unexhausted by any interpellation" (*Psychic Life* 131).

Butler's account of subjectivity and *Jerry Maguire*'s narrative of self-transformation are revealing for the ways in which both critical and mainstream culture understand self- or subjecthood: its constitution, its capacity for autonomous agency, and its opportunities for transformation. Like *Revolutionary Road*, both *Jerry Maguire* and Judith Butler imagine the

17. Jerry realizes he has become "just another shark in a suit." *Jerry Maguire* (1996). Sony Pictures.

subject in fundamentally performative terms. And though Judith Butler speaks of the poststructuralist subject and *Jerry Maguire* evokes a pop-psychologized identity, both are also committed to imagining ways that performative subject or self might become a project through transformative action. For Butler, this requires revising Althusserian interpellation to produce a subject with the capacity to reconfigure its own identity. Her work proposes that repetitive action, previously understood as the means through which identity is imposed and naturalized, instantiates as well the subject's capacity for agency. It produces both the interpellated subject and the agency capable of revising those interpellations. For *Jerry Maguire*, the problem of agency is more literally engaged. Fired from his job at Sports Management International, Jerry decides to open his own sports agency, which becomes an effort to create *agency* as such: over his career, his family, and most important himself. As in *Revolutionary Road*, that project takes place primarily in the world of business, though unlike Frank Wheeler—who at best only dimly perceives the role his work performance plays in his transformation—Jerry is fully self-conscious of his efforts to change. Dedicating its lead character both to reforming his business and re-creating his identity, the movie figures the two efforts as precisely the same project and locates agency in self-institutionalization, in the fledgling company Jerry Maguire Inc.

From one perspective, then, Judith Butler and the film seek the same end by different means; while the former investigates the constitution of the subject, the latter narrates the connection between institutions and individuals to theorize a subject with the capacity for agency. Yet those means are not equally successful, and what follows is ultimately concerned with the way that *Jerry Maguire* emerges as both a demonstration and a critique of Butler's account of subjectivity. There are two moments of transformation in the film: the first, a mystified account of catching a touchdown pass, stages the moment of interpellation in narrative time and thus exposes the "temporal suppression" (Althusser 175) that both Althusser and Butler rely upon to theorize an "always-already constituted" subject (Althusser 176). True to the temporality in which subjectivity is inevitably enacted, *Jerry Maguire* articulates a problem at the center of Butler's interpretation of Althusser: namely, how can a wholly interpellated subject retain an aspect of self-determination? Is there a subject prior to performance?

If this first transformation demonstrates the difficulty of imagining a purely constitutive repetition, the second transformation — an illustration of Jerry's dual successes in business and marriage — provides a solution by taking at face value what in Althusser is merely a rhetorical device: the conflation of a person (the policeman) with an institution (the Ideological State Apparatus). Situating *Jerry Maguire* amid contemporaneous writing on corporate identity and the marketing concept of the brand, the film, like much recent business writing, collapses the distinctions between persons and corporations. It redirects Jerry's project away from his own identity, over which the subject may not have any influence, and toward the identity of his company, an area in which the subject's ability to act is not a priori at question. The movie thus avoids the problems of agency that plague Butler's account but retains a means whereby Jerry might be transformed through his interpellation by the very agency that Jerry himself created. To put this slightly differently, as Jerry creates an agency he also creates agency itself. The result is a continual circuit between Jerry and his company, the subject and his institution, in which the former determines the identity of the brand he founds and the latter constructs the former as "the me [he'd] always wanted to be" (38).

To theorize a subject with the capacity for transformative agency, Butler examines the role that conscience plays in Althusser's account of subject formation; conscience both compels the turn toward the law that constitutes and guarantees one's subjection and impels the mastery of a set of social skills (social, linguistic, productive, etc.), where that mastery is paradoxically "'at the same time, a reproduction of [the subject's] submission to the rules of the established order' . . . [so that] the more a practice is mastered, the more fully subjection is achieved" (*Psychic Life* 116). For example, it is Frank Wheeler's guilty conscience about April's insistence that he had

18. Rod Tidwell lies unconscious in the end zone while the crowd cheers for him. *Jerry Maguire* (1996). Sony Pictures.

"worked like a dog year after year" (Yates 124) that results in the *Speaking of* brochure; his mastery of that form produces requests for further forms, which then produce his promotion, and so on. However, Butler's emphasis is less on the "lived simultaneity of submission as mastery and mastery as submission" (*Psychic Life* 117) than on the notion of repetition as crucial to subject formation. Repetition in Butler guarantees that one is what one does; moreover, it is only by way of what one does that one is at all. By performing again and again the various social and productive skills through which identity is composed and conferred — skills of language, of labor, of social interaction — the subject emerges and is recognized as such.

How, precisely, is repetition constitutive of the subject? *Jerry Maguire* itself illustrates how repetition might be said to be transformative; it is the vehicle whereby Jerry and his only client, Rod Tidwell (Cuba Gooding Jr.), an underpaid and unappreciated professional football player, metamorphose into the persons they desire to become. Fired from Sports Management International for circulating his "touchy-feely" (38) mission statement to the rest of the employees, Jerry convinces Rod and Dorothy to join "something real and fun and inspiring and true in this godforsaken business" (70), an independent agency. The movie recounts each man's efforts to achieve completion, the state of being that the movie imagines to come from the full integration of one's professional and personal life, in which what one does and who one is cannot be separated. For Jerry, the problem is the personal. He is good at inspiring people, a quality the film deems essential for professional success, but he has trouble in romantic relationships. He is, he admits to Dorothy, "great at friendship, [but] bad at intimacy" (163) and fears he is not "built that way" (162). Rod, by

19. Shot from Rod Tidwell's point of view as he awakens from unconsciousness to see the doctor leaning over him. *Jerry Maguire* (1996). Sony Pictures.

comparison, has "heart" in his marriage to Marcee but lacks it professionally. "You are a *paycheck* player," Jerry explains. "You play with your *head*, not your heart. In your personal life—heart. But when you get on the field, it's all about what you didn't get, who's to blame . . . [and] that is not what inspires people."[13] With mirrored and inverted stories, the men embody both sides of the movie's commitment to imagining neither the professional nor the personal realms as enough.

Even in Hollywood, merely desiring change is not enough to make it happen, and if the film's frequent scenes of heart-to-heart talks between Jerry and Rod, Jerry and Dorothy, Rod and his wife Marcee, and Dorothy and her sister Laurel seem repetitious, it is, as Butler might argue, repetition with a purpose. In a second montage sequence similar to the movie's opening, *Jerry Maguire* stages the same commitment to reiteration as Butler deems crucial to interpellation. The segment shows repeated shots of Jerry on the telephone and Rod catching footballs and getting sacked while Paul McCartney's "Momma Miss America" plays in the background, as if to suggest that even the most glamorous career might be reduced to a set of quotidian, ever-recurring tasks.[14] Yet the sequence emphasizes most of all that the men are trying: trying to jump-start the new agency and Rod's career, trying to achieve intimacy with each other and with their wives, trying to become "complete" (177). If their success is not guaranteed (save by the generic requirements of a Hollywood feel-good movie), at the very least, the film suggests, everyone really *wants* to change.

Needless to say, all this wanting and repeating does pay off, literally. In the first of what will be two moments of transformation, Rod catches the game-winning, playoff-slot-securing pass on *Monday Night Football*.[15] Knocked unconscious in the end zone, he lies on the field while the movie

20. Rod Tidwell opens his eyes in response to the hails from the crowd. *Jerry Maguire* (1996). Sony Pictures.

alternates among shots of Rod surrounded by doctors, Jerry on the sidelines, and Marcee and her family watching at home. But the movie places the viewer within Rod's experience for the actual moment of transformation; in a close-up of Rod's unconscious face, all background sound is filtered out until the requisite lone voice from the stadium calls "We love you Rod!"[16] The camera then cuts directly to Rod's point of view to show the doctor's hands clapping in slow motion above him. The extradiagetic music swells, and in a second close-up, the camera shows Rod slowly opening his eyes. In a spasm of joy at being loved, at being hailed as a star by the institution of sports celebrity, Rod dances around the stadium in front of the crowd. This, it seems, is playing with "heart" and "inspir[ing] people" (158), the qualities that Jerry insisted were necessary for athletic stardom. As a result the audience loves him, the press loves him, and the Arizona Cardinals management is compelled to fork over $11.2 million for four more years.[17]

By narrating the precise moment of Rod's transformation from his point of view, *Jerry Maguire* thoroughly mystifies the source of this transformation. Unconscious, not even Rod knows what happened to him at the moment of interpellation. Surely all that practice played a role in his subsequent success, but the actual circumstances — a close game, a great pass, a near-fatal accident, a hail of love from the stadium — suggest that something more is involved. This something more is itself represented metaphorically in the extradiagetic music; the implication is that the unconscious quite literally takes over and produces the star quality that had previously eluded Rod. Yet occurring as it does in narrative time, rather than in the "always-already" temporality that Butler inherits from Althusser, the film underscores the difficulty of imaging a purely constitutive repetition.

Something (or someone?) runs for the ball over and over again, if only to be conveniently knocked unconscious, before a football star is produced in its (his?) place. Without a preperformative subject, or at least some form of preperformative agency, it is not clear why all that running and catching would occur.

Butler herself is no more specific about the means whereby repetition mysteriously spawns a subject without a preexisting motivation and yet not mechanistically. She explains,

> What leads to this reproduction? Clearly, it is not merely a mechanistic appropriation of norms, nor is it a voluntaristic appropriation. It is neither simple behaviorism nor a deliberate project. To the extent that it precedes the formation of the subject, it is not yet of the order of consciousness, and yet this involuntary compulsion is not a mechanistically produced effect. The notion of ritual suggests that it is performed, and that in the repetition of performance a belief is spawned, which is then incorporated into the performance in its subsequent operations. But inherent to any performance is a compulsion to "acquit oneself" and so prior to any performance is an anxiety and a knowingness which becomes articulate and animating only on the occasion of the reprimand. (*Psychic Life* 119)

Defining by exclusion the motivation for such repetition — whatever it is, it is not "mechanistic," it is not "voluntaristic," nor is it a "deliberate project" though its results ultimately produce them — Butler rewrites reproduction as ritual and thus obscures the origin of either the action or the belief. However, it remains unclear what makes ritual different from mere action or a series of actions. What makes the ritual of catching a ball, say, distinct from the act of catching a ball? Presumably, it is the fact that it is done over and over again. Yet to catch a ball over and over again is from one perspective merely a series of actions; there is no obvious reason that an action performed ten times is more ritualistic than an action performed once. The promise would seem to be that ritual is more than just doing something over and over again, but what differentiates it from an action repeatedly performed if not the belief that motivates it?

The value of ritual as a model for subject formation lies in its ability to make belief and practice inseparable and thus to obfuscate the question of whether a subject is required prior to performance. It is only when such repetition is specifically enacted that the conceptual difficulty of Butler's project is laid bare, as Rod's example shows. Elsewhere in the text, Butler accounts for this difficulty through paradox; in her words, "The story by which subjection is told is, inevitably circular, presupposing the very subject for which it seeks to give an account" (*Psychic Life* 11). For Butler this is less a problem of subject formation than of language. The grammar through which one would account for the subject must presuppose that subject to make sense. It is grammar that requires there be a "doer behind the deed," and the anxiety about agency that stems from this grammatical fact is itself misplaced. As she states, "To literalize or to ascribe an ontological status to the grammatical requirement of 'the subject' is to presume a mimetic relation between grammar and ontology which misses the point, both Althusserian and Lacanian, that the anticipations of grammar are always and only retroactively installed" (124).

This may be the case, but the linguistic contortions that result underscore the difficulty of Butler's project. Without a subject, actions begin to look self-motivating, rather like subjects themselves. In *Bodies That Matter* (1993), Butler defines what agency might mean in the absence of the preperformative subject. She states,

> "Agency" would then be the double-movement of being constituted in and by a signifier, where "to be constituted" means "to be compelled to cite or repeat or mime" the signifier itself. Enabled by the very signifier that depends for its continuation on the future of that citational chain, agency is the hiatus in iterability, the compulsion to install an identity through repetition, which requires the very contingency, the undetermined interval, that identity insistently seeks to foreclose. (220)

Agency thus lies in the capacity to resignify identity categories, to shift the content of the signifier "queer," for example, away from its "place within a homophobic strategy of abjection and annihilation" (233) and toward a meaning that includes the power of radical critique, so that one might talk, as Butler does, about being "critically queer" (223). The above quotation illustrates the difficulty of this proposition, however, where to avoid providing a substantial agency to a subject, Butler is required to posit agency within the signifier itself—a signifier that can be understood as "depending" upon continuation, that can desire to "secure its future" even if that future is revision. The subject is relegated to the passive voice — "to be constituted," "to be compelled" — while the signifier and identity do all of the work. It is the "signifier of identity" that commits a "disloyalty against identity"; it is identity that "seeks to foreclose" on contingency. The subject is merely along for the ride. Allowing for a moment the possibility that signifiers in fact care about their future, or that identities can be invested in their continuation, the above illustrates the need to anthropomorphize linguistic categories so as to retain agency while depriving the subject of any ontological claim on the capacity for action.

From Butler's perspective, it may not be crucial to determine whether in fact there can be a performance without a motivating intention, whether the "preconscious" "compulsion" to repeat can be characterized as neither mechanistic nor motivated, or, ultimately, why Butler is so invested in holding neither position. This point returns below. Returning to Butler's earlier discussions of gender identity, it becomes clear that her work has been most invested in performativity itself, as opposed to the status of the preperformative subject. As Butler explains in *Gender Trouble*, "The challenge for rethinking gender outside of the metaphysics of substance will have to consider the relevance of Nietzsche's claim in *On the Genealogy of Morals*, that 'there is no "being" behind doing, effecting, becoming; "the doer" is merely a fiction . . . the deed is everything'" (25). What appears striking in this formulation is the extent to which "doing" starts to look less like action and more like creation. That is, Butler dismantles identity, claiming that it is only performance, only to reinstate it as performance's proper outcome. As a result, the deeds that are "everything" take as their primary purpose the construction of the very identities they purported to replace.

The project that Butler outlines involves using one's identity to resignify the terms through which that identity is itself constituted, so that "the subject who is 'queered' into public discourse through homophobic interpellations of various kinds *takes up* or *cites* that very term as the discursive basis for opposition" (*Bodies* 232, emphasis in original). To return to *Jerry Maguire*, one could argue that the project of the movie involves precisely this type of resignification: Jerry, realizing he does not like the identity signified by "Mr. Maguire," transforms it from a shark in a suit to an agent who keeps the best interests of his client in mind and a husband who is completed by his wife. It is worth noting that this resignification of terms may not in fact easily constitute the type of opposition that Butler imagines. The problem for queer politics is not that the word "queer" means to one individual deviant, unnatural, and punishable, and to another radical, critical, and engaged. The problem is that some individuals think homosexuality is wrong, and that gay and lesbian men and women (not to mention the transgendered and transsexual) should be denied basic political protections as a result. It is the beliefs, not the words, that matter. Certainly the latter has a significant *role* in constituting the former, but it is far from the only player. Changing the meaning of the word "queer" will not automatically or uncomplicatedly change the opinions of an unfortunately significant portion of the population. Individuals who are opposed to gay civil rights may well just come up with another word.

Yet in advocating identity itself as a proper realm for political advocacy, Butler imagines a world in which the deeds that are "everything" take as their primary purpose the construction of the very identities they purported to replace.[18] As such, this world is no different from the type of existence imagined in *Jerry Maguire* and the contemporary self-help movement. For Butler, the type of "completion" offered in *Jerry Maguire* is impossible and naïve; the self will never fully inhabit the identities it works so hard to perform. There are, in fact, only failed performances. The fact of one's failure is not to be understood as a deterrent, however, not because one has no choice but to perform (although she imagines one does not), but rather because, even with "resources infinitely impure," it is still better to try (*Bodies* 241). From one perspective, then, the example provided in *Jerry Maguire* proves significantly more appealing. At least in Hollywood one might succeed at resignification. Why work so hard at a performance that is doomed to failure? And if such failure is inevitable, why is identity so idealized? The very analysis that proves identity to be an illusion serves primarily to reify it as the object of infinite pathos. The "difficult task of forging a future" within the "ambivalent condition of the power that binds" (*Bodies* 241, 242) is from Butler's perspective inescapable and tragic — inescapable, because Butler imagines there is no option other than to perform with no "hope of ever fully recognizing oneself in the terms by which one signifies" (*Bodies* 242), and tragic, because even so such an option is to her mind still desirable.

The mystification of Rod's transformation makes a certain amount of sense; taking place entirely internally and metaphysically, it depends on the filmic rhetoric of close-ups, point-of-view shots, slow motion, and extra-diagetic sound, even as Butler's argument defines the motivation/mechanization of repetition by explaining what it is not. By comparison, Jerry's project of transformation is rooted in the relation between individuals and institutions and is represented in far more concrete terms, suggesting a possible solution to the dilemmas of agency discussed above. Though he begins the movie obsessed with the question of "who had [he] become?" (36), Jerry realizes two facts early in the film. First, transformation of any type will not be tolerated while he works for Sports Management International. He is promptly fired with the explanation, "You did this to yourself" (58). Second, it is very difficult to focus on self-improvement and corporate success at the same time. But as Jerry's project to transform his identity is overtaken and finally replaced by his project to establish his sports agency, the movie imagines the means whereby that self-transformation can occur all the same: through the interpellative relation between individuals and institutions that Althusser originally proposed. That is, Jerry's agency with regard to his own identity may be open to dispute but, as the movie reminds us, that he would have influence over his company is not theoretically out of the question.[19]

At first glance, it may seem as unlikely to imagine that an individual and an agency might be similar enough entities that the concerns for one could be substituted with the concerns for the other. The project of the film, however, is dedicated to imagining the ways that individuals and the companies that employ them are essentially comparable and fundamentally inseparable. Furthermore, contemporary writing on the nature of service labor tends to agree. As noted above, the work of C. Wright Mills, William Whyte, and David Riesman all discuss the profound influences that corporations have on the individual employees, yet it is in service labor where that influence is perceived most powerfully. For example, C. Wright Mills discussed the economic shift from manufacturing to services and observed that such economies tend to create "a personality market" in which the distinction between what a person does and who a person is becomes increasingly difficult to maintain (*White* 182). Unlike manufacturing, which primarily emphasizes "manual skills," service employment requires "the art of 'handling,' selling, and servicing people," with the result that "personal or even intimate traits of the employee are drawn into the sphere of exchange" (182). A salesperson, for example, cannot lower prices to make a sale, so "she uses her 'personality'" (183) to persuade her customers to buy. Her success at her job depends upon her ability to make that personality "an instrument of an alien purpose" (184). When unemployment is down, salespeople might relax the standards of performance, but if unemployment rises, "the salespeople must again practice politeness," and in this way "the laws of supply and demand continue to regulate . . . the kind of personality he may develop and display" (184).

From one perspective, Mills's description of service labor ultimately looks not unlike an early version of interpellation, in which the need "for workers with a pleasant manner" affects first business-training enterprises and public education. These "new ways are diffused by charm and success schools and by best-seller literature" until "the sales personality . . . has become a dominating type, a pervasive model for imitation for masses of people in and out of selling" (*White* 187). Yet for Mills the issue is not agency and the possibility of transforming action, but rather alienation and the inclusion of personality traits in the means of production. His account assumes a substantive or preperformative subject that in making "an instrument of himself" can be "estranged from It also" (188). This is not an assumption—about either the self or the estrangement—that Judith Butler or *Jerry Maguire* necessarily shares. What makes his explanation of the personality market useful is twofold: first, it illustrates the continuities between discussions of corporate life in the 1950s and the 1990s, continuities that make *Jerry Maguire* and *Revolutionary Road* seem surprisingly similar; second, it elaborates the conflation of the worker and the work inherent in service employment, a conflation upon which *Jerry Maguire*'s account of the self or subject ultimately relies.

For Jerry, the idea that he must make "an instrument of himself" (Mills, *White* 188) to provide a service successfully is hardly new. The self-proclaimed "Lord of the Living Room," Jerry is attentive to the fact that his skills at "'handling,' selling, and servicing people" (182) are a significant part of his success.[20] When he pitches his services to a client, he describes as much who he is as what he will do. "I want you to know I'm about personal attention," he explains. "This is my life. I'm available to you twenty-four hours a day."[21] Jerry thus seems aware of marketing consultant Harry Beckwith's recent observation about the service economy: "You buy products based on your feelings about the product[;] you choose your services based on your *feelings* toward the providers" (*Clients* 195).[22] "The problem with services," according to Beckwith, is that "[y]ou can't see them — so how do you sell them?" (*Selling* xiii). "A product is tangible. You can see it and touch it"; but a service "is intangible" (xv), leaving open the question of what a consumer actually purchases. The operating assumption has been that in the service economy the client buys the provider's expertise, but Beckwith notes that clients are rarely in a position to evaluate that expertise. Since "today's clients cannot choose among services and products [because] they cannot gather all the information," they increasingly "*choose among people*" (*Clients* 47). A successful service enterprise must cultivate a series not of clients but of "loving relationships" (195). To use the phrase from *Jerry Maguire*, "the key to this job is personal relationships" (37). After all, as Beckwith reminds us, "*we love people, not institutions*" (*Clients* 195).

In a company the size of Jerry's, the fact that individuals "love people" rather than institutions would not seem to be much of a problem. With only two employees, the association of Jerry Maguire the person with Jerry Maguire Inc. is easy to make. As Rod himself acknowledges, he retains Jerry Maguire Inc. primarily because of Jerry himself: "I like you. My wife likes you. You're good to my wife."[23] When the service provider is a large company, however, these "loving relationships" are arguably harder to create. Does the fact that "*we love people, not institutions*" (Beckwith, *Clients* 195) preclude the types of "loving relationships" upon which Beckwith insists? How can a company make its clients love it like a person?

Interest in such questions has dominated business-marketing literature throughout the 1990s and has produced "in recent years" what John Hancock CEO David D'Alessandro calls "a kind of brand mania in American business" that "more than any other business concept of the day ... has infiltrated the culture" (xii, xiii). The concept of the brand refers not to products and services per se, but rather to the "psychological concept held in the mind of the public" about the company that provides those products or services (Bedbury 15). In the words of Scott Bedbury, chief of marketing at Nike and then at Starbucks, if "a product is no more than an artifact around which customers have experiences," a brand is defined "by the sum total of those experiences, rather than the products or services themselves" (16). Brands encapsulate "the emotional reasons for people's buying" a product. Companies should pursue relationships that are "so emotionally grounded that . . . your customers can honestly defend their choice by saying, 'I don't know, I just like it better'" (Moser 72).

The value for corporations of branding stems from precisely this "emotional realm." As a "living concept that we hold in our minds for years" (Bedbury 20), brands provide the basis for the type of "loving relationship" Beckwith imagines to be so difficult and so crucial for institutions. Yet it does so by encouraging customers to imagine those brands — and by extension, the institutions they personify — as persons themselves. "Struck by the similarities between defining a person and defining a brand" (19), Bedbury argues that every brand has a "genetic structure" (28) or "brand DNA" (29). Cracking that "genetic code . . . is about tapping into an essence and an ethos that defines who you are" (41). Of course, the "you" refers to a corporate rather than an individual entity, yet the generality of the pronoun, applying both to the company whose brand is under consideration as well as to the employees who work there, underscores the metaphor established by the phrase "brand DNA." Even more explicitly, Mike Moser argues in *United We Brand* that "it is impossible for a company not to have a personality, just as it's impossible for a person not to have a personality" (67). The best way to conceive of a brand is by acknowledging this fact up front. If you "[t]hink of your company as a person" (176), Moser claims, you will be more likely to "create a [brand] personality that connects with people" and thus "create your own brand community" (77–79).

From a professional perspective, it seems obvious why Jerry would want to establish the "Jerry Maguire brand." According to these authors, brands are the single most important aspect of contemporary marketing. Besides, having written his mission statement, Jerry has already done the majority of the work. Establishing the "brand message" (D'Alessandro 26), "brand essence" (Bedbury 28), or "core brand values" (Moser 11) is the most crucial part of branding, and it is easy enough to chart the progress of Jerry's business project alongside the "ten rules" (D'Alessandro), "eight principles" (Bedbury), and "five steps" (Moser) the authors offer to guide one's efforts. Yet the logic of branding has its place in the metaphysical side of Jerry's project as well. As it turns out, brands and the companies they stand for can also help produce "the me [Jerry had] always wanted to be" (Crowe 38). Where Moser and Bedbury focus on how brands embody corporate identities, D'Alessandro imagines that brands provide a means to define not only the corporations that make one's favorite products but also one's own identity through their use.

Downplaying the traditional identity categories of "geography, pedigree, race, or religion," D'Alessandro argues that individuals increasingly define themselves "by education and accomplishment," values made tangible "by the things we consume" (22). Using Daniel Boorstin's analysis of late-nineteenth- and early-twentieth-century "consumption communities" as the basis of his argument, D'Alessandro asks, "With whom are you more likely to share what Boorstin calls 'certain illusions, hopes, and disappointments'? With someone 3,000 miles away, who drinks the same brand of microbrewed beer that you do, or with the 'Bud' drinker who lives right next door?" (22). Though it is not entirely clear what differentiates these "consumption communities" from the more familiar category of class affiliation (unless it is to specify it further), D'Alessandro's point is less about how a person defines his identities — racially, ethnically, regionally, or socioeconomically — than about the ways in which consumer brands have become a part of that process. Like the hailing that "promises identity" (Butler, *Psychic Life* 108), "Brand[s] offer trust, comfort, convenience and identity in an increasingly complicated world" (D'Alessandro 23).

The concept of the brand provides a way in which transforming a company — Jerry Maguire Inc. — and transforming a person — Jerry Maguire — can become precisely the same project. That is, once Jerry establishes the corporate identity or brand of Jerry Maguire Inc., that institution is then in a position to interpellate the customers who consume its services and the employees who work on its behalf, including presumably its CEO. In a world where one builds brands as if they were identities and builds identities by way of one's favorite brands, Jerry's efforts to define the identity of his company end up as efforts to determine the nature of his self. In an odd echo of Butler's commitment to repetition as a vehicle for interpellation (and of performance theory more generally), Beckwith himself argues that companies produce the employees they require: recommending a system of daily "mantras" to remind staff members of the

21. The camera begins its close-up of Jerry Maguire as he watches Rod speak with Marcee. *Jerry Maguire* (1996). Sony Pictures.

importance of customer service, he comments that these mantras "become practices and practices soon become habits [until . . .] eventually, those habits become part of the employee's way of thinking and working . . . Mantras change our actions and then those actions change our attitudes. We become what we do" (*Clients* 240–41). To put it more concisely, Jerry abandons his concern for the self in favor of his concern for the company, and then that company produces the self he wanted all along.[24]

From this perspective, it becomes clear why Rod's transformation from a "*paycheck*" (Crowe 157) to a "marquee player" (120) necessarily precedes Jerry's metamorphosis from "a shark in a suit" (36) to a man capable of intimacy. Though the audience has no literal account of why Rod metamorphosed when he did, he is certainly not the only one who benefits from it. The agency too derives an advantage that is represented by the opposing team's quarterback, who admires Rod and Jerry's extended hug outside the locker room after the game. Demanding of his own agent, "Why don't we have that kind of a relationship?" (175), he is shown observing Rod and Jerry with a thoughtful expression. Only after this player's comments imply the long-term success of Jerry Maguire Inc. does the movie represent Jerry's transformation into the "man he almost is."[25] This second transformation appears in far less romanticized terms than Rod's: no one loses consciousness, the camera never overtly enters Jerry's point of view, there is no slow motion, and the only outward sign that Jerry has developed the capacity for intimacy is his assumption that when his phone rings it is a call from his estranged wife. The film emphasizes instead Jerry's *realization* of his transformation, which is represented in a thirteen-second cut-in that ends in a close-up of Jerry's face; as the camera moves in, his expression turns pensive and then he suddenly turns to run home to Dorothy.[26]

22. The camera ends in a close-up of Jerry's face as he realizes he loves Dorothy. *Jerry Maguire* (1996). Sony Pictures.

The lack of a concrete instant of the type that Rod experienced speaks to the film's efforts to see the success of Jerry's self-transformation in terms that remind us more of Althusser than of Hollywood—of the self as process rather than the self as project. That is, Jerry has no moment comparable to Rod's because Jerry's moments have been happening all along through his efforts to produce a successful business institution. While Jerry made a project of his agency, his agency made a process out of Jerry, interpellating him as its CEO. Furthermore, if the difficulty from Althusser's perspective is that subject has no agency with regard to his own identity, the film's point is that he does not need it. He need only have agency with regard to the type of brand identity he creates. The inevitable relation between individuals and institutions will take care of the rest. The creation and success of Jerry Maguire Inc. produces subjective agency in and of itself. This model of procedural selfhood likewise suggests a reason to care about identity despite its illusoriness: while the subject may have little reason to resignify identities that never truly existed, corporations have every incentive to do so since identities play a crucial role in the marketing of their products and services.

In the final scenes of the movie, Jerry's return to Dorothy is played out against the chorus of a divorced women's group and is preceded by an older woman's explanation for the repeated failure of relationships: "The neural pathways are set and that's why it's hard for people to change. That's why people don't change very often."[27] This faith in neurology and formative environments is immediately contradicted by Jerry's declaration that he is a changed man, yet he cannot explain that transformation outside of the company that produced it. "[T]onight, our little project, our company," he tells Dorothy, "had a very big night," but it "wasn't complete" because he "couldn't share it with [her]" (177). The phrasing leaves ambiguous what precisely is not complete: Is it the night? Is it Jerry himself? Is it the company? But if the distinction between Jerry and his agency is impossible to maintain, Dorothy appears not to care, and the film doesn't offer a clue. The epilogue of the movie finds the now-completed Maguire family returning from the zoo; when Jerry discovers that Dorothy's four-year-old son has athletic ability, he promptly suggests a training regimen to cultivate his talent.[28] As there is no difference between building a better agency and becoming a better person, so too there is no difference between raising a child and representing a client. With the creation of Jerry's agency, in both senses of the term, the hitherto disparate spheres of work and home are merged: what one does and who one is may again coexist without conflict.

CONCLUSION: "COLLAGE IS THE ART FORM OF THE TWENTIETH CENTURY"

IN *Jerry Maguire*, "completion" is imagined to be possible: the self or subject that one struggles to create actually comes into being through a (good) marriage, after which (the movie suggests) one's proper role is to assist one's children in their own becoming. As discussed at the end of the last chapter, the epilogue of the movie suggests that the corporate and the domestic spheres might finally merge through four-year-old Ray's burgeoning athletic ability. As Ray's father/agent, Jerry need no longer see his professional and his personal lives as distinct. He and Rod can be all "heart" in both realms. Yet the movie's endorsement of completion as an achievable goal — an endorsement that Butler would quite legitimately deride as simplistic — is itself undermined through the very repetition that performance theory understands as constitutive of the subject. At various points during the movie, the narrative is punctuated by brief interjections from Jerry's sports-agent mentor, "the late great Dicky Fox," who offers such stale career advice as "the key to this job is personal relationships" (37) and "unless you love everybody, you can't sell anybody."[1] These moments are comedic; the actor (Jared Jussim) playing the part looks like an old guy who would give stale advice, and audiences frequently laugh when he appears. But his use of cliché — like the performative subject itself, the product of repetition — underscores the naiveté of Jerry's search. It suggests that the movie, if not the audience, is too sophisticated to be taken in by Jerry's fantasy of self-actualization. The final goal of the movie is thus simultaneously to idealize and ironize Jerry's project of becoming.

Dicky Fox's hallowed chestnuts are not the only clichés in *Jerry Maguire*. Early on in the film, when Jerry prepares his mission statement

23. The close-up of the cover of Jerry Maguire's memo. *Jerry Maguire* (1996). Sony Pictures.

for distribution to his colleagues (the move that leads first to his termination and then transformation), he gives it a simple cover with the title, "The Things We Think But Do Not Say," centered above a solid blue background. He proudly declares, "Even the cover looked like *The Catcher in the Rye*."[2] The reference is obvious—the dark red paperback edition of Salinger's novel that had been a primary high school text throughout the 1980s—and analogizes Jerry's fantasy of a company devoted to "less money, fewer clients" to Holden's dream of a world without phonies: confused, impractical, and adolescent. The subsequent uncertainty over the genre of Jerry's manuscript—he insists it is a "mission statement," but everyone else calls it a "memo" (48)—itself speaks to Holden's dilemma about phoniness. Jerry writes his fantasy of a company that is outside of any existing model, free from cynicism and the taint of social compromise, whereas those who read it see only a variation on a form. This is a Butler-like critique of the Cartesian subject (or the Cartesian corporation), which imagines that an original subject might exist. And Jerry's final success, illustrated by his acceptance of the term "memo" in the second-to-last scene, though compromised in his own terms, is a Butler-like success.[3] It acknowledges both the possibilities within and the limitations of one's constitution within pre-given forms.

The presence of Holden Caulfield in *Jerry Maguire* is hardly unique, providing only one example of the ambiguous status Salinger's novel held at the end of the twentieth century.[4] Frequently, illusions to Holden and the novel more generally mark a fantasy of authenticity that has been abandoned, in which the innocence one associates with Holden's search (and adolescence more generally) has been replaced by a weary sophistication that fondly recollects its own naiveté.[5] As this volume has uncovered, the mid-century's concept of authenticity was far more complicated than it may appear when it is invoked at a comfortable distance of a half-century or more. At various points, writers and social critics imagined authenticity in a number of ways: there was the Caulfieldian authenticity — in which the self must possess an inner core and an outer façade, the latter of which is mutable and deployed by the former for its own purposes. There was the paradoxical *inauthentic* authenticity of the real phony — an individual who was constructed entirely within the social realm and thus could not count either as real *or* as false. And there was the American version of existentialist authenticity (in works by Kazan, Percy, Highsmith, among others), in which the authentic self was less a state to be realized than a process to be lived. Yet what importantly bound together these disparate variations was a profound commitment to the concept of authenticity as something that separated the self from a social realm, begrudged even a hint of cultural construction, and viewed individuals who appeared genuinely to be like their peers as inevitably mistaken about themselves and their wants — and as inevitably coerced. Authenticity in the postwar period defined the self in opposition to, rather than as the product of, or even in symbiosis with, the cultural circumstances through which the self or subject came into being.

Holden's reemergence at the end of the twentieth century was not only an exercise in sophisticated nostalgia. It likewise marked the restoration of the very authenticity that postmodernity and performance theory purported to abandon. Thus what looks at first like wistful longing for a time when authenticity might be invoked without irony actually constitutes the rehabilitation of the term under different auspices. In a representative example, John Guare's play *Six Degrees of Separation* (1990) — itself a meditation on the consequences of performativity — uses the novel *The Catcher in the Rye* to introduce con-man Paul Poitier's discourse on the transformative power of the imagination. An approximately college-age black adolescent who refashions himself from a street hustler into Sidney Poitier's son, Paul talks his way into the world of Ouisa and Flan Kittredge — wealthy New Yorkers ensconced on the Upper East Side of Manhattan. He arrives at their penthouse apartment with a (self-inflicted) knife wound in his side, convinces them that he knows their children from prep school, claims (untruthfully) to be Sidney Poitier's son, cooks them dinner and describes his thesis, a meditation on *The Catcher in the Rye*. At first, neither Flan nor Ouisa would seem susceptible to appeals based on Holden Caulfield. A private art dealer, Flan embodies the postmodern collapse of "aesthetic production . . . into commodity production generally" (Jameson, *Postmodernism* 4). He is simultaneously and without contradiction adoring of and utterly mercenary about the art he brokers. Ouisa's fondness for puns that turn on the juxtaposition of political upheaval and upper-class consumerism — she comments, for example, "The phrase — striking coal miners — I see all these very striking coal miners modeling the fall fashions" (Guare 11) — betrays a calloused if clever wit.[6] Yet despite being "smart, sophisticated, tough New Yorkers" (93), Paul's exposition of the novel affects them deeply, and not just as a nostalgic reminder of idealisms past.

The Catcher in the Rye, Paul claims, is about "paralysis . . . the great modern theme" and illustrates "one of the great tragedies of our times, the death of the imagination" (Guare 33). It is the imagination, Paul argues, that "teaches us our limits and then how to grow beyond these limits"; it "is the voice that sees clearly and says 'Yes, this is what I want for my life'" (62).[7] By Paul's account, imagination is what Holden does not have in *The Catcher in the Rye*, committed as he is to a clear distinction between phonies and authentic persons — to the idea that everyone possesses an authentic self that he is in constant danger of betraying. From one perspective, Paul stands as proof that Holden's ideas are at the very least outdated if not outright erroneous. With the help of Trent Conway, a prep school classmate of the Kittredge children, who picks Paul up on a dark street corner and takes him home to his dorm room for sex, Paul transforms himself. Over and over, he practices the vocabulary, accent, and behaviors of the upper classes. Within three months — Ouisa marvels, "Can you believe it? Three months! . . . Trent Conway, the Henry Higgins of our time" (81) — he learns enough about the social mores of the upper classes to become "a guest in their houses" (79). Yet from a different angle, it is not clear that Paul's version of performativity avoids the fantasy of authenticity to which Holden stubbornly clings. Rather, the switch to a performative account of the subject makes authenticity no less important. It just defines authenticity differently, as a becoming rather than a being, the realization of a project of self (or subject) rather than the embodiment of an essence. To put it slightly differently, if as Paul explains it, "the imagination is another phrase for what's most uniquely *us*" (34, emphasis in original), then one's most unique self is defined not by the "me that I am," as Holden Caulfield would have it, but rather as Jerry Maguire might: in terms of the "me I most want to be." Jean-Paul Sartre, with his theorization of authenticity as process of both recognizing one's situation and then one's freedom within it, might well have been pleased.

Thus, performativity, which purports to have rendered authenticity obsolete by obliterating the notion of a stable subject, in fact reestablishes it as a standard of evaluation by imagining as authentic that which most closely resembles the self or subject of one's desires. Instead of signifying one term in an opposition — in which one was either phony or authentic, a representation or real — authenticity at the end of the century operated as one end of a continuum on which representations themselves are to be evaluated. Herbert Marcuse maintained in 1955 that the United States "has individuality . . . in name only, in the specific representation of types" (*Eros* 103). To Marcuse, no one could genuinely be a "he man" or a "vamp" because no one could authentically inhabit a social role; any such habitation was a denial of what makes each individual *essentially* unique. Anyone who appeared as a he-man or vamp must be a real phony — unaware of his or her construction within social forms (what makes one real) and yet still invalidated by that cultural construction (what makes one phony). But in the 1990s, the issue is not the avoidance of typage, since everyone is already perceived to have been constructed within precisely the systems of types that Marcuse finds so degrading. What matters instead is the success of any particular embodiment. The performance theorists' claim that there are only failed performances illustrates how perfect inhabitation of a type is impossible. Authenticity instead becomes the tool whereby one's inevitably relative success is judged. One speaks of performances that are themselves more or less authentic in comparison to the self or subject of one's imaginative longing.

This is not to say that *Six Degrees of Separation* presents no limits to the individual's imaginative capacity to remake him- or herself in the world. Indeed, the play itself encodes a critique of Paul's own imaginative philosophy, and of the kind of economic and racial/ethnic position one needs to put that philosophy successfully to work. In Paul's final conversation with Ouisa, *Six Degrees* illustrates the crucial importance both of race, ethnicity, and class position in one's ability to project oneself into the life one wants.

After Paul has disappeared and is sought for police questioning, he calls Ouisa to ask for her help.[8] She insists he go to the police, and he agrees, provided she and Flan will accompany him to the police station, because he'll "be treated with care if [they] take [him]." Ouisa does not believe her presence would make any difference. "Mrs. Louisa Kittredge," Paul flatly states, "I am black" (110). In this brief moment, Paul acknowledges all the race and class markers away from which he has had, and will continue to have, a hard time imagining himself.[9] His subsequent loss to Ouisa in the bureaucracies of the justice system — "we didn't know Paul's [real] name," Ouisa explains, "We weren't family" (116), and without his name there is no way to locate him in the myriad of holding jails in New York City — is in this sense a commentary on the limits of Paul's own teachings. Flan insists, "He'll be back. We haven't heard the last of him. The imagination. He'll find a way" (119). Perhaps. But there is no question that, when it comes to imaginative re-creation, some people will have an easier time than others.[10]

Ouisa herself is in a far better position to refashion herself than Paul ever could be: an upper-class, educated white woman, there are far fewer limitations placed on her imagination than on that of a twenty-something poor and undereducated black man. Ouisa acknowledges this difference when, at the end of the play, she comments on how simultaneously privileged and "paltry" her life with Flan actually is. After Paul has been arrested and Ouisa seeks fruitlessly to locate him, she struggles to describe why his loss is so important to her:

> He wanted to be us. Everything we are in the world, this paltry thing — our life — he wanted it. He stabbed himself to get in here.... And we turn him into an anecdote to dine out on. Or dine in on. But it was an experience. I will not turn him into an anecdote. How do we fit what happened to us into life without turning it into an anecdote with no teeth and a punch line you'll mouth over and over for years to come? "Tell us the story about the imposter who came into your lives—." "This reminds me of the time this boy—." And we become these human juke boxes spilling out these anecdotes. But it was an experience. How do we keep the experience? (117–18)

Ouisa's plaint is based in an apparent opposition between anecdote and experience; she then parallels that opposition to one between "human juke boxes" and (one presumes) actual humans. What are the differences? Clearly an anecdote is a version of an experience — it is a representation of an experience — and by extension one can assume a human jukebox is a version of a human, only one who has replaced consciousness and feeling with mechanized automation. In the former case (anecdote versus experience), Ouisa's concern is with the difference between experience and representation itself, in which any representation (an anecdote, say, or a painting) fails to embody adequately the event (or object) that inspired it. Her protest is from this perspective one that Holden would appreciate, addressing the inevitable disparity between reality and any depiction of it. In Holden's case, this concern appears, appropriately enough, at the theater; he complains, "It was supposed to be like people really talking and interrupting each other and all. The trouble was, it was *too* much like people talking and interrupting each other" (126). He maintains that the quality of performance undermines those moments when, outside of the theater, talking and interrupting happen. Similarly, in repeating her anecdote, Ouisa fears she does more than tell the story of an experience; she believes that she diminishes that experience, removing its "teeth," and finally loses whatever it was the anecdote was intended to portray in the first place.

In the latter case (human jukeboxes versus humans), however, Ouisa opposes automation with consciousness, and in so doing rehabilitates representation under certain circumstances. It seems unlikely that humans, as opposed to "human juke boxes," never represent; among other things, this would mean they never use language. Rather, Ouisa's distinction turns on the *integration* of experiences. If experience can be "fit into life," in Ouisa's words, then presumably it does not matter if one represents it or not. Ouisa's emphasis on anecdotes as opposed to, say, stories, is telling in this context. An anecdote implies a degree of repetition that a story does not; it suggests a story turned to more than once, "to dine out on or dine in on"; it evokes a story that has become a ritual that one "mouth[s] over and over for years to come," a recited script, or even a cliché.[11] What for Butler guarantees the inseparability of the performer and her performance, the means whereby the performance comes to inhabit the subject and the subject to inhabit the performance, for Ouisa results in precisely the opposite. Repetition for Ouisa is what severs an experience from its subject, replacing imminence with automation. To "fit [an experience] into life," the guarantee of authentic as opposed to automated humanity, requires that it retain an immediacy that anecdotes do not possess.

Thus, to fit an experience into life does not mean never to *represent* it, but rather to retain a certain relationship to it (both the experience and the representation) and by extension to the life of which it forms a part. This relationship separates performance of the type Paul engages in from mere acting. The actor, Paul explains, "has no life — he has no memory — only the scripts producers send him through his agents" (31) — whereas at his best the imaginative performer is able, as Paul explains, to "use all the parts of myself" (107). Crucially, those "parts" are not some inner qualities or essences. When Ouisa admires his Salinger lecture, Paul admits it was a "[g]raduation speech at Groton two years ago" and that his cooking is "[o]ther people's recipes." It seems that with the Kittredges, Paul used all of the parts of himself, as well as the parts of a few others. Yet why this borrowing does not constitute precisely the type of phoniness that Holden (at very least) abhors is open to question. The answer lays in the particular definition of "life" advocated in *Six Degrees of Separation*.

Quoting from Donald Barthelme, Paul declares that "collage is the art form of the twentieth century," though when faced with Ouisa's admission that "Everything is somebody else's," he responds, "Not your children. Not your life" (107). Paralleling the three, collages, children, and life become the same because all are understood as something the individual *makes*. The implication is that collage and life are in some fundamental sense the same thing — creations — and representation need not be harmful to experience because at its best experience is *itself representation*. This implication is made explicit in the final moments of the play when Flan comments that Cezanne "would leave blank spaces in his canvasses if he could not account for the brushstroke, give a reason for the color," and Ouisa responds: "Then I am a collage of unaccounted for brush-strokes. I am all random" (118). The harm of anecdotes is thus not that they are representations — all life, it will turn out, is a representation — but rather that they are "unaccounted for" or "random." Her subsequent challenge to Flan, "how much of your life can you account for?" valorizes intentionality and self-consciousness above all else; and Flan's response of "All! I am a gambler" (118) is in some sense a contradiction in terms. How can a gambler account for a bad role of the dice? Even allowing for the fact that the art of bluffing means in gambling that the player with the best hand does not always win, gambling still allows for the random in a way that Cezanne would not, and helps to explain Flan's earlier dream when he remembered himself "as [he] was. A painter losing a painting" (46). By comparison, Ouisa recalls a trip to the top of the scaffolding during the restoration of Michelangelo's Sistine frescoes. Encouraged by the cleaners, she high-fives God's outstretched hand. Like Adam, reaching up for the life that God offers him, Ouisa is a deliberate partner in her own creation.[12]

The valorization of self-consciousness and intent as a guarantor of authenticity might seem at first counterintuitive. It is the aforementioned actors' self-consciousness, after all, that identifies them as phony for Holden. He comments, "they acted more like they knew they were celebrities. . . . If you do something *too* good, then after a while, if you don't watch it, you start showing off" (126). And what is a show-off but someone self-conscious of her own abilities, performing with the intent to impress? Yet what in *The Catcher in the Rye* signals *phoniness* — an awareness of how one is received in a social context and a careful tailoring of one's performance to that audience — emerges in *Six Degrees of Separation* as the very mark of authenticity. In the play, if everything is a performance, then at the very least one should perform *deliberately*, with a direction and a goal, and with an eye toward what one wants to be. It bears noting that Holden's own self-consciousness makes him fear that he himself is no better than the actors he so strictly judges. But from the perspective of the late twentieth century, he worries for no reason. From that perspective, Holden's hyper-self-consciousness (of everything except his own performative brilliance) shows him not to be a hero of adolescent rebellion, exposing adult hypocrisy, but rather to be a pioneer of performativity — Paul Poitier's ancestor in self- or subject-realization. If Holden had walked the streets of New York long enough, he might have run into Paul on his way to the Kittredges'. This helps explain Paul's affection for Holden (despite Holden's lack of imagination), and for *The Catcher in Rye* more generally, which — though its fans and critics alike are accustomed to viewing it as the standard for traditional notions of authenticity — emerges, almost as if despite itself, as a foundational performative text.

Yet self-consciousness does more than just rehabilitate Holden as an authentic performer in late-twentieth-century understanding. It likewise allows the concept of authenticity and its opposites to perform the same work that they did at mid-century, just under different terms. As this volume has illustrated, in the immediate postwar period, authenticity separated the individual from his social context. So, too, did phoniness. By suggesting that conformity to social norms was a behavior rather than a being, phoniness suggested that the individual who engaged in its practice knew that there was a difference between himself and his context, and altered his behavior accordingly. Though that phony might be ethically reprehensible, he likewise illustrated that the self might still be thought *essentially* individual — that the self's interior maintained a crucial distance from the contexts through which it inevitably moved. Authenticity in the postwar period was a means to differentiate between the individuals who were constructed entirely by cultural forms (the real phonies), and those who were not (the authentic, who remained ethically committed to their individuality, and the phonies, who did not). As such, it allowed writers, filmmakers, social critics, and the like to maintain a belief in the longstanding ideology of American individualism.

Authenticity at the end of the century does the same type of cultural labor. Instead of valuing the individuated self over the constructed one, the concept values the knowing subject over an unknowing one, but the result — a faith in the individual's distance from her cultural contexts — remains fundamentally the same. If authenticity at the turn of the twenty-first century represents an acknowledgment of the perceived inevitability of cultural construction — a scaling back of that "less acceptant and genial view of the social circumstances of life" which, for Lionel Trilling, defined the mid-century's commitment to authenticity (11) — then it also provides a way to retain the notion of individual separateness through one's awareness of that construction. Allowing for the inescapable impact of cultural forms on the subject, the late-century individual is inevitably a real phony. But the subject who recognizes this fact, and who might manipulate it through recourse either to an imagination (to adopt Paul's terms), or a capacity to "outrun... the condition of its emergence" (to adopt Butler's), suggests a psychic distance from that cultural realm. That person possesses the "attitude" of detachment (in Menand's terms) that promises a (perhaps illusory) distance. The real phony becomes more real by being aware of one's own construction; authenticity now recognizes cultural authority, but still valorizes the individual within it.

NOTES

Introduction

1. Unless otherwise noted, all italics are from the original text.

2. Other historians — in addition to Halberstam and Diggins — who address the inaccuracy of contemporary stereotypes of the 1950s include Chafe, L. May, Meyerowitz, and Patterson. For an insightful discussion of the failures of contemporary scholarship to break through these stereotypical configurations, see Joel Foreman's Introduction to *The Other Fifties: Interrogating Midcentury American Icons* (1997).

3. These texts are by no means the only ones. For example, other psychology texts would include B. F. Skinner's *Walden Two* (1948), whose extreme version of behaviorism results in a notion of authenticity that looks remarkably like that espoused by performance theorists and others fifty years later, and also Norman O. Brown's *Life against Death: The Psychoanalytical Meaning of History* (1959). Theologian Paul Tillich, in *The Courage to Be* (1952), considers the historical genealogy of two alternative types of courage: the courage to be as a part (embodied in democratic conformism) versus the courage to be as oneself (as suggested by modern individualism) — as a struggle between "the loss of the self in collectivism and . . . the loss of the world in Existentialism" (154).

4. Nabers's observation was part of a seminar he organized on "Postwar American Literature and the Sociological Imagination" for the first *Post-45* symposium, held at Concordia University in November 2006. I am very grateful to the members of that seminar, and to the literary and cultural scholars who participate in *Post-45* more generally, for their unstinting assistance in formulating these arguments.

5. For example, in Morris Dickstein's analysis, the organizational and bureaucratic structures that World War II put into place never fully dissipated during peacetime. Dickstein convincingly argues that the war novels of the immediate postwar period feared "victory over Fascism abroad had been purchased at the cost of intolerance and

regimentation at home. These war novelists' nightmare was a world threatened not by foreign tyrants and obvious villains but by large, impersonal social organizations (30).

Similarly, Leerom Medevoi credits Fordist economic systems derived from the World War II economic mobilization with "a new mode of regulation of labor . . . modeled on a wartime precedent" (16). The resulting intellectual criticism of these systems produced numerous "forays against the Fordist world" in which "the new system of mass consumption was [pictured as] depriving Americans — and most vitally its men — of their hitherto distinctive autonomy" (21). In *Rebels: Youth and the Cold War Origins of Identity*, Medevoi examines the ways in which the rebellious adolescent of the postwar years "heralded new historical conditions that would soon inaugurate what we now call the 'politics of identity'" (1). While I agree with many of Medevoi's conclusions about the cultural work performed by the rebel, this project is committed to exploring the ways in which Holden Caulfield, and the figure of the teenager more generally, stages and then resolves larger cultural questions about authenticity and uniformity in the postwar period. This means situating that teenager alongside such relevant postwar characters as the mentally ill, the corporation man, and so on.

Andrew Hoberek provides a powerful corrective to studies that imagine the fears of the middle class to be largely illusory by tracing the important economic "transition from small-property ownership to white-collar employment as the basis of middle class status" (8). This shift makes possible a view of the pervasive anxieties of middle-class Americans "in class terms rather than individual ones, and historically rather than existentially" (11). With various shadings, all of these works make convincing arguments for the sources of mid-century anxiety in the dramatic historical changes to U.S. political, social, and psychic life in the years after World War II.

6. As Riesman takes pains not to attach an ethical valence to inner- versus other-directed persons, he is likewise careful to point out that "no one could be completely characterized by any one of these terms. . . . Even the insane person is not anomic in every sphere of life; nor could an autonomous person be completely autonomous." He argues, however, that "we can characterize an individual by the way in which one mode of adaptation predominates, and when we study individuals, analysis by such a method provides certain helpful dimensions for descriptive and comparative purposes" (243).

7. Critiques of the idea of a unique self — with its "unique personality and individuality, which can be expected to generate its own unique vision of the world and to forge its own unique, unmistakable style" (Jameson, *Cultural* 6) — have emerged from a variety of disciplines, including philosophy, linguistics, psychoanalysis, anthropology, literature, and theater. In the words of Patrick O'Donnell: "As different as theoretical conceptions of postmodern subjectivity may be, a remarkable number of them engage in the liquefaction of the postmodern subject/body — a fluidity that marks both its

supposed freedom and commodification. Whether it is Luce Irigaray's gendered subjectivity as 'fluid,' Deleuze and Guattari's nomadic 'BwO' (body without organs), Lyotard's 'great ephemeral skin,' Kristeva's 'abject,' or Haraway's 'cyborg,' identity in these conceptions is, by terms, amoebic, fractal, mutative, provisional, or multiple" (23–24).

8. For a compelling discussion of the uses of authenticity in the production and reception of ethnic fiction, see Jeff Karem, *The Romance of Authenticity: The Cultural Politics of Regional and Ethnic Literatures* (2004). Karem historicizes the fascination with ethnic cultural production alongside the early-twentieth-century interest in regional writing. He documents well the pervasive belief that "some forms of writing, identity, and cultural practice are 'truer' to one's group than others" (205), and the cumulative effect of his evidence suggests that, in endorsing a multiethnic approach to literary scholarship, literary critics have only exchanged one set of limitations for another. I agree with Karem's conclusions about the pervasive use of authenticity as a litmus test for ethnic writing. Yet concerns about the authenticity of texts cannot be separated from — and indeed are entirely dependent on — concerns about the authenticity of persons that extend beyond the boundaries of ethnicity that delineate Karem's examination.

9. For example, see Ihab Hassan, *Selves at Risk: Patterns of Quest in Contemporary American Letters* (1990); Jerome Klinkowitz, *Structuring the Void: The Struggle for Subject in Contemporary American Fiction* (1992); Tom LeClair, *The Art of Excess: Mastery in Contemporary American Fiction* (1989); and *In the Loop: Don DeLillo and the Systems Novel* (1987); Timothy Melley, *Empire of Conspiracy: The Culture of Paranoia in Postwar America* (2000); Patrick O'Donnell, *Latent Destinies: Cultural Paranoia and Contemporary U.S. Narrative* (2000); Gabriele Schwab, *Subjects without Selves: Transitional Texts in Modern Fiction* (1994); Mark Seltzer, *Serial Killers: Death and Life in America's Wound Culture* (1998); Joseph Tabbi, *Postmodern Sublime: Technology and American Writing from Mailer to Cyberpunk* (1995).

10. Emphasis in original. This project has benefited from Melley's sophisticated study. Melley identifies a collection of postwar narratives that are "deeply invested in a traditional concept of individual autonomy and uniqueness . . . [and] reveal this investment through nervousness about its viability" (3). He theorizes this nervousness as "agency panic": an "intense anxiety about an apparent loss of autonomy or self-control — the conviction that one's actions are being controlled by someone else, that one has been 'constructed' by powerful external agents" (12). Such panic stems from the attempt "to conserve a long-standing model of personhood — a view of the individual as a rational motivated agent with a protected interior core of beliefs, desires, and memories" (14). The problems of agency that Melley identifies and critiques in postwar texts are in many ways similar to the problems of authenticity here described, insofar as

both deal with the consequences of new ideas about persons and their susceptibility to exterior influence.

11. For example, one might consider the relation between *Invisible Man* and works like historian Stanley M. Elkins's *Slavery: A Problem in American Institutional and Intellectual Life*. One of Elkins's central questions directly addresses the intersection of race, self, and authenticity. Asking, "is it possible to deal with 'Sambo' as a type? . . . Was he real or unreal?" (82), Elkins questions whether Sambo should be understood as a product of race (biology), of social institutions (slavery) that form or deform individual character, or as a deliberate deception (phoniness) enacted "'in order to win maximum rewards within the system'" (83 [interior quote from Kenneth Stamp]). These same questions are likewise considered narratively in Ellison's *Invisible Man*, which evokes different possible models of the self at various points. Biological models are referenced in the racism that the narrator encounters on virtually every page of the novel. The "phony" model appears in the portrayal of Dr. Bledsoe, the manipulative president of the black college that the narrator briefly attends. Bledsoe declares, "I's big and black and I say 'Yes suh' as loudly as any burrhead when it's convenient, but I'm still the king down here" (142) before he expels the novel's narrator. The relation of the self to class position is considered during the long section of the novel in which the narrator works for the Communist Party recruiting new members in Harlem. Models of cultural construction are evoked when the narrator acknowledges his southern heritage while purchasing cooked yams from a street vendor. "They're my birthmark," he says to the peddler: "I yam what I am!" (266). Shortly after making his purchases, the narrator questions the authenticity of his likes and dislikes in terms very similar to those Holden Caulfield evokes in *The Catcher in the Rye* (as discussed in chap. 1): "What and how much had I lost by trying to do what was expected of me instead of what I myself had wished to do? . . . But what of those things which you actually didn't like, not because you were not supposed to like them, not because to dislike them was considered a mark of refinement and education—but because you actually found them distasteful? The very idea annoyed me. How could you know?" (266). At moments like these, the narrator's problem is not the pressures of conformity ("you were not supposed to like them") but the reality of uniformity ("you actually found them distasteful"). How can the narrator prove his authenticity—his individuality—when he prefers the more refined choice? What does individuality mean, if it is not defined in opposition to cultural mores? That the narrator figures this dilemma as an epistemological problem—"how could you know?"—suggests a further alignment with the type of dilemmas that appear throughout *The Catcher in the Rye* and *Breakfast at Tiffany's*. The criticism on *Invisible Man* is too varied and voluminous to list here; however, for discussions that consider the role that selfhood or identity plays in the novel, see the article by Jonathan Arac and

chapters in books by Dickstein and Hoberek. These works have been particularly useful for this consideration of authenticity in the postwar period.

Chapter One. Postwar Teenagers and the Attitude of Authenticity

1. The film's legendary status as a representation of youth culture has lasted at least until the early twenty-first century, in which the same broad plot outlines — including the time spent in the abandoned mansion — were recycled in the first two episodes of the first season of the teen television drama *The O.C.* Part of this status is no doubt attributable to James Dean's celebrated method acting performance in the role, and the actor's sudden death three days before the film was released. For discussions of Dean's performance, see Pomerance and Braudy.

2. For example, Robert Linder, whose 1944 case study of an incarcerated youth offender provided the title of the film, asserts in *Must You Conform?* (1956) that both homes and "schools have become vast factories for the manufacture of robots" (168): "the school takes up where the parent leaves off; and the children who emerge from it with a few shreds of individuality clinging to their blue jeans or bobby-socks are rare birds, indeed" (169). Linder advocates a "positive rebellion" as a necessary corrective to the uniforming influences of social institutions. The positive rebel "is essential to our society. The maintenance of our values and their realization depends upon him" (189). Parents and schools must adopt a new orientation, "the pedagogy of freedom" as opposed to the "myth of adjustment" (210). Nicholas Ray himself claimed that Linder did little more than provide the title for the film, though he met with the author when Linder was in Los Angeles lecturing for *Must You Conform?* (Ray 33). However, the ideas expressed in Linder's writing bear a close resemblance to the picture of the rebel that emerges in the film as a whole. Whether this was a result of the residual influence of Linder's work on the screenwriters or because the terms through which adolescence and juvenile delinquency were understood during the period remained consistent across various cultural fields is open to debate. That juvenile delinquency was very much a popular concern in the early to mid-1950s is well established. As J. David Slocum observes, "The very tangle of voices involved in the film's preproduction enriched the eventual production but also reflected the complicated contemporary concerns over the causes and social significance of juvenile delinquency" (2). See Gilbert, Medevoi, and Devlin for a more complete analysis of the cultural concern with juvenile delinquency in the period.

3. This brief summary and analysis overlooks many important aspects of the film's representation of mid-century American teenagers, not the least of which is the way the film asserts the importance of traditional gender roles, particularly within the family.

After arguing with his parents, Jim escapes with Judy and Plato to an abandoned mansion where they establish an idealized family. Jim is the strong, "gentle and sweet" father; Judy is the mother who wants only "to love someone"; and Plato, whose parents divorced and left him to be raised by a maid, and whose closeted homosexuality is variously and repeatedly coded in the film, is the child they put to bed with a lullaby. Plato obviously feels his father's absence strongly, and his openly expressed wish that Jim be his father suggests the latter's desertion as a possible source of his homosexuality. After Plato's death, Jim, wearing his father's sports coat, introduces his parents to Judy: their implied union rehabilitates the American family and its conventional gender divisions over the body of the dead gay teen. J. David Slocum's edited collection of essays provides a number of excellent analyses of the complicated gender politics of the film.

4. The idea of adolescence as a specific developmental stage is generally thought to have been invented at the beginning of the twentieth century in response to demographic changes that advanced the onset of puberty but significantly delayed marriage. Educators and social reformers thus became increasingly concerned with the regulation of premarital sexuality, and the concept of the adolescent—sexually of age, but not yet married—was born. For a meticulous discussion of the link between the emergence of the adolescent and the development of abstinence and sex-education movements, see Moran. But if adolescence as such was invented at the beginning of the twentieth century, the term "teenage" was first used in 1921, and in the years after World War II the teenager came to signify a distinct category of being, with its own cultural practices and prerogatives. For a larger history of adolescence in the United States, see Kette. For analyses of the turmoil surrounding youth culture and teenage consumerism in the 1950s, see Gilbert, Hine, and Palladino. For a valuable account of the development of the concept of "market segmentation" more generally during the immediate postwar years, see L. Cohen. For a discussion of the youth market and the emergence of "teen-picks" as a distinct Hollywood genre, see Doherty.

5. Lawrence J. Friedman's biography of Erik Erikson discusses the importance of his elaborations on neo-Freudian thought.

6. For an excellent account of the history of *The Catcher in the Rye*'s reception and canonization, see chap. 2 of Medevoi's *Rebels: Youth and the Cold War Origins of Identity* (2005). Medevoi provides a detailed discussion of the criticism to argue that the novel's "hypercanonization" (56) is linked to the rise of the "identity novel" and "identity criticism," in which novels like *The Catcher in the Rye*, *Invisible Man* (1952), and Saul Bellows's *The Adventures of Augie March* (1953) were read as Cold-War national allegories. Representative essays on the novel since its publication include Baumbach, Lundquist, Miller, Ohmann and Ohmann, Pinsker, and Wells. Helpful critical collections include those edited by Bloom, Salzman, and Steed. In particular, works by

Cowan, Freedman, Seelye, and Steinle proved thought-provoking. In addition, chapters in Dickstein and Nadel have been particularly useful to this project.

7. The six essays that comprise Trilling's *Sincerity and Authenticity* were given as the Charles Eliot Norton lectures at Harvard University in the spring of 1970. Although the timing of these lectures places Trilling's observations outside the scope of this particular chapter, I include them for two reasons: first, because Trilling is here discussing works (Sartre's *Being and Nothingness*, Marcuse's *Eros and Civilization*, R. D. Laing's *The Divided Self*, and Norman O. Brown's 1960 Phi Beta Kappa address at Columbia University) that are themselves from the period; and second, because these essays elucidate Trilling's attitude toward the concept of authenticity throughout his career, explicitly stating opinions inferable from earlier works.

8. Unless otherwise noted, all italics are from the original text.

9. Unless otherwise noted, all emphasis in quotes from Sartre's works is from the original text.

10. For extremely useful accounts of the American reception of Sartre in particular, and existentialism more generally, see Fulton as well as Cotkin, chaps. 5 through 13. Fulton focuses on the specifically philosophical response, charting the academic reaction to Sartre's philosophy in the postwar years as it evolved from a profound skepticism (due, she argues, in part to existentialism's mainstream popularity and in part to the unavailability in English of *Being and Nothingness* until 1956) to a gradual acceptance of his work as a legitimate philosophical contribution. Cotkin focuses more broadly on existentialism's reception in mainstream intellectual culture: the New York intellectuals, the literary community, and the student movements of the 1960s.

11. As Ann Fulton notes, *Existentialism and Humanism* is considered to be a somewhat superficial distillation of Sartre's far more complicated account of human ontology. She quotes Sartre scholar Joseph Fell, who observed, "It is unfortunate that that the first and only work of Sartre's that most students and many professing philosophers in this country read . . . was the Existentialism is a Humanism lecture — a drastically oversimplified exposition that Sartre himself regrets having published" (27).

12. Though selections from *L'Être et le Néant* (1943) appeared earlier, the volume was not completely translated and published in English as *Being and Nothingness* until 1956.

13. As Trilling rightly points out, "Sartre deals with the theory of psychoanalysis in a relatively early stage of its development," and "the good faith of psychoanalysis is not impugned if the situation it postulates is that of being two consciousnesses (the ego and the superego), one of which is not accessible to the other by intuition" (147, 149).

14. For an analysis of the intellectual development of the ideas ultimately expressed in *Childhood and Society* see Friedman, chaps. 4 and 5; a discussion of the critical and

popular reception of *Childhood and Society* can be found on pp. 237–41. For a thorough and persuasive analysis of Erikson's work in general, and *Childhood and Society* in particular, as foundational texts for the development of not only the concept of identity as such but also the phenomenon of identity politics that descended from it, see Medevoi, esp. chap. 1. Medevoi's analysis of the historical roots of identity as a concept has been particularly helpful to this analysis.

15. The surprising emergence of the Jew as the representative American during this period is discussed at length in chap. 4 of this volume.

16. There is limited critical work on *Breakfast at Tiffany's*. Recent articles include Bibler, Cornut-Gentille, Krämer, Hassan ("Birth"), and Pugh. *Breakfast at Tiffany's* is also included among the texts discussed in the collection edited by Waldmeir.

17. In the movie version of *Breakfast at Tiffany's* (1961), directed by Blake Edwards, this ending is substituted by the Hollywood-requisite romantic one. Yet the commitment to a happy ending results in significant alterations to both the letter and the metaphysical spirit of the novel. After Holly (Audrey Hepburn) is arrested and Paul Varjak (George Peppard) announces that he loves her, Holly responds by claiming "I'm not Holly. I'm no Lulamae either. I don't know who I am. I'm like Cat here. We're a couple of no-named slobs." Paul's answer to "Miss Whoever-you-are" claims for Holly precisely the substantive self that the novel is committed to denying, a self that can only be discovered through love and the fact that "people belong to each other." He argues, "You're terrified somebody's going to stick you in a cage? Well baby, you're already in that cage. You built it yourself. . . . It's wherever you go. Because no matter where you run you just end up running into yourself." A model in which one can run into oneself suggests not only that the authentic self does exist, but that it continually sabotages her efforts to deny it. The final moments of the film, when Holly silently acquiesces to Paul's love and together they find the cat (amid a thunderous downpour) suggests her ultimate acceptance of this authentic self as the "only chance anybody's got for true happiness."

18. This in and of itself is not surprising. One might easily imagine a situation in which certain individuals could only experience themselves as authentic if they committed ritualized murder; naturally, a society might have an investment in such individuals not being authentic in quite that way. Ritual or serialized murder is considered as a question of authenticity at length in chap. 3.

Chapter Two. From Madness to the Prozac Americans

1. Unless otherwise noted, ellipses and emphases come from the original text. There has been a wide range of criticism on the film and its various remakes. The film is analyzed in relation to a number of discourses, with genre studies (science fiction and

horror), Cold-War politics, the HUAC investigations, 1950s American culture, and gender studies being the most common. Particularly useful analyses for this project include the collection by LaValley, and articles and chapters by Rogin, Badmington, and Mann.

2. Unless otherwise noted, all emphasis in quotes from Percy's works is from the original text.

3. The pods are instantly self-conscious of the change that has taken place, however, and know as well of both the overall plan and the need for secrecy. As the offensive progresses, their need to conceal their true natures becomes less important, culminating with Dr. Kaufman's open declaration to Dr. Bennell of their intent to repopulate the world. For the majority of the movie, the pods are seen as surreptitiously advancing their cause, suggesting less an invasion than an infiltration.

4. That Esther is depressed is readily apparent in the novel, but critics have claimed as well that Plath's imagery provides an "unerring description of schizophrenic perception: a hallway becomes an menacing tunnel, a person approaching has an enormity that threatens to engulf the viewer the closer they come, objects loom out of all proportion, the alphabet letters on a page become impossible to decipher, and virtually everything seems both unreal and dangerous" (McCullough xiii).

5. Compelling accounts of the ineffectiveness of these centers, despite the good intentions behind their creation and the best efforts of the individuals employed within them, may be found in Gillon, Grob, and Torrey.

6. Unless otherwise noted, all emphasis from the original text.

7. Unless otherwise noted, all emphasis from the original text.

8. This discussion of *The Bell Jar* and the mid-century's climate of anti-institutionalization is indebted to Maria Farland's thorough and compelling analysis in "Sylvia Plath's Anti-Psychiatry." Farland examines the ways in which *The Bell Jar* simultaneously critiques middle-class conformity while endorsing the middle-class privilege of private asylums, exposing the novel's own complicity with the class-based assumptions of the antipsychiatry movement. Other discussions of *The Bell Jar* and Sylvia Plath more generally that have been of particular help to this analysis include Baldwin and Nelson ("Plath").

9. Unless otherwise noted, all emphasis in quotes from Derrida's works is from the original text.

10. This analysis of *The Thanatos Syndrome* benefited from the analysis of Percy's work performed by Desmond ("Holocaust" and *Walker Percy*), the collection edited by Gretlund and Westarp, as well as the article by Martin.

11. Certainly, the civil rights violation implicit in the wholesale medication of an unknowing population is alarming irrespective of any social benefits thereby derived.

Percy pays homage to such concerns by invoking both the fluoridation programs of the late 1940s and the anxieties expressed (or parodied) by such postwar cult classics as *Invasion of the Body Snatchers* (1955), *Dr. Strangelove, or How I Learned to Quit Worrying and Love the Bomb* (1963), and *The Stepford Wives* (1975) — *there's something in the water supply* — as his vehicle of transmission. But Percy shifts the debate surrounding Na-24 away from both an obvious question of social harm and a more abstract evaluation regarding civil rights and liberties. Rather, he uses the conspiracy to stage questions more ethical than either a practical evaluation of consequences or a theoretical evaluation of means. This commitment to ethical as opposed to legal questions is illustrated in a secondary plot involving the "Qualitarian Life Centers" — federally funded clinics that Percy imagines open in response to a Supreme Court decision allowing limited euthanasia of the terminally ill, the elderly, and "unwanted or afflicted infants" (35). When Tom suggests that the center be turned into a hospice, Dr. Bob Comeaux — one of the coconspirators — claims that to change the center's purpose is "violating the law of the land." Tom responds "the law of the land does not require gereuthanasia of the old or pedeuthanasia of pre-personhood infants. It only permits it under certain circumstances" (334). He thus carefully delineates the difference between the legal and ethical spheres. One might imagine a similar argument in which abortion would continue to be legal, but a significant portion of the population refrained from any part in the procedures in a form of conscientious objection.

12. As in *The Catcher in the Rye*, while it is not necessary to understand desires as commensurate with selfhood, Percy imagines the two to be inextricable. Percy suggests that changes in or the disappearance of the self renders itself most readily apparent in changes in the nature or content of desires.

13. This imagined reversion to so-called traditional forms of artistry implies that certain cultural manifestations — the various forms of artistic expression common to certain cultural groups — are biologically encoded in much the same way that a predisposition to certain skin tones is genetically determined. As Percy implies that such a reversion is in fact a regression — evolution in reverse — it is hard to hypothesize how it avoids partaking of racist assumptions about African versus European American culture and African versus European American genes. At the very least, Percy seems to posit some sort of essential difference between the genes of African and European descendants. Certainly neither Mickey, Ella, nor Donna decorates her home with Masai vegetation — nor, for that matter, do they begin weaving cloth in the ostensible tradition of the Anglo or Saxon tribal communities. The fact that Percy is obviously satirizing the conspirators and their racial attitudes here and elsewhere in the text — as manifested by Tom's horrified disbelief at Comeaux's paternalistic racism — does not necessarily exculpate Percy from charges of racial insensitivity.

14. As Nathan Glazer observes in *We Are All Multiculturalists Now*, the phenomenon

of multiculturalism and its related curricular reform, though applicable to any ethnic category, was "given its force and vigor by our greatest domestic problem, the situation of African-Americans" (10) and, not surprisingly, the resulting Afrocentric curriculums bore the brunt of the backlash.

15. Percy is generally characterized as an existentialist although he himself may have disagreed with the characterization. He discusses his dispute with Jean-Paul Sartre over ontology in greatest detail in "Symbol as Hermeneutic in Existentialism" and also in "Naming and Being" (1960) and "Is a Theory of Man Possible?" The dispute itself is helpfully discussed by Kathleen Scullin in "*Lancelot* and Walker Percy's Dispute with Sartre over Ontology." In Scullin's words: "Percy maintains . . . that Sartre's emphasis on the human predicament amounts to an elevation of psychology over ontology, that is, mistaking how it *feels* to be human with what it *is* to be human. For Sartre, the self, alone and empty, can sustain itself only by seizing the freedom to create a self out of its own nothingness. Other persons constitute a threat to that self-creation. For Percy, the self is rooted in connectedness with others and sustained in celebrating that connectedness — in language, in commitments to others, and in sacramental signs connecting one to God" (110–11, emphasis in original).

16. In "Diagnosing the Modern Malaise," Percy offers a number of phrases intended as diagnoses — "rootless and isolated consciousness" (209), "loss of community, loss of meaning, inauthenticity" (210) — of the twentieth-century spiritual decline in an effort to proscribe the proper role of the artist, and particularly the novelist, as "diagnostic at the outset, and in the end, one hopes, therapeutic" (205).

17. It is uncertain whether Percy, as a trained (though not practicing) psychiatrist, would have heard of fluoxetine's preliminary success in drug trials conducted by Eli Lilly (the drug's manufacturer) and the Food and Drug Administration in advance of Prozac's general availability.

18. Cooper provides a particularly helpful account of the Jekyll/Hyde question, and the existentialists' response to it, to which this analysis is indebted. He argues that "the obsession with providing a criterion for self-identity betrays a failure to be rid of the traditional view of the human being as a substantial subject. The demand for a criterion of self-identity suggests that there is a true or false answer to the question of whether Pierre is the same person after the brain transplant or after imbibing the potion. But the suggestion is mistaken, for what would be called for in such bizarre circumstances are decisions on how to *describe* them." While "such decisions need not, of course, be arbitrary," they are importantly outside the realm of existentialist concerns. What the existentialist wants to avoid is "the pretence that the decision taken is really a discovery of a deep fact about the nature of the self" (98–99, emphasis in original).

19. When a cancer victim is understood to be altered by her disease, the alteration is generally attributed to the medications prescribed (most notably, painkillers) and

not to the disease itself. Two notable exceptions occur in the cases of victims suffering from various brain cancers, in which the location of the tumors can cause a variety of neurological effects (impaired sight or balance, mood disorders, and others), and from Alzheimer's disease with its drastic consequences for memory and behavior. An interesting discussion of the philosophical implications of the latter occurs in Michael Ignatieff's novel *Scar Tissue* (1994).

20. It is important to note that once the hype surrounding Prozac died down, its limitations as an antidepressant became clear: not everyone experienced the dramatic turnaround recounted by the most successful candidates, and many depressives found it helpful only in conjunction with other drugs (such as Wellbutrin and other psychopharmaceuticals). Even the "good responders," in Peter Kramer's phrase, experienced side effects such as a diminished libido that detracted from Prozac's overall appeal. What this analysis argues, however, is that Prozac provided, if not a cure to depressive symptoms, then an opportunity to imagine what such a cure would look like and, more important, what the self would look like if the symptoms of depression should disappear. Curiously enough, for Wurtzel at the very least, that self appears to change little, if at all.

21. It is difficult to determine whether Kramer and Wurtzel are correct in their opinions. Certainly the number of people taking antidepressants as a family of pharmaceuticals has risen in the past decade, but the release of new medications such as Paxil, Wellbutrin, and Effexor (among others) that were not available when Kramer and Wurtzel were writing has meant that Prozac no longer dominates the field.

22. The publication of *Bitch* (1998) suggests that Wurtzel did succeed in creating just that "whole new personality," or identity, she needed. The book's cover, complete with a topless photograph of its author giving the finger to her reader (while surely a publicity stunt), makes clear that the relationship between Wurtzel and her subject matter can only be seen as one of identity. As she explains, "The one statement a girl can make to declare her strength, her surefootedness, her autonomy — her self as a *self* — is to somehow be bad, somehow do something that is surely going to make her parents weep" (3, emphasis in original). The content of Wurtzel's observations on bitch identity and popular culture is less interesting than her need to make every assertion of identity publicly — in the form of self-revealing memoir after self-revealing memoir — but to focus on the quality of her analysis as opposed to the mere fact of her compulsion to identify sidesteps the issue that makes her work representative of a generation of memoirs that explore, implicitly or explicitly, an author's identification with and negotiation of a range of cultural categories (an extremely limited list might include *An Unquiet Mind* [1997] by Kay Redfield Jamison, *Girl, Interrupted* [1993] by Susanna Kaysen, and *Wasted* [1998] by Marya Hornbacher). The salient point is not Wurtzel's understanding

of the bitch identity but rather her investment in identity as such — bitch, depressive, or whatever.

23. In *Black Skin White Masks*, Franz Fanon engages in a similar fantasy when he suggests "for several years laboratories have been trying to produce a serum for 'denegrification'" (111) and uses this fantasy to explore the extent to which black Africans and their descendants are "overdetermined from without." As Fanon explains in a statement that draws an implicit contrast with Sartre's Jew, "I am the slave not of the 'idea' that others have of me but of my own appearance" (116).

Chapter Three. "They Didn't Do It for Thrills"

1. Unless otherwise noted, the emphasis in quotes from Harris's works is from original texts.

2. Starling's status as a female agent investigating crimes against women within the decidedly male institution of the FBI is deliberately explored by the novel. Although this point is not the focus of this particular chapter, Starling's female status is importantly discussed in other works on both the novel and film versions of *The Silence of the Lambs*. See, for example, Tasker and Robbins.

3. This emphasis on the impossibility of change argues against the claims of those critics who accuse both Thomas Harris and Jonathan Demme (the director of the film version of *The Silence of the Lambs*) of perpetuating gay stereotypes. Not only does Lecter repeatedly emphasize that Gumb is not a transsexual but also remembers (in the novel) a conversation in which a patient observes, "Jame is not really gay, you know, it's just something he picked up in jail. He's not anything, really" (172). Critics who acknowledge these moments counter by claiming that because Gumb *believes* he is both gay and a transsexual and presents himself as such (particularly in the movie, which reveals him cross dressing, mimicking female voices, and cavorting in an exaggerated manner), the audience will assume that he is, doing damage to the cause of gay rights despite Lecter's protestations. But the ontology of serial killing that the novel and film provide actually favors the cause of gay rights, as discussed later in this chapter.

4. The line "one thousand times more savage" is taken from the film version of *The Silence of the Lambs* rather than the novel. The line is quoted here because it states explicitly an idea implied throughout the novel.

5. Philip Jenkins's *Using Murder: The Social Construction of Serial Homicide* (1994) is only one of a collection of texts addressing the sociology, psychology, and neurology of serial murder that have been extremely useful. Other examples are: John Douglas and Mark Olshaker, The *Anatomy of Motive: the FBI's Legendary Manhunter Explores the Key to Understanding and Catching Violent Criminals* (1999); James Alan Fox and

Jack Levin, "Multiple Homicide: Patterns of Serial and Mass Murder" (1998); Ronald M. Holmes and Stephen T. Holmes, *Serial Murder* (1998); Elliot Leyton, *Hunting Humans: The Rise of the Modern Multiple Murderer* (1986); Joel Norris, *Serial Killers* (1988); Anne Rule, *The Stranger beside Me* (1980); and Terry Sullivan and Peter T. Maiken, *Killer Clown: The John Wayne Gacy Murders* (1983).

6. All of these assertions are strongly debated, raising valid questions about definitions, the accuracy of reporting, and the retrospective recategorization of crimes.

7. These representations have also been the subject of rising critical interest. Recent book-length works on cultural representations of serial killing include Seltzer and Simpson. *Post-Script: Essays on Film and the Humanities* devoted its Winter/Spring 2003 issue to essays that explore the genre, thematics, and conventions of serial-killer narratives. Particularly provocative and helpful essays from that collection include: Gates, Goldberg and Crespo, Hantke, Hemmeter, and Rombes. Other helpful articles include Dyer, Gomel, Nixon, Taubin, and Staiger.

8. One example of this elision appears in Seltzer's book, which provides a compelling literary critical analysis of a number of serial-killing narratives. Viewing serial killing as a privileged site for popular anxieties about media technology, trauma psychology, and social constructionist ideas about the self, Seltzer theorizes an American "wound culture," which accounts for not only the phenomenon of serial killing but also the contemporary fascination with it, arguing "the spectacular public representation of violated bodies . . . has come to function as a way of imagining and situating our notions of public, social, and collective identity" (21). This chapter has been particularly aided by Seltzer's analysis of the conflicting tendency to view serial killers as simultaneously antisocial and oversocialized. Claiming "The serial killer . . . is in part defined by such a radicalized experience of typicality within," he argues that "'murder by numbers' (as serial murder has been called) is the form of violence proper to statistical persons. That such a generalized experience of a generality within is insupportable may go some way in explaining the explosive violence through which it becomes visible and its localization, and pathologization, in the figure of the serial killer" (30–31). He thus locates the violence of serial killing in a conflict between the socially constructed self—the "generalized generality" or what I am calling the real phony—and a residual (but nonessential) self that resists this "insupportable" reduction and retaliates by asserting its subjecthood in the form of an externalized display. The present volume argues that this residual self is itself *historically* determined as a consequence of a commitment to modernist ontologies of persons; as contemporary interest shifted away from existentialist toward poststructural analyses of being, so definitions of serial killers deemphasized the specific acts of the acting subject in favor of expressive accounts focusing on a particular type of person.

9. The official FBI victim estimate is listed by Ann Rule as 36, but when confronted with this number Bundy is reported to have said "add one digit" (414), leaving open the question of whether he meant 37, 136, or 360.

10. Holmes and Holmes here differentiate serial killing from other forms of multiple homicide: mass murder, "the killing of three or more people at one time and in one place" (11), as in the case of Richard Speck, who killed seven nurses in Chicago, Illinois, in 1966; and spree murder, "the killing of at least three people within a thirty-day period" (17) as in the case of Andrew Cunanan, who killed six people in the spring of 1997, including fashion designer Giovanni Versace.

11. The (most likely specious) theory that Bundy killed in response to a failed relationship is taken from Ann Rule, who argues, "The victims were all prototypes of Stephanie [not her real name]. The same long hair, parted in the middle, the same perfectly even features. . . . they all resembled Stephanie, that first woman who had pierced Ted's carefully constructed façade and revealed the yawning vulnerability beneath. The damage to Ted's ego could never be forgiven. None of the crimes filled the emptiness. He had to keep killing Stephanie over and over again" (401).

12. Unless otherwise noted, all emphasis is from the original text. Douglas's comparison of a modus operandi and a signature aptly illustrates the link between motive and identity emphasized here: while the former is "dynamic. . . . [and] evolves as the offender learns more and gets better at what he's doing," the latter is "an aspect of the crime that emotionally fulfills the offender, and so . . . remains relatively the same" (55). Like the signature in contemporary legal culture, which is understood to be an identifying mark that represents the being of its author, the criminal signature, Douglas explains, "is a critical clue in coming up with the [unknown subject's] personality and motive" (55).

13. In *The Talented Mr. Ripley*, Ripley kills only two people, and thus would not be categorized as a serial murderer under at least the Holmeses' definitions of the term. Ripley is included in this study for three reasons: first, because in 1955 the contemporary definition of serial killer itself did not exist; such killers were termed "multiple murderers," a category into which Ripley would fit. Second, the reasons the term "serial killers" would not have been used in the 1950s is suggested by Highsmith's representation. Finally, Highsmith continues Ripley's murderous career over a series of five novels written from 1955 through 1991, by the end of which Ripley's status as a serial murderer is more than justified. The other novels in the series are *Ripley under Ground* (1970), *Ripley's Game* (1974), *The Boy Who Followed Ripley* (1980), and *Ripley under Water* (1991). For an interesting discussion of the link between the term "serial killers" and the genre of episodic narratives (in this case, television adventure serials), to which the Ripley novels belong, see Seltzer (64).

14. Unless otherwise noted, all emphasis is from the original text.

15. *Double Indemnity* never provides a satisfactory account of Huff's murderousness, though at various points both Huff and his employer/nemesis Keyes blame the novel's femme fatale for inspiring Huff. Keyes excuses Huff's behavior by explaining that Huff "just got [him]self tangled up with an Irrawaddy cobra, that's all. That woman — it makes my blood run cold just to think of her. She's a pathological case, that's all. The worst I ever heard of" (105). Keyes's analogy suggests two things: first, that murderousness is a product of one's *nature* (an Irrawaddy cobra); and second, that one's nature is susceptible to influence (getting "tangled up"). This is similar to Lou Ford's original positioning of the prostitute Joyce Lakeland as the source of his pathology; when he first runs into her in the course of his professional duties, he claims, "I knew what was going to happen if I didn't get out, and I knew I couldn't let it happen. I might kill her. It might bring *the sickness* back" (11). Ultimately, Joyce Lakeland is replaced by an earlier femme fatale and emerges as more of the victim than the instigator of Ford's violence, but the association of female sexuality and murderousness remains the same.

16. For a compelling account of *Double Indemnity*'s relation to Poe's fiction and to the concept of professionalization in 1930s' crime novels more generally, see John T. Irwin's "Beating the Boss: Cain's *Double Indemnity*."

17. The similarities between Highsmith's opening plot and that of Henry James's *The Ambassadors* are explicitly made when Mr. Greenleaf, delighted that Tom has agreed to his subterfuge, comments, "I'll write [Dickie] about you — not telling him that you're an emissary from me" (22) and recommends that Tom "read a certain book by Henry James" (23). As in the James novel, the difficulty of standing in for an absent self — of *representing* as opposed to *being* someone else — is made rapidly clear, as discussed in detail in what follows. For a discussion of the use of *The Ambassadors* in the novel, and its film adaptations by Clément and Minghella, see Golsan.

18. *The Talented Mr. Ripley* is not the first book in which Highsmith plays out questions about actions and the self through the concept of motivation. In her debut novel, *Strangers on a Train* (1950), she presents two characters with diametrically opposed accounts of selfhood: Guy Haines, who believes in "character" in the strong sense of the word and imagines he is "not [the] kind of person" who could commit murder; and Anthony Bruno, who argues that "any kind of person can murder" and that it has "not a thing to do with temperament" (29). The novel then investigates the implications of each of these positions as Bruno murders Guy's wife and coerces Guy into killing his (Bruno's) father. In this earlier novel, neither position is fully endorsed or entirely dismissed. Guy, who believes character is fixed and determined, is shown constantly questioning the reasons for his actions ("what was it that he liked?" [56], "why didn't he turn him in?" [102], "Whatever had possessed him to buy tickets to Verdi?" [142], "why

had he been so mad to think he didn't want to see her?" [143]); Bruno, who argues that character is purely a matter of circumstance and choice, is consistently on the verge of utter dissolution.

19. Unless otherwise noted, all emphasis is from the original text.

20. That there is a connection between sex, particularly homosexual sex, and the destruction of boundaries between persons is by now a critical commonplace. *The Talented Mr. Ripley* is itself saturated with references to Tom's possible homosexuality, which, in combination with Patricia Highsmith's lesbianism, suggests a productive area for further research. Yet to read Ripley as a repressed homosexual, whose thwarted love for Dickie leads to murder, works against the characterization of Ripley put forth in the novel as a whole. Ripley displays no sexual interest in either men or women; as Marge writes to Dickie in a letter, "All right, [Tom] may not be queer. He's just a nothing, which is worse. He isn't normal enough to have *any* kind of sex life" (123). It's worth noting that "nothing" or "not anything" describes Jame Gumb in *The Silence of the Lambs* as well; what marks the killer in at least these two cases is not sexuality per se, but rather its absence, and of the self more generally. For discussions of Ripley's potential homosexuality, particularly with regard to the Clément and Minghella film adaptations of the novel, see Shannon, Straayer, and Williams.

21. The connection between Highsmith and Camus is also noted in Russell Harrison's *Patricia Highsmith* (1997), particularly with regard to Highsmith's novel *The Tremor of Forgery* (1967). This novel, Harrison argues, revisits the central motif of Camus' novel *The Stranger*: it is set in northern Africa and takes as its subject a French writer who may or may not have murdered an Arab he believes is trying to rob him.

22. This interest in the hands as the differentiating feature of selfhood appears again in the second of the Ripley novels—*Ripley under Ground*—when Ripley impersonates the painter Derwatt as part of an art fraud only to be recognized by his hands. The narrator states, "Murchison looked at Tom's hands, his face, back to his hands again. 'Was it *you* impersonating Derwatt? Yes, I noticed Derwatt's hands. . . . You can't put a beard on those, can you?'" (69). Needless to say, Tom murders Murchison on the spot so as to avoid being exposed.

23. Writing in 1989, DeLillo spoke specifically of the Manson murders as a twentieth-century incarnation of an obsession with millennial or apocalyptic violence that has reappeared throughout human history. Commenting that "the stranger the material, the more it fits the pattern" (351), DeLillo argues that cults like the Manson Family, the white supremacist organization *Bruder Schweigen*, the Crusades of the Middle Ages, and the Germans under the Nazi government are evidence of "what remains of the wilderness . . . a pulse in the brain that beats for desolation. Bring it all down" (350). Lyricism aside, it is worth noting that DeLillo's interest in the cult in *The Names* is as

much in the fact of a cult as in its murders; the issue of what people will do in groups (in comparison to what they might do on their own) reappears throughout DeLillo's oeuvre.

24. Specific references to writing and to the violence of language are constant throughout the novel, with a particular focus on the nature of carved writing and of the rituals associated with the places where the writing can be found. To list a few examples: letters have been "cut" into the rock at archaeological sites (36); the ancient languages have been "subdued and codified, broken down to these wedge shaped marks" (80); and the letters represent "the mystery of alphabets, the contact with death and oneself, one's other self, all made stonebound with a mallet and chisel" (284).

25. The analysis of language as a system in *The Names* has been aided by Joseph Tabbi's chapter on DeLillo from *Postmodern Sublime* (1995), in which Tabbi argues that DeLillo's "formal preoccupations are those of the late modernist writer who is becoming ever more separated from the age's dominant energies, and who must live amid technological forces and corporate systems that have grown too complex for any single mind or imagination to comprehend." The characterization of DeLillo as a "late modernist" suggests Tabbi's conviction that, for DeLillo, the self remains a viable ontological category. The artist's job, therefore, is "to build himself back into a culture that tends to exclude him, aesthetically making a virtue of one's cognitive limitations" (176). But in *The Names* at least, the possible difference between ontological and phenomenological selfhood is precisely what is under investigation by the cult, if no one else. Other analyses that discuss DeLillo's use of language in the novel include Berger, Cowart, and Foster.

26. Jameson is correct to note that *The Names* is less the story of the cult than the story of James Ashton, particularly in relation to his family; the cult serves as a way of foregrounding certain questions about the possibilities of love, intimacy, and identity that are acted out within the family unit. But language does not itself exist only as a screen for something else. Rather it serves as the most literal example of systems that can (and do) take on many forms.

27. Again, David Cooper's reconstruction of existentialism provides a helpful gloss to this notion. Explaining that since "Human existence is embodied in Being-in-the-world: so persons may be identified through their bodies. The important thing . . . is to resist the temptation to treat the continuity of Pierre's body as *evidence* for a further, deeper identity of his person or self" (99, emphasis in original). That this particular body is the one who committed these murders is reason enough for Dolarhyde to be held accountable for them, but it is not reason enough to think he is the same person he was when he committed them or that he will commit a similar crime again.

28. Emphasis added.

29. The interior quote is taken from Raymond Thompson's autobiography, *What Took You So Long? A Girl's Journey to Manhood* (177).

30. This essentialist version of transsexuality continues to receive harsh criticism from those scholars who favor a performative model of gender, arguing that transsexuals, in the words of Marjorie Garber, "*essentialize* their genitalia" (98, emphasis in original), with implications for those individuals trying move away from gender models based on predetermined physical or psychic sexing. While it may be true that "being trapped in the wrong body is simply what transsexuality feels like," as Prosser claims (69), it does not follow that this is what transsexuality *is* (ontology) — just that this is how transsexuality is experienced (phenomenology). However, in the absence of a definitive answer to these questions (or even a clear consensus on what the questions should be), the phenomenological experience of transsexuals deserves place in the debate.

31. Those studies that maintain there are many serial killers or protoserial killers who either are in jail for other crimes or never break into violence advocate biological or sociobiological accounts of violence, for obvious reasons. A notable example is Joel Norris's *Serial Killers*, which strongly favors neurological accounts of behavior and argues: "It may be that many individuals are able to navigate through life on the border between incipient violence and normal behavior. . . . Although these people may demonstrate some of the biological and psychological symptoms of the serial killer syndrome, they will spend their lives as carriers of the disease and may never emerge as violent criminals" (219). The final chapter of Norris's book provides a list of symptoms that suggest a predilection to serial murder; while Norris acknowledges the potential civil rights violations inherent in labeling certain members of a community in advance of any violent behaviors, he argues "when these forces can be detected individually, especially in children who have not yet confronted the juvenile justice system, it is likely that any potential criminal or antisocial behavior can be short circuited at the start" (249).

32. This idea of "passing" as applied to serial murderers appears most frequently in descriptions of serial murderers as chameleons who by all accounts appear as normal, functioning persons. This tendency is explored at length in Seltzer, who comments, "One refrain in coverage of serial killing is the just this dead average and look-alike character of the killer. . . . there is something uncanny about how these killers are so much alike, living composites, how easily they blend in" (10, and throughout).

33. By offering an expressive model of identity based not in acts but in being, Harris endorses precisely the same ontology of the self put forth by a subset of gay advocacy groups in their efforts to secure civil rights protection — a fact that may prove surprising both to gay activists and to Harris himself. When homosexuality stops being

a behavior and becomes a form of being, its behaviors are most easily understood as entitled to protection under the Fourteenth Amendment. The similarities between the two movements (one highly fanciful, the other genuine) begin and end with this observation, however. It is worth noting as well that homosexuality need not be characterized as a form of being to be granted protection. One only need determine that, as an *act*, homosexuality is in no way harmful to either the individual or the society of which he is a part to ensure that one could not discriminate against it. This solution tends to be viewed as less politically viable than the above.

34. The idea of "officially designated prejudices" — or, alternatively "officially protected identities" — is of crucial importance to Jacobs and Potter, who are interested in the idea that some groups are protected and others are not. They discuss in particular the omission of crimes against women from federal statutes, ostensibly because "the federal government already collect[s] statistics on rape and domestic violence" (72). Both Jacobs and Potter maintain that the real reason gender crimes are not included is because "If a significant percentage of crimes by men against women were to count as hate crimes, then victims of other hate crimes would get less attention, and the significance of their victimization and the force of their moral claims would be diminished" (78). That is, crimes against women would so overwhelm the statistics that the other categories of hate crime — against African Americans, against Latinos/as — would appear insignificant by comparison. While this complaint is legitimate, the interest in hate crimes here discussed focuses less on the difficulties inherent in defining them than on the particular position they assume with regard to motive.

35. Importantly, the FBI's categorizing techniques are designed for apprehension, not punishment, the area in which hate-crime laws matter. One can imagine that motive would be an important part of solving a crime but play little role in its prosecution and punishment, where acts and acts only would be considered, to avoid punishing a person for who they are rather than what they've done. Indeed, prosecutors are not required to prove motive in criminal cases. But as Douglas observes, "the main thing that the prosecution wanted from me or my people was an answer to the question *Why?* . . . it is a very important consideration when prosecuting a case in court. Juries often have a difficult time convincing themselves that someone committed a particularly heinous act if they can't figure out what the motive was" (73).

36. Of course, this analysis presumes that Bundy and Gacy are correct in their own interpretations of their motives. Like Jame Gumb, however, both Bundy and Gacy are commonly understood to be mistaken about why they killed: possible interpretations range from the psychiatric (each man murdered in an extreme desire for control) and the biologic (the men suffered from brain damage) to the religious (the men were fundamentally evil).

37. Notably, in July 1999 Benjamin Smith engaged in a spree killing in Illinois and

Indiana that took the lives of two people and hospitalized eight; Smith's ostensible motive was racial hatred—his victims were African American, Jewish, and Asian American—and he was known to belong to a white supremacist group, the World Church of the Creator. Although he is not available for prosecution or sentence enhancement (he committed suicide during a police chase), his crimes were categorized as hate crimes by local law enforcement, the media, and the FBI.

38. The presence of expressive content provides another link between serial murder and hate crimes; as James Alan Fox and Jack Levin observe, "while the range of motives for serial homicide is quite broad . . . [f]or these killers, murder is a form of expressive, rather than instrumental violence" (415).

39. A parallel instance is found in Katherine K. Baker's analysis of Rule 413 of the Federal Rules of Evidence, which makes prior acts of sexual assault by alleged rapists admissible in criminal sexual assault cases. Baker comments on this rule's tendency to view rape as an expressive crime that illustrates the "character" of the accused, arguing, "Is someone who has raped more of a 'rapist' than someone who has killed is a 'murderer' or that someone who has lied is a 'liar'? Are all rapists alike in an essential way that makes them 'rapists'?" (566). In a similar discussion, Rachel Hill reviews the "aberrant behavior" departure of the U.S. Sentencing Guidelines that allows the courts to bypass mandatory sentencing requirements if they find evidence that the crime is "a single act of aberrant behavior" (975). Hill, who unlike Baker (one might infer) favors a character-theory of criminal responsibility, argues "a character-based approach to sentencing . . . means that 'good' people are less likely than 'bad' people to commit dangerous or undesirable acts in the future. . . . Similarly, character theory furthers the rehabilitative aim of punishment because 'good' people *are* 'good' and do not need to become 'good' through 'educational or vocational training, medical care, or other correctional treatment'" (987; the internal quote is taken from the U.S. Criminal Code).

40. *Bruders Schweigen* is perhaps best known for the 1984 murder of talk-radio host Alan Berg in Denver. Their oath is thought to be based on the fictional pledge taken by Earl Turner in *The Turner Diaries*, Andrew Macdonald's apocalyptic novel about race war. The novel itself is believed to have been part of the inspiration for both Berg's murder and the 1993 bombing of the Murrah Building in Oklahoma City.

41. As mentioned above, these laws do not necessarily require that the legal system imagine that attacking minority victims is more reprehensible than majority ones. The nature of the perpetrator, not the victim, is the relevant factor. But in establishing certain prejudices as particularly socially damaging (and thus requiring sentence enhancement), these laws make it worse to hate certain kinds of persons than others, which reinforces the belief in, say, racial difference even as it punishes those who believe in it.

Chapter Four. Assimilation, Authenticity, and "Natural Jewishness"

1. In *The Holocaust in American Life*, Novick provides a forceful argument about the lack of a cultural or political engagement with the Holocaust in the United States during the 1940s and 1950s. Novick's project overall is to uncover the political motivations for either the suppression or deployment of Holocaust discourse at various points in the second half of the twentieth century. For the immediate postwar period, see in particular chaps. 4 through 6. I am indebted to my colleague Louis Schwartz for directing me to Novick's work.

In an analysis that builds off of Novick's work, Kirsten Fermaglich argues that the years between 1957 and 1965 — "the turn of the 1960s" — saw an awakening of Holocaust awareness in American intellectual life, as embodied in its use as metaphor in works ranging from Stanley Elkins's *Slavery: A Problem in American Institutional and Intellectual Life* (1959) to Bette Friedan's *The Feminine Mystique* (1963). Fermaglich argues that, though "men and women of different political persuasions had used brief, angry rhetoric that compared various components of American politics to the travesties of the Nazi German regime" (3), not until 1957 does "the Nazi destruction of European Jewry become a dominant presence in the discussion of world events, in film, and in literature" (18). The emergence of these discussions was itself a continuation of "the dominant intellectual paradigms at the height of the Cold War. Intellectuals at the turn of the 1960s were still, for example, preoccupied with the dangers posed to an individual in a mass society that had featured so prominently in works such as David Riesman's *The Lonely Crowd* (1950), William Whyte's *The Organization Man* (1956), and C. Wright Mills's *The Power Elite* (1956) and *White Collar* (1951)" (8).

2. In fact, Novick is explicitly critical of the deployment of Holocaust discourse during the 1970s and 1980s, arguing that the "Holocaust framework allowed one to put aside as irrelevant any legitimate grounds for criticizing Israel, to avoid even considering the possibility that the rights and wrongs were complex. In addition, while American Jewish organizations could do nothing to alter the recent past in the middle east, and precious little to protect its future, they *could* work to revive memories of the Holocaust. So the 'fading memories' explanation offered an agenda for action" (155, emphasis in original). While Novick is certain that this is not the appropriate place of the Holocaust in American life, he does not suggest what role, if any, it might legitimately play — a point upon which reviewers were quick to comment.

3. For a useful discussion of mid-century suburbanization and the attendant anxiety it produced over conformity and uniformity see Jurca, particularly chap. 5, and Patterson, chap. 11.

4. It is not Daniel Bell but rather Nathan Glazer—another mid-century Jewish sociologist—who Herberg cites in relation to this more general attitude. Herberg quotes from Glazer's article, "What Sociology Knows about American Jews": "'A social group with clearly marked boundaries exists, but the source of the energies that hold [it] separate, and of the ties that bind it together, has become completely mysterious'" (198).

5. By the late 1940s, the point-of-view shot had been established within the Hollywood repertoire, as demonstrated most notably through the 1947 film *The Lady in the Lake*, directed by Robert Montgomery, which was filmed entirely from the point of view of the main character, Philip Marlowe (Robert Montgomery). Kazan himself employed point of view shots most memorably in the final scenes of *On the Waterfront* (1954), when Terry Malloy walks up to the shipping boss to lead the workers back into the shop.

6. Interestingly, the one character in the film that is represented as avowedly Jewish is Dave Goldman, whose status as a Jew is indicated to the audience before his character appears. Moreover, the character of Dave Goldman is played by John Garfield, the one actor whom the audience might have known to be Jewish in advance of the film's release.

7. In his review of *Gentleman's Agreement*, Elliot E. Cohen comments on the ostensible absence, if not of the Jew, than of the idea of Jewish difference in the film as one of two "shortcomings" in the film. He writes: "To make tolerance conditional on uniformity is risky for groups, and for America, too. . . . But to most Jews being Jewish is more than being religious in the creedal sense, or standing one's ground negatively against anti-Semitism. Dave is visibly different from Phil, as you can see in the picture; his son, too, will be noticeably different from Phil's" (56). Though Cohen may refer only to the ethnic traditions associated with Jewish life, his reference to visible signs of group affiliation suggests that he employs a racial definition of Jewishness.

8. This ending can be productively compared to Arthur Miller's 1945 novel *Focus*, the other narrative of gentile passing from the immediate postwar period. In *Focus*, the laughable premise is that the lead character, Lawrence Newman, gets continually mistaken for Jewish after beginning to wear glasses that "seemed to draw his flat, shiny-haired skull lower and set off his nose, so that where it had once appeared a trifle sharp it now beaked forth from the nosepiece. . . . [H]is teeth which had always been irregular now seemed to insult the smile and warped it into a cunning, insincere mockery of a smile, an expression whose attempt at simulating joy was belied, in his opinion, by the Semitic prominence of his nose, the bulging set of his eyes, the listening posture of his ears" (25). Formerly the personnel director of a large company whose job it was to screen out Jewish applicants, Lawrence is promptly fired when he wears his glasses at the office, and he likewise cannot stay at hotels that formerly admitted him without

protest. The novel compares Lawrence's previous casual anti-Semitism with his dawning awareness of its costs once he himself is taken for Jewish. The climax of the novel comes after he is beaten along with a(nother) Jew in his neighborhood and he identifies himself as Jewish to the police when he makes his report. In this narrative, there is no returning to the previous status as gentile, perhaps because the mistake of his identity will continue to be made as long as he continues to wear the glasses. Because Phil doesn't look especially Jewish, his Jewishness must be positively asserted and will disappear once he stops stating it: because Lawrence's ostensible Jewishness is written on his face, there is no way to escape it.

9. Brodkin's analysis traces the connections between racial and class status in the United States, arguing that, as the Jews rose in class during the middle of the twentieth century, Jewishness evolved from a race to an ethnicity. In particular, she traces the ways in which various federal agencies included Jews and excluded blacks from programs designed to provide important tools for upward mobility such as education and housing. She argues, "The myth that Jews pulled themselves up by their own bootstraps ignores the fact that it took federal programs to create the conditions whereby the abilities of Jews and other European immigrants could be recognized and rewarded rather than denigrated and denied" (50). For an exhaustive and compelling account of the entangled histories of blacks and Jews in the United States after 1945, see Sundquist.

10. That the Jew can take on this representative status for Americans stems, to Fiedler's mind, from "the gradual breaking up of the Anglo-Saxon domination of our imagination; the relentless urbanization which makes rural myths and images no longer central to our experience; the exhaustion as vital themes of the Midwest and of the movement from the provinces to New York or Chicago or Paris; the turning again from West to East, from our own heartland back to Europe; and the discovery in the Jews of a people essentially urban, essentially Europe-oriented, a ready-made image for what the American longs to or fears he is being forced to become" (Fiedler 109–10). Fiedler differentiates with precision among the various classes of Jewish literary production in the mid-1950s, noting, "What Saul Bellow is for high-brow literature, Salinger is for upper-middlebrow, Irwin Shaw for middle middlebrow, and Herman Wouk for lower middlebrow" (110).

11. The fact of Wilhelm's assimilation has produced two contrary tendencies in the criticism of this novel—tendencies that Hoberek's analysis suggests might be applied to *The Adventures of Augie March* as well. On the one hand, some critics who follow Bellow's own lead in their interpretations of the text tend to emphasize the universal aspects of the novel (Eichelberger, Kazin, and Fuchs, for example). Another strain of criticism locates Jewish references and thematics throughout the text, as exemplified most clearly in Budick, Costello, Simmons, and the essays in M. Kramer's collection.

12. As Brodkin writes: "The United States emerged from the war with the strongest economy in the world. Real wages rose between 1946–1960, increasing buying power a hefty 22 percent and giving most Americans some discretionary income. American manufacturing, banking, and business services were increasingly dominated by large corporations and these grew into multinational corporations. Their organizational centers lay in big, new urban headquarters that demanded growing numbers of clerical, technical, and managerial workers. The postwar period was a historic moment for real class mobility and for the affluence we have erroneously come to believe was the American norm. It was a time when the old white and the newly white masses became middle class" (37–38).

13. Unless otherwise noted, all emphasis is in the original.

14. For an interesting analysis of Riesman's work in *The Adventures of Augie March*, see Hoberek, chap. 3.

15. As Nathan Glazer writes, "In Germany, the Jewish middle class paralleled a German middle class, using the same language, having the same cultural attributes, and differing, it would seem, only in religion. It was reasonable for German Jews to think that Reform Judaism, in modifying these differences of religion, would enable them to become an accepted part of the German middle class, and, consequently, of the German nation" (*American* 64). Once in the United States, Glazer argues, German Jews in the early twentieth century worked to Americanize newer Eastern European Jewish immigrants because "[t]he coming of the East European Jews, they believed, had adversely affected the social position of the upper-class Jewish families in New York. After all, were they not all Jews, Germans and East Europeans alike, and would not the ordinary American, who cared little for fine distinctions, think of all Jews as crude and radical?" (74).

16. Though Bellow is broadly grouped amid the postwar American trend toward existential thought, in this Foreword he criticizes academics "even those calling themselves existentialists, [who] very seldom offer themselves publicly and frankly as individuals, as persons" (12). Whether this is a complaint with existentialist philosophy or with the academics that purport to follow it and yet allow themselves to be merely representative of a subject position constructed out of race, class, gender, and orientation, is unclear.

17. Kramer also notes that Bellow's refusal to see the fact of his Jewishness as constitutive of either his writing or himself has the effect of reproducing Jewishness as a racial category—as does Fiedler's (and one assumes Herberg's) insistence on the American Jew as the American Everyman. Kramer writes, "Having offered himself as the model American, the Jew as Bellow and his fellows saw him and valued him *had* virtually vanished. . . . For if the Jew is Everyman and Everyman is the Jew, then ethnic difference rhetorically loses its cultural and spiritual dimension and is effectually reduced

to genealogy, to descent — which is to say, strictly speaking, to race" (18, emphasis in original). In other words, "[w]ithout a racial *fundamentum*, 'non-Jewish Jew' is but a contradiction in terms" (19). Kramer's analysis usefully traces Bellow's own writing on his ostensible Jewishness throughout his career.

18. In both "A Philosophy for 'Minority' Living: The Jewish Situation and the 'Nerve of Failure'" and *The Lonely Crowd*, Riesman uses the example of Aldous Huxley's *Brave New World* to illustrate his point about individual and minority resistance, further suggesting the connection between the earlier and the later work.

19. *Marjorie Morningstar* was a New York Times best-seller (Shapiro 157). *The New York Times* reviewed it twice: once in the Books of the Times column (by William du Bois), and once on the cover of the *Times Book Review* (by Maxwell Geismar).

20. Unless otherwise noted, all emphasis in quotes from Wouk's works are from the original text.

Chapter Five. "The Man He Almost Is"

1. Citations are to the published screenplay, *Jerry Maguire*, by Cameron Crowe. When the spoken lines in the film differ from the published text, the film's lines are quoted and the written version is provided in an endnote.

2. The Afterword is not paginated in the Thunder Mouth Press edition of the novel from 2002. It originally appeared as an Introduction to the 1983 edition.

3. There is less literary criticism on *Revolutionary Road* than one might expect given that it was nominated for the National Book Award in 1961. The most insightful and useful analyses for this project include Castronovo, Klinkowitz, and Moreno.

4. Unless otherwise noted, all emphasis is from the original text.

5. For a compelling analysis of the representations and realities of postwar American domesticity and suburbanization, see in particular Cootz, Jackson, and E. May. For discussions of the effects of such domesticity on the ideology and institutions of masculinity, see Corber, Ehrenreich, Faludi, Medevoi, and Moreno.

6. Moreno's article, "Consuming the Frontier Illusion: The Construction of Suburban Masculinity in Richard Yates's *Revolutionary Road*," argues that the novel reveals "the origins of male consumer identity and the disappearance of the frontier/war hero by the onset of the Cold War — all the while illustrating the crisis of contemporary tensions of masculinity" (93). This chapter differs in arguing that masculinity, first, is represented as primarily performative and, second, is part of an overall investigation into the nature of self and performance on the part of the novel. For additional discussions on the development of the postwar consumer, see Cohen.

7. Hence, in Goffman's analysis, the crucial place granted to the con man who embodies the type of cynical performer whose role-playing has tangible and unambiguous

NOTES TO CHAPTER FIVE

real-world consequences for his victims. For Goffman, the problem is not that the con man dissimulates (everyone does), but that his dissimulations are in service of crimes.

8. Unless otherwise noted, all emphasis is from the original text.

9. The screenplay reads, "The answer was fewer clients. Caring for them, caring for ourselves, and the games, too" (38).

10. The screenplay reads, "the guy he wants to be . . . and the guy he almost is" (137).

11. The screenplay does not include the line "It's what I do."

12. The subject is "always-already" constituted in Althusser, and the policeman's hail serves only to represent or make apparent an interpellation that has previously taken place. As he states, "I must now suppress the temporal form in which I have presented the functioning of ideology, and say: ideology has always-already interpellated individuals as subjects, which amounts to making it clear that individuals are always-already interpellated by ideology as subjects, which necessarily leads us to one last proposition: *individuals are always-already subjects*" (175–76 — emphasis in original). This temporal suppression is what enables an individual (the policeman) to allegorize the role of an institution (the law enforcement apparatus). This "temporal suppression" is discussed in greater detail in this chapter.

13. The lines appear in the written text as "You are a *paycheck* player. You play with your *head*. Not your heart. In your personal life? Heart. But when you get on the field — you're a businessman. It's wide-angle lenses and who fucked you over and who owes you for it. That's not what inspires people" (157–58).

14. The montage sequence is only briefly described in the screenplay as focusing primarily on Rod (152).

15. The movie continues to emphasize the importance of repetition even after Rod is unconscious; cutting to a close-up of the Tidwell's living room television (where his family gathered to watch the game), Crowe juxtaposes shots of Rod's wife on the telephone to Jerry with shots of the broadcast replaying Rod's final fall over and over again in quick succession.

16. The line does not appear in the written text. The direction for this scene reads, "The Trainer leans in close, bellowing, he spreads his hands to clap right in front of Rod's still face. His hands head toward each other . . . closer . . . bringing with them the first inkling of sound . . . getting closer and then finally coming together, bringing with him the sounds of the stadium" (172).

17. The published screenplay lists Rod's salary at $10.2 million (178).

18. The basis for this tendency can perhaps be traced to performance theory's use of transsexuality as the model of all gender identity. The pressure on transsexuals to inhabit more completely the traditional gender categories — pressure that for the majority of the population is experienced as a more or less compelling desire to be more

masculine or feminine—often results in identity becoming precisely a project: the project to align more closely the psyche with the body, to become what one already is. But desires do not have to, and frequently do not, become projects, as the many individuals who choose not to have cosmetic surgery—transsexual, transgendered, or otherwise—can attest. As a very helpful reader for *Arizona Quarterly* pointed out to me, however, this resistance to identity-as-project may well transform into the project of "identity-as-resistance."

19. Of course, this is not to say that all subjects will have the capacity to go out and start successful sports agencies that somehow manage to compete despite having only one client. The marketplace obviously favors the efforts of some individuals over others, and that favoring is most likely influenced by the identities through which those subjects have been and continue to be interpellated. The fact that Jerry Maguire is white, male, heterosexual, highly educated (law school), and good looking no doubt has an enormous amount to do with his ultimate success. Rather, there is no clear theoretical reason why a wholly interpellated subject would not have the agency to create a company, regardless of the various practical factors that may impede his efforts. For an excellent discussion of the ways in which nonmale, nonwhite bodies are interpellated as brands in the marketplace, see Lauren Berlant's "National Brands/National Body: *Imitation of Life*."

20. The phrase is originally coined by Jerry's former fiancée, Avery (Kelly Preston), who describes Jerry as "King of Housecalls! Master of the Living Room!" (79). Jerry repeats the phrase when he is speaking to Dorothy, though it does not appear in the published script.

21. The line does not appear in the published screenplay.

22. Unless otherwise noted, emphasis appears in the original text.

23. The line appears in the written text as "I like you, you're nice to my wife" (68).

24. The idea that, in focusing on developing his company, Jerry ends up transforming his self is taken to its logical extreme in Robin Fisher Roffer's book *Make a Name for Yourself*. Noting that "only recently has a brand become more than just a mark, or a word, or a logo" (3), Roffer describes an experience surprisingly similar to Jerry Maguire's in which she was introduced at a cocktail party as "Robin Fisher, the Sweepstakes Queen of Cable!" Having "never thought of [herself] as the sweepstakes queen," Roffer too wonders, in Jerry's phrase, "who had [she] become?" (Crowe 36). But Roffer phrases her realization in the language of contemporary marketing: "I had been *branded*," she explains, "and branded as someone I didn't want to be" (1). The moment makes her realize that "If [she] wanted to become the person [she] would be proud to be [she] would have to begin to reflect my values and passions and my authentic self in everything [she] did—in my word, message, action and style—from then on" (3). Like

Jerry Maguire, Roffer is an independent brand strategist and the president of her own company; to transform her personal brand she first begins to expand her company's brand. As she explains, though "I am talking about *success in the workplace*, as symbolized by financial reward and/or professional respect," she also understands this process as "self-actualization. The process of branding allows you to become the person you are meant to be" (8, emphasis in original).

25. In case the audience misses that Rod's success has solidified Jerry's, the film brings in real-life quarterback Troy Aikman as a member of the studio audience during Rod's triumphant ESPN interview. Aikman is introduced to Jerry by a mutual friend and makes the point of saying that he "enjoyed [Jerry's] memo." The line does not appear in the published screenplay.

26. The written directions for the shot are: "Standing against the wall, just another fan in this crowded hallway, Maguire feels a deep and unexpected loneliness. . . . Jerry turns and heads down the hallway, gaining speed as he walks. . . . Jerry Maguire sprints through the empty airport, heading for the flight out of town. Music" (175–76).

27. The line does not appear in the published screenplay.

28. The explicit discussion of Ray's abilities does not appear in the published screenplay, which directs: "Jerry and Dorothy stop, looking at Ray, who has just shown shocking natural ability. They are quiet for a moment, then turn slowly to look at each other. And then, not ready to deal with it, not even close to ready to deal with it, they say quickly to the boy: (Jerry) Come on, Ray. (Dorothy) Ray, let's go. Happily, Ray joins them as they walk to the car. A family" (180).

Conclusion

1. The line "unless you love everybody, you can't sell anybody" does not appear in the published screenplay.

2. The line, "Even the cover looked like *The Catcher in the Rye*" does not appear in the published screenplay.

3. The moment where Jerry accepts the description of his mission statement as a memo in conversation with Troy Aiken does not appear in the published screenplay.

4. Another example is the 1997 film from Warner Bros., *Conspiracy Theory*, in which Mel Gibson plays an amnesiac taxi driver obsessed with an assistant district attorney played by Julia Roberts. This movie draws upon the coincidence that both Mark Chapman (who murdered John Lennon) and John Hinckley (Reagan's attempted assassin) referred to the novel when asked why they did it; the movie claims that *The Catcher in the Rye* was used as part of mind-control experiment to produce assassins and Mel Gibson is the botched product of this program. Gibson's character himself

finds the novel strangely comforting; it is both the clue to his missing identity and also the means through which he is eventually tracked by the mysterious agents who wish to silence him (led by Patrick Stewart). What makes *Conspiracy Theory* more than just a typical recasting of traditional conspiracy tropes is the role it assigns to *The Catcher in the Rye* as an instrument of socialization — or in the movie's terms, brainwashing. It cleverly plays off of the most interesting fact about the novel: the book that ostensibly derides the sameness of American teens is the one book that every adolescent of at least two generations was required to read.

5. In Cameron Crowe's *Almost Famous* (2000), Holden Caulfield has been replaced by Atticus Finch as the symbol of youthful idealism: the movie opens in flashback with the young William Miller (Patrick Fugit) describing Finch as the man he most wants to be. As William matures, Finch is replaced by pioneering rock journalist Lester Bangs (Philip Seymour Hoffman), who instructs William of the pitfalls of the trade. Bangs insists that one must not socialize with one's subjects, that the rock stars are "fake friends who will try to corrupt you" and "get you to write sanctimonious shit about the genius of rock musicians" but that this represents "the death of real rock and roll." Authentic journalism — and by extension, "real rock and roll" — Bangs argues comes in the form of a prose that is "honest and merciless" about its subjects.

6. Another example of Ouisa's wit occurs later on in the play when she describes a sign in a store window that reads "cruelty-free cosmetics." When her daughter insists, "Mother, that is such a beautiful thing. Do you realize the agony cosmetic companies put rabbits through . . . ?" Ouisa responds, "Dearest, I know that. I'm only talking about the phrase. Cruelty-free cosmetics should take away all evidence of time and cellulite and — " (95–96). That one can talk only about the phrase and not what the phrase conveys — the word rather than the thing — is crucial to Ouisa's worldview.

7. The play makes uncertain whether Paul actually says the latter two lines or whether Ouisa Kittredge dreams them; regardless, they are consistent with Paul's own statements at other points.

8. The police search for him not because he scammed the rich New Yorkers, but rather because a twenty-something young man killed himself after spending time with Paul. The young man's suicide — he jumped from a window — itself stems from his fear that having sex with Paul made him gay. As he explains, "What have I done? What did I let him do to me? I wanted experience. I came here to have experience. But I didn't come here to do this or lose that or be this or do this. . . . I didn't come here to be *this*" (91, emphasis in original). With more faith in Paul's treatise on the imagination, he would not have had to believe that one experience made him any kind of a person. His mistake, like Holden's, lies in believing in an innate or fundamental self, outside of his control.

9. In the film version, this scene presents Paul dressed far differently from when he conned the Kittredges. Inexpensive-looking, dirty clothes and unkempt hair suggest he has been sleeping on the streets. Though presumably he might adopt the carefully intonated speech of the upper classes that he used during his performances, the police would be hard-pressed to see him as upper class given his manner of dress.

10. In Jennie Livingston's 1990 documentary *Paris Is Burning*, the young men and women of Harlem's drag balls suggest both the power and the difficulty of putting Paul's philosophy into play as race, class, and sexual minorities. The performers at "Paris Is Burning" compete in both familiar categories — showgirl, Hollywood star, diva, etc. — and unfamiliar ones — executive, college student, military officer — and are judged on what they describe as their "realness." As veteran performer Dorian Corey explains it, "If you can pass the untrained eye, or even the trained eye, and not give away the fact that you're gay, that's realness. The idea of realness is to look as much as possible as your straight counterpart. The realer you look means you look like a real woman or you look like a real man, a straight man." Such performances are not just about men passing as women or women passing as men; the performances involve class passing as well. Corey continues, "In a ballroom, you can be anything you want. You're not really an executive, but you're looking like an executive. And therefore you are showing the straight world that I can be an executive. If I had the opportunity I could be one. Because I can look like one . . ." Realness, then, is not about a putative state of being, but rather a quality of representation. The difficulty of sustaining those performances in the world outside of the drag balls, at the end of the twentieth century — a difficulty that Livingston documents at various points, most notably when Octavia St. Laurent attends an open call for models — in no way diminishes the performers' enthusiasm for the project.

11. In the movie of *Six Degrees of Separation*, the sections of the script that Flan and Ouisa speak directly to the audience are refigured to emphasize Ouisa's sense of anecdote as something to "dine out on"; each section of the play is set at a different social event — weddings, dinners, cocktail parties — with a different group of listeners gathered around Flan and Ouisa in rapt attention.

12. None of which saves Ouisa, or *Six Degrees* more broadly, from further charges of classism — or at least class insensitivity. As Paul must remind Ouisa that he "is black" (110) and will not get the same treatment at the police office alone as he would receive with her, so too Ouisa can analogize her life to a Cezanne painting, or make a symbol out of her trip to the Sistine Chapel. If all life is art, and collage is the art form of the twentieth century, then it helps to have really nice things to put into it, and the script makes clear that Ouisa can purchase the good stuff.

WORKS CONSULTED

Almost Famous. Dir. Cameron Crowe. 2000. DVD. Dreamworks Video, 2001.
Althusser, Louis. "Ideology and Ideological State Apparatuses." 1970. In *Lenin and Philosophy.* Trans. Ben Brewster. New York: Monthly Review Press, 1971. 127–86.
Ames, Lois. "Biographical Note to *The Bell Jar.*" In Plath. 247–64.
Anshen, David. "Clichés and Commodity Fetishism: The Violence of the Real in Jim Thompson's *The Killer inside Me.*" *Journal of Narrative Theory* 37.3 (Fall 2007): 400–426.
Arac, Jonathan. "Toward a Critical Genealogy of U.S. Discourse on Identity: *Invisible Man* after 50 Years." *Boundary 2: An International Journal of Literature and Culture* 30:2 (Summer 2003): 195–216.
Armstrong, Nancy, and Leonard Tennenhouse. "Representing Violence, or 'How the West Was Won.'" In *The Violence of Representation: Literature and the History of Violence.* Ed. Nancy Armstrong and Leonard Tennenhouse. New York: Routledge, 1989. 1–26.
Asante, Molefi Kete. *The Afrocentric Idea.* Philadelphia: Temple UP, 1987.
———. *Afrocentricity.* 1980. Trenton, NJ: Africa World, 1988.
Austin, J. L. *How to Do Things With Words.* 1962. 2nd ed. Ed. F. O. Urmson and Marina Sbisà. Cambridge, MA: Harvard UP, 1999.
Badmington, N. "Pod Almighty! or, Humanism, Posthumanism, and the Strange Case of *Invasion of the Body Snatchers.*" *Textual Practice* 15 (2001): 5–22.
Baker, Katherine K. "Once a Rapist? Motivational Evidence and Relevancy in Rape Law." *Harvard Law Review* 110 (1997): 563–624.
Baldwin, Kate A. "The Radical Imaginary of *The Bell Jar.*" *Novel: A Forum on Fiction* 38.1 (Fall 2004): 21–40.
Barkun, Michael. *Religion and the Racist Right: The Origins of the Christian Identity Movement.* Chapel Hill: U of North Carolina P, 1997.

Baumbach, Jonathan. "The Saint as a Young Man." *Modern Language Quarterly* 25 (1964): 461–72.
Beckwith, Harry. *Selling the Invisible: A Field Guide to Modern Marketing*. New York: Warner, 1997.
———. *What Clients Love: A Field Guide to Growing Your Business*. New York: Warner, 2003.
Bedbury, Scott, and Stephen Fenichell. *A New Brand World: 8 Principles for Achieving Brand Leadership in the 21st Century*. New York: Viking, 2002.
Bell, Daniel. "Reflections on Jewish Identity." *Commentary* (June 1961): 471–78.
Bellow, Saul. *The Adventures of Augie March*. 1953. New York: Penguin, 1999.
———. "Foreword." *The Closing of the American Mind*. By Allan Bloom. New York: Simon and Schuster, 1987.
———. *Seize the Day*. 1956. Intro. Cynthia Ozick. New York: Penguin Modern Classics, 2001.
Bennett, Lerone, Jr. "Nat's Last White Man." In Clarke. 3–16.
Berger, James. "Falling Towers and Postmodern Wild Children: Oliver Sacks, Don DeLillo, and Turns against Language." *PMLA: Publications of the Modern Language Association of America* 120.2 (March 2005): 341–61.
Berlant, Lauren. "National Brands/National Body: Imitation of Life." In *Comparative American Identities: Race, Sex, and Nationality in the Modern Text*. Ed. Hortense J. Spillers. New York: Routledge, 1991. 110–40.
Bibler, Michael P. "Making a Real Phony: Truman Capote's Queerly Southern Regionalism in *Breakfast at Tiffany's: A Short Novel and Three Stories*." In *Just below South: Intercultural Performance in the Caribbean and the U.S. South*. Intro. Jessica Adams. Ed. Adams, Michael P. Bibler, and Cécile Accilien. Charlottesville: U of Virginia P, 2007. 211–38.
Blackboard Jungle. Dir. Richard Brooks. 1955. DVD. Warner Home Video, 2005.
Bloom, Harold, ed. *J. D. Salinger*. New York: Bloom's Literary Criticism, 2008.
Bordwell, David, Janet Staiger, and Kristin Thompson. *The Classical Hollywood Cinema Film Style and Mode of Production to 1960*. New York: Columbia UP, 1985.
Boyer, Paul. *By the Bomb's Early Light: American Thought and Culture at the Dawn of the Atomic Age*. Chapel Hill: U of North Carolina P, 1994.
Boynes, Roy. *Foucault and Derrida*. 1990. New York: Routledge, 1996.
Braudy, Leo. "'No Body's Perfect': Method Acting and 50s Culture." *The Movies: Texts, Receptions, Exposures*. Ed. Laurence Goldstein and Ira Konigsberg. Ann Arbor: U of Michigan P, 1997. 275–99.
Breakfast at Tiffany's. Dir. Blake Edwards. 1961. DVD. Paramount, 2006.

Brodkin, Karen. *How the Jews Became White Folks and What That Says about Race in America*. New Brunswick, NJ: Rutgers UP, 1998.
Brown, Norman O. *Life against Death: The Psychoanalytical Meaning of History*. 1959. 2nd ed. Middletown, CT: Wesleyan UP, 1985.
Budick, Emily Miller. "*Yizkor* for Six Million: Mourning the Death of Civilization in Saul Bellow's *Seize the Day*." In *New Essays on* Seize the Day. Ed. Michael P. Kramer. The American Novel. Emory Elliott, gen. ed. New York: Cambridge UP, 1998. 93–109.
Butler, Judith. *Bodies That Matter: On the Discursive Limits of "Sex."* New York: Routledge, 1993.
———. *Gender Trouble: Feminism and the Subversion of Identity*. New York: Routledge, 1990.
———. *The Psychic Life of Power: Theories in Subjection*. Stanford, CA: Stanford UP, 1997.
Cain, James M. *Double Indemnity*. 1936. New York: Vintage, 1992.
———. *Mildred Pierce*. 1941. New York: Vintage, 1989.
Camus, Albert. "The Myth of Sisyphus." In *The Myth of Sisyphus and Other Essays*. 1955. Trans. Justin O'Brien. New York: Vintage–Random House, 1991. 1–138.
Capote, Truman. *Breakfast at Tiffany's*. 1958. New York: Modern Library, 1994.
Castronovo, David. *Beyond the Gray Flannel Suit: Books from the 1950s That Made American Culture*. New York: Continuum, 2004.
Catch Me If You Can. Dir. Steven Spielberg. 2002. DVD. Dreamworks Video, 2003.
Clarke, John Henrik, ed. *William Styron's Nat Turner: Ten Black Writers Respond*. Boston: Beacon, 1968.
Cohen, Elliot E. "An Act of Affirmation: Editorial Statement." *Commentary* (November 1945): 1–3.
———. "The Intellectuals and the Jewish Community." *Commentary* (July 1949): 20–30.
———. "Jewish Culture in America." *Commentary* (May 1947): 412–20.
———. "Mr. Zanuck's 'Gentleman's Agreement': Reflections on Hollywood's Second Film about Anti-Semitism." *Commentary* (January 1948): 51–56.
Cohen, Lizabeth. *A Consumers' Republic: The Politics of Mass Consumption in Postwar America*. New York: Knopf, 2003.
Conspiracy Theory. Dir. Richard Donner. 1997. DVD. Warner Home Video, 1997.
Coontz, Stephanie. *The Way We Never Were: American Families and the Nostalgia Trap*. New York: BasicBooks, 1992.
Cooper, David E. *Existentialism: A Reconstruction*. Oxford: Basil Blackwell, 1990.

Corber, Robert J. *In The Name of National Security: Hitchcock, Homophobia, and the Political Construction of Gender in Postwar America*. Durham, NC: Duke UP, 1993.

Cornut-Gentille, Chantal. "Who's Afraid of the Femme Fatale in *Breakfast at Tiffany's*? Exposure and Implications of a Myth." In *Gender, I-Deology: Essays on Theory, Fiction and Film*. Intro. Chantal Cournut-Gentille. Foreword by José Angel García Landa. Ed. Cournut-Gentille and García Landa. *Postmodern Studies* 16. Amsterdam: Rodopi, 1996. 371–85.

Costello, Patrick. "Tradition in *Seize the Day*." *Essays in Literature* 14.1 (Spring 1987): 117–31.

Cotkin, George. *Existential America*. Baltimore, MD: Johns Hopkins UP, 2003.

Courtney, Susan. *Hollywood Fantasies of Miscegenation: Spectacular Narratives of Gender and Race, 1903–1967*. Princeton, NJ: Princeton UP, 2005.

Cowart, David. "DeLillo and the Power of Language." In *The Cambridge Companion to Don DeLillo*. Ed. John N. Duvall. Cambridge: Cambridge UP, 2008. 151–65.

Crowe, Cameron. *Jerry Maguire and a Jerry Maguire Journal*. London: Faber and Faber, 1998.

D'Alessandro, David. *Brand Warfare: 10 Rules for Building the Killer Brand*. New York: McGraw-Hill, 2001.

DeLillo, Don. *The Names*. 1982. New York: Vintage–Random House, 1989.

———. "Silhouette City: Hitler, Manson, and the Millennium." 1989. In *White Noise*. Ed. Mark Osteen. Viking Critical Library Edition. New York: Penguin, 1998. 344–52.

Derrida, Jacques. "Cogito and the History of Madness." In *Writing and Difference*. Trans. Alan Bass. Chicago: U of Chicago P, 1978. 31–63.

———. *Of Grammatology*. 1976. Trans. Gayatri Chakravorty Spivak. Corrected ed. Baltimore, MD: Johns Hopkins UP, 1998.

———. "Signature Event Context." In *The Margins of Philosophy*. 1972. Trans. Alan Bass. Chicago: U of Chicago P, 1982. 307–30.

Desmond, John F. "Walker Percy and Writing the Holocaust." *Religion and Literature* 38.2 (Summer 2006): 101–16.

———. *Walker Percy's Search for Community*. Athens: U of Georgia P, 2004.

Devlin, Rachel. "Female Juvenile Delinquency and the Problem of Sexual Authority in America, 1945–1965." In *Delinquents and Debutantes: Twentieth-Century American Girls' Cultures*. Ed. Sheerie Inness. New York: New York UP, 1998. 83–106.

Dickstein, Morris. *Leopards in the Temple: The Transformation of American Fiction 1945–1970*. Cambridge, MA: Harvard UP, 2002.

Diggins, John Patrick. *The Proud Decades: America in War and in Peace, 1941–1960*. New York: W. W. Norton, 1989.

Doherty, Thomas Patrick. *Teenagers and Teenpicks: The Juvenilization of American Movies in the 1950s.* Rev. and exp. ed. Philadelphia: Temple UP, 2002.

Douglas, John, and Mark Olshaker. *The Anatomy of Motive: The FBI's Legendary Mindhunter Explores the Key to Understanding and Catching Violent Criminals.* New York: Scribner, 1999.

Doxey, William, ed. "*The Catcher in the Rye* Issue." *Notes on Contemporary Literature* 32 (2002): 1–8.

Dr. Strangelove, or How I Learned to Quit Worrying and Love the Bomb. Dir. Stanley Kubrick. 1964. DVD. Sony Pictures, 2001.

Du Bois, William. "Books of the Times." *The New York Times* 1 Sept. 1955: 21.

Duvall, John N., ed. *The Cambridge Companion to Don DeLillo.* Cambridge: Cambridge UP, 2008.

Dyer, Richard. "Kill and Kill Again." *Sight and Sound* 7.9 (September 1997): 14–17.

Ehrenreich, Barbara. *The Hearts of Men: American Dreams and the Flight from Commitment.* New York: Anchor, 1983.

Eichelberger, Julia. *Prophets of Recognition Ideology and the Individual in Novels by Ralph Ellison, Toni Morrison, Saul Bellow, and Eudora Welty.* Southern Literary Studies. Baton Rouge: Louisiana State UP, 1999.

Elkins, Stanley M. *Slavery: A Problem in American Institutional and Intellectual Life.* 1959. 3rd ed. Chicago: U of Chicago P, 1976.

Ellison, Ralph. *Invisible Man.* 1952. New York: Vintage International–Random, 1995.

Erikson, Erik. *Childhood and Society.* 1950. New York: Norton, 1993.

Faludi, Susan. *Stiffed: The Betrayal of the American Man.* New York: W. Morrow, 1999.

Fanon, Franz. *Black Skin White Masks.* 1952. New York: Grove, 1967.

Farland, Maria. "Sylvia Plath's Anti-Psychiatry." *Minnesota Review* 55–57 (2002): 245–56.

Fermaglich, Kirsten. *American Dreams and Nazi Nightmares: Early Holocaust Consciousness and Liberal America, 1957–1965.* Waltham, MA: Brandeis UP, 2006.

Fiedler, Leslie. "Saul Bellow." 1957. In *A New Fiedler Reader.* Amherst, NY: Prometheus, 1999. 108–16.

Fish, Stanley. "The Common Touch, or, One Size Fits All." In Gless and Hernstein. 241–66.

Fitch, Robert E. "The Bourgeois and the Bohemian." *Antioch Review* 16.2 (1956): 131–45.

Ford, Richard. Introduction to *Revolutionary Road.* By Richard Yates. 1961. New York: Random–Vintage, 2000.

Foreman, Joel, ed. *The Other Fifties: Interrogating Midcentury American Icons.* Urbana: U of Illinois P, 1997.

Foster, Dennis. "Alphabetic Pleasures: *The Names*." In *Introducing Don DeLillo*. Ed. Frank Lentriccia. Durham, NC: Duke UP, 1991. 157–73.

Foucault, Michel. *Madness and Civilization: A History of Insanity in the Age of Reason*. 1965. Trans. Richard Howard. New York: Vintage, 1988.

Fox, James Alan, and Jack Levin. "Multiple Homicide: Patterns of Serial and Mass Murder." In *Crime and Justice: A Review of Research*. Vol. 23. Ed. Michael Tonry. Chicago: U of Chicago P, 1998. 407–55.

Freedman, Carl. "Memories of Holden Caulfield and of Miss Greenwood." *J. D. Salinger: Bloom's Modern Critical Views*. Ed. Harold Bloom. New York: Bloom's Literary Criticism, 2008. 175–90.

Freud, Sigmund. *Civilization and Its Discontents*. 1930. Trans. and ed. James Strachey. 1961. New York: Norton, 1989.

Friedan, Betty. *The Feminine Mystique*. 1963. Intro. Anne Quindlen. New York: Norton, 2001.

Friedenberg, Edgar Z. *The Vanishing Adolescent*. Intro. David Riesman. 1959. Boston: Beacon, 1964.

Friedman, Lawrence J. *Identity's Architect: A Biography of Erik H. Erikson*. New York: Scribner, 1999.

Fromm, Erich. *The Sane Society*. 1955. New York: H. Holt, 1990.

Fuchs, Daniel. *Saul Bellow, Vision and Revision*. Durham, NC: Duke UP, 1984.

Fulton, Ann. *Apostles of Sartre: Existentialism in America, 1945–1963*. Evanston, IL: Northwestern UP, 1999.

Fuss, Diana. *Essentially Speaking: Feminism, Nature, and Difference*. New York: Routledge, 1989.

Garber, Marjorie. *Vested Interests: Cross-Dressing and Cultural Anxiety*. New York: Routledge, 1992.

Gates, Henry Louis, Jr. "The Master's Pieces: On Canon Formation and the African-American Tradition." 1990. In Gless and Smith. 95–117.

Gates, Philippa. "Manhunting: The Female Detective in the Serial Killer Film." *Post Script: Essays in Film and the Humanities* 24 (2004): 42–61.

Geismar, Maxwell. "The Roots and the Flowering Tree." *New York Times Book Review* 4 Sept. 1955: BR1.

Gentleman's Agreement. Dir. Elia Kazan. 1947. DVD. Twentieth Century Fox, 1999.

Gersh, Harry. "The New Suburbanites of the '50s: Jewish Division." *Commentary* (March 1954): 209–221.

Gilbert, James. *A Cycle of Outrage: America's Reaction to the Juvenile Delinquent in the 1950s*. New York: Oxford UP, 1986.

Gillon, Steven M. *That's Not What We Meant to Do: Reform and Its Unintended Consequences in the Twentieth Century.* New York: Norton, 2000.
Glazer, Nathan. *American Judaism.* 1957. 2nd ed. rev. Chicago: U of Chicago P, 1988.
———. "The Jewish Revival in America: I. A Sociologist's Report." *Commentary* (December 1955): 493–99.
———. "The Jewish Revival in America: II. Its Religious Side." *Commentary* (January 1956): 17–24.
———. *We Are All Multiculturalists Now.* Cambridge, MA: Harvard UP, 1997.
———. "What Sociology Knows about American Jews." *Commentary* (March 1950): 275–84.
Gless, Darryl J., and Barbara Hernstein Smith, eds. *The Politics of Liberal Education.* Durham, NC: Duke UP, 1992.
Goffman, Erving. *The Presentation of Self in Everyday Life.* Garden City, NY: Doubleday, 1959.
Goldberg, Carl, and Virginia Crespo. "A Psychological Examination of Serial Killer Cinema: The Case of *Copycat.*" *Post Script: Essays in Film and the Humanities* 22 (2003): 55–63.
Golsan, Katherine. "Adaptation as Forgery: The Case of *The Talented Mr. Ripley.*" *Post Script: Essays in Film and the Humanities* 23.3 (Summer 2004): 19–35.
Gomel, Elana. "Written in Blood: Serial Killing and Narratives of Identity." *Post Identity* 2.1 (Winter 1999): 24–70.
Gretlund, Jan Nordby, and Karl-Heinz Westarp. *Walker Percy: Novelist and Philosopher.* Jackson: UP of Mississippi, 1991.
Grob, Gerald N. *From Asylum to Community: Mental Health Policy in Modern America.* Princeton, NJ: Princeton UP, 1991.
Guare, John. *Six Degrees of Separation.* 1990. New York: Vintage Books–Random House, 1994.
Halberstam, David. *The Fifties.* New York: Villard, 1993.
Hamm, Mark S. *American Skinheads: The Criminology and Control of Hate Crime.* Westport, CT: Praeger, 1993.
Hantke, Steffen. "Monstrosity without a Body: Representational Strategies in the Popular Serial Killer Film." *Post Script: Essays in Film and the Humanities* 22 (2003): 34–54.
Harris, Thomas. *Red Dragon.* New York: Bantam Doubleday Dell, 1981.
———. *The Silence of the Lambs.* New York: St. Martin's, 1988.
Harrison, Russell. *Patricia Highsmith.* New York: Twayne, 1997.
Hassan, Ihab. "Birth of a Heroine." In Waldmeir and Waldmeir. 109–14.

———. *Selves at Risk: Patterns of Quest in Contemporary American Letters*. Madison: U of Wisconsin P, 1990.

Hemmeter, Thomas. "Horror beyond the Camera: Cultural Sources of Violence in Hitchcock's Mid-Century America." *Post Script: Essays in Film and the Humanities* 22 (2003): 7–19.

Herberg, Will. *Protestant–Catholic–Jew: An Essay in Religious Sociology*. 1955. New intro. Martin E. Marty. Chicago: U of Chicago P, 1983.

———. "The 'Triple Melting Pot': The Third Generation: From Ethnic to Religious Diversity." *Commentary* (August 1955): 101–08.

Highsmith, Patricia. *The Boy Who Followed Ripley*. 1980. New York: Vintage Crime/Black Lizard–Random House, 1993.

———. *Ripley's Game*. 1974. New York: Vintage Crime/Black Lizard–Random House, 1993.

———. *Ripley under Ground*. 1970. New York: Vintage Crime/Black Lizard–Random House, 1992.

———. *Ripley under Water*. 1991. New York: Vintage Crime/Black Lizard–Random House, 1993.

———. *Strangers on a Train*. 1955. New York: W. W. Norton, 2001.

———. *The Talented Mr. Ripley*. 1955. New York: Vintage Crime/Black Lizard–Random House, 1992.

———. *The Tremor of Forgery*. 1969. New York: Atlantic Monthly, 1988.

Hill, Rachel. "Character, Choice, and 'Aberrant Behavior': Aligning Criminal Sentencing with Concepts of Moral Blame." *University of Chicago Law Review* 65 (1998): 975–99.

Hine, Thomas. *The Rise and Fall of the American Teenager*. 1999. New York: Perennial, 2000.

Hoberek, Andrew. *Twilight of the Middle Class: Post–World War II American Fiction and White-Collar Work*. Princeton, NJ: Princeton UP, 2005.

Hobson, Laura Keane Zametkin. *Gentleman's Agreement: A Novel*. 1946. Atlanta: Cherokee, 2007.

Holmes, Ronald M., and Stephen T. Holmes. *Serial Murder*. Thousand Oaks, CA: Sage, 1998.

Hornbacher, Marya. *Wasted: A Memoir of Anorexia and Bulimia*. New York: HarperCollins, 1998.

Ignatieff, Michael. *Scar Tissue*. New York: Farrar, Straus and Giroux, 1994.

Invasion of the Body Snatchers. Dir. Don Siegal. 1956. DVD. Republic Pictures. 1998.

Irwin, J. T. "Beating the Boss: Cain's *Double Indemnity*." *American Literary History* 14.4 (Summer 2002): 255–83.

Jackson, Kenneth T. *Crabgrass Frontier: The Suburbanization of the United States.* New York: Oxford UP, 1985.

Jacobs, James B., and Kimberly Potter. *Hate Crime: Criminal Law and Identity Politics.* New York: Oxford UP, 1998.

Jameson, Frederic. *The Cultural Turn: Selected Writings on the Postmodern 1983–1998.* London: Verso, 1998.

———. *Postmodernism, or the Cultural Logic of Late Capitalism.* Durham, NC: Duke UP, 1991.

———. Rev. of *The Names*, by Don Delillo. *Minnesota Review* 22 (1984): 116–22.

Jamison, Kay Redfield. *An Unquiet Mind.* New York: Knopf, 1995.

Jenkins, Philip. *Using Murder: The Social Construction of Serial Homicide.* New York: Aldine De Gruyter, 1994.

Jerry Maguire. Dir. Cameron Crowe. 1996. DVD. Sony Pictures, 1997.

Joyce, James. *A Portrait of the Artist as a Young Man.* 1916. Ed. Seamus Deane. New York: Penguin Classics, 2003.

Jurca, Catherine. *White Diaspora: The Suburb and the Twentieth-Century American Novel.* Princeton, NJ: Princeton UP, 2001.

Karem, Jeff. *The Romance of Authenticity: The Cultural Politics of Regional and Ethnic Literatures.* Charlottesville: U of Virginia P, 2004.

Karenga, Maulana. *Introduction to Black Studies.* Los Angeles: Kawaida, 1982.

Kaysen, Susanna. *Girl, Interrupted.* New York: Turtle Bay, 1993.

Kazin, Alfred. *Bright Book of life: American Novelists and Storytellers from Hemingway to Mailer.* Boston: Little Brown, Atlantic Monthly, 1973.

Kette, Joseph F. *Rites of Passage: Adolescence in America, 1970 to the Present.* New York: Basic, 1977.

Klinkowitz, Jerome. *Structuring the Void: The Struggle for Subject in Contemporary American Fiction.* Durham, NC: Duke UP, 1992.

Knapp, Caroline. *Drinking: A Love Story.* New York: Bantam, Doubleday Dell, 1996.

Knox, Israel. "Is America Exile or Home?" *Commentary* (November 1946): 401–08.

Kramer, Michael P. "The Vanishing Jew: On Teaching Bellow's *Seize the Day* as Ethnic Fiction." In *New Essays on* Seize the Day. Ed. Michael P. Kramer. The American Novel. Emory Elliott, gen. ed. New York: Cambridge UP, 1998. 1–24.

Kramer, Paul. *Listening to Prozac.* New York: Viking Penguin, 1993.

Krämer, Peter. "The Many Faces of Holly Golightly: Truman Capote, *Breakfast at Tiffany's* and Hollywood." *Film Studies–Oxford* 5 (2004): 58–65.

Lady in the Lake. Dir. Robert Montgomery. 1947. DVD. MGM/UA Home Video, 2006.

Laing, R. D. *The Divided Self: An Existential Study in Sanity and Madness.* 1960. New York: Penguin, 1990.

LaValley, Al, ed. "Continuity Script." In *Invasion of the Body Snatchers, Don Siegel, Director*. New Brunswick, NJ: Rutgers UP, 1989. 31–109.

———. "*Invasion of the Body Snatchers*. Politics, Psychology, Sociology." *Invasion*, 3–17.

LeClair, Tom. *The Art of Excess: Mastery in Contemporary American Fiction*. Champaign-Urbana: U of Illinois P, 1989.

———. *In The Loop: Don DeLillo and the Systems Novel*. Champaign-Urbana: U of Illinois P, 1988.

Lee, Robert. "'Flunking Everything Else Except English Anyway': Holden Caulfield, Author." In *Critical Essays on Salinger's* The Catcher in the Rye. Ed. Joel Salzberg. Boston: Hall, 1990. 185–97.

Levin, Meyer. "The Writer and the Jewish Community." *Commentary* (June 1947): 526–30.

Lévi-Strauss, Claude. *Tristes Tropiques*. Trans. John and Doreen Weightman. 1973. New York: Penguin, 1992.

Leyton, Elliot. *Hunting Humans: The Rise of the Modern Multiple Murderer*. 1986. Toronto: McClelland and Stewart, 1995.

Lhamon, W. T., Jr. *Deliberate Speed: The Origins of a Cultural Style in the American 1950s*. 1990. Cambridge. MA: Harvard UP, 2002.

Linder, Robert. *Must You Conform?* New York: Reinhart, 1956.

Lundquist, James. "Against Obscenity: *The Catcher in the Rye*." In *J. D. Salinger*. New York: Frederick Ungar, 1979. 37–68.

MacDonald, Andrew. *The Turner Diaries*. 1978; New York: Barricade Books, 1996.

MacDonald, Dwight. "A Theory of Mass Culture." In *Mass Culture: The Popular Arts in America*. Ed. Bernard Rosenberg and David Manning White. New York: Free Press, 1957. 59–73.

———. "Masscult and Midcult." In *Against the American Grain: Essays on the Effects of Mass Culture*. 1952. New York: Random House, 1962. 3–75.

The Manchurian Candidate. Dir. John Frankenheimer. 1962. DVD. MGM (Video & DVD), 2004.

Mann, K. "'You're Next!': Postwar Hegemony Besieged in *Invasion of the Body Snatchers*." *Cinema Journal* 44 (2004): 49–68.

Marcuse, Herbert. *Eros and Civilization: A Philosophical Inquiry into Freud*. Boston: Beacon, 1955.

Martin, Richard T. "Language Specificity as Pattern of Redemption in *The Thanatos Syndrome*." *Renascence: Essays on Values in Literature* 48.3 (Spring 1996): 208–23.

May, Elaine Tyler. *Homeward Bound: American Families in the Cold War Era*. New York: Basic, 1988.

May, Lary, ed. *Recasting America: Culture and Politics in the Age of the Cold War*. New ed. Chicago: U of Chicago P, 1989.

McCarthy, Mary. "J. D. Salinger's Closed Circuit." In *The Writing on the Wall and Other Literary Essays*. New York: Harcourt Brace and World, 1962. 35–41.

McCullough, Frances. Foreword to *The Bell Jar*. By Sylvia Plath. 1972. New York: Perennial-HarperCollins, 1999.

McFadden, Robert D. "Laura Z. Hobson, Author, Dies at 85." *New York Times* 2 March 1986, Late City Final ed.: sec. 1: 40.

McHale, Brian. *Postmodernist Fiction*. New York: Methuen, 1987.

Medevoi, Leerom. *Rebels: Youth and the Cold War Origins of Identity*. Durham, NC: Duke UP, 2005.

Melley, Timothy. *Empire of Conspiracy: The Culture of Paranoia in Postwar America*. Ithaca, NY: Cornell UP, 1999.

Menand, Louis. "Holden at Fifty: 'The Catcher in the Rye' and What It Spawned." *The New Yorker* 1 Oct. 2001: 82–87.

Meyerowitz, Joanne, ed. *Not June Cleaver: Women and Gender in Postwar America, 1945–1960*. Philadelphia: Temple UP, 1994.

Miller, Arthur. *Focus*. 1945. New York: Penguin, 2001.

Miller, James E., Jr. "Catcher in and Out of History." *Critical Inquiry* 3 (1977): 599–603.

Mills, C. Wright. *The Power Elite*. New York: Oxford UP, 1956.

———. *The Sociological Imagination*. 1956. 40th anniversary ed. Oxford: Oxford UP, 2000.

———. *White Collar: The American Middle Classes*. New York: Oxford UP, 1951.

Moi, Toril. "What Is a Woman? Sex, Gender, and the Body in Feminist Theory." In *What Is a Woman? And Other Essays*. Oxford: Oxford UP, 1999. 3–120.

Moran, Jeffrey P. *Teaching Sex: The Shaping of Adolescence in the 20th Century*. Cambridge, MA: Harvard UP, 2000.

Moreno, Michael P. "Consuming the Frontier Illusion: The Construction of Suburban Masculinity in Richard Yates's *Revolutionary Road*." *Iowa Journal of Cultural Studies* 3 (2003): 84–95.

Moretti, Franco. *The Way of the World: The Bildungsroman in European Culture*. 1987. Trans. Albert Sbragia. New ed. London: Verso, 2000.

Moser, Mike. *United We Brand: How to Create a Cohesive Brand That's Seen, Heard, and Remembered*. Boston: Harvard Business School Press, 2003.

Nadel, Alan. *Containment Culture: American Narratives, Postmodernism, and the Atomic Age*. Durham, NC: Duke UP, 1995.

Nelson, Deborah. "Plath, History and Politics." *The Cambridge Companion to Sylvia Plath*. Ed. Jo Gill. Cambridge: Cambridge UP, 2006. 21–35.

———. *Pursuing Privacy in Cold War America*. New York: Columbia UP, 2002.

Nixon, Nicola. "Making Monsters, or Serializing Killers." in *American Gothic: New*

Inventions in a National Narrative. Ed. Robert K. Martin and Eric Savoy. Iowa City: U of Iowa P, 1998. 217–36.

Norris, Joel. *Serial Killers*. New York: Doubleday, 1988.

Novick, Peter. *The Holocaust in American Life*. Boston: Houghton Mifflin, 1999.

O'Donnell, Patrick. *Latent Destinies: Cultural Paranoia and Contemporary U.S. Narrative*. Durham, NC: Duke UP, 2000.

Ohmann, Carol, and Richard Ohmann. "Universals and the Historically Particular." *Critical Inquiry* 3 (1977): 773–77.

On the Waterfront. Dir. Elia Kazan. 1954. DVD. Sony Pictures, 2001.

One Flew over the Cuckoo's Nest. Dir. Milos Forman. 1975. DVD. Warner Home Video, 2002.

Ozick, Cynthia. "Introduction: Saul Bellow's Broadway." In *Seize the Day*. By Saul Bellow. 1956. New York: Penguin Modern Classics, 2001.

Palladino, Grace. *Teenagers: An American History*. New York: Basic, 1996.

Paris Is Burning. Dir. Jennie Livingston. 1990. DVD. Miramax Home Entertainment, 2005.

Patterson, James T. *Grand Expectations: The United States, 1945–1974*. Vol. 10 of the Oxford History of the United States. New York: Oxford UP, 1996.

Payne, Kenneth. "The Killers inside Them: The Schizophrenic Protagonist in John Franklin Bardin's *Devil Take the Blue-Tail Fly* and Jim Thompson's *The Killer inside Me*." *Journal of Popular Culture* 36.2 (Fall 2002): 250–63.

Percy, Walker. "The Coming Crisis in Psychiatry." 1957. In *Signposts*. 251–62.

———. "Diagnosing the Modern Malaise." 1985. In *Signposts*. 204–21.

———. "Is a Theory of Man Possible?" N.d. In *Signposts*. 111–29.

———. *The Moviegoer*. New York: Knopf, 1961.

———. "Naming and Being." 1960. In *Signposts*. 130–38.

———. *Signposts in a Strange Land*. Ed. and intro. Patrick Samway. New York: Farrar, Straus and Giroux, 1991.

———. "The State of the Novel: Dying Art or New Science?" 1977. In *Signposts*. 139–52.

———. "Symbol as Hermeneutic in Existentialism." In *The Message in the Bottle, How Queer Man Is, How Queer Language Is, and What One Has to Do with the Other*. New York: Farrar, Straus & Giroux, 1975. 277–87.

———. *The Thanatos Syndrome*. New York: Ballantine, 1987.

Pinky. Dir. Elia Kazan. 1949. DVD. Twentieth Century Fox, 2005.

Pinsker, Sanford. *The Catcher in the Rye: Innocence under Pressure*. Twayne's Masterwork Studies 114. New York: Twayne, 1993.

Plath, Sylvia. *The Bell Jar*. 1963. New York: Perennial–HarperCollins, 1999.

Podhoretz, Norman. "The Jew as Bourgeois." *Commentary* (February 1956): 186–88.
Pomerance, Murray. "Stark Performance." In *Rebel without a Cause: Story of a Maverick Masterwork*. Ed. J. David Slocum. Albany: State U of New York P, 2005. 35–52.
Poussaint, Alvin F. "The Confessions of Nat Turner and the Dilemma of William Styron." In Clarke 17–22.
Prosser, Jay. *Second Skins: The Body Narratives of Transsexuality*. New York: Columbia UP, 1998.
Pugh, Tison. "Capote's *Breakfast at Tiffany's*." *Explicator* 61.1 (Fall 2002): 51–53.
Ray, Nicholas. "Story into Script." In *Rebel without a Cause: Story of a Maverick Masterwork*. Ed. J. David Slocum. Albany: State U of New York P, 2005. 25–34.
Rebel without a Cause. Dir. Nicholas Ray. 1955. DVD. Warner Bros. Pictures, 2005.
Regester, Charlene. "Miss Em's Voyeuristic Gaze of Pinky — White Desire for Blackness." *Popular Culture Review* 14.1 (February 2003): 67–85.
Riesman, David. "A Philosophy for 'Minority' Living: The Jewish Situation and the 'Nerve of Failure.'" *Commentary* (November 1948): 413–22.
———, with Nathan Glazer and Reuel Denny. *The Lonely Crowd: A Study of the Changing American Character*. 1953. Abridged ed. New Haven, CT: Yale UP, 1961.
Robbins, Bruce. "Murder and Mentorship: Advancement in *The Silence of the Lambs*." *Boundary 2: An International Journal of Literature and Culture* 23.1 (Spring 1996): 71–90.
Roffer, Robin Fisher. *Make a Name for Yourself: 8 Steps Every Woman Needs to Create a Personal Brand Strategy for Success*. New York: Broadway, 2002.
Rogin, Michael Paul. "Kiss Me Deadly: Communism, Motherhood, and Cold War Movies." In *Ronald Reagan, the Movie and Other Episodes in Political Demonology*. Berkeley: U of California P, 1987. 236–73.
Rombes, Nicholas. "A through S(e7en): A Racial Taxonomy of Serial Killer Cinema." *Post Script: Essays in Film and the Humanities* 22 (2003): 81–91.
Rosenbaum, D. L. "On Being Sane in Insane Places." *Science* 179 (January 1973): 250–58.
Rosenberg, Harold. "Does the Jew Exist?" *Commentary* (January 1949): 8–18.
Rossman, Evelyn N. "The Community and I. Belonging: Its Satisfactions and Dissatisfactions." *Commentary* (November 1954): 393–405.
———. "The Community and I. Two Years Later: The Wine, or the Blessing?" *Commentary* (March 1956): 230–38.
———. "The Community and I. Part III: Judaism in Northrup." *Commentary* (November 1957): 383–91.
———. "Decade in Northrup: A Natural Jewishness Emerges." *Commentary* (September 1959): 214–22.

Rothenberg, Molly Anne, and Joseph Valente. "Fashionable Theory and Fashionable Women: Returning Fuss's Homospectatorial Look." In *Identities*. Ed. Kwame Anthony Appiah and Henry Louis Gates Jr. Chicago: U of Chicago P, 1995. 413–23.

Rule, Anne. *The Stranger beside Me*. 1980. New York: Signet, 1989.

Salinger, J. D. *The Catcher in the Rye*. Boston: Little, Brown, 1951.

Salzman, Jack, ed. *New Essays on* The Catcher in the Rye. New York: Cambridge UP, 1991.

Sartre, Jean-Paul. *Anti-Semite and Jew*. Trans. George J. Becker. New York: Schocken, 1948.

———. *Being and Nothingness*. Trans. and intro. Hazel E. Barnes. 1956. New York: Washington Square, 1992.

———. *Existentialism and Humanism*. Trans. and intro. Philip Mairet. London: Methuen, 1948.

———. *Existential Psychoanalysis*. Trans. Hazel E. Barnes. 1953. Reprint. Intro. Rollo May. New York: Regency, 1996.

Schaub, Thomas Hill. *American Fiction in the Cold War*. Madison: U of Wisconsin P, 1991.

Schwab, Gabriele. *Subjects without Selves: Transitional Texts in Modern Fiction*. Cambridge, MA: Harvard UP, 1994.

Scullin, Kathleen. "Lancelot and Walker Percy's Dispute with Sartre over Ontology." In Gretlund and Westarp. 110–18.

Seelye, John. "Holden in the Museum." In Salzman. 23–33.

Seltzer, Mark. *Serial Killers: Death and Life in America's Wound Culture*. New York: Routledge, 1998.

Shannon, Edward A. "'Where Was the Sex?' Fetishism and Dirty Minds in Patricia Highsmith's *The Talented Mr. Ripley*." *Modern Language Studies* 34.1–2 (Spring–Fall 2004): 16–27.

Shapiro, Edward S. *A Time for Healing: American Jewry since World War II*. Vol. 5 of The Jewish People in America. Baltimore, MD: Johns Hopkins UP, 1992.

Simmons, Gaye McCollum. "Atonement in Bellow's *Seize the Day*." *Saul Bellow Journal* 11.2/12.1 (1993–94): 30–53.

Simpson, Philip L. *Psycho Paths: Tracking the Serial Killer through Contemporary American Film and Fiction*. Carbondale: Southern Illinois UP, 2000.

Six Degrees of Separation. Dir. John Schepsi. 1993. Video and DVD. MGM. 2000.

Skinner, B. F. *Walden Two*. 1948. Reprint ed. New York: Hackett, 2005.

Sklare, Marshall. *Conservative Judaism: An American Religious Movement*. Glencoe, IL: Free Press, 1955.

Slocum, J. David, ed. *Rebel without a Cause: Story of a Maverick Masterwork*. Albany: State U of New York P, 2005.

Sontag, Susan. "AIDS and Its Metaphors." 1989. In Sontag, *Illness*.
———. *Illness as Metaphor and AIDS and Its Metaphors*. New York: Anchor, 1990.
Staiger, Janet. "Taboos and Totems: Cultural Meanings of *The Silence of the Lambs*." In *Reception Study: From Literary Theory to Cultural Studies*. Ed. James L. Machor and Philip Goldstein. New York: Routledge, 2001. 282–93.
Stampp, Kenneth M. "The Historian and Southern Negro Slavery." *American Historical Review* 57.3 (1952): 613–24.
Steed, J. P. *The Catcher in the Rye: New Essays*. New York: Peter Lang, 2002.
Steinle, Pamela Hunt. "*The Catcher in the Rye* as Postwar American Fable." *J. D. Salinger; Bloom's Modern Critical Views*. Ed. Harold Bloom. New York: Bloom's Literary Criticism, 2008. 129–43.
———. *In Cold Fear: The Catcher in the Rye, Censorship Controversies and Postwar American Character*. Columbus: Ohio State UP, 2000.
The Stepford Wives. Dir. Bryan Forbes. 1975. DVD. Paramount, 2004.
Straayer, Chris. "The Talented Poststructuralist: Heteromasculinity, Gay Artifice, and Class Passing." In *Masculinity: Bodies, Movies, Culture*. Ed. Peter Lehman. New York: Routledge, 2001. 115–32.
Styron, William. *The Confessions of Nat Turner*. 1967. New York: Vintage International–Random, 1992.
———. *Darkness Visible: A Memoir of Madness*. New York: Random House, 1990.
———. "Nat Turner Revisited." Afterword. In *Confessions* 433–55.
———. *Sophie's Choice*. 1976. New York: Vintage-Random, 1992.
Sullivan, Terry, and Peter T. Maiken. *Killer Clown: The John Wayne Gacy Murders*. 1983. New York: Pinnacle, 1993.
Sundquist, Eric J. *Strangers in the Land: Blacks, Jews, Post-Holocaust America*. New York: Belknap, 2005.
Szasz, Thomas S. *The Myth of Mental Illness: Foundations of a Theory of Personal Conduct*. New York: Paul B. Hoeber-Harper, 1961.
Tabbi, Joseph. *Postmodern Sublime: Technology and American Writing from Mailer to Cyberpunk*. New ed. Ithaca, NY: Cornell UP, 1995.
The Talented Mr. Ripley. Dir. Anthony Minghella. 1999. DVD. Paramount, 2000.
Tasker, Yvonne. *The Silence of the Lambs*. London: British Film Institute, 2002.
Taubin, Amy. "Grabbing the Knife: *The Silence of the Lambs* and the History of the Serial Killer Movie." In *Women and Film: A Sight and Sound Reader*. Ed. Pam Cook and Philip Dodd. Philadelphia: Temple UP, 1993. 123–31.
Thompson, Jim. *The Killer inside Me*. 1952. New York: Vintage, 1991.
Thompson, Raymond, and Kitty Sewell. *What Took You So Long? A Girl's Journey to Manhood*. London: Penguin, 1995.
Tillich, Paul. *The Courage to Be*. 1952. 2nd ed. New Haven, CT: Yale UP, 2000.

Torrey, E. Fuller. *Out of the Shadows: Confronting America's Mental Illness Crisis.* New York: Wiley, 1997.

Tribe, Laurence H. "The Mystery of Motive, Private and Public: Some Notes Inspired by the Problems of Hate Crime and Animal Sacrifice." *Supreme Court Review 1993.* Ed. Dennis J. Hutchinson, David A. Strauss, and Geoffrey Stone. Chicago: U of Chicago P, 1993. 1–36.

Trilling, Lionel. *Sincerity and Authenticity.* Cambridge, MA: Harvard UP, 1971.

Waldmeir, Joseph J., and John Christian Waldmeir. *The Critical Response to Truman Capote.* Westport, CT: Greenwood, 1999.

Wells, Arvin R. "Huck Finn and Holden Caulfield: The Situation of the Hero." *Ohio University Review* 2 (1960): 31–34.

Whitfield, Stephen J. *The Culture of the Cold War.* 2nd ed. Baltimore, MD: Johns Hopkins UP, 1996.

Whyte, William H., Jr. *The Organization Man.* New York: Simon and Schuster, 1956.

The Wild One. Dir. Laslo Benedek. 1953. DVD. Sony Pictures, 1998.

Williams, Michael. "*Plein soleil* and *The Talented Mr. Ripley*: Sun, Stars and Highsmith's Queer Periphery." *Journal of Romance Studies* 4.1 (Spring 2004): 47–62.

Wilson, Sloan. *The Man in the Gray Flannel Suit.* 1955. New York: Four Walls Eight Windows, 2002.

Wisconsin v. Mitchell. 113 S Ct 2194 (1993).

Wolfe, Cary, and W. J. T. Mitchell. Foreword. *Animal Rites: American Culture, the Discourse of Species and Posthumanist Theory.* Chicago: U of Chicago P, 2003.

Wouk, Herman. *Marjorie Morningstar.* Boston and New York: Little Brown, 1955.

———. *This Is My God.* 1959. New York: Back Bay/Little, Brown, 1988.

Wright, Richard. *Native Son.* 1940. New York: HarperCollins, 2003.

Wurtzel, Elizabeth. *Bitch: In Praise of Difficult Women.* New York: Doubleday, 1998.

———. *Prozac Nation: Young and Depressed in America.* New York: Houghton Mifflin, 1994.

Yates, Richard. *Revolutionary Road.* 1961. New York: Random-Vintage, 2000.

Young, Jeff. *Kazan: The Master Director Discusses His Films. Interviews with Elia Kazan.* New York: Newmarket, 1999.

INDEX

action: continual re-creation through, 110; naming, 129–30; representation of self through, 132–40; serial killing as related to, 107–9, 121–26, 133

adolescence: attitude of modest contempt in, 24–25, 27–28, 41, 45, 55, 78, 103, 182; and bad faith versus falsehood, 42–45; *Breakfast at Tiffany's* on progression to self-knowledge in, 14–18, 27–29, 42–55; and *The Catcher in the Rye* and deaf-mute solution, 1, 14, 18, 25, 29–42; and existential emergence as way of life, 28; *Weltschmerz* concept of, 34

adolescents: Erikson's developmental concept of, 27–28, 45–51, 254n4; reconciliation to adulthood realities by, 25–26; representation of authentic, 18, 23–25, 26

Adorno, Theodor, 46

African Americans: "black" versus "Afro-American" versus, 101; "denegrification" of, 261n23; *Pinky* on passing by, 157–61, 162, 163, 166, 167; social exclusion (1950s) of, 30; *The Thanatos Syndrome* on, selfhood, and Afrocentricity, 83–86. *See also* race

Afrocentricity, 83–86

agency. *See* performative agency

Age of Reason, The (Sartre), 42

Almost Famous (Crowe), 278n5

Althusser, Louis: "Ideology and Ideological State Apparatuses," 193; on state transformation of individuals into subjects, 220–23

Alvarez, A., 65

"always-already" subjects, 233, 275n12

Ambassadors, The (James), 264n17

American culture: adolescent-created subculture in, 26; adolescent dual representation in, 25–26; *Breakfast at Tiffany's* on, and self, 35, 52–55; developmental interaction between, and evolving self, 45–48; impact of, on inauthentic identity, 47–48; inclusion of Judaism along with Christian faiths in, 144–45; mad cogito determined by, 65–78, 103; mental illness response to conformity/uniformity of, 69–79; "nerve of failure" in, 176–78; reshaping of perceptions of serial killing in, 109–40. *See also* cultures

American identity: other cultures compared with, 48–49; "predetermined," 46–48. *See also* identity; middle-class identity

American individualism: Marcuse's analysis of inauthentic, 9–11, 198, 243; "other-directed" betrayal of, 7; social efficacy of, 13, 197–98; Whyte's analysis of, 198
American Jews (Glazer), 273n15
American psyche: and media response to conformity of 1950s, 6–9; recasting conformity of 1950s, 6
anecdote-experience opposition, 244–46
angst, 52–53
antidepressants, 89–94, 260nn20–21
Anti-Semite and Jew (Sartre): existential model of self in, 20, 28; *Gentleman's Agreement* as fictional counterpart to, 148–49, 150–57, 159, 160–67; radical self-making advocated in, 38–39
Arab-Israeli War (1973), 143
Arendt, Hannah, 46
Armstrong, Nancy, 126–27
Aryan groups, 138
Asante, Molefi Kete, 84
assimilation: by Jewish Americans, 147–49, 161; of Jewish identity in Germany, 173–74; *Marjorie Morningstar* on, and phony Jews, 180–90; melting pot "starched uniformity" of, 177–78; *Pinky* on African American passing as, 157–61, 162, 163, 166, 167; and *Seize the Day*, 168–69, 173–74; *The Thanatos Syndrome* on Jewish, 188
attitude of modest contempt, 24–25, 27–28, 41, 45, 55, 78, 103, 177, 182, 201, 218, 248
authenticity: through absence of unified self, 16–17; correlation of mental illness with, 56–57, 59–65; cultural context of, 15–16; depression as form of, 19, 69–70, 80–83, 89; ethnic fiction use of, 251n8; evolution of, into standard of belonging, 4; examination of, and Jewish identity, 144–50, 167–80; as index to one's uniqueness, 3–4; innermost being in relation to, 86; internal versus superficial, 50; media representation of adolescent, 18, 23–25, 26; narrative genres manifesting cultural history of, examined, 17–22; performance theory solution to, and agency, 21–22, 194–95, 204–12, 222; phoniness as index used to access, 3, 14–15; postwar definition of, 248; reexamination of concepts of, during postwar period, 4–22; restoration of, in postmodernity, 241–43; Sartre's theorization of, 38–40, 86, 164–65, 243; self-consciousness and intent of, 247–48; three observations by Trilling on, 32–33. *See also* inauthenticity; phoniness
authenticity models: and adolescent struggle as developmental problem, 28; self-contradictions in history of, examined, 28–29
autonomous/adjusted/anomics individuals, 12–13, 36, 78, 218, 250n6

bad faith versus falsehood, 42–45
Beauvoir, Simone de, 42
Bedbury, Scott, 233, 234
Being and Nothingness (Sartre), 20, 38–39, 42, 44, 86, 133, 152–54, 175, 211, 255n7, 255n10
"being-in-the-world," 68, 69
"being-seen-by-the-Other," 152–53

INDEX

Bell, Daniel: on *embourgeoisement* of American Jewishness, 142, 149–50, 182; Jewish "crisis of identity" analysis by, 21, 141–42, 146–47
Bell Jar, The (Plath), 18, 58; *The Catcher in the Rye* compared with, 65–66, 78; mad cogito imagined in, 65–78, 103; madness examined in, 76–78, 80; metaphor use in, 70–71, 76; on pressures of conformity and uniformity on mental illness, 69–70
Bellow, Saul, 4, 85; on construction of self, 175; *Seize the Day*, 21, 167–80
Benedek, Laslo, 23
Berg, Alan, 269n40
Berkowitz, David, 108
Beyond the Pleasure Principle (Freud), 113
bildungsroman: *Breakfast at Tiffany's* focus on, 53–54; *The Catcher in the Rye* in context of, 18, 41; on human-nature-and-society conflict, 34–35
Bitch (Wurtzel), 260n22
Bloom, Allan, 175
Bodies That Matter (Butler), 228, 230
Boorstin, Daniel, 235
branding: *Jerry Maguire* on value of, 234–38; value for corporations of, 232–34
Brave New World (Huxley), 13, 274n18
Breakfast at Tiffany's (Capote): and adolescent postwar phoniness, 14, 18, 42–55; angst in, 52–53; on mass culture producing real phoniness, 35, 52–55; movie version's happy ending for, 256n17; problem of uniformity and phoniness in, 52–55
Brodkin, Karen, 144, 166, 272n9, 273n12
Brontë, Charlotte, 126

Bruders Schweigen (Silent Brotherhood or The Order), 138, 269n40
Budick, Emily Miller, 168
Bundy, Ted, 108, 111–12, 136, 137, 140, 263n11, 268n36
Butler, Judith, 4, 220–21; on Althusser's Ideological State Apparatus, 220–23; on subject formation and role of repetition, 223–24, 227–28
— works of: *Bodies That Matter*, 228, 230; *Gender Trouble*, 229. See also *Psychic Life of Power, The*

Cain, James M.: *Double Indemnity*, 117–18, 264n16; *Mildred Pierce*, 200
Camus, Albert, 123
Capote, Truman, superficial authenticity examined by, 4, 14, 30. See also *Breakfast at Tiffany's*
Cartesian cogito, 72
Catcher in the Rye, The (Salinger): adult readers of, 29; attitude of modest contempt shown in, 24–25, 27–28, 41, 45, 55, 201; authentic behavior presented in, 24–25; *The Bell Jar* compared with, 65–66, 78; bildungsroman context of, 18, 34–35, 41; deaf-mute solution of, 37–38, 39–41; death of imagination revealed by, 242–43; *Jerry Maguire* references to, 240–41; *Marjorie Morningstar* compared with, 182; McCarthy's critique of, 29–31; as new literary genre, 34; phoniness of self defined in, 1, 14, 18, 30–31, 55; reconciliation solution in, 25, 29–42; as restoring authenticity abandoned by postmodernity, 241–43; *Revolutionary Road* as echoing themes of, 204–5;

Catcher in the Rye, The (continued)
revulsion from adult life realities in, 35; self-knowledge examined in, 35–38, 40; in *Six Degrees of Separation*, 241–42; social-interaction approach advocated in, 41–42
Catch Me If You Can (film), 15
Cheney, Lynne, 85, 86, 101
Childhood and Society (Erikson), 18, 45–49
Civilization and Its Discontents (Freud), 7
class: connections between, and race, 272n9; markers of, 243–44; *Six Degrees of Separation* charged with classism, 279n12
Closing of the American Mind, The (Bloom), 175
Cobain, Kurt, 99
Cohen, Elliott E., 142, 143, 271n7; "The Intellectuals and the Jewish Community," 143; "Jewish Culture in America," 143
Cohen, L., 26
Cold War: fears associated with, 143, 203; fiction related to, 254–55n6
"Coming Crisis in Psychiatry, The" (Percy), 57, 63, 64, 80
Commentary (American Jewish Committee), 141, 143, 189
Confessions of Nat Turner, The (Styron), 102
conformity: definition of, 4–5; identity versus, 91; mental illness due to, and uniformity, 70–79; "protective coloration" as positive form of, 5, 193–94, 198–99; and religion, 145, 187; uniformity compared with, 8–13, 46, 55, 61–63, 78, 116, 184–85, 193, 198–99, 248, 252n11, 257n8, 270n3; and women, 50. *See also* uniformity
Conspiracy Theory (film), 277–78n4
Cooley, Charles H., 210
Cooper, David E., 89
corporate life: alienating conditions of modern, 214; attitude of contempt toward, 201; branding component of, 233–38; *Jerry Maguire*'s self-transformative narration on, 218–27, 229–38; *The Man in the Gray Flannel Suit* narrative of, 191–92, 195, 199–201; "personality market" of, 231–33; as regulating intimate life-fate of individual, 194; *Revolutionary Road* on contaminating effects of, 201–2. *See also* institutional influence on self
Courtney, Susan, 159
Crime and Punishment (Dostoyevsky), 113
Crowe, Cameron, 278n5. *See also Jerry Maguire*
Cultural Turn, The (Jameson), 16, 82, 250n7
cultures: assumptions about, and artistry, 258n13; created by adolescents, 26; curriculum accommodating multicultural, 258–59n14; identity in different, compared, 46–49. *See also* American culture

D'Alessandro, David, 233, 234, 235
Darkness Visible (Styron), 19, 58, 92–96, 98, 100–102
deaf-mute solution, 37–38, 39–41
Dean, James, 253n1
"Decade in Northrup" (Rossman), 189–90
DeLillo, Don, 4. *See also Names, The*

INDEX

"denegrification," 261n23
depression: biological models of, 90–95; as form of authenticity, 19, 59–60, 61–63; homosexuality as analogous to, 95–96; identity as, 99–101; identity as opposite to, 91–92; as inauthenticity, 59; as interfering with capacity of self to be itself, 94–95; medicalization of, 89–91, 92–94; *The Thanatos Syndrome* on cure for, 19, 58, 79–89, 98. *See also* mental illness
Derrida, Jacques, 4, 75, 129–30, 131–32
Descartes, René, 72, 73, 74
developmental models: on changes to self over time, 32, 35–37; Erikson's adolescence, 27–28, 45–51, 254n4; of evolving self and culture, 45–47; and existentialism, 27–28, 41; life cycle, 48
Dickstein, Morris, 8
différance concept, 130–32
Diggins, John Patrick, 6
Divided Self, The (Laing), 6, 19, 67–69, 72
Dostoyevsky, Fyodor, 113
Double Indemnity (Cain), 117–18, 264n16
Douglas, John, 112–13
Durkheim, Émile, 12

Elkins, Stanley M., 252–53n11, 270n1
Ellison, Ralph, 17, 252–53n11
embourgeoisement, 142, 149–50, 182, 186
Emerson, Ralph Waldo, 2
Enlightenment, 2, 13
Erikson, Erik: *Childhood and Society*, 18, 45–49; concept of adolescent development by, 27–28, 45–51, 254n4; life cycle of, 48
Eros and Civilization (Marcuse), 6, 9–11, 13, 198, 243

ethnic fiction, 251n8
ethnicity, markers of, 243–44. *See also* race
Existentialism and Humanism (Sartre), 39, 42
Existentialist Psychoanalysis (Sartre), 42
existential model of self: "being-seen-by-the-Other" truth of "seeing-the-Other," 152–54; commitment to individual transcendence as outgrowth of, 86; Highsmith's interpretation of, 19–20, 107, 110–11, 113, 121–26, 124–26, 131–32; Holden's deaf-mute solution using, 37–38, 39–40; mental illness examined using, 68–69; and the Other, 152–54; radical self-making approach of, 38–39; relation of, to adolescent development, 27–28; Sartre's description of, 20, 27–28, 41, 42–45, 152–54, 167; *Seize the Day*'s examination of, 149, 171–72. *See also* self
experience: opposition of, and anecdote, 244–46; performance versus, 246–47; repetition as creating automation from, 245–46; as representation, 246–47

"Family of Man, The" (Steichen), 142
Farland, Maria, 70, 77
Federal Rules of Evidence, 269n39
Feminine Mystique, The (Friedan), 50, 216
fiction: Cold-War national allegories in, 254–55n6; ethnic, 251n8
Fielder, Leslie, 142, 165, 167–68, 169, 272n10, 273n17
Fitch, Robert E., 181
Flanner, Janet, 42
Flies, The (Sartre), 42

Focus (Miller), 165, 271–72n8
Foucault, Michel, 19, 57, 67, 74–76
Frankenheimer, John, 62–63
Freud, Sigmund, 7, 9; *Beyond the Pleasure Principle*, 113; *Civilization and Its Discontents*, 7
Freudian model: on conscious and unconscious life, 32–33; dyad of self and other, 43–44; on repression of individual instincts, 9; social theory on inauthencity, 33
Friedan, Bette, 28, 50–51; *The Feminine Mystique*, 50, 216
Friedenberg, Edgar Z., 26, 28
Friedman, Lawrence J., 46, 47, 48, 254n5, 255–56n14
Fromm, Erich, 7, 34, 36
Fuss, Diana, 86–87

Gacy, John Wayne, 108, 136, 137, 268n36
Gates, Henry Louis, Jr., 85
Gender Trouble (Butler), 229
Gentleman's Agreement (Hobson novel), 150
Gentleman's Agreement (Kazan film), 20–21; anti-Semitism examined by, 150–57, 159, 160–67; authentic living examined in, 148–49; criticism on, 271n7
Germany: Jewish assimilation in, 173–74, 273n15; *Kristallnacht* attack on Jews in, 185. *See also* Holocaust
Gersh, Harry, 143
Glazer, Nathan: *American Jews*, 273n15; "The Jewish Revival in America," 143; *We Are All Multiculturalists Now*, 258–59n14; "What Sociology Knows about American Jews?" 271n4

Goffman, Erving, 6, 21, 192–93, 194, 209, 274–75n7
Gooding, Cuba, Jr., 224
Guare, John, 4; *Six Degrees of Separation*, 15, 16, 241–46

Halberstam, David, 6
happiness, 9–11
Harris, Thomas, changed approach to serial killing by, 105–7. *See also Red Dragon*; *Silence of the Lambs, The*
Harrison, Russell, 265n21
hate crimes, 132–40, 268n34, 268–69nn37–38. *See also* race
Herberg, Will, 142; *Protestant-Catholic-Jew*, 144–46, 167–68, 186; "'The Triple Melting Pot,'" 144
Highsmith, Patricia, 4; existentialist ontology of self by, 124–26
— works of: *Ripley under Ground*, 265n22; *Strangers on a Train*, 264–65n18; *The Tremor of Forgery*, 265n21. *See also Talented Mr. Ripley, The*
Hoberek, Andrew, 8, 148, 168
Hobson, Laura, 150
Holden Caulfield. *See Catcher in the Rye, The*
Holly Golightly. *See Breakfast at Tiffany's*
Holmes, Ronald M., 112
Holmes, Stephen T., 112
Holocaust: "fading memories" explanation for deployment of discourse on, 270n2; as killing Jewish identity, 97–98, 99, 143, 166; lack of postwar political engagement on, 270n1; as metaphor for Jewish assimilation, 188–89; and *The Thanatos Syndrome*, 88–89. *See also* Germany

INDEX

homosexuality: and depression, 95–96; as form of being, 267–68n33; as identity, 135–36; *The Silence of the Lambs* stereotypes of, 261n3; *The Talented Mr. Ripley* references to, 265n20
Huxley, Aldous, 13, 274n18

identity: American, 46–49; branding as form of, 233–38; cultural creation of inauthentic, 47–48, 49–50, 52–53; culture and bitch, 260–61n22; depression as, 99–101; depression as opposite of, 83–86, 91–92; as more powerful than race, 101–2; "predetermined," 47–48, 49–51; Prozac American, 102–3; *The Thanatos Syndrome* on linguistics and Jewish, 87–89. *See also* Jewishness/Jewish identity; middle-class identity
Ideological State Apparatus, 220–23
"Ideology and Ideological State Apparatuses" (Althusser), 193
Illness as Metaphor (Sontag), 93
inauthenticity: depression as symptom of, 52, 59–60, 61–63; Marcuse's analysis of, and American individualism, 9–11, 198; Sartre on state of, 38–39, 40, 41, 42–43, 44–45, 48, 164–65; Trilling on ethical problem of, 32–33. *See also* authenticity; phoniness
inner core metaphor, 2–3
institutional influence on self: academic scholarship on, 192–93; the brand in relation to, 235–36; Ideological State Apparatus form of, 220–23; *Jerry Maguire*'s self-transformation narrative of, 218–27, 229–38; *The Lonely Crowd* analysis of, 6–7, 8, 11–13, 36, 178, 195–96, 197, 198, 209, 218; *The Man in the Gray Flannel Suit* on, 191–92, 194–202; *The Organization Man* analysis of, 5, 193–94, 196–200, 209; *Revolutionary Road* analysis of, 201–18; trained "from the outside inward" by, 213–14; *White Collar* analysis of, 194, 195, 209, 213, 214, 231–32. *See also* corporate life; middle-class identity; self; subject formation
"Intellectuals and the Jewish Community, The" (Cohen), 143
Invasion of the Body Snatchers (Siegel): and correlation of authenticity with insanity, 56–57, 59–62, 63–65; on mass hysteria response, 63–65, 80; self-consciousness of need for secrecy in, 257n3
Invisible Man (Ellison), 17, 252–53n11
"Is America Exile or Home?" (Knox), 143

Jacobs, James B., 137
James, Henry, 264n17
Jameson, Fredric, 81–82, 131; *The Cultural Turn*, 16, 82, 250n7; *Postmodernism*, 242
Jane Eyre (Brontë), 126
Jenkins, Philip, 108, 109
Jerry Maguire (Crowe): *The Catcher in the Rye* references in, 240–41; "completion" of transformation in, 238, 239; on institutional influence on self, 193, 194–95; "personality market" concept examined in, 232–33; pop-psychologized identity evoked by, 21–22, 221; on problem of performative agency, 222–23; on role of repetition in transformation, 224–25; self-transformation narrative of, 218–27, 229–38

Jewish Americans: "crisis of identity" of contemporary, 141–42; cultural responsibilities of, 143–44; *embourgeoisement* of, 142, 149–50, 182, 186; examination of postwar, 143–45; *Marjorie Morningstar* on real phony, and Jews, 180–90; "natural Judaism" compared with experience of, 187–88; passing or assimilation of, 147–49, 161, 173–74, 177–78, 180–90; and "predetermined" identity, 47–48; social exclusion (1950s) of, 30; suburban life of, 189–90; *The Thanatos Syndrome* identity of, 87–89

Jewish assimilation: in America, 147–49, 161; Holocaust metaphor of, 188–89; of Jewish identity in Germany, 173–74, 273n15; melting-pot "starched uniformity" of, 177–78; *The Thanatos Syndrome* on, 188

"Jewish Culture in America" (Cohen), 143

Jewishness/Jewish identity: *embourgeoisement* of, 142–43; examination of, and authenticity, 144–50; generational differences in, 170–72; *Gentleman's Agreement* on, and anti-Semitism, 150–67; and German assimilation, 173–74; Herberg's analysis of, 146; *Kristallnacht* attack on, 185; *Marjorie Morningstar* and phoniness of, 180–90; natural, 189–90; Nazi Holocaust as killing, 97–98, 99, 143, 166, 188; and "pretender soul," 172–73; *Seize the Day* on, and authenticity of failure, 167–80; Wurtzel on, and depression, 97–99; and *Yiddishkeit* of Eastern European, 142–43, 174, 180. *See also* identity

"Jewish Revival in America, The" (Glazer), 143

Joyce, James, 34

Judaism: inclusion of, in American culture, 144–45; "natural," 187–88; and *yizkor* (prayers for the dead), 141

Jurca, Catherine, 8, 144, 193

Karem, Jeff, 16, 251n8
Karenga, Maulana, 84
Kazan, Elia, 4. See also *Gentleman's Agreement*; *Pinky*
Killer inside Me, The (Thompson), 19, 107, 110, 113–17, 118–20
Knapp, Caroline, 96
Knox, Israel, 143
Kramer, Peter, 90–92
Kristallnacht (Germany), 185

Laing, R. D., 65; *The Divided Self*, 6, 19, 67–69, 72; on mental illness treatment, 68–69, 75; on unembodiment of self, 72
language: *The Bell Jar* and orthographically correct, 76–77; and grammatical requirement of subject, 228–30; *The Names* use of violence related to, 129–32, 266nn24–25; and naming, 129–30; representational capacities of, 87–88; *The Thanatos Syndrome* and representational capacities of, 87–88
Levi, Primo, 92, 94
Lévi-Strauss, Claude, 129
Levin, Meyer, 143
Linder, Robert, 253n2
Listening to Prozac (Kramer), 90–92
Livingston, Jennie, 279n10
Lonely Crowd, The (Riesman): on

autonomous individuals, 12–13, 36, 78, 218, 250n6; "From Morality to Morale" chapter in, 171; on generational shift from inner- to other-directed, 11–12, 171; on middle-class homogeneity due to institutional influence, 6–7, 8, 11, 13, 178; on other-directed individuals, 7, 11–13, 15, 141, 145, 149, 171, 196, 209, 218, 250n6; on relation of social character and society, 195

MacDonald, Andrew, 269n40
madness: *The Bell Jar*'s examination of, 76–78, 80; Foucault's analysis of, 19, 57, 67, 74–76; mass hysteria form of, 63–65, 80; medicalization of, 79–81, 82–83, 102–3; mental illness versus, 78, 80, 103–4; shift from, to Prozac Americans, 103–4. *See also* mental illness
Madness and Civilization (Foucault), 19, 57, 67, 74–76
Make a Name for Yourself (Roffer), 276–77n24
Manchurian Candidate, The (Frankenheimer), 62–63
Man in the Gray Flannel Suit, The (Wilson): anti-institutional way of thinking presented in, 204; corporate narrative of, 191–92, 193; on "honesty" guarantee against phoniness, 200–201; as model of social ethic, 199–200; *Revolutionary Road* compared with, 194–95, 204; on social character relationship to society, 195–202
Manson murders, 127, 128, 265–66n23
Marcus Aurelius, 105, 134

Marcuse, Herbert, 46, 59; American individualism analysis by, 9–11, 198, 243; *Eros and Civilization*, 6, 9–11, 13, 198, 243
Marjorie Morningstar (Wouk), 21; *The Catcher in the Rye* compared with, 182; *embourgeoisement* of, 149–50; on phony Jews, 180–90; on role of institutions in authenticity, 150; *Weltanschauung* revealed through, 181–82
mass hysteria, 61–62, 63–65, 80
materialism, and inauthencity, 9–10
McCarthy, Mary, 29–32
McCullough, Frances, 65
Medevoi, Leerom, 8, 249–50n5
medications: alteration due to, 259–60n19; antidepressants, 92–94, 260nn20–21; Prozac treatment of mental illness, 89–104
Melley, Timothy, 8, 16
Menand, Louis: on adolescent attitude as authentic, 24–25, 27, 41, 45, 78, 103, 177, 182, 201, 218, 248; on adult readers of *Catcher in the Rye*, 24–25, 29, 182; and *bildungsroman* genre, 34
mental illness: biological models of, 90–95; correlation of, and authenticity, 56–58, 59–65; deinstitutionalization of patients with, 66–67; Descartes on, 72, 74; examination of diagnoses of, 56–57; existential consideration of, 68–69; Foucault's approach to, 19, 57, 67, 74–75; and mad cogito, 65–78, 103; madness versus, 77–78, 80, 103–4; mass hysteria form of, 63–65, 80; metaphors using cures of, 70–71, 76; movement from madness to, 57–58;

mental illness (*continued*)
　pressures of conformity and uniformity leading to, 69–79; problems with treating, 67–69; Prozac treatment of, 89–104. *See also* depression; madness
Mental Retardation and Community Mental Health Centers Construction Act (1963), 66–67
middle-class identity: American, 46–49; performative agency and authenticity of, 21–22, 194–95, 205–18, 222; and phoniness as form of social good, 193–94; and "protective coloration," 5, 193–94; relationship of society to social character of, 195–202; resistance to institutions grounding, 193–94; shift from Protestant ethic to social ethic in, 196–97; "white plight" of, 203. *See also* identity; institutional influence on self
Mildred Pierce (Cain), 200
Miller, Arthur, 165, 271–72n8
Mills, C. Wright: on alienating conditions of modern work, 214; on institutional influence on self, 6, 192, 193, 195, 209, 213, 214, 231–32; on "personality market," 231–32; *White Collar*, 6, 192, 193, 194, 195, 209, 213
Mitchell, Wisconsin v., 137
Moreno, Michael P., 203, 274n6
Moretti, Franco, 34–35, 37, 41
Morrison, Toni, 85
Moser, Mike, 234
motivation: causal methodology to uncover, 105–7, 111–13, 134–35; of cult/Manson murders, 127–28; for hate crime, 136–40; and repetition, 227–28, 231; serial killing component of, examined, 111–13, 116–19, 128, 136–37, 264–65n18
Moviegoer, The (Percy), 58, 89
Must You Conform? (Linder), 253n2
Myth of Mental Illness, The (Szasz), 19, 67
"Myth of Sisyphus, The" (Camus), 123

Nabers, Deak, 7
Names, The (DeLillo): serial killing examined in, 18, 20, 107, 111, 127–32, 265–66n23; U.S. and Greek cult killings compared in, 127–29; violence of, 127–32
naming: loss of self-presence through, 130; process of, 129–30. *See also* language
National Endowment for the Humanities, 85
Native Son (Wright), 200
natural Jewishness, 189–90
"natural Judaism," 187–88
"nerve of failure," *Seize the Day* and the, 176–80
"New Suburbanites of the 50s, The" (Gersh), 143
New Yorker (magazine), 42
New York Times, 42, 92, 150, 274n19
Nietzsche, Friedrich, 229
No Exit (Sartre), 42
Notebooks on an Ethics (Sartre), 39
Novick, Peter, 143

O.C., The (TV show), 253n1
Olshaker, Mark, 113
"On Being Sane in Insane Places" (Rosenbaum), 65
One Flew over the Cuckoo's Nest (film), 65

On the Genealogy of Morals (Nietzsche), 229
Organization Man, The (Whyte): on institutional influence on self, 5, 6, 192, 193–94, 196–200, 209; uniformity analyzed in, 196–97, 199–200
Other, the, 152–54
"Other-directed" individuals, 7, 11–13, 15, 141, 145, 149, 171, 196, 209, 218, 250n6
outer-façade metaphor, 2–3
Ozick, Cynthia, 169–70

Paris Is Burning (Livingston), 279n10
passing: applied to serial murderers, 267n32; in *Gentleman's Agreement*, 154–57, 161; by Jewish Americans, 147–49, 161; *Pinky* on African American, 157–61, 162, 163, 166, 167. See also race
Patricia Highsmith (Harrison), 265n21
Percy, Walker, 57, 59; on continual recreation of self, 110; dispute of, with Sartre, 259n15
— works of: "The Coming Crisis in Psychiatry," 57, 63, 64, 80; *The Moviegoer*, 58, 89. See also *Thanatos Syndrome, The*
performance: experience versus, 246–47; of other-directed individuals, 209; as presenting idealized versions of self, 210–12; *Revolutionary Road* examples of, 194, 205–9; and transsexual model of gender identity, 275–76n18. See also social character
performative agency: *Jerry Maguire* on problem of, 222; as means to authenticity, examined, 21–22, 194–95, 209–13, 222; and "personality market," 231–33; *The Presentation of Self in Everyday Life* analysis of, 209–12; in *Six Degrees of Separation*, 242–44
"personality market," 231–33
phoniness: accessing authenticity through, 3, 14–15, 18; Holden Caulfield's definitions of, 1–2, 29–31; "honesty" as guarantor against, 200–201; inner core and outer façade components of, 2–3; and Jewish identity, 146–47, 172–73, 180–90; and mental illness, 60–63; middle-class identity role of, 193–94; postwar definition of, 248; reexamination of concepts of, during postwar period, 2, 4–22; of serial killers, 114–16, 119–23; uniformity in relation to, 50–55, 198–99. See also authenticity; inauthenticity
Pinky (Kazan): on African American passing, 148, 157–61, 162, 163, 166, 167; slavery left unexamined in, 166, 167
Plath, Sylvia, 18, 58, 65. See also *Bell Jar, The*
Podhoretz, Norman, 181
Portrait of the Artist as a Young Man, The (Joyce), 34
Postmodernism (Jameson), 242
postmodernity: death of subject as consequence of, 81–82; ontologies from theorization of, 16; radical social constructivism of, 85; restoration of authenticity abandoned by, 241–43
postwar period: anxieties expressed in cult classic films of, 257–58n11; concepts of phoniness and authenticity during, 2, 4–22; concern with conformity during, 6; definition of authenticity and phoniness during, 248; Jewish Americans during,

postwar period (*continued*)
examined, 30, 143–45; lack of political engagement with Holocaust in, 270n1; recent literary criticism on, 7–8, 249–50n5; strong U.S. economy of, 273n12

Potter, Kimberly, 137

Presentation of Self in Everyday Life, The (Goffman): institutional influence of self analyzed in, 6, 192–93, 194; performance agency analyzed in, 209–12

Prosser, Jay, 134

Protestant-Catholic-Jew (Herberg), 144–46, 167–68, 186

Protestant ethic–social ethic shift, 196–200

Prozac American identity, 102–3

Prozac Nation (Wurtzel): on biological model of mental illness, 90–91; on identity as depression, 99–101; on Jewishness and depression, 97–99; on loss of self through depression, 96–97; mental illness examined in, 19, 58, 59

Psychic Life of Power, The (Butler), 21, 193; performative agency in, 220–24, 227–28, 235

psychotherapy: challenges and failures of, 67–69, 77; as mental illness treatment, 59, 89

race: and Bellow's construction of self, 175; connections between, and class, 272n9; and construction of self, 175; depressive identity as more powerful than, 101–2; language depicting, 101; and *Six Degrees of Separation*, 243–44; *The Turner Diaries* on war over, 269n40. *See also* African Americans; hate crimes; passing

Ray, Nicholas, 23–25

Rebel without a Cause (Ray), 23–25, 253n1, 253–54n3

Red Dragon (Harris): causal narrative of, 133; serial killers examined in, 20, 105, 108, 112; *The Silence of the Lambs* compared with, 105–7, 133–35

repetition: as replacing experience with automation, 245–46; ritual compared with, 227–28, 231; transformation role of, 223–25

Reprieve, The (Sartre), 42

Revolutionary Road (Yates), 21, 193; anti-institutional way of thinking in, 204; *The Catcher in the Rye* echoed in, 204–5; on contaminating effects of corporate life, 201–2; on institutional influence on self, 201–18; male consumer identity revealed in, 274n6; *The Man in the Gray Flannel Suit* compared with, 194–95, 204; on patriarchal gender relations, 203–4; performance agency staged in, 205–9; on role of conscience in subject formation, 223

Riesman, Dave: on adjusted/anomic/autonomous individuals, 12–13, 36, 78, 218, 250n6; homogeneity of U.S. analysis by, 11–13; *The Lonely Crowd*, 5, 6, 8, 11, 13, 36, 78, 171, 178, 209; on "the nerve of failure," 176–78; on other-directed individuals, 11–13, 15, 141, 145, 149, 171, 196, 218, 250n6; on social importance of self, 178; theories of middle-class American character by, 145–46

INDEX

Ripley under Ground (Highsmith), 265n22
Roffer, Robin Fisher, 276–77n24
Rosenbaum, D. L., 65
Rosenberg, Harold, 142, 161–62
Rossman, Evelyn N.: "Decade in Northrup," 189–90; on suburban Jewish life, 189
Rothenberg, Molly Anne, 85
Rousseau, Jean-Jacques, 2

Salinger, J. D., 4, 5. See also *Catcher in the Rye, The*
Sane Society, The (Fromm), 7, 34, 46
Sartre, Jean-Paul: on bad faith versus falsehood, 42–45; existential model of self by, 20, 27–28, 38–39, 41, 42–45, 152–54, 167; Percy's dispute with, 259n15; on performance of self, 211–12; "seeing-the-Other," 152–53; theorization of authenticity process by, 243
— works of: *The Age of Reason*, 42; *Being and Nothingness*, 20, 38–39, 42, 44, 86, 133, 152–54, 175, 211, 255n10; *Existentialism and Humanism*, 39, 42; *Existentialist Psychoanalysis*, 42; *The Flies*, 42; *No Exit*, 42; *Notebooks on an Ethics*, 39; *The Reprieve*, 42. See also *Anti-Semite and Jew*
Seize the Day (Bellow), 21; authenticity of failure examined in, 167–80; existentialist model of self examined by, 149
self: action related to, 107–9, 110, 121–26, 132–33, 138–40; authenticity in the absence of unified, 16–17; body in relation to, 63–64, 71–73, 82–83; critiques of idea of unique, 250–51n7; cultural impact on, 35–36, 52–55, 83–86; depression as interfering with capacity of, 94–95; developmental changes over time to, 32–34, 35, 49–50, 52–55; developmental interaction between culture and evolving, 45–47; dyad of, and other, 43–44; hate crime and representation of, 132–40; hierarchy of identic categories of, 86–87; performative agency as related to authentic, 21–22, 194–95, 204–12; phoniness problem of, 1, 14, 18, 30–31, 55, 222; presenting idealized versions of, 210–12; radical self-making of existential, 38–39; social, cultural, racial construction of, 175; social importance of, 178; *The Thanatos Syndrome* question on, 80–83; "unembodiment" of, 72. See also existential model of self; institutional influence on self
self-consciousness, 81, 247–48
self-knowledge: on adolescent progression to, 14–18, 27–29, 42–55; *The Catcher in the Rye* examination of, 35–38, 40
self-transformation: "completion" of, 237–38, 239; grammar and language role in, 228–30; *Jerry Maguire*'s narrative of, 218–27, 229–38; realization of successful, 236–37; repetition rituals in, 223–25, 227–28, 231; role of branding in process of, 233–38; role of conscience in, 223; *Six Degrees of Separation*'s examination of, 15, 16, 242–43
Seltzer, Mark, 115–16, 120, 251n9, 262n8, 267n32
serial killers: Harris's two alternative explanations for, 107, 133–35;

serial killers (*continued*)
"passing" applied to, 267n32; phoniness of, examined, 114–16, 119–23; relevant question to ask about, 111; reshaping of perceptions on, 109–40; self- or subjecthood in relation to, 107–9; transformation of imagined murderers into, 19–20

serial killing: biological or sociobiological accounts of, 267n31; differentiated from other homicides, 263n10; motivation in relation to, 111–13, 116–19, 128, 136–37, 264–65n18; other crimes compared with, 111–12; as product and critic of social mores, 120; relationship of action to selfhood of, 107–9, 121–26; and representation of self and hate crime, 132–40, 268n34, 268–69nn37–38; research on social problem of, 108–9; violence of, 262n8; and violence of language, 129–32, 266nn24–25. *See also* violence

sexual assault crimes, 269n39

Siegel, Don, 56. *See also Invasion of the Body Snatchers*

Silence of the Lambs, The (Harris): causal nature methodology of, 105–6, 134–35; gay stereotypes accusation against, 261n3; *Red Dragon* compared with, 106–7, 133–35; serial killers examined in, 20, 105, 108, 111, 112–13

Simmons, Gaye McCollum, 176

Six Degrees of Separation (Guare): on anecdote and experience opposition, 244–46; audience spoken to directly by actors in, 279n11; *The Catcher in the Rye* in, 241–42; class insensitivity accusations against, 279n12; performative agency in, 242–44; on role of race, class, and ethnicity in presenting self, 243–44; self-transformation examined in, 15, 16, 241–43

Slavery (Elkins), 252–53n11, 270n1

slavery, *Pinky*'s neglect to mention, 166, 167. *See also* African Americans

Smith, Benjamin, 268–69n37

social character: adjusted/anomic/autonomous, 12–13, 36, 46, 71, 78, 218, 250n6; relationship of society to, 195–202. *See also* performance

social class. *See* class

social ethic: *The Man in the Gray Flannel Suit* as model of, 199–200; shift from Protestant ethic to, 196–97

society: class divisions of, 243–44, 272n9, 279n12; relationship of social character to, 195–202; shift of, from Protestant ethic to social ethic, 196–200

Sontag, Susan, 93

Spielberg, Steven, 15

"starched uniformity," 178

Steichen, Edward, 142

Strangers on a Train (Highsmith), 264–65n18

Styron, William: *The Confessions of Nat Turner*, 102; *Darkness Visible*, 19, 58, 92–96, 98, 100–102

subject formation: branding component of, 233–38; grammatical requirement of subject in, 228–30; Ideological State Apparatus in, 220–23; *Jerry Maguire*'s self-transformation narrative of, 218–27; role of conscience in, 223; role

of grammar and language in, 228–30; role of repetition in, 223–25, 227–28, 231. *See also* institutional influence on self
superego repression, 9
surface uniformities, 5, 198–99
Szasz, Thomas, 65, 77; *The Myth of Mental Illness*, 19, 67

Talented Mr. Ripley, The (Highsmith): *The Ambassadors* compared with, 264n17; existentialist ontology of self in, 19–20, 107, 110–11, 113, 121–26, 131–32; homosexual references in, 265n20; motivation examined in, 112–13, 264–65n18; *The Names* compared with, 131–32; on self determined by action, 132–33; serial killer label applied to, 263n13
Tennenhouse, Leonard, 126–27
Thanatos Syndrome, The (Percy): mental illness examined in, 19, 58, 79–89, 98; mental illness versus madness debate in, 103–4; nature of self examined in, 82–83; on selfhood and Afrocentricity, 83–86; on psychotropic medication as kind of holocaust, 188
This Is My God (Wouk), 187–88
Thompson, Jim, 4; *The Killer inside Me*, 19, 107, 110, 113–17, 118–20
Thoreau, Henry, 2
transsexuality, 267n30, 275–76n18
Tremor of Forgery, The (Highsmith), 265n21
Tribe, Lawrence H., 137–38, 139
Trilling, Lionel, 4, 32–33, 248, 255n7, 255n13

"'Triple Melting Pot, The'" (Herberg), 144
Tristes Tropiques (Lévi-Strauss), 129
Turner Diaries, The (MacDonald), 269n40

unembodiment of self, 72
uniformity: assimilation as "starched" form of, 177–78; conformity compared with, 8–13, 46, 55, 61–63, 78, 116, 184–85, 193, 198–99, 248, 252n11, 257n8, 270n3; definition of, 5; mental illness due to, and conformity, 70–79; 1950s adolescence in context of, 18; problem of, and phonies, 52–55, 198–99; protective coloration of surface, 5, 193–94; traditional description of 1950s, recast, 6. *See also* conformity
unique self, 250–51n7
United We Brand (Moser), 234
Updike, John, 85

Valente, Joseph, 85
violence: biological or sociobiological accounts of, 267n31; and evidence rules on rape, 269n39; and hate crime, 132–40; *The Names* use of language relationship to, 129–32, 266nn24–25; of serial killing, 262n8. *See also* serial killing
Violence of Representation, The (Armstrong and Tennenhouse), 126–27

We Are All Multiculturalists Now (Glazer), 258–59n14
Weltanschauung, 181–82
Weltschmerz concept, 34

"What Sociology Knows about American Jews?" (Glazer), 271n4
White Collar (Mills): on alienating conditions of modern work, 214; on institutional influence on self, 6, 192, 193, 195, 209, 213, 214, 231–32
"white plight," 203
Whyte, William, Jr.: on American individualism, 198; on institutional influence on self, 5, 193–94, 196–200, 209; *The Organization Man*, 5, 6, 192, 196–97, 199–200; on performative agency, 209; on protective coloration of, 5, 193–94, 210, 218; uniformity analyzed by, 196–97, 199–200
Wild One, The (Benedek), 23
Wilson, Sloan, 4; *The Man in the Gray Flannel Suit*, 191–92, 193, 194–95, 199–201, 204
Wisconsin v. Mitchell, 137
Wouk, Herman, 142, 145; *Marjorie Morningstar*, 21, 149–50, 180–90; *This Is My God*, 187–88
Wright, Richard, 200
"Writer and the Jewish Community, The" (Levin), 143
Wurtzel, Elizabeth, 4; *Bitch*, 260–61n22. See also *Prozac Nation*
Wuthering Heights (Brontë), 53

Yates, Richard, 4, 223. See also *Revolutionary Road*
Yiddishkeit culture, 142–43, 174, 180
yizkor (prayers for the dead), 141

CPSIA information can be obtained
at www.ICGtesting.com
Printed in the USA
BVOW04s2059180517
484460BV00003B/1/P